Jordan's
GUIDE
· to ·
GOOD
WINES

Jordan's GUIDE · to · GOOD WINES

Brian Jordan

with photographs by the author

H.F. & G. Witherby
LONDON

By the same author

WINE – Which? What? Where? When? Why?
Jordan's Supermarket Wines
Jordan's High Street Wines

First published in Great Britain in 1990 by
H.F. & G. WITHERBY LTD
14 Henrietta Street WC2E 8QJ

British Library Cataloguing in Publication Data

Jordan, Brian
    Jordan's guide to good wines.
    1. Wines
    I. Title
    641.22

ISBN 0-85493-184-8

ACKNOWLEDGEMENTS

My thanks are due to
D.J., J.J., G.R. and D.S. for their
help, advice, guidance and forbearance
– as appropriate! And to my stalwart editor
and inventive designer for
making a book out of
mere words.

Edited by Penny Clarke

Designed by Roger Kohn

Cover photo by Steven Morris
taken at Shoppenhangers Manor Restaurant,
Maidenhead
by kind permission of Crest Hotels

Photo on pages 236–7 also taken by Steven Morris

Maps drawn by Malcolm Porter

Typesetting by Florencetype Limited

Printed and bound in Singapore by Imago Publishing Ltd

*Previous pages Part of the Marlborough
vineyard on the north coast of South Island,
New Zealand.*

CONTENTS

FOREWORD

Ask a dozen wine writers how they came to be doing the job they do, and you'll more than likely be given a dozen different answers. Brian Jordan and I, however, are both members of a small group that came to wine writing via the sharpish end of the business – running a restaurant and filling its wine cellar.

In Brian's case, he did both with such skill that, just two years after first opening the doors of Bowlish House in 1978 when, as he says now, he knew 'absolutely nothing about food or wine', his restaurant featured in the *Good Food Guide*, and had won the coveted Wine List of the Year award.

We first met in 1980, at around the time that he was quoted in Jancis Robinson's first edition of the *Which? Wine Guide* as 'tending to move away from the "classic" wines. Of course we stock them, and present them as carefully as they deserve, but if asked for a recommendation, we steer customers towards value-for-money areas of South Europe and the New World'.

Today, new and unusual wines from Australia, Spain and California are almost as commonplace in restaurants as they are on the shelves of Britain's better wine merchants, but back at the beginning of the 1980s Brian Jordan's attitude was very much that of a pioneer. Those were the days when, for most people, red wine came in a handful of styles: Bordeaux, Burgundy, Beaujolais, Barolo – and the obligatory Châteauneuf-du-Pape. To offer Carbernet Sauvignons from California, Australia and Chile as well was little short of revolutionary.

Brian Jordan's attitude towards pricing was similarly unusual. While other restaurants were unashamedly charging £5 for the most basic of wines, the Bowlish House list offered no less than 15 priced at £3.50 a bottle, ranging from 1978 Beaujolais to 1974 Dão.

Brian Jordan's view was quite simply that while wine used to be a mark of privilege, and consequently a product for which the privileged often thought they had to be prepared to pay through the nose, times had changed. The wine drinkers of the 1980s had become far more critical, more adventurous, and more aware of the value-for-money aspect of the stuff in the glass – however smart its label.

Eight years after that first encounter, Brian volunteered to help me run the 1988 *WINE Magazine* International Challenge, the world's biggest comparative wine tasting and the wine world's answer to the Royal Tournament. That year, some 2400 different wines had to be sorted into logical tasting order and set before several hundred of the wine trade's most exacting palates. The qualities Brian exhibited then – and the following year when the number had risen to 3200 – were precisely the same as the ones that made him so successful as a restaurateur: a level head, common sense and a boundless enthusiasm for the sheer variety and unexpected joy of wine.

Since switching roles, from restaurateur to wine writer, Brian has sought to share those qualities with a growing number of wine lovers. With this book, I am sure that a great many more people will be infected by his enthusiasm and, through its pages, be led to explore and discover for themselves literally hundreds of glorious and good value wines of which they were previously quite unaware.

ROBERT JOSEPH 1990

INTRODUCTION

The drinking of wine, like so many so-called social graces, has become surrounded by humbug. The self-styled wine expert, the wine bore and the wine snob are all with us, all tending to confuse what is already a potentially confusing subject. It is all too easy to lose sight of the fact that the 'bottom line' of wine drinking is the paying of money to fill a glass with an alcoholic beverage you are hoping to enjoy. Thus, there is really only one good wine and that's the wine you enjoy. Equally, if you are given an expensive wine – and some can work out at around £40.00 a glass or £5.00 per mouthful! – and you don't enjoy it then, as far as you are concerned, it's not good wine.

Wine drinking is all about enjoyment and committing a large sum of money to purchasing a bottle is not a direct guarantee of increased enjoyment. The law of diminishing returns applies very positively to wine quality and, although the tax laws do serve to complicate the issue, once a wine is about plonk level and is of acceptable quality, then each perceptible improvement in taste and enjoyment is normally accompanied by a very marked increase in price. The whole purpose of this book is to encourage and direct the reader to wines which offer low cost and high enjoyment.

Beware of 'experts'. There are very few who are, indeed, expert in this complex subject and to retain an up-to-date authority needs knowledge of not only grapes, weather patterns, regional variations and changes in wine laws affecting quality, but also the movement of international exchange rates, taxation alterations and other financial changes which affect the final cost of wines. An expert must see both sides of the equation – the quality of a particular wine versus the cost of that wine – and good value for money should be the standard used in assessing any particular wine. A wine is not automatically good because it is expensive and it is not automatically dull because it is cheap, neither is it automatically good because it comes from an established growing area or inferior because the country of origin is little known as a wine production area. Every wine should be assessed on its individual merit related to the price asked. Enjoyment versus cost is the criteria.

'God made only water, but man made wine'
Victor Hugo, *'Les Contemplations'*, 1856

Before going any further it might be sensible to define 'wine'. The *Oxford English Dictionary*'s definition is 'fermented grape juice as an alcoholic drink'. That is the traditional view. The more modern definition, which I follow in this book, defines wine as 'the fermented juice of grapes with no flavouring additives'. That's the theory, but what, in practical terms, for the customer and the consumer is included and what excluded?

Included are:
● *fortified wines* that is ports, sherries, madeiras, malagas and all other wines fortified by the addition of spirits
● *wood-aged wines* wines which have beneficial flavours of wood introduced by ageing in wooden casks or barrels – or achieved by modern alternative methods
● *retsina* included for historic reasons although the addition of pine essence should disqualify it. Frankly, the pine essence practically disqualifies it from most people's enjoyment anyway!

Excluded are:
● *country wines* made from fruits and herbs
● *fruit wines* recently introduced, these are wines, often sparkling, to which a considerable amount of fruit juice is added. Peach juice was the most popular addition to begin with, but now a whole range of alternatives are available
● *vermouths* although basically fortified wines, they have considerable quantities of herbs, roots, spices and the like added
● *British wines* or *made wines* produced by adding water to imported dried or otherwise compressed grape crush and fermenting the resulting juice
● *Pineau de Charentes* this saddens me for not only am I a great Pineau lover, but have had the honour of Chevalier de la Confrérie due Franc-Pineau conferred on me. In theory this whole family of drinks should be included as they qualify for taxation and for export as fortified wines. However, that is a cheat. They are really brandies with grape juice added. To qualify for the more advantageous taxation classification

the grape juice is fermented to 1% alcohol and then brandy is added, thus technically becoming fortified wine, even though the 'wine' that is fortified is of a very low alcohol level.

These definitions are, for most people, merely a matter of interest, the point to remember is that wine is fun. It is not meant to be a source of social one-upmanship. There are few 'experts' and it is most unlikely that you will meet any of them. What you are in danger of meeting is the wine-snob with a little card giving the 'good' years in Bordeaux and Burgundy – and it is almost certainly worth taking the advice of such a self-appointed connoisseur with a large pinch of salt.

Experimenting is the best way of learning. Simple varietal wines – that is wines with labels that tell you WHAT grape has been used rather than WHERE the wine was made – can be bought for a very modest outlay. Find out what types of wine and, therefore, what types of grape please you. Do your own research, for that's when the fun begins!

Our per capita consumption of wine has increased regularly each year but we still have a very long way to go to reach the levels achieved by many of our European neighbours. However, although they may consume much larger quantities than us, their drinking is of a very different type. A Frenchman will not be drinking Spanish wines; an Italian will not have German wines available; the Portuguese know nothing of the wines of Alsace. The traditional wine producers of Europe drink their own national products and see little need to import from their competitors.

Historically though, the UK has had many years of intimate involvement with the wine and spirit trade of Europe. Our influence was, and in many cases still is, keenly felt in Bordeaux, in areas of fortified wine production and in the production of spirits. Names like Barton in Bordeaux; Hine, Hardy and Hennessey in Cognac; Dow's, Cockburn, Graham and Taylor in Oporto; Wisdom and Warter, Garvey and Harvey in Jerez all attest the early influence of the UK in these areas – names which still appear on bottles of wines and spirits on our supermarket shelves.

Our membership of the Common Market has committed us to closer trading relationships with our European partners and this, coupled with ease of travel for continental holidays during the past two decades, has increased the acceptance and consumption of wine as a part of everyday life. In addition we have our common language, our membership of the Commonwealth and our old political and trading ties with former members of the British Empire, all of which encourage wine imports from those sources. Again, a common language and historic ties with the United States facilitates the import of wine from that country while our relatively high standard of living and lack of allegiance to a national wine production industry has made us a significant outlet for producer nations from the eastern bloc. Hungarian, Yugoslav and, most especially, Bulgarian wines have all found a receptive market in Britain.

Wines from all the major source areas are readily available and, while it is perhaps less common to find wines from Chile, China, the Lebanon or India, these too are available to the inquisitive without too much effort. The world is very much our oyster when it comes to choosing wine, but that, at the same time, can make choosing a wine much more difficult. We are often spoilt for choice, hence the new-found thirst for knowledge and guidance and, in consequence, the proliferation of wine books, articles and radio and TV programmes on the subject of wine. In such a sea of complexity a little basic knowledge can prove extremely useful!

On the continent, where wine is a more everyday drink, wine books are less necessary. A Frenchman gradually gains his knowledge of the wines available to him as he matures – probably local wines for everyday drinking and from further afield for special occasions. He grows up to know what type of taste awaits him when he opens a bottle of red burgundy or a dry white bordeaux and he does not need to know what type or types of grape were used in their production. For us, with literally thousands of wines from across the world, we need all the help we can get . . . And the simple solution to the problem is 'know your grapes'.

PART 1

KNOW YOUR GRAPES

VINES

The grape vines that produce 99% of the world's wine are of the species *Vitis vinifera*, but in virtually every vineyard in the world this species is grafted onto rootstock of such indigenous American species as *Vitis riparia*, *Vitis labrusca*, *Vitis rupestris*, *Vitis berlandieri* and so on. The grafting is to prevent attack by the American root louse *Phylloxera vastrix* which, between 1850 and 1920, decimated almost all the world's vineyards.

Vitis vinifera is just one of a vast genus, or family, of plants which includes such unlikely relatives as the Virginia creeper. The varieties of *Vitis vinifera* which, together with variations of soil and climate, give us the range of flavours of different wines, number thousands, more than 4,000 being individually named. However, only 400 or so are sufficiently important for international consideration and about 40 produce virtually all the wine we are likely to meet.

The cultivation of *Vitis vinifera* is thought to have originated in the eastern Mediterranean, in Caucasia or Mesopotamia around 6000 BC. Egyptian paintings from 1500 BC show grapes being trodden to make wine and 500 years later,

▲ *Picking Merlot grapes at Château Laroque, St-Emilion. In France this back-breaking work is* traditionally done by migrant Spanish workers who start in the south and work north.

around 1000 BC, the Greeks fostered the spread of the vine and of viniculture. In southern France, at Marseilles and in the Languedoc, there is firm evidence of Greek-originated vine plantings, but it was the Romans who really developed the vine in Europe.

The Romans wrote so much about wine production in their homeland, that we can place at least 60 of their vineyards. The Romans' progress across Europe brought the vine to Bordeaux about AD 50, to Burgundy by AD 150, to the Loire 100 years later, the Rhine and Mosel around AD 300 and Champagne by AD 350. Of the major modern French wine-growing areas, only Alsace had to wait – the vine arriving there about AD 800.

As with any crop, the vine-grower has to produce as profitably as possible. Over the centuries, this has lead to certain types of indigenous vines in some areas being replaced or superseded by other varieties with, perhaps, a more popular flavour, greater resistance to disease or heavier cropping characteristics. Thus, with the many changes that have taken place over the centuries, we find that some grapes now grown a thousand miles apart, and for long thought to be indigenous to one particular area, may actually be genetically related. Experts can still disagree, even in this age of microbiology and genetic engineering, but some amusing relationships have been found. For example, it appears that the Riesling, the king of grapes in Germany and Alsace, is also the Alvarinho of the Minho in northern Portugal where it produces Vinho Verde, the Sercial of Madeira and the Pedro Ximenez of Andalucia, a constituent of sherry and the producer of both malaga and montilla!

However, with modern advances in plant technology, ingenious ways to resolving the centuries-old problem – that heavier crops from more prolific varieties seem invariably to produce lower quality wines – are being explored. We may yet see the development of a 'super-grape', disease resistant, early ripening, full of flavour and uncaring of soil or aspect – but until that time, we shall still enjoy the services of varieties like the Syrah (or Shiraz), the Muscat, the Malvasia and others that have remained virtually unchanged since the beginnings of civilisation.

GRAPES

Traditionally, the Old World wine-growing areas of Spain, France, Germany and Italy have named wine geographically – a Rioja, from that region in northern Spain: a Volnay, from the village of the Côte de Beaune in Burgundy; Piesporter Michelsberg, from the Michelsberg group of vineyards at Piesport on the Mosel. In other words, *where* the wine was grown was deemed more important than the grapes it was made from. However, the pursuit of excellence by the vineyards of the New World and the advances made in the new growing areas of the Old World has completely changed this. *What* grapes have been used to make the wine is now regarded as at least as important as where the wine is made. This change is reflected in the labels on wine bottles, though you'll still be more likely to find the really helpful labels stating what grapes were used to make the particular wine you're considering on bottles from the newer wine-producing areas.

In the past, the fact that a wine was a claret, a burgundy or whatever was seen as some sort

of quality assurance. Not so nowadays. The dual effect of improved wine-making techniques in newer growing areas and the proliferation of wine scandals in the older growing areas of Europe has made the assurances implied in the fact that an area has produced wine for hundreds of years much less valid.

The taste of any wine is a reflection of the grape variety or varieties that were used in its production. Other factors can modify the taste – the position of the vineyard, the climatic conditions during the growing period, the number of bunches produced by each vine, how early or late the grapes were picked and so on – but these are only modifications of the basic flavour of the grape. Thus, if you find an exciting Bulgarian wine produced from the Sauvignon Blanc grape, it follows that an Australian Sauvignon Blanc, a Californian Sauvignon Blanc, indeed a Sauvignon Blanc from almost anywhere in the world, should share the same crisp, grassy, gooseberry-like, tangy freshness that is characteristic of this variety.

Knowing the taste of the eight or ten most basic and most commonly used grapes is like having a series of hooks to hang your hat on. Most of the 'younger' growing areas in the world use the name of the grape variety somewhere on their labels and even the wine-makers of the 'old' growing areas are being forced to use 'varietal' labelling (page 11) to maintain sales. The analogy to a food menu is useful. If faced with a dish simply called 'Summer Stew' it would be difficult to decide whether it might be enjoyable. If, however, the menu read 'Summer Stew, a casserole of diced pork, mushroom and sweet green peppers' then, because the taste contribution of each of the constituents can be imagined from the taste 'index' we all carry in our heads, a decision whether that particular dish is likely to please is that much easier.

Confronted by a bottle labelled Murrumbidgee Red and without further information, one could be excused for passing along the shelf and selecting something more familiar. But given the title Murrumbidgee Cabernet-Sauvignon/Shiraz and knowing that the Cabernet Sauvignon is the taste signature of Bordeaux and the Shiraz (or Syrah in France) is responsible for the flavour of the excellent wines of the northern Rhône, then a wine tasting like a mix of Bordeaux and Rhône will probably be just the thing for the weekend beef or the summer barbecue.

▼ *Small-berried Cabernet Sauvignon grapes grown by Montana Wines at their* *Marlborough vineyards on the northern tip of South Island, New Zealand.*

VARIETAL LABELLING

Varietal labelling, that is labelling that gives prominence to the name of the grape contributing the flavour to the wine, is now very common. In fact it is more useful these days to know what flavour each major type of grape variety contributes to a wine than to know, for example, that 1972 was a poor year in Bordeaux!

I'll end with three more examples of varietal labelling: Gamay de Touraine is a red wine made from the Gamay Noir grape grown in Touraine in France. And when you appreciate that the Gamay is the grape that gives the characteristic taste to Beaujolais, then you have some idea of what the wine may taste like. Similarly, if a wine is labelled Svichtov Cabernet Sauvignon or Khan Krum Chardonnay, knowing that the Cabernet Sauvignon is the key to the taste of claret and that the Chardonnay gives the flavour to white burgundy, may persuade you to try these excellent Bulgarian wines.

WHITE WINE GRAPES

There are four outstanding varieties of grape from which white wines are made: the Chardonnay, Muscat, Riesling and Sauvignon Blanc.

CHARDONNAY

In a sense the Chardonnay is the white grape equivalent of the Cabernet Sauvignon in that it can produce superlative wines in most of the major growing areas of the world. Reputed to have originated in the Lebanon, it is best known for the delights of Burgundy, Chablis, Champagne and Pouilly-Fuissé, but its popularity in the US and the relative strength of the dollar has pushed prices for these better-known French Chardonnay wines through the roof.

Luckily for us, there are other areas in France and other countries around the world whose Chardonnay wines rival the classics for quality and affordability. From Bulgaria to New Zealand and from the Tyrol to Australia's Hunter Valley great wines are being produced in the full range of Chardonnay styles.

Cooler climates tend to produce steely Chablis tastes reminding the drinker of green apples and lemon; warmer growing areas tend to give fuller flavours which, coupled with ageing in oak barrels, produce an intense, buttery, toasty combination of flavours which, for many, represents the ultimate drinking experience – the delights of Burgundy Corton, Montrachets and Meursault – if one has a limitless pocket, or the pleasures of Rosemount Show Reserve Chardonnay, McWilliams Mount Pleasant Chardonnay from Australia or Edna Valley Vineyards Chardonnay from California if one is more economically minded.

Chardonnay wines fall neatly into two broad types, the lighter wines from cooler growing areas and the fuller, fatter wines from areas richer in sunlight. The lighter wines are sometimes overshadowed by the luscious buttery versions, but both have their part to play when matching wine to occasion. First-class lighter Chardonnays are produced in Sudtirol, that part of Italy that thinks of itself as Austrian and where many of the inhabitants speak German as their first language. Lageder and Tiefenbrunner are two names to look out for in this area. Bulgaria has a large Chardonnay production and has no less than three different Chardonnays out of the 16 varietal wines imported into the British Isles. The Novi Pazar Chardonnay is a lighter variety whilst the Khan Krum Reserve Chardonnay is deeper, fuller and more buttery.

Germany has flirted with the Chardonnay, but here it is often confused with the near relative, the Pinot Blanc or Weissburgunder and, in any case, the results have not been sufficiently attractive to the commercially minded Germans. Some good results have been achieved in Spain, where both the Torres family and Jean Leon in Penedés, and Raimat in Lérida have produced exceptionally satisfactory wines. It is, however, in the New World that the Chardonnay has been developed to its full potential.

Australia has taken to the Chardonnay like a new-found lover. Before the 1970s this grape was almost unused in Australia, but now it is the success story of the decade. The Lower Hunter Valley, 100 miles north of Sydney, seems to be the best growing area – the extreme heat of the summer is alleviated somewhat by frequent cloud cover and the rain which often arrives at harvest times seems to affect this variety less than others. Rothbury Estate, Tyrrell, Wyndham Estate, Rosemount and McWilliams are the best known in the UK and most of these companies produce a whopping oak-aged

◀ *Frost-dispersing propellers, so common in California's Napa Valley, are now being introduced in Burgundy.*

prestige version which can make the similar wines of Burgundy look pretty silly at three to four times the price.

American successes have been overshadowed by the Australians but here again their oak-aged wines are a match for the very best of France and, in spite of a strong dollar, good value for money.

MUSCAT

This wonderful grape – the grapiest of grapes and one of the few wine grapes that is good to eat – is thought to have been brought back from 'the lands of the Saracens' by the Crusaders and was first planted at the foot of the Pyrenees, whence today we obtain Muscat de Frontignan and Muscat de Rivesaltes.

The 'ancient tribe of Muscats', as Hugh Johnson describes them, now consists of two major varieties: Muscat of Alexandria and Muscat Blanc à petit Grains.

Muscat of Alexandria generally thought the inferior of the two, but, due to its higher yield, increasingly usurping the better variety. Best examples are Moscatel do Setubal from Portugal, a fortified wine produced from old, un-grafted, pre-phylloxera vines; Malaga, a raisiny fortified wine from southern Spain; Vin Doux from Rivesaltes in France; Brown Brothers honeyed Late Harvest Muscat from victoria in Australia and the rare Zibibbo, Moscato di Pantellaria, from the tiny island of Pantellaria between Sicily and Tunisia.
Muscat Blanc à petit Grains also known as Schmeckende, Tamyanka, Sargamuskotaly, Zutimuscat . . .! Particularly good examples of wines from this grape are dry Muscat d'Alsace, the sweet Beaumes de Venise from the Rhône and Muscat de Frontignan from the Pyrenees; Samos from the island of the same name in Greece; Mondavi's Moscato d'Oro from the Napa Valley and the liqueur Muscats from Australia.

Two other varieties of Muscat are in limited use, the Muscat Alupka in Russia (where all their wines are sweet to European tastes) and the Muscat Ottonel in Austria, Hungary and Yugoslavia, but none of these areas produce classic wines.

Naturally sweet dessert wines are a comparative rarity – most require some degree of fortification. However, the Muscat is the grape that can, in hot growing conditions, produce the genuine article – a wine made from grapes so sweet when picked that the process of fermentation produces a sufficiently high alcohol level and yet the resulting wine is still sweet enough to be classed a dessert wine.

In days gone by the Muscat produced one of the legendary dessert wines of the world – the Czars of Russia had a great penchant for ultra-sweet wines and alongside Château d'Yquem, Tokay Essencia and the old Malmseys from Madeira, they drank the famed Constantia from South Africa. This was produced from Muscat grapes at the Groot Constantia Estate just south of Capetown, founded in 1679 by Simon van der Stel – now, sadly, just a museum to its former glories.

Some dry Muscat wines are produced, most notably in Alsace and by João Pires in Portugal, but also in Tunisia. These wines, however, tend to taste like a paradox – one is aware of drinking a dry wine yet, at the same time, the heady, soft, pungent, grapey bouquet suggests a rich sweetness on the nose contrasting and, to some, conflicting with the dry palate.

RIESLING

Today, the Riesling is not so much a grape as a large family of relatives due to the extensive work which has taken place in the last century to try to 'improve' the original. This versatile variety, thought to have originated from the wild vines of the Rhine Valley, offers drinkers a wide range of wines from steely dry right through to heavily honeyed viscous dessert wines. It is grown throughout the world in cooler climates and enjoys at least 35 alternative names – however, it is extremely dependent on good weather which, for the Riesling, means an unusual mix of a warm, but not hot, late spring and summer followed by a mild autumn. Poor weather in autumn has a disastrous effect on this late-ripening grape, and, for this reason, hybridisation with earlier ripening grape varieties has been taking place since the mid 1800s.

A complete solution to the late ripening characteristic was thought to have been found in 1883 by Dr Müller of the village of Thurgau in Switzerland who successfully crossed the Riesling with the early-ripening Sylvaner. The resultant Müller-Thurgau did, indeed, ripen earlier – but produced far duller wine.

◀ *Tractor-mounted equipment being used to tie back long vine tendrils at the Louis Gisselbrecht vineyard in Alsace. This seasonal work is usually carried out in early summer.*

The Sylvaner was, for a long time, the most important grape variety in Germany and is planted extensively throughout the world, but it is a workhorse grape, lacking in flavour and complexity. Probably originating in Austria, the Sylvaner gives big crops but bland wine and this contribution to the Müller-Thurgau offspring of its marriage to the Riesling has doomed drinkers in many parts of the world, not least the UK, to less than exciting wines for far too long. Naturally the growers prefer this unexciting grape, it seems to give them everything they ask, but drinkers come off second best, as it gives them nothing they desire! The Müller-Thurgau is a sort of processed-cheese type of grape and the search for more exciting, flavoursome hybrids has been continuous.

Some of the better known recent successes are:

Schonburger M–T × (Sylvaner × Riesling)
Bacchus M–T × (Sylvaner × Riesling)
Optima M–T × (Sylvaner × Riesling)
Septimer M–T × Gewürztraminer
Wurzer M–T × Gewürztraminer
Perle M–T × Gewürztraminer
Faber M–T × Weissburgunder (Pinot Blanc)
Morio Muskat Sylvaner × Weissburgunder

The fact that more effort has been spent to try to improve on the growing habits of the Riesling whilst retaining its individual flavour than with any other variety is the greatest endorsement of its near-perfect balance. It is a shame that many people assume that all German wine is a product of the Riesling when, in practice, only the best will be Riesling – and the grower will proudly publicise the fact by putting 'Riesling' on the label after the vineyard name and before the sweetness grading.

Some of the best examples now come from Alsace, with the cooler areas of Australia, New Zealand and the northern states of the US also producing worthwhile examples.

SAUVIGNON BLANC

The name, which derives from 'Sauvage' or wild, well describes the flavours which vary from light and aromatic through to heavier, more Chardonnay-like tastes. This grape provides a complement to some of the new, lighter styles in cooking and, besides the traditional areas of cultivation in France, has now been planted in virtually every major wine-producing area of the world as the demand for light, flavoursome white wines increases.

The upper Loire around Sancerre and Pouilly-sur-Loire, together with neighbouring Reuilly, Quincy and Menetou-Salon, produces wines regarded as the benchmark for dry Sauvignon Blanc. Crisply dry with a fresh grassy tang and a refreshing gooseberry-like flavour, the wines from this area of France also show the slightly smoky overtones which have given the grape its other name: Blanc Fumé (or Fumé Blanc).

New plantings in the USA, Australia, New Zealand, Bulgaria, north-eastern Italy, Chile and around Penedés in Spain all aim at a sort of Pouilly-Blanc-Fumé effect, a sort of blackcurranty flinty lightness, and of these Montana and Cloudy Bay in New Zealand must be judged the most successful.

In California this grape has recently become more fashionable although, in spite of using the name Fumé Blanc, the style is more often akin to the dry whites of Bordeaux than the classic wines of the upper Loire. Robert Mondavi, that pioneering genius of the Napa Valley, produces wines with a richness that almost, but not quite, detracts from the crispness. Other excellent examples come from Beringer, Buena Vista and Christian Brothers where Brother Timothy gives a slightly oaked flavour to his version as well as Sterling Vineyard. In Livermore Valley Concannon and Wente Brothers both produce outstanding versions.

The Torres family at Penedés near Barcelona, as revered for their dedication and innovation as the Mondavi family in the Napa, also use Sauvignon Blanc grapes to good effect. Their top white wine, Gran Vina Sol Green Label is a combination of the local Parellada grape with Sauvignon Blanc and is given a degree of oak-ageing to produce a delightful wine, well rounded yet crisp, full of flavour yet refreshingly dry.

In Australasia the Sauvignon Blanc has not enjoyed the following it should. Few vineyards in Australia itself bother, although those that do, notably McWilliams and Rosemount, certainly produce excellent examples. The successes 'Down-under' have been from New Zealand, most notably the Marlborough Vineyard Sauvignon Blanc from Montana Wines and Cape Mentelle's Cloudy Bay. Cooks' Sauvignon Blanc is another very worthwhile wine while, also from the Hawkes Bay area, Mission Vineyard's version has a definitive Fumé Blanc style comparable with the best of the Loire.

The Sauvignon Blanc is also a major contributor to some of the world's finest sweet wines. Used in conjunction with the Sémillon and a little Muscadelle it produces the honeyed delights of Sauternes and Barsac and Late Harvest versions in the New World.

This grape has been the subject of some interesting research at Jekel vineyard in Monterey, south of San Francisco. By varying the numbers of bunches per vine and by pruning for leaf cover and by altering the amount of light reflected from the ground they produced, without any other action and without modifying the fermentation conditions, a complete spectrum of wines from the one vineyard, from bone dry, grassy wines through to deep, golden versions, rich although not sweet. These experiments may well point the way to future developments in vine growth – producing the wine on the vine rather than by amending fermentation conditions later.

Less important but common white grape varieties include:

Aligoté As Merlot is to Cabernet Sauvignon and Sylvaner to Riesling, Aligoté is to Chardonnay – the bridesmaid rather than the bride. Most French plantings are in Burgundy; Bulgaria has more than twice the French area and even Russia has extensive plantings. In many areas used as a good basis for sparkling wine.

Chenin Blanc The grape of the middle Loire. Sadly this grape, almost by virtue of its versatility, seems destined to produce dull wines virtually everywhere. This is probably due to the naturally medium-sweet wine it tends to produce – it appeals to unsophisticated palates so growers take less trouble. However, treated with respect, the Chenin Blanc gives amazingly complex wines in Savenniéres and rich sweet wines on the Coteaux du Layon, a tributary of the Loire. A large proportion of the vineyards of the middle Loire produce grapes destined to make sparkling Saumur. Elsewhere in the world it is similarly undervalued. Some worthwhile examples are produced in South Africa where it is known as the Steen and other good wines can be found in Australia and the USA.

Gewürztraminer Taking its name from Tramin in the Italian Tyrol, the Gewürz addition means 'spicy'. Some doubt exists whether the Traminer and the Gewürztraminer really are the same grape, but all examples, however labelled, possess the spicy perfume often likened to that of lychees. Best known are the wines of Alsace, but other good examples, albeit with less 'Gewürz', come from northern Italy, from parts of Germany and from Austria, while unsuccessful examples come from New World vineyards.

Malvasia or *Malvoisie* One of the oldest grapes originating, allegedly, in Monemvasia in the Greek Peloponnese. It is white port, it is malmsey, it is white Rioja, it is grown in southern Spain as a concentrated sweetener for blending and in Italy it is blended into Chianti as well as producing sweet, dry and sparkling wines. Is it versatile!

Müller-Thurgau Although developed in 1882 it was not until the post Second World War replantings that the Müller-Thurgau came into its own in Germany. The bulk of the tidal wave of cheaper German wines are of Müller-Thurgau stock for it represents a quarter of the planted vineyard area and even more of the output – hardly surprising when yields as high as 400 hl per hectare are achievable. See also Riesling.

Muscadet Thought to have originated in Burgundy – hence the proper name Melon de Bourgogne – it apparently replaced red grapes around the mouth of the Loire late in the 17th century due to pressures from Dutch traders presumably looking for lighter, more distillable, wines for brandy production. All too often anaemic or downright dull in spite of allegedly being the 'perfect' accompaniment for seafood.

Palomino Best known as the major constituent of sherry, this is really the only true glory of the grape. Dull table wines are produced in Jerez in addition to sherry, and also in Portugal, the Midi in France, and to a limited extent, in California. In South Africa and in Australia the grape is used for local sherry-style products.

Pinot Blanc A probable mutation of Pinot Noir – or even of Pinot Gris (see next). A grape with more problems than most over naming. Auxerrois in Alsace although the name Clevner or Klevner is also used. In Italy it has long been confused with Chardonnay which, of course, was for long thought to be a Pinot itself. Significant in East Germany and in Austria and increasingly in Chile. Its real strength is its suitability for sparkling wines.

Pinot Gris One of many mutations of the Pinot Noir. This strain is hardly white at all as, in many areas, the skins are definitely red hued. At its best in Alsace where, until EEC ruling forbade it, the wine was called Tokay d'Alsace, and in northern Italy where the name Tocai was used rather than Pinot Grigio. To further complicate the name issue, it is grown and respected in Hungary – home of the genuine Tokay – where it is known as the Szürkebarat or Graver Mönch.

Sémillon A complex grape and very underrated. It is one half of the Barsac/Sauternes production team but elsewhere in the world it has little opportunity to realise its potential. In Australia and New Zealand there are signs of serious attempts to capture the complex flavours in dry white wines and in California they are producing some pretty genuine-tasting 'Sauternes'.

Sylvaner Famous as the other parent of the Riesling crossing that produced the Müller-Thurgau hybrid. In its own right it is very widely planted, being popular for its high yields. However, as is so often the case, high yields make dull uninspiring wine. The best Sylvaners come from Alsace where some individuality and distinction is achieved.

Trebbiano A workhorse grape. Known as the Ugni Blanc and the St-Emilion in France, it is the main brandy grape in Charente for cognac. In Italy it produces Frascati and Orvieto among others as well as Tuscany's sweet Vin Santo. Very widely planted throughout the world, but usually producing unremarkable wines.

Welschriesling Almost, and undeservedly, a dirty word. Does well in central Europe, especially Romania, and could probably do well in many other areas if only growers would appreciate its real attributes rather than simply take advantage of its high yields. Widely planted throughout central Europe, there are a few high spots of sweet wines and a flood of indifferent sickly Yugoslavian cheapies.

RED WINE GRAPES

Of all the red grape varieties that are used to produce red wine, three are supreme: the Cabernet Sauvignon, Pinot Noir and Syrah or Shiraz.

CABERNET SAUVIGNON

Just as the Chardonnay is the most widely admired white grape, so the Cabernet Sauvignon is of the reds – admired by growers and drinkers alike for the richness of flavour and, in the newer growing areas, relative ease of production leading to realistic prices.

In Bordeaux it plays the major part in the classic Cabernet Sauvignon/Merlot/Cabernet Franc and/or Petit Verdot blend of the Médoc, while it is the lesser, but still significant, partner in the wines of St-Emilion and Pomerol.

The Cabernet Sauvignon produces later ripening grapes which are thick-skinned and

▲ *The tower of Château Latour. Probably best-known of all the 1re Crû (1st growth) Médoc properties, Latour is owned by sherry-shippers John Harvey, part of the British Allied-Lyons group.*

small berried – the low ratio of juice to skin producing a high tannin level which gives the prodigious ageing potential of the greatest Bordeaux wines. These long-lived wines do, of course, need several or, in some cases, many, years to come to maturity and for the youthful excess of acidity to diminish and mellow. Unfortunately this maturing process is necessarily expensive due to the capital tied up for long periods.

The less-than-great châteaux of Bordeaux use less Cabernet Sauvignon in their blends and more of the soft Merlot and the larger berried Cabernet Franc to overcome the initial high acidity of the Cabernet Sauvignon and to produce drinkable wines sooner.

A comparative graph of the maturing curves for wines of a premier crû château and wines from a crû bourgeois property shows the former as being almost undrinkable for about five years while the latter will start off easier to drink from the outset and will have peaked in about five years – and will be past its best in maybe 15 years, whereas superlative vintages of the greatest properties can live for centuries.

Unlike the Pinot Noir and the Gamay, the Cabernet Sauvignon when grown in warmer climates can produce sensational results. The higher levels of sunlight when combined with good wine-making techniques balances the tannin level with a greater sugar content to reproduce the effect achieved in matured Bordeaux from only the very greatest vintages. But the conditions can be reproduced virtually every year, so the wine is much softer and the expensive maturing periods can be reduced.

This ability to produce great wines that are soon ready for drinking is hastening the demise of the great Médoc properties as the greatest red wine producers of the world. The strength

▲ *Young vines developing in the nursery at the Yalumba vineyard in the* *Barossa Valley, Australia. Clonal selection ensures that* *suitable strains of grape can be matched to vineyard conditions.*

of the US dollar in the late 1980s, and the social snobbery too often found in the USA, has left their reputation as the most expensive of red wines relatively untouched, but they now have many first-rate competitors at a fraction of their prices.

The flavour to look for from this grape is predominantly that of blackcurrants. When growing areas are cool this will be a fresh, minty sort of taste, but in warmer regions this flavour is more intense – a sort of cassis flavour. As most Cabernet Sauvignon wines are oak-aged there is usually an overlay of vanilla – a whiff of the cigar-box – about the wines and this is pretty well common throughout the world.

PINOT NOIR

The main red grape of Burgundy and Champagne, the perverse Pinot Noir, can, given the most perfect conjunction of many, many variables, produce wine that is a pure joy – but the many factors so rarely coincide that the world has, for years, paid high prices for relatively indifferent and unimaginative wines.

If yields were higher then costs would be lower – but high yields and cool weather mean there is insufficient sugar in the grapes to produce an acceptable alcohol level. For years this problem was overcome by bringing in millions of litres of high alcohol, well coloured wine from Algeria and, after Algeria's independence, from around the northern shores of the Mediterranean. The EEC has savagely reduced the permitted levels of 'cutting wine' and the alternative method of increasing the alcohol level, that of adding sugar to the fermenting must, is now all too common and normally results in coarse, dull wine lacking the delicate subtlety that should be the hallmark of the Pinot Noir.

Newer growing areas in the world assumed that this problem would be overcome given sunnier growing conditions – higher levels of grape sugar removing the low alcohol/poor colour difficulties of the Burgundians. This assumption was wrong – more sunshine merely lead to overblown wines similar to those suffering from over sugaring in France.

The taste of Pinor Noir is difficult to describe – raspberries in manure is one suggestion – certainly the mix is like soft fruit with deeper vegetal undertones, but above all the taste is delicate and subtle. One thing it has never been is deep, rich and velvety – such Burgundies

imported (or concocted here) were more the product of the cutting wine and less the produce of true Pinot Noir.

There is no doubt that the Pinot Noir does not have the immediate appeal of, say, a fruity Gamay, a luxuriant Cabernet Sauvignon or a rich, earthy Syrah – and when one considers the generally thin, unremarkable wines now coming from Burgundy one wonders why people pay the quite extraordinary prices asked. Sadly, the story of the Pinot Noir still has to concentrate on Burgundy, for nowhere else in the world is yet worthy of comment, although growers still try for to produce a really good Pinot Noir at economic prices would be the vinous equivalent of finding the Holy Grail or the philosopher's stone!

SYRAH OR SHIRAZ

Probably one of the oldest varieties in the world, its origins can be traced back to the city of Shiraz in ancient Persia. Today, the strongholds of the Syrah are the Rhône valley and Australia where it is known as the Shiraz. Few Australian growers, however, are concerned with the production of quality Shiraz wine, the majority of the output goes to make bulk wines sold in boxes or other large volume containers. Of the few quality producers, Penfold must be the leader for, among others, their outstanding Magill Vineyard Grange Hermitage.

In France the cheaper Rhône wines contain almost no Syrah. However, as the price of the wine increases so does the proportion of Syrah it contains until, at the very peak of Rhône output, the wines of Côte Rôtie and Hermitage are 100% Syrah for the red grape component (white grapes can be added in small proportions to modify the concentrated fruit and darkly tannic nature of the Syrah).

In the Lebanon, Serge Hochar uses around 20% Syrah for his legendary Chateau Musar blends, with Cabernet Sauvignon and Cinsault as the other constituents. There are hopeful signs that California may yet produce quality wines from this grape, although here, too, there will no doubt have to be other varieties of grape blended with the uncompromising Syrah/Shiraz.

Well loved he garleek, onyons and eek lekes,
And for to drinken strong wyn as red as blood.
Geoffry Chaucer 1340–1400
The Canterbury Tales: The Prologue

Less important but other common red grape varieties include:

Barbera One of the world's most planted grapes. In Italy the plantings exceed that of Sangiovese (see opposite) and even in California more than 10% of that state's red grapes are Barbera. Often underrated and even more often badly treated, in the north-west of Italy it finds sympathy and understanding and produces easy drinking wines of character.

Cabernet Franc The often overlooked third member of the Médoc blend; also used as a single variety in the Loire, producing light-bodied wines, the best have great charm but, more often, lack flavour. Many Italian wines labelled 'Cabernet' are Cabernet Franc not Cabernet Sauvignon.

Carignan A large volume producer in southern France and also grown in Sardinia. Originated in Cariñena in Aragon where it still grows, but now widespread in Catalonia. Best examples come from Fitou in southern France.

Cinsault High crop yields, tough skins, resistance to disease, good colour, early ripening and, best of all, ease of machine-harvesting, make this a popular grape with many growers. It has swept through the southern French vineyards. Capable of producing everything from rosé to rock-solid reds, the Cinsault is usually best in a blend.

Gamay or *Gamay Noir* The splendid red grape of Beaujolais. On the sandy, stony granite-based soil of the area it gives one of the most agreeable and justly popular wines of France. Fruity, tender, ready early, better without bottle age except in a few cases. The most friendly of all reds. Also good in the Loire, but attempts to grow it elsewhere have met with little success.

Grenache An amazingly adaptable variety. Grown throughout southern France, northern Spain, north Africa – all the hotter growing areas. Best known as a major part of the Châteauneuf-du-Pape cocktail of permitted

RECOMMENDED WINES

PRICE BANDS – *prices are based on those prevailing at 1.6.90*

A	CHEAP	*Under £2.50*
B	INEXPENSIVE	*£2.50 – £4.00*
C	AVERAGE	*£4.00 – £6.00*
D	PRICEY	*£6.00 – £10.00*
E	EXPENSIVE	*£10.00 – £20.00*
F	VERY EXPENSIVE	*Over £20.00*

These wines are recommended as providing good examples of the characteristics of the more important grape varieties. Purists might be surprised at some of the following choices, but in every case I have tried to recommend wines which are distributed by at least one of the national chains, be they supermarkets or high street retailers. In some cases they are, perhaps, not the most perfect specimens one could find, but they all share the benefit of being excellent value. I can see little point, for example, in recommending Sassicaia as the best example of Cabernet Sauvignon wine (which it arguably is!) when it is virtually unobtainable and very highly priced.

WHITE GRAPES

Chardonnay Khan Krum Reserve Chardonnay (Bulgaria) **B**
Vin de Pays d'Oc Chardonnay, Hugh Ryman (France) **B**
Jeunes Vignes, La Chablisienne (France) **C**
Raimat Chardonnay (Spain) **C**
Lowengang Chardonnay, Alois Lageder (Italy) **D**

Sauvignon Blanc Most New Zealand examples, especially
Montana Sauvignon Blanc **C**
or, from other countries,
Ch la Jaubertie Sauvignon, Nick Ryman (France) **B**
Sauvignon du Haut-Poitou, Caves Co-op du Haut-Poitou (France) **B**

Riesling German-style, medium-sweet
Scharzhofberger Riesling, Bernd Van Volxem (MSR Germany) **B**
Eitelsbacher Marienholz Riesling, Bischofliches Konvikt (MSR Germany) **B**

varieties, but provides the bulk of most of the Rhône output as well as rosé wines from Listrac and Tavel and sweet wines from Banyuls. Sound but undistinguished.

Merlot Best known as the other half of the Médoc 'double act' where the soft plumminess of this grape balances the initial hardness of the Cabernet Sauvignon. It is, however, the predominant grape of Pomerol and St-Emilion and is bottled by itself to great effect in California and Bulgaria and with less distinction in Italy.

Nebbiolo 'Nebiolium' is mentioned in the early 16th century in what is now Barolo and it is suggested that the ancestry of the grape extends back at least to Roman times. However, with the exception of the north-western corner of Italy, few growers anywhere respond to the uncompromisingly dry acid attack of this variety. Careful wine-making and lengthy ageing are essential and many nowadays lack the patience.

Sangiovese Provides the backbone of the great reds of central Italy, Chianti and Brunello di Montalcino. Noted for fullness of flavour and rich, deep colour, it is also used for less prestigious wines across the whole of northern and north-central Italy. Less successful elsewhere in the world. The name allegedly derives from 'Sanguis Jovis' or Jupiter's blood!

Tempranillo Temprana, Spanish for early, is the origin of the name. In spite of romantic stories about this grape starting as a Pinot Noir or a Cabernet and brought to Spain by pilgrims, this is a genuinely indigenous Spanish grape. A 40% participant in the wash of wines from the Rioja, it is actually a somewhat flavourless grape. Does well in Valdepeñas and some fine wines also come from Penedés and, especially, Raimat in Lérida. Also found in Portugal and in Argentina.

Zinfandel Thought of as indigenous to California, but probably the Primitivo from Sicily. Can be all things to all producers, often abused but, when treated with respect, gives a rich, spicy taste with plummy overtones.

RED GRAPES

Riesling Drier style
Riesling, La Decapole, Turckheim Co-op (Alsace) **B**
Riesling d'Alsace, Gisselbrecht (Alsace) **B**
Plus practically any Australian Rhine Riesling, normally **B** or **C**

Chenin Blanc Sweeter styles (moelleux)
Moulin Touchais, Coteaux du Layon, Touchais (France) **C**
Ch Bellerive, Quarts de Chaume (France) **D**

Chenin Blanc Normal style, off-dry or medium
Ch Moncontour, Vouvray (France) **B**
Domaine des Ambuisieres, Vouvray (France) **C**

Sémillon Go for Australian versions – Tolley's, Saltram, Piggot Hill, Brown Bros., Mitchelton etc – all are excellent **C**s

Cabernet Sauvignon Many, if not most, Californian or Australian versions at all prices
Orihovitza Reserve Cabernet Sauvignon (Bulgaria) **B**
Raimat Cabernet Sauvignon (Spain) **C**

Merlot Safeway's Hungarian Merlot **A**
Firestone Vineyards Merlot (California) **C**

Pinot Noir Difficult to recommend. Oregon examples such as Erie Vineyards, Adelsheim and Knudsen Erath very good but difficult to find. For more than a hint of the real thing try Hungarian Pinot Noir (sometimes labelled Nagyburgundi) **B**

Syrah/Shiraz Most unblended Australian examples, particularly Penfolds Bin 2 or Bin 28 Shiraz or Brown Brothers Shiraz all **B**
French examples with enough Syrah in the blending to discern the true flavour do not start until category **E** with the best in **F** – see recommendations for the Rhône, pages 74–80.

WINE PRODUCTION

THE VINEYARDS OF THE WORLD

These are mainly located in two bands – in the northern hemisphere between latitudes 35° and 52° and between 30° and 45° in the southern hemisphere. The distance from the equator is only one of many factors that determine temperature suitability for growing vines whose grapes are destined for wine production. Altitude plays a big part – nearer the equator grapes still develop well at higher altitudes, as the best vineyards in Sicily, Australia, Morocco and

LUXEMBURG p176
GERMAN p10

ENGLAND p173
SWITZERLAND p176
FRANCE p43
ITALY p119
SPAIN p137
PORTUGAL p165
ALGI p1
MOROCCO p190
TUN p

CANADA p210

USA p193

MEXICO p210

☐ Main wine regions

PERU p214

CHILE p212
BRAZIL p214
URUGUAY p214
ARGENTINA p211

Algeria, confirm. Proximity to the moderating influence of large bodies of water also helps to modify the effect of what might otherwise be an environment unsuitable for quality grape production – the effects of the mists of San Francisco Bay on the Napa Valley and from the Gironde on Bordeaux vineyards are scientifically established and well documented.

Soil with good drainage is another advantage. This normally means gravel, slate, schist or limestone, although volcanic soils are also good. It is a commonly heard expression that 'vines need to fight' – an oversimplification, but it is generally true that forcing vines to drive their tap roots deep to find sustenance does have a beneficial effect on grape quality. To see the state of the top-soil of many of the world's greatest vineyards would be to wonder how anything could grow, never mind a vine expected to produce masses of fruit.

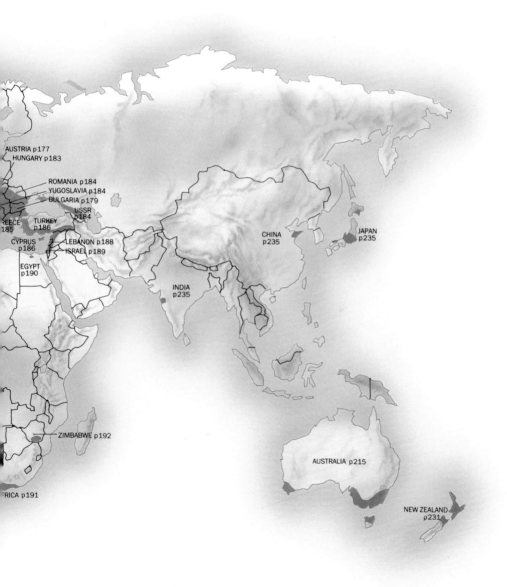

AUSTRIA p177
HUNGARY p183

ROMANIA p184
YUGOSLAVIA p184
BULGARIA p179
USSR p184

REECE 185
TURKEY p186

CYPRUS p186
LEBANON p188
ISRAEL p189

EGYPT p190

INDIA p235

CHINA p235

JAPAN p235

ZIMBABWE p192

AUSTRALIA p215

RICA p191

NEW ZEALAND p231

MAKING WINE

Over the centuries that man has produced wine there has been a sort of gradual natural selection: if grapes grew better in one area than another then that tended to become the grape growing area and, similarly, the vines that produced the best crops were favoured over types that were less successful. Nowadays science has reached such a level of exactitude that potential vineyards can be surveyed and a decision made, not just about the best variety, but precisely the best strain, clone or hybrid. Happily, because so many variables are involved in the making of wine this scientific precision has not (yet) resulted in anonymous alcoholic beverages.

Grapes have been grown around the Mediterranean for both wine production and eating at least since 3000 BC and by AD 500 viniculture had spread across Europe in the wake of the Roman conquerors. Almost all the main production areas in Europe today can trace their ancestry back to the Romans, if not beyond. However, wine production was very haphazard and relied almost entirely on the ability of grape juice to ferment naturally. It was not until the work of Louis Pasteur in the mid 1800s that the essential part played by yeasts in the fermentation process was understood.

The production methods used down the centuries had been crude. Crushing was by treading or pressing; the uncontrolled fermentation by the natural yeasts continued until either the sugar was used up, in which case a dry wine resulted, or the alcohol level was high enough to stop the yeasts converting more sugar to alcohol, in which case a semi-sweet or sweet wine resulted. The importance of temperature was not understood, and sometimes fermentation stopped because temperatures became too high.

Pasteur's work enabled wine-makers to improve on their previous primitive methods, and greater understanding of the fermentation process produced a continual flow of modifications and improvements for the next 100 years. This, allied to improvements in the basic technology and materials – stainless steel superseding wood, for example – and the genetic engineering of plants, now enables us to drink well balanced and stable wines with clear characteristics and stable composition from any of the world's production areas.

◀ *Boring post-holes for a new vineyard at the Maculan property at Breganze in the Veneto region of Italy. The posts mark the end of each new row of vines and will anchor the network of wires on which the vines are trained.*

▶ *'Museum' of old and rare vintages, Marqués de Riscal, Elciega, Rioja, Spain.*

METHODS OF PRODUCTION

The basic requirements for wine production are:

● a method of separating the grape juices with their natural sugars from the stalks, skins and pips which contain colouring and tannins
● a container to hold the fermenting grape juice
● some form of stoppered vessel to contain the wine.

The first requirement, that of separating the juices, normally takes two separate machines: a destalker and a press.

Destalkers are most often in the form of a revolving perforated drum through which the grapes are pushed by centrifugal force leaving the stalks behind.

Presses crush the grapes, letting the juices flow into a vat, leaving the skin and pips behind. They may be either horizontal or vertical.

Horizontal presses are most often used for white wines and take one of two forms. In the first a circular disc or discs work their way along a central screw squeezing the grapes against the end plate or plates, the juice running off into a trough under the press. In the second type a

▲ *Sauvignon Blanc grapes being discharged into a light crusher* *at Marqués de Riscal in Rueda.*

central inflatable bladder squeezes the grapes against slatted drum sides forcing the juices out between the slats into the trough.

Vertical presses are mainly used for red wines. A vertical cylindrical basket is filled with grapes and a circular plate on a threaded screw is pressed down from above. The juices are squeezed out through slatted sides to collect in the bottom and be run off through a tap.

Several pressings are needed to extract all the available juice, but the best wines result from using only the juice of the first pressing. Also, the less time that juice and air are in contact the better as the juice quickly oxidises and eventually will turn brown with prolonged air contact. For this reason some modern white wine presses allow no air contact at all until the juice is in the fermentation vat.

Unless the wine-maker prevents it, fermentation starts immediately the grapes burst open and the juice comes into contact with the yeasts on the grape skins, so controlled fermentation normally follows immediately after pressing. For centuries wooden vats varying in size from a barrel to giant containers holding thousands of gallons have been used with clay or concrete vats as an alternative in some areas. This type of vat is still in use, although now with specially developed epoxy resin paint coating the sides, but the usual practice today is for fermentation to take place in a large stainless steel cylinder equipped with a system for cooling the outer skin. Water flowing down the outside is the simplest method, while the more sophisticated vats have glycol or ammonia circulating through tubes around the outside of the vat, often linked to temperature probes in the fermenting liquid so that the fermentation temperature is maintained to within one or two degrees of what the wine-maker considers the optimum.

Nowadays every stage of the wine-making process can be controlled, modified or altered. For example, some wine-makers centrifuge the pressed juice to remove the natural yeasts and then introduce specially developed cultures with better characteristics to start the fermentation process. Strangely, but reassuringly, this has lead to local and regional styles and flavours becoming more pronounced, rather than creating one standardised wine taste which was the fear of the old-time producers when faced with the modern techniques.

After the wine is produced, it will either be stored to allow taste characteristics to develop or to allow the introduction of outside flavours such as the taste of oak, or else it will be put into its container immediately. Today these containers may be glass or plastic, ring-pull cans or bag-in-the-boxes. However, quality wine is still only sold in conventional glass bottles stoppered with a fully inserted cork which is protected by a foil.

MAKING WHITE WINE

Not everyone realises that all grape juice is white or, more accurately, colourless. The colouring in red or rosé wines comes from the skins of black grapes so, provided care is taken to reduce or prevent skin contact, white wine can be produced from any colour of grape. The very best champagnes, for example, can contain over 50% juice of black grapes, but, as a general rule, most white wine is produced exclusively from white grapes.

The methods used to produce a typical, good quality regional white wine are the same almost everywhere.

The juice is separated from the skin and the pips as quickly as possible and is then left for up to 24 hours for any residues to sink to the bottom of the holding vat. The clear juices are then pumped into the fermentation vat. If the juice has become especially cloudy, a fining agent is passed through the juice to collect the heavier particles or else centrifuging is used. Both methods produce a totally clear juice but also remove the natural yeasts, so the juices are seeded with new yeast cultures.

Fermentation then begins and the chemical reaction produces heat which should be controlled. A temperature of around 20°C/68°F seems to be ideal for white wines, although there are some variations according to type of grape and the wine-maker's preference.

The vast majority of white wines are expected to be light and fresh tasting. To help achieve this the wine-maker will store them for as short a time as possible before bottling and he may introduce a malolactic fermentation to soften the wines by converting the sharper malic acid to softer lactic acid – but whether or not this secondary fermentation is introduced, wines will normally be bottled immediately after their final cleaning by filtration, fining, a second fining, or the use of a centrifuge.

Modern bottling techniques also call for a cold-stabilisation process before actual bottling where the wine is chilled to just above freezing

▼ *Wine containers for fermentation or storage can be of wood, concrete, stainless steel or* *fibreglass, as are these in the Huesgen cellars at Traben-Trarbach, Moselle.*

for several days to encourage tartrate crystals to precipitate out of the wine and fall to the bottom of the tank. In times past, when wines were often stored for years in cool cellars, these crystals formed on the inside of the storage barrels, but due to faster modern methods of production and distribution, crystals sometimes form in the bottle – especially if storage conditions are not good with varying temperatures and exposure to sunlight. These crystals are tasteless and odourless and do no harm whatsoever, but they can be unsightly and can lead to customers rejecting an otherwise perfect bottle of wine because of the 'sugar' in it.

Some of the finest white wines, most especially those produced from the Chardonnay grape, can benefit from ageing in oak barrels – the oakiness complementing the other, natural, grape flavours and adding another dimension to a quality wine. Apart from these exceptional, big, oakey whites, the rule of thumb should be produce quickly and drink quickly.

The full range of white wines is:

PLAIN, DRY WHITE WINES
Usually made from non-grapey grapes – grapes which have no pronounced special taste characteristics of their own and typified by Muscadet, Soave or Vinho Verde. These are wines which give pleasure by their youthful freshness, often aided by the slight prickle of dissolved carbon dioxide present. Modern production methods now exclude air as much as possible.

DRY, GRAPEY WHITE WINES
These will be distinctly aromatic, as in good quality wines from Germany or Alsace. However, greater care has to be exercised to choose the correct moment to pick the grapes to ensure maximum sugar content. Considerable effort is made to preserve the individual character of the grapes during processing and to bring out the flavours of grapes like Gewürztraminer, Riesling, Sauvignon Blanc and so on.

FULL DRY WHITES, OFTEN OAK-AGED

Sometimes made with red-wine style skin contact during fermentation and often at higher temperatures in wooden casks. Ageing in barrel for up to 12 months is not uncommon. The Chardonnay grape is the most popular for this type of treatment, white burgundies being the best known and by far the most expensive examples of wines made in this way.

SEMI-SWEET WHITE WINES

Cheaper German-style wines of this type are now normally fermented through to dryness and then have unfermented grape juice (sussreserve) added. 'Back-blending', as this technique is called, lowers the alcohol level and produces the smooth, sweeter styles popular with unsophisticated wine drinkers. True semi-sweet wines are produced from other varieties of grape, the Chenin Blanc for example.

MEDIUM-SWEET WHITE WINES

Like semi-sweet white wines these are produced from grapes with a high sugar content so that fermentation can be stopped at a point where the alcohol level is sufficiently high, but sufficient sugar remains unfermented to produce a medium-sweet wine.

SWEET DESSERT WINES

The grape sugar is concentrated to a degree that allows fermentation to the required alcohol level and yet allows sufficient sugar to remain for a sweet wine to result.

SWEET WINES

Why are sweet wines sweet? A simple question, but one with a complex answer. Of course, the straightforward response is that they are sweet because they contain sugar – but only as a result of considerable labour and significant cost.

All grapes contain natural sugars which provide the 'food' on which the yeasts feed to produce alcohol and carbon dioxide during fermentation. If the grape sugar levels are low when the crop is picked then all the sugar available will be used up during fermentation and a dry wine will result. To achieve a naturally sweet wine, it follows that the sugar levels must be high enough to allow fermentation to the desired level of alcohol, yet with enough sugar remaining to render the wine sweet.

If the sugar levels are sufficiently high to allow fermentation to go on to finality this is normally reached at an alcohol level of 16%–17% alcohol at which point the yeasts are 'stunned' by the alcohol and no further fermentation occurs. Under certain exceptional conditions the actual concentration of sugar in the grape also inhibits the action of the yeast – some massively sweet Trockenbeerenauslesen will only ferment to 5%–6% alcohol. But, for sweet wine producers, successful production depends principally on good sunshine levels to produce a high sugar content in the crop and then on further events, some natural, some artificial, to concentrate these grape sugars still more.

Luckily nature, given the right conditions, provides an excellent means of concentrating the sugars through the action of the benign mould we call noble rot – *pourriture noble* in French, *edelfaule* in German, *Botrytis cinerea* in Latin. This mould, which is naturally present in vineyards, will, following suitably moist, misty mornings and bright, fine days, develop on the berries and start its beneficial work. The mould feeds on the sugars and the tartrates in the grape pulp and makes the skin permeable, so allowing the water content to evaporate. Unfortunately, this process is seldom uniform throughout the vineyard, or even through each bunch of grapes, so that repeated pickings are necessary. The workers may go around a vineyard perhaps ten times between September and November to pick the fully ripened/rotted berries at their peak. In addition there is also the danger that October rain will wipe out the harvest, or that conditions will not encourage noble rot anyway. The cost of this is obviously very high and, in practice, is only carried out by the most expensive properties. Other growers simply wait to pick until they feel that the optimum balance has been achieved between, on the one hand, decayed berries and, on the other hand, berries insufficiently affected. The alternative to using berries wholly or partially affected by noble rot is to increase the sugar level artificially. In the simplest cases this just means adding sugar and the lack of subtlety always shows.

Air-drying (Italian reciotos) or freezing (German and Austrian eisweins) the grapes increases the concentration of sugar. In the first case the raisin-like berries produce a liquorous dark, syrupy wine, while eiswein is the exact opposite – delicate, fragrant and light.

FORTIFIED WINES

Another option is available to the maker of sweet wines. If the grapes are reasonably sweet then alcohol can be added part-way through fermentation – this raises the alcohol level, stuns the yeasts and stops fermentation with the majority of the natural sugars still present. This process, called fortification, is used for many south European dessert wines as well as for port (page 170) and, with modification, for sherry (page 160) and vermouths.

If a quantity of pure spirit or brandy is added to unfermented grape juice, the resultant mixture is called a vin de liqueur – the best-known example of which is Pineau de Charentes from the Cognac region in France. On the other hand, spirits are sometimes added to wines after fermentation to act as a preservative, as in the case of sherry.

But the main reason for adding spirits or brandy to a partially fermented wine is the preservation of a proportion of the grape sugar by arresting fermentation. The French call their wines of this type 'vins doux naturels', which is somewhat inaccurate as the name implies that they are naturally sweet which they are not!

SPARKLING WINES

There is evidence that Limoux, near Carcassonne, produced sparkling wines at least a century before Champagne – and Champagne has been producing them for over 200 years!

Three systems exist to promote bubbles in wine, the simplest being the injection of carbon dioxide as in lemonade or Coca Cola. However, the mousse, or pattern of bubbles, is coarse and quickly dissipates. Inducing a secondary fermentation in the wine is a more satisfactory method and this can be done in a sealed vat (cuvée close) from which the wine is bottled while still under pressure or in each individual bottle, the méthode champenoise (below). In each case the wine has a carefully calculated amount of a sugar and yeast mixture added to start the secondary fermentation. The comparative ease of doing this in vat compared with in bottle is accurately reflected in the prices of these two types of sparkling wine. The carbon dioxide which bubbles out of any sparkling wine is, however, only a part of that which is dissolved in the wine. Much remains in solution until the wine is drunk – giving the attractive prickle in the mouth and, perhaps more important, speeding the absorbtion of alcohol into the bloodstream and accelerating its passage to the brain.

THE MÉTHODE CHAMPENOISE – HOW CHAMPAGNE IS MADE

Méthode champenoise is the inducing of secondary fermentation in individual bottles by the addition of carefully measured amounts of yeast and sugar. After this addition the bottles are stored in cold limestone caves at around 4°C/38°F and, during this storage, the first two to three months completes the secondary fermentation. Regulations require further ageing – a minimum of two years for non-vintage champagne and four years for vintage – for the longer the ageing, the deeper the flavour gained by the wine from the lees in the bottle. After ageing this sediment is persuaded down the inverted bottle either by manual or mechanical means until it has collected over the cork. To remove this sedimentation the inverted bottles are then passed through a freezing brine solution so that when the cork is removed the sediment shoots out as a frozen plug adhering to the cork.

The bottle is then topped up with a liqueur d'expedition or dosage which is a mixture of sweetener and champagne brandy – the final sweetness of the product is thus determined by the degree of extra sweetening added – see page 66. Méthode champenoise produces a mousse of columns of fine bubbles which last longer than either of the other methods.

▲ *Gyropallets are used in the making of méthode champenoise wines to ease the sediment in the bottle on to the cork.*

MAKING RED WINE

The essential difference between red and white wine production is the use of the skins, pips and stalks of black grapes to add colour and tannin. The colouring also contributes to both taste and flavour and the tannins are important in promoting longevity.

As most red wines are dry, the actual date of picking tends to be a little less critical than for white wine, but from the time the grapes are picked the maker of red wine has to make more choices and decisions than his opposite number making white wine.

The first is about which form of pressing and fermentation to use: macération carbonique, thermovinification or vat fermentation and pressing.

MACÉRATION CARBONIQUE

This method of fermentation is used to produce easy drinking, soft, fruity wine – short-lived but fun. The technique was developed by Professor Michel Flanzy and others in France in 1935, and it has been surprisingly slow to gain acceptance considering the very real benefits it offers.

Whole bunches of grapes are put, with as little damage as possible, into a vat which is then sealed. The weight of the mass will burst some grapes, so starting a spontaneous fermentation. This causes the production of carbon dioxide which, as it cannot escape, surrounds the grapes, creating a spontaneous fermentation within the whole grapes, which leads to flavour and colour being extracted from the inner skin. The process is allowed to continue for several days before the juices are run off and the remaining mass in the vat is lightly pressed to produce some more juice. Fermentation is then completed in a separate vat, but does not take long because most of the sugar has already become alcohol.

THERMOVINIFICATION

An alternative to macération carbonique for producing well-coloured, soft red wines. In this method the grapes are heated in an oxygen-free atmosphere, which removes the colour from the skins. The grapes are then cooled, pressed and fermented off the skins as if making white wine. Cheap Beaujolais Nouveau is often produced in this way.

VAT FERMENTATION AND PRESSING

The arguments about leaving the stems on grapes when making red wine are many. Some growers do, some sometimes do and some never do, but whatever the grower's policy on de-stemming, there is one natural phenomenon which occurs during fermentation that must be overcome. The mass of skins and stalks in the vat floats to the surface during fermentation supported by carbon dioxide bubbles. This cap of skins has to be broken up, sometimes by men with long poles, but more often by pumping juice from the bottom of the vat and spraying it over the cap of skins on the surface. When fermentation is finished the juice is pumped out into another vat and the remaining matter (the 'marc') is pressed. The first, gentle, pressure will give a wine which can usefully be added to the free-run juices, but the second, more vigorous, pressing only produces wine fit for cheap blending or distillation into brandy – hence 'Marc de Bourgogne', 'Marc de Champagne'.

Other processes are now necessary, or may be chosen, to ensure that the final produce accurately reflects the wine-maker's intentions regarding the finished taste of his wine.

RACKING

The technical name for the process of clearing all particles from wine to leave it clear. Older, traditional, methods were the use of coagulants, such as isinglass, whipped egg whites, blood or gelatine. As they sank to the bottom of the vat these products attracted floating particles. Mineral powders such as bentonite – a powdery clay from Wyoming – or potassium ferrocyanide are also used. Once the heavy sediment or gros lies has fallen, the wine can be poured into barrels for ageing. However, the wine will continue to throw (release) a sediment, frequently necessitating transfer from barrel to barrel sometimes via a closed pipe and sometimes, if the wine-maker thinks that oxygenation would be beneficial, through open troughs.

MALOLACTIC FERMENTATION

In times past it was noted that fresh activity would develop in wine stored in cellars. This activity used to occur in the spring and as it seemed to be a revival of fermentation, it was assumed to be some sort of rapport between the wine and the season. After the activity the wine tasted softer, less sharp. This is due to bacteria changing the malic (apple) acid in the wine to the less sharp lactic (milk) acid and giving off some carbon dioxide at the same time. The process is now encouraged, and often artificially induced, when the normal fermentation takes place.

BLENDING

Some grapes seem to produce a better wine when bottled on their own, others are definitely improved by mixing with other varieties. The Pinot Noir of Burgundy and the Riesling of Germany are seldom better when blended but the Cabernet Sauvignon is a prime example of a grape often improved by blending. As a general rule, most of the red wines of the Old World are blends, but blending is less prevalent in the newer growing regions in America and Australia, for example. However, even if a wine is labelled as a varietal wine – the produce of just one grape variety – it is very seldom 100% of that variety, and would often be the poorer if it was! Until 1983 California only required 51% of a variety of grape for a wine to be labelled as being of that grape although since 1983 the proportion must be 76%, which is a more general minimum around the world. The minimum to comply with EEC regulations is 85%.

AGEING

There are two types of ageing. One, oxidative ageing, occurs when oxygen is present, as in a barrel. In the other, reductive ageing, oxygen is almost completely excluded, as in a wine bottle. The balance between these two effects can be critical and is often specified in the wine production regulations for a particular area or region.

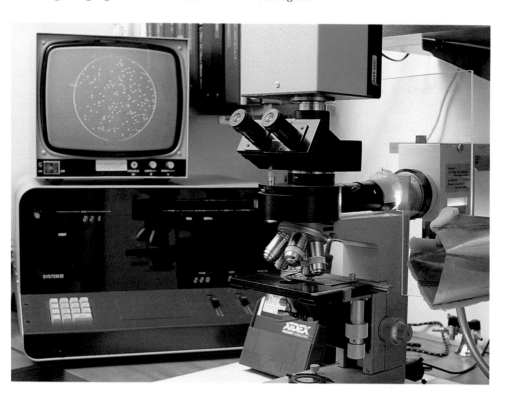

▲ *Few facets of wine production escape analysis these days. Optical and electronic analytical equipment in the laboratory of Smith & Son, now run by the Hill-Smith family, Barossa Valley, Australia.*

The full range of red wines is:

LIGHT, FRUITY RED WINES

Normal fermentation and pressing but very limited contact with the skins. These are fresher and less astringent than other reds, but lack their longevity as the protective (and bitter) tannins are very much reduced.

SOFT, RICH, FRUITY RED WINES

The products of macération carbonique (page 30) or thermovinification (page 30). Short-lived wines, but full and rich, very approachable, although normally lacking in complexity and subtlety.

FULLY AGED RED WINES

Produced by normal vat fermentation and prolonged skin contact, which can vary from three weeks in relatively sunless Bordeaux to three days in the more favoured Napa Valley in California. Ageing in oak barrels is followed by ageing in bottle before the wine is sold.

MAJOR EXCEPTIONS

Lambrusco and Rotwein Sekt. Frothy, lightly fizzy Italian and German red wines.
Reciotto della Valpolicella (Amarone). Reciotto is produced by air drying grapes from the ripest part of bunches of grapes left on the vines after the first picking. This concentration produces a sweet red wine. When some of this wine is allowed to ferment as far as it will go the result is a massive alcohol level over 16% and a dry wine with huge body and great depth. This is Amarone, a bitter or dry version of Reciotto.

ROSÉ WINES

Few rosé wines aspire to any sort of prestige, the majority being simple wines produced for quick, easy, summer drinking – picnic and patio rather than dining room.

The production technique is simple. A red grape, usually light bodied such as the Gamay or the Cabernet Franc, is pressed and fermented with some or all of the skins in the fermentation vat for as long as it takes to colour the wine to the desired intensity. Care has to be exercised as too prolonged a contact will sharpen the taste of what is normally expected to be a fairly bland, middle-of-the-road flavour.

The actual shade of a rosé's pink can vary from the lightly tinted 'blush' or 'partridge eye' wines of California through the orangey shades of Tavel to the light reds of Haut-Poitou Cabernet or Spanish Clarete.

The bulk of rosés, ignoring the commercial chemical confections of Portugal, are produced in Anjou on the Loire, and if called simply Rosé d'Anjou are produced from the undemanding and unexciting Groslot grape. More interesting rosés from around the world include:
Anjou Cabernet Rosé using the more flavoursome Cabernet Franc grape
Rosé de Riceys Pinot Noir rosé from Champagne, rare and expensive
Rosé de Marsannay another rare Pinot Noir rosé, this time from Dijon
Lirac and Tavel rosés well flavoured, with tangerine colours
Chiaretto del Garda an Italian cocktail of Gropello, Sangiovese, Barbera and Marzemino grapes
Cendre de Novembre (Embers of November) from the Jura and the Poulsard grape, though here rosé wines are known as vins gris, grey wine!

The Californian 'blush' wines are a response to changing tastes. Faced by a market drinking less and less red wine and more and more white wine the Californians, in desperation, are producing as white a wine from red grapes as they can manage. As these wines inevitably have a hint of red no matter how they try, they have made a virtue of necessity and coined the marketing name 'blush' wines. The benefit is that the wines, being produced from such substantial, flavoursome red grapes as Cabernet Sauvignon and Zinfandel, have good depth of flavour and a reasonable bouquet, characteristics rare in European rosés.

OAK-AGED WINES

Oak flavouring is virtually the only extraneous flavour voluntarily introduced into both red and white wines to add to those produced naturally by sun, soil and fruit.

Oak ageing, where wines are stored in young oak barrels so that the wine will leach out the tannins naturally present in the wood, has been carried out for centuries, but in the past the practice was one of necessity rather than choice. Wine had to be matured and stored somewhere and the most convenient vessels were hardwood barrels of around 200 litres – the size that one man could roll or two carry. However, necessity has now given way to choice as plastic barrels can easily be produced at a fraction of the cost of hardwood, but the

taste of oak is valued in addition to those tastes naturally present in the wine.

The flavouring leached out of the wood is mainly that of vanillin, the vanilla-tasting tannin, although many other scents and tastes are also gained in the process and the contribution made by each barrel is at its height in the first two years of use. After this period a skin of tartrate crystals forms on the surface of the wood, reducing the contact of wine and wood.
This skin can now be removed, so extending the period for which the barrel can be used to impart flavour to the wine. Old barrels can, however, still play a useful part in the ageing process of wine. If, for example, the wine is to be matured for a number of years, as in the case of Gran Reserva Riojas, then the use of new barrels throughout this period would overwhelm the wine with the woody taste. Wine-makers therefore move maturing wines from new to old casks to achieve the desired balance of flavouring in the wine.

Only wines from grapes of pronounced character will benefit from ageing in this way. Grapes such as Chardonnay, Cabernet Sauvignon, Syrah/Shiraz and the Rioja blending

▲ *Only the largest wine-producers still make their own barrels. Here, at Herpe near Narbonne in the Corbières region of France, reconditioned barrels are steam cleaned before re-use.*

of Tempranillo and Garnacha all benefit from oak – but the sources of the 'best' oak is a matter of some dispute. Most valued are woods from Limousin, Nevers and Tronçais in France and Kentucky (long used for Bourbon ageing) in the USA although German, Baltic and Balkan oaks also have their adherents.

The process is naturally expensive and the high cost of the barrels, together with their fairly short life, has led to short cuts. Oak chips may be added which, due to their large surface area quickly impart flavour, or, alternatively, wine may be pumped through a bed of oak chips. Liquid additives, usually prepared by boiling oak chips and shavings with wine or weak brandy (called Boisé in Cognac) are also sometimes used. Few growers will admit to using these additives, but they are harmless, generally beneficial and keep costs down – which benefits the wine drinker.

WINE AND FOOD

Wine and food seem to have such a natural affinity. It is difficult to drink a full red wine without wishing there were some cheese and biscuits to nibble and dessert wines seem to cry out for peaches, nectarines or strawberries as an accompaniment. Most people, however, plan the dinner menu first and chose wines to accompany the food rather than vice-versa.

Before suggesting wines to complement various dishes let us first look at some conventions of wine drinking at mealtimes that have stood the test of time. Convention is, perhaps, a dangerous word to use, for one of the great problems surrounding the matching of wine and food is that people are often inhibited from branching out and exploring different combinations, by a fear of 'doing the wrong thing'.

When choosing wine for any given occasion remember the Three Cs: convention, custom and common sense! And of the three common sense is the most important. Most drinkers know more than they realise, but the inhibitions due to mumbo-jumbo and snobbery induced by the so-called mystique of wine knowledge make people self-conscious.

A wine drinker saying 'I'm no connoisseur, but I know what I like' should not regard this as an admission of defeat, but as a starting point for exploration:

● if two bottles of red wine are selected then it is wise to have both of the same style of wine. Two wines of the Bordeaux blend of grapes; two bottles of Syrah/Shiraz, and so on.
● serve the younger or lighter red wine first.
● it is more interesting if the two wines can be contrasted in some way, two bottles from neighbouring properties; two different vintages from the same property etc.
● if two bottles of white wine are chosen then the lighter or drier should be served first; a Sauvignon Blanc before a Chardonnay; an un-aged Chardonnay before one that has had oak-ageing.
● champagnes and sparkling wines make excellent aperitifs but poor accompaniments to food. There are many who insist that champagne can be drunk throughout a meal, but the lack of body and the excess of bubbles seems to conflict with interesting dishes.

If you are starting with a rich country game terrine or a rich dish of kidneys then a red wine would be a more reasonable accompaniment to the first course than a white and, by the same token, if the main course is a delicate chicken or poussin dish then a flavoursome white would probably be far more pleasing than a heavy red. Remember also that where a restaurant offers you good house wines by the glass this facility can be used to produce a better balance. You can drink different wines with each course and can utilise a dessert wine by the glass list to produce a wine programme for the whole meal to suit the individual dishes in a far more logical way than the selection of one single bottle could ever hope to achieve. At home, though, this opportunity does not occur.

There is a convention that Muscadet or Gros Plant is good with a fish starter. Treat this one with caution for, while it is a good pairing with Breton Fruits de Mer, this dish is essentially a shellfish not a fish dish. Served with a fish dish, especially if there is a flavoursome sauce, the lack of body and flavour can reduce the effectiveness of this wine to a point where water might be just as interesting. Equally, some fish can make red wines taste metallic.

Fish does require care. Strong sauces, especially if they are oniony or garlicy, need decisive wines. Gewürztraminer, old Rioja, dry sherry even. At the fishiest end of the scale kippers, anchovies and the like are disaster to wine. Better to leave the bottle unopened!

Very rich meat sauces need a red wine with some balancing acidity – something Bordeaux often has far too much of. On the other hand some of the more modern reds – Californian or Australian Cabernet Sauvignons or Bulgarian reds like the Controliran red wines from Orihovitza and Svichtov – can have an excess of fruit and fall away too quickly in the mouth with little back-bite.

Sadly, few people offer cheese after the main course. This is a shame for it takes so little preparation, there does not need to be a large amount, and it is the perfect way to finish off what should have been the best bottle of red wine served. However, the cheese, if it is not to destroy the delicacy of a good wine, should be a mild variety – too strong and the wine cannot compete.

Sweet wines are an excellent way to accompany the dessert, but are not advisable through the meal simply because the sweetness clogs the tastebuds and dampens the appetite. That's fine at the end of a meal, but is somewhat counter-productive before the last course.

Chocolate desserts can overwhelm most of the lighter dessert wines. All eisweins, Loire dessert wines and most Sauternes come off second-best when faced with heavy chocolate puds. Muscat dessert wines are reasonably safe but fortified dessert wines are safest of all.

Whether you are eating at home or in a restaurant any suggestions for matching wines and foods must, of necessity, be subjective but here are some ideas:

FOODS	CONVENTIONAL APPROACH	UNCONVENTIONAL APPROACH
Soups	Dry white wine	Dry sherry, Montilla, Manzanilla
Sea foods	Muscadet	Rich whites like German Spatlesen, Gewürztraminers, Californian or Australian Chardonnays
Smoked fish	Bourgogne Aligoté or Muscadet	Alsace Pinot Blanc or Gewürztraminer; rich old-style white Rioja; dry sherries
Meat terrines or liver pâté	First course white wine	Bulgarian Merlot, Hungarian Cabernet Franc, Loire Gamay, light Zinfandels, Valpolicella
Kidney or liver	First course white wine; big fruity reds	Lively reds from Crete or Morocco, Nebbiolos from Italy, Australian Shiraz
Salads	Crisp dry white, eg Fumé Blanc	Vinegar in a salad dressing kills the taste of any wine, serve Perrier or iced water
Rich aubergine or courgette dishes	Dry or medium whites	Zinfandel, young Chianti, Portuguese Dão or Bairrada
White fish, sole, plaice, monkfish with light cream sauces	White burgundy	Good German Kabinett wines or Rieslings from California and Australia, Bourgogne Aligoté
Fresh salmon	Good white wines	The *best* white wines!
Chicken, poussin	Light red wines, Beaujolais	Big white wines: old Rioja or Dão, Chardonnay from Australia
Pork or veal	Fruity red wines, Beaujolais etc	Good neutral background to any quality wines, both red and white, the sauce should govern the choice
Rich casseroles	Big red wines, clarets etc	Australian Shiraz, Reserva Rioja, Taurasi or Sicilian red wines
Boeuf Stroganoff	Main course red wine claret or burgundy	Very big reds, Recioto Amarone della Valpolicella, Barolos
Grilled or fried fillet or sirloin	Main course red wine claret or burgundy	Mavrud, Californian Cabernet Sauvignon, Sassicaia, Gran Coronas Black Label, Venegazzù

RESTAURANT WINE LISTS

Unlike their Continental neighbours, the British were slow to appreciate the pleasures of eating out regularly – or perhaps it just reflected the fact that there was nowhere for them to go. But times are changing. Not only are we now eating out more, but we are increasingly interested in what we are eating and drinking, hence the proliferation of restaurant guides, books and newspaper columns on those twin subjects: food and wine. The increased interest is also shown in the amount of wine the British are drinking which has doubled in the last seven years.

In general the wine trade has been more than happy to respond to this growing interest which, after all, means greater profits for them. More people are buying wine than ever before. Most of this wine is bought in supermarkets and off-licences and while the majority of such outlets cannot provide knowledgeable staff to advise coustomers, they are using the wine bottles themselves to very good effect. The back labels on many bottles of wines you'll find in the big chains provide a great deal of useful information. They expand on the information, often rather cryptic, on the front labels and may also include the Wine Development Board's symbols (page 253).

Sadly the catering trade has not yet caught up with this new, informative approach to wine drinking. It is as if most of the profession is living in a time-warp and still insists on presenting their wine lists as they would have done before the 1970s – which is when the wine and food boom really took off. The standard image of the wine list in a British restaurant as '6 French, 2 German, 2 Italian, 1 Spanish' is based on depressingly common fact.

In addition to such an unimaginative parade of veterans, the list will probably be distinguished by its total lack of information about the wines. All too often they will be described merely as 'Chablis', 'Beaujolais' or 'Châteauneuf-du-Pape', with, perhaps, a vintage stated but with no

details of producer, wine style, quality standard or of suitability for certain dishes. What a contrast this attitude is to the ready acceptance of the latest culinary fads – cuisine nouvelle, cuisine minceur and the like. Food fashions come and go and restaurants are seldom backward in rapidly incorporating much of the best, and often much of the worst, of these ever-changing gastronomic styles. And you'd be forgiven for thinking that if they can do it for one part of the business they could do it for the other – but somehow it doesn't seem to work like that!

I have repeatedly emphasised that forward-thinking, modern wine-producers use varietal labelling (page 11) for their wines. And there is no good reason why hotels and restaurants should not adopt this same helpful, approach when making up their wine lists.

A few do and their lists stand out like the proverbial good deed in a naughty world. Among these are Crest Hotels. Crest have followed this new helpful approach, giving sensible, factual and non-pompous information on their wine lists. They also aim to give their customers a good spread of wines from around the world (see below). Interestingly, their carefully kept sales profile of customer orders shows exactly what one would expect: that given half a chance the British public is not over-awed or inhibited when faced with a wine list that includes wines from, among other places, New Zealand, Texas and Israel.

Fortunately times are changing. The number of hotels and restaurants that provide good wine service is increasing – if only slowly – and while few of us like to spoil an occasion by complaining, we do have one very strong card in our hand – we need not return to a restaurant. So next time you are confronted with a wine list of the old variety resolve not to return to that restaurant. And who knows, if enough customers do not return, the stick-in-the-muds might even mend their ways. Vive la revolution!

Champagne

White
1. **Boizel Réserve, Brut, N.V.**
   Clean, fresh and fragrant – represents outstanding value
2. **G.H. Mumm, Cordon Rouge, N.V.**
   Soft bouquet and taste, a little milder than other well known Brut champagnes
3. **Moët et Chandon, Brut Impérial, N.V.**
   Fully fresh, not too dry, with good balance
5. **Bollinger Grand Année, 1983**
   A wine of great finesse with perfect balance between roundness and elegance

Rosé
6. **Lanson Rosé, Brut, N.V.**
   Classic pink champagne. Full flavour and dry on palate

Sparkling Wines

White
7. **Saumur Brut, Ackerman Laurence, A.C. N.V.**
   Pure, clean and refreshing taste; quite dry. Made by the champagne method
8. **Asti Martini, Consorzio Dell' Asti, D.O.C. N.V.**
   Slightly aromatic flavour, fairly sweet, but well balanced

Bordeaux

Red
9. **Château du Juge, Premières Côtes de Bordeaux, A.C. 1987/88**
   Good fruit and easy drinking
10. **Mouton Cadet, Sélection Baron Philippe de Rothschild, A.C. 1985/86**
    Round and full of fruit, with plenty of classic Bordeaux character
12. **Médoc Baron Philippe, La Baronnie, A.C. 1986**
    Subtle, fine wine of character, typical of the Médoc
15. **Château Brown, Graves, A.C. C.B. 1985**
    A classic wine – dry on the palate with plenty of fruit and tannin – marvellous aroma
16. **Château Laroque, St. Emilion Grand Cru, A.C. C.B. 1983**
    Rich, round and full flavoured, with good aftertaste
18. **Château Mouton Baronne Philippe, 5ème Cru Pauillac, A.C. C.B. 1983**
    Rounded, soft and well-balanced. Drinking well
19. **Château Lascombes, 2ème Cru Margaux, A.C. C.B. 1979/81**
    Classic Margaux – mature and well-rounded, with an excellent finish

White
21. **Mouton Cadet Blanc, Sélection Baron Philippe de Rothschild, A.C. 1986/87**
    Supple and well balanced; dry but without excess acidity
22. **Graves Baron Philippe, La Baronnie, A.C. 1987**
    Fresh and full of fruit, which balances its dryness. Excellent with seafood
24. **Château Coutet, Premier Cru, Barsac, A.C. C.B. 1984**
    Complex, rich and harmonious. Excellent acidity prevents this honeyed dessert wine from being excessively sweet

Rosé
25. **Rosé Baron Philippe, La Baronnie, A.C. N.V.**
    A light, dry, elegant and aromatic wine

Burgundy

Red
27. **Beaujolais Villages, Pasquier-Desvignes, A.C. 1988**
    Well-balanced, with good fruit and long flavour
28. **Brouilly, Château de St. Lager, Cru Beaujolais, Pasquier-Desvignes, A.C. 1988**
    Deep flavoured, this single estate wine is of excellent quality
29. **Côte de Beaune Villages, Jean Germain, A.C. N.V.**
    Elegant and well-balanced, very enjoyable with meat dishes and cheese
30. **Gevrey Chambertin, Domaine des Varoilles, A.C. D.B. 1985**
    Smooth and medium-bodied, with good fruit
31. **Nuits-St-Georges, Jules Normand, A.C. 1981**
    Fairly full-bodied with perfumed aroma, reminiscent of woodland fruits

White
32. **Macon Clessé, Jean Thevenet, A.C. D.B. 1986/87**
    Traditional Burgundy, with very fine depth; creamy fruit, good acidity and excellent finish
33. **Chablis St. Martin, Henri Laroche, A.C. 1988**
    Crisp, dry wine of elegance and character with a distinctive bouquet
34. **Meursault, Les Narvaux, Jean Germain, A.C. D.B. 1986/87**
    Well-balanced wine, with smooth orchard fruit on nose and palate
35. **Puligny Montrachet, Jean Germain, A.C. 1986**
    Excellent quality: firm well-flavoured fruit, with depth

Rhone

Red
36. **Côtes du Rhône, Pasquier-Desvignes, A.C. 1988**
    Full bodied red wine with plenty of flavour from the Rhone valley
37. **Crozes Hermitage, Delas Frères, A.C. 1987**
    Full bodied, fragrant red wine with a slight spiciness on aroma and taste
38. **Châteauneuf du Pape, Medaillon, Delas Frères, A.C. 1986**
    Robust and powerful red wine, richly alcoholic and well-balanced

Loire

Red
40. **Bourgueil, Domaine Audemont, J. Dumont, A.C. 1988**
    Light, dry red wine with a fruity flavour. Made from Cabernet Franc grape

White
41. **Muscadet Sèvre-et-Maine, Château de la Ragotière, Sur Lie, A.C. D.B. 1987/88**
    Light, fresh, fragrant white wine with well-balanced acidity
42. **Sancerre, Les Montachins, Fouassier, A.C. D.B. 1988**
    Rich, ripe white wine with pungent and distinctive fruit and flavour. Made from Sauvignon grape

Alsace

White
43. **Pinot Blanc Mise du Printemps, Josmeyer, A.C. 1987**
    Delicate fragrant nose with a lively clean palate
45. **Gewürztraminer Cuvée des Folastries, Josmeyer, A.C. 1986/87**
    Dry, spicy flavour and rich aroma which combines well with smoked fish
46. **Riesling Les Pierrets, Réserve, Josmeyer, A.C. 1983/86**
    Mature dry Riesling with richness and finesse; long lasting flavour

Moselle

White
48. **Deinhard Green Label, Bereich Bernkastel, QbA 1987/88**
    Balance of delicate fruit with crisp finish. Refreshing with lasting flavour
49. **Brauneberger Juffer Riesling Spätlese, Deinhard, QmP 1985**
    A delicate balance of acidity and sweetness of late harvested Riesling grapes. Ideal with fish dishes or light meals
50. **Leiwener Laurentiuslay Riesling Kabinett, Halbtrocken, Franz Reh, QmP 1987**
    Light 'semi dry' wine with delicate ripe fruit and refreshing acidity; a wine of great quality from the Josenfinengrund Estate

Rhine

White
51. **Blue Nun, Liebfraumilch, Rheinpfalz, Sichel, QbA 1987**
    Easy drinking, well-balanced medium dry wine
52. **Johannisberger Erntebringer Riesling Kabinett, Rheingau, Sichel, QmP 1988/89**
    Straw yellow with greenish tinge. Classic Riesling style with good balancing acidity

Italy

Red
53. **Valpolicella Classico Superiore, Masi, Veneto, D.O.C. 1986/87**
    Medium weight, with fair depth of fruit flavour
56. **Barolo, Fontanafredda, Piedmont, D.O.C.G. 1983/85**
    Dark, rich, dry wine with a deep flavour. Highly rated
57. **Tavernelle Cabernet Sauvignon, Castello Banfi, Tuscany, Vino da Tavola, 1984/85**
    Elegant wine with good fruit and acidity, a silky texture and smooth taste

White
59. **Frascati Superiore Satinata, Colli di Catone, Latium, D.O.C. 1988**
    Full flavoured, dry, and with character
61. **Gavi, Principessa Gavia, Villa Banfi, Piedmont, D.O.C. 1988**
    Dry, crisp and fresh, with depth and good ripe flavour
62. **Lowengang Chardonnay, Alois Lageder, Alto-Adige, D.O.C. 1985/86**
    Pale gold with green tinges, an aromatic Chardonnay with a hint of oak
63. **Torcolato, Maculan, Veneto, Vino da Tavola, 1986**
    Golden colour, rich velvety grapey flavour. A dessert wine of high quality

Spain

Red
64. **Torres Coronas, Miguel Torres, Penedes, 1986**
    Made from Tempranillo variety, this wine has a pleasant mellow maturity and a lasting flavour
66. **Coto de Imaz, Rioja, Gran Reserva, Bodegas El Coto, D.O. 1981**
    A classic Rioja from an excellent year; full flavoured and smooth, this red wine is aged for five years in bottle and cask

White
67. **Torres Gran Viña Sol, Miguel Torres, Penedes, 1988**
    Silky, well-balanced dry white wine with a flowery, spicy aroma and lingering flavour

Portugal

Red
68. **Tinto da Anfora, Joao Pires, Palmela, 1984/85**
    A deep purple wine with ripe, rich fruit. Full bodied and well rounded

White
70. **Pires Moscato Branco, Joao Pires, Palmela, 1988**
    Refreshing dry white wine with intense bouquet from the Muscat grape. Mouthfilling flavour, yet balanced with spice, freshness and acidity

Australia

Red
72. **Koonunga Hill Shiraz-Cabernet Sauvignon, Penfolds, Barossa Valley, 1987**
    This blend produces a full bodied red wine, rich in flavour and packed with fruit
73. **Yellow Label Cabernet Sauvignon, Wolf Blass, Barossa Valley, 1985**
    Velvety and smooth red wine with a touch of oakiness and long finish. Highly recommended

White
74. **Bin 65 Chardonnay, Lindemans, Victoria, 1987/88**
    A soft dry white wine with the buttery aroma and flavour of ripe Chardonnay grapes
76. **Noble Riesling, Brown Brothers, Victoria, 1982**
    Classic dessert wine made from Riesling grapes affected by Noble Rot. Rich, complex nose with impressive length and firm finish

New Zealand

White
77. **Chardonnay, Montana, Marlborough, 1988/89**
    Traditional fruity aroma and flavour associated with Chardonnay but lighter and more elegant in style than Australian examples
78. **Sauvignon Blanc, Montana, Marlborough, 1988/89**
    This light, fragrant, dry wine has the intense and distinctive aroma and flavour of Sauvignon grapes
79. **Sémillon-Chardonnay, Babich, Gisborne, 1988/89**
    A crisp, aromatic dry wine, resulting from a careful blend of Sémillon and Chardonnay grape varieties

United States of America

Red
80. **Cabernet Sauvignon, Wente Bros, California, 1985**
    Deeply coloured red wine, aged in oak and matured in the bottle. Beautiful bouquet

White
81. **Chenin Blanc, Domaine Cordier, Texas, 1988**
    Pale yellow, lively fresh bouquet reminiscent of soft fruits
82. **Chardonnay, Wente Bros, California, 1987**
    Full bodied white wine with a rich, buttery flavour and delicate fruit

Rosé
83. **White Zinfandel, Wente Bros, California, 1988**
    A blush wine from California. Delicate pale pink in colour, light dry style and very fruity

Chile

Red
84. **Antiguas Reservas Cabernet Sauvignon, Cousiño Macul, Maipo Valley, 1982**
    Made exclusively from Cabernet Sauvignon, grown on the Cousiño family estate, this wine is round and full of flavour

White
85. **Torres Sauvignon Blanc, Miguel Torres, Curico, 1988**
    A well made Sauvignon wine which is soft, dry with a fresh, clean flavour

SERVING WINE

TEMPERATURE FOR WHITE WINE

Beware of over chilling white wines. More white wines are spoilt by the drinker's desire to see frost forming on the outside of the bottle than ever by being too warm.

The best temperature range for white wine is between 5° and 10°C – temperatures lower than these will reduce the ability of the wine to 'open out' and numb the taste buds to a point of non-receptiveness. If wine is standing in an ice bucket be especially careful of the over chilling effect on the last two glassfuls in the bottom. It is sometimes a wise precaution after pouring out glasses three and four, to leave the bottle on the table for, by then, the bottle will be sufficiently cold to keep the remainder of the wine cool.

To cool wine, a fridge, a freezer or ice and water are the methods normally available. A freezer is not very much quicker than ice and

water – and the danger of forgetting the bottle and the loss of wine or, worse, a broken bottle if the cork is too strong to be forced out when the wine has frozen solid, makes the benefit not worth the risk. A fridge at the normal domestic temperature range will chill a bottle from 18° to 13°C in about one hour, whilst immersion in ice and water will accomplish the same temperature drop in 8–10 minutes.

To maintain the temperature the modern 'Vinicool'-type product is quite efficient. They work on the principle that the bottle takes up most of the space inside the Vinicool, what little air remains is quickly cooled by the bottle, and the cold is not lost as the double skinned container acts as a basic thermos while the colder air inside the body of the Vinicool stays where it is being heavier than the surrounding air.

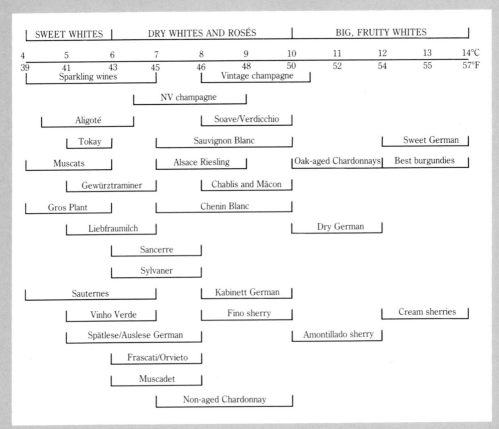

SWEET WHITES		DRY WHITES AND ROSÉS				BIG, FRUITY WHITES			
4	5	6	7	8	9	10	11	12	13	14°C
39	41	43	45	46	48	50	52	54	55	57°F

Sparkling wines
Vintage champagne
NV champagne
Aligoté
Soave/Verdicchio
Tokay
Sauvignon Blanc
Sweet German
Muscats
Alsace Riesling
Oak-aged Chardonnays
Best burgundies
Gewürztraminer
Chablis and Mâcon
Gros Plant
Chenin Blanc
Liebfraumilch
Dry German
Sancerre
Sylvaner
Sauternes
Kabinett German
Vinho Verde
Fino sherry
Cream sherries
Spätlese/Auslese German
Amontillado sherry
Frascati/Orvieto
Muscadet
Non-aged Chardonnay

TEMPERATURE FOR RED WINE

'The little sentence "have the chill taken off" has done more harm to good wine than it is possible to imagine'

X. Marcel Boulestin in
Simple French Cooking for English Homes

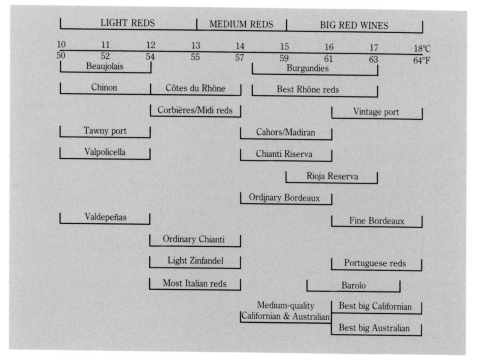

Beware of overheating red wine. Overheated red wine suffers from excess volatility, it loses flavour and the excessive evaporation of alcohol will mask the scent. Each variety of grape seems to have a critical temperature range and this range remains surprisingly constant for the same grape varieties produced in different areas. In addition, all red wine temperatures must be seen in relation to the temperature of the room in which they are served – and the temperature generally climbs during the evening. The ideal would be a maximum of around 18°C, but that might seem quite arctic if you have American guests!

The best methods of warming red wine are a bucket of warm water or a microwave oven. The former will take about as long as ice and water takes for the reverse effect: water of about 23°C will raise the temperature of a standard sized wine bottle by around 6°C in 10 minutes.

If you have a microwave, then the temperature of red wines can easily be adjusted upwards. A wine which needs decanting should be decanted first, but if there is no sedimentation and the wine does not need any oxygenation then the bottle can be laid on its side on a cloth and 45 seconds will bring the temperature up from cellar temperature of 10°C to just over 16°C – a good serving temperature compromise for most reds. In spite of manufacturers' recommendations about metal in microwaves, I have never experienced trouble with lead foils around the neck. The only time metal has been a problem is with the sort of wire mesh that some Riojas are decorated with – this sort of external wire-work should definitely be removed. Obviously, if a wine has been decanted then the decanter should simply be popped in for the necessary length of time.

BREATHING AND DECANTING

Many tests have been carried out both in the UK and the USA, to try to quantify the beneficial (or otherwise) effect of letting red wines 'breathe' – that is, removing the cork well before serving to bring fresh air in contact with the wine. These tests have firmly concluded that such 'breathing' has no perceptible effect. This is supported by none other than the great Professor Emile Peynaud of Bordeaux who is on record as saying 'If it is necessary to decant [at all], one should always do it at the last possible moment, just before moving to the table or just before serving [the wine]; never in advance.'

I agree that the concept of letting wine 'breathe' by simply removing the cork is not worth the effort, for there is only a minute circle of wine in the neck of the bottle that is actually in contact with the air. On the other hand, most reds are improved by decanting, or even double decanting, just before serving; it seems that the flavours and the scents become more obvious and are released beneficially. But let's be clear that we are talking about decanting to oxygenate the wine – many reds will in any

case need decanting to release the wine from the sediment formed in the bottle.

Decanting is a simple process, but, for some reason, fills people with apprehension. The essentials of successful decanting are simple. The bottle should have been stored on its side with the label facing upwards, this allows you to see the label more clearly and ensures that you know where the sediment is lying – opposite the label. Stand the bottle upright slowly and gently and, by revolving the bottle with a sharp knife held against the top ridge of the neck, remove the top of the lead foil. Ingenious foil-cutters like that from Screwpull are both inexpensive and efficient. If the top of the cork is mildewed or mouldy, wipe this with a paper napkin, taking care not to jog the bottle in the process, and draw the cork. Designs of corkscrew vary enormously, just ensure that the corkscrew has enough length for the cork you are drawing – port and top quality Bordeaux wines have the longest corks – and try not to move the bottle too much.

Light a candle and place it between your bottle and the decanter and start to pour the wine gently into the decanter with the shoulder of the bottle between you and the flame. You

▲ *A decanting cradle being used for 25 year-old*   *Morgon at Jean-Ernest Descombes, Villié-Morgon*   *in Beaujolais.*

should pour slowly to start with as some bubbling-back will take place and, if too violent, will disturb the sediment and cloud the wine. Continue, more swiftly if you like after the risk of back-bubbling has passed, until the 'finger' of sediment is visible in the lighted area of the shoulder of the bottle, then pour slowly until the sediment just reaches the neck of the bottle.

The whole pouring motion should be steady and progressive and, if everything has gone according to plan, there should be little more than an inch of wine left in the bottom of the bottle which, of course represents very little wine as the depression takes up so much space in the bottom. The acid test comes when the decanter is held in front of the candle flame – one should be rewarded by a clear rich red wine, one of the most attractive sights possible! If, however, you are pouring a bottle of red wine into a decanter simply to give the wine some oxygen, then the precautions against sedimentation are unnecessary and the wine can be poured in without too much ceremony.

Old burgundies are the most difficult of all wines to decant for their sediment is extremely fine and comes over more as a cloud of tiny particles than a dark finger. Discretion has to be used, to stop too soon will leave quite a lot of expensive wine in the bottle, whilst too late and cloudy wine will result. Rely on your judgement, but once you have stopped, that's it!

GLASSES

Two principles apply to the selection of glasses: choose large clear ones. Try to buy glasses with curved-in tops to trap the bouquet and, for preference, with thin walls, although too delicate and you scare your guests and washer-up!

Glasses need not be expensive. Some stores sell excellent simple champagne flutes and most of the larger chain stores in big cities have good, inexpensive ranges of glassware, often of French manufacture.

Never use those so-called champagne glasses shaped like saucers and supposedly modelled on Marie Antoinette's breast. If they were, then the poor lady must have been remarkably flat chested and somewhat deformed, but, in fact, they were in use well before Marie Antoinette was alive. Why it has become the custom to use the one type of glass most totally unsuited to enjoyment of this expensive beverage is a puzzle.

Cut glass or glass with designs moulded-in are claimed to reflect more light from the many facets, so making the wine glitter more – I wonder.

Glasses with coloured stems allegedly reflect that colour up into the wine – traditionally Alsacian and German wines are served in glasses with stems of green, gold or light brown glass. Try to avoid following this practice.

It is the custom to use a smaller glass for white wines than for red, largely because red wines have a larger bouquet and therefore need more space in the glass. Stems that are too fine should be avoided. Apart from the greater risk of breakage they are more difficult to hold, and holding glasses by the stem is to be encouraged when drinking white wines so as not to warm up the wine with the hand – the opposite to the brandy glass which is specially designed with a short stem to encourage cupping in the hand.

For sherry the traditional copita-shaped glasses are essential for a true appreciation of the wine. Do not fill more than two-thirds full – after all, sherry has an inviting bouquet to be savoured too! Port and madeira can also be served in such glasses.

TASTING WINES

Too many people feel that wine tastings are the exclusive province of the expert, the connoisseur, the wine buff. But with some of the more forward thinking retail chains now offering wines for tasting to the general public it is time that the ordinary enthusiast learnt some of the tricks of the trade. Just what is it that the professionals look for in a wine?

Pleasant taste obviously. If a wine is unpleasant there is either a fault in the wine, or it is simply a wine that's outside your range of enjoyment. The poor members of the wine trade have to soldier on with wine they don't necessarily like but, as an amateur, you have the chance to spit it out and simply write it off. Taste should tell something of the grape and the sort of growing conditions and, as already mentioned, it is important to begin to recognise at least the seven major grape varieties in use around the world so that a judgement of a particular Cabernet Sauvignon, say, can be made by referring to a sort of mental taste profile of Cabernet Sauvignon.

To judge the other qualities of a wine needs a procedure which has been evolved over the

◄ *The stylish and spacious new tasting room at Raimat, Costers del Sagre, Spain. This is a part of the company's unusual, semi-underground new bottling and storage complex (see also page 158).*

years. The visual and nasal senses are used before any wine even reaches the mouth and the routine is as follows.

Pour enough wine into a large, clear glass to fill it barely a quarter full. Tilt the glass away from you and over a white surface so that the colours at the edge of the wine rim can be clearly seen. Then swill the wine around in the glass and, by practically inserting your nose into the glass, sniff the bouquet. Swill the wine around in the glass again and watch the sides of the glass where the wine has washed and the way the wine returns to its natural level in the glass. Savour the bouquet again and then, finally, sip some of the wine into your mouth. Now comes the difficult, and potentially messy, bit. Try to suck some air into the mouth over the wine which should lie in the front of the mouth. It's a bit like gargling in the mouth and not in the throat and the sound should be pretty much like someone slurping soup. In fact, it is exactly the same process as slurping soup but, instead of the air being dragged across the surface of the soup to cool it down, it is dragged across the surface of the wine to release the aroma into the mouth. Finally, spit it out. (Or, if it is a very good wine, cheat and swallow it!)

What should we learn from these manoeuvres?
● *Colour* this will indicate age – young wines are always a bright colour, with greenish tinges in a white wine and a cherry-red with purply overtones if a red. White and red wines both move into a brown-tinted colour rim with advancing years. Old reds will have a noticeable orange/brown rim when well matured.

● *Aroma* this will give the first hint of the grape type and there should be no trace of sherry-like odours or vinegary smells. The first would indicate that the wine is becoming oxydised while the latter would suggest that the wine is 'over the hill'. The fruitiest aromas come from Beaujolais Nouveau, but all wines have a message to impart from their bouquet – not least of which is to provoke a Pavlovian response of heightened anticipation.
● *Body* the wine will leave characteristic 'legs' down the glass. These will be more marked in a heavy wine which will have a higher glycerine content. Heaviest of all are fortified wines such as port and sherry although dessert wines high in sugar also display 'strong legs'.
● *Taste* this is the most complex part of the drinking experience, but can be split into components. Sweetness or acidity should be easily established and acidity is a normal, and essential, part of the taste of any wine. Only when there is excess acidity without balancing fruitiness or grapiness does a wine become unpleasant. The reverse is also true, a wine with insufficient acidity will be like drinking fruit juice and will tend to clog the palate.
● *Length* even after wine is swallowed or spat out there will be, or should be, a lingering taste and this should not deteriorate in quality. It should not, for example, turn metallic or in any way diminish the enjoyment of the mouthful.

All of these qualities and characteristics, taken together, constitute the balance of a wine and, as with so many of the finer things of life, good balance is a sure endorsement of quality.

PART 2

FRANCE

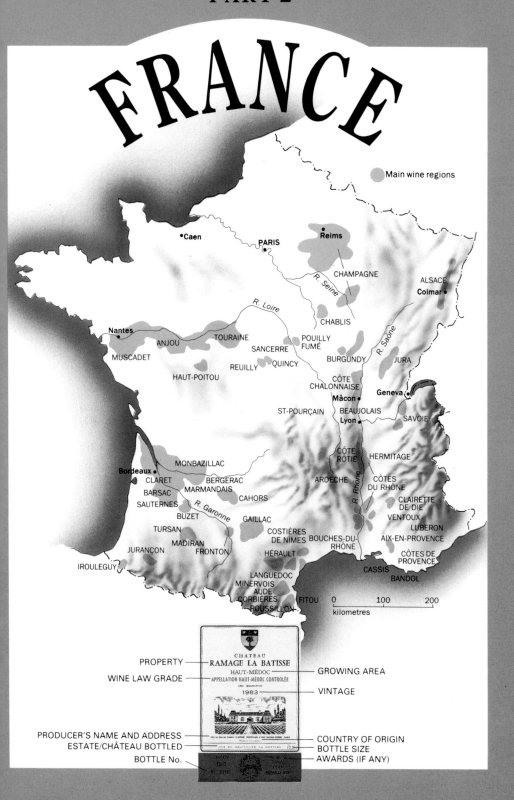

Main wine regions

Caen •PARIS •Reims

CHAMPAGNE ALSACE Colmar•

R. Seine

R. Loire CHABLIS

Nantes R. Saône

ANJOU TOURAINE POUILLY FUMÉ

MUSCADET SANCERRE BURGUNDY JURA

REUILLY QUINCY

HAUT-POITOU CÔTE CHALONNAISE

ST-POURÇAIN Mâcon Geneva•

BEAUJOLAIS SAVOIE

Lyon•

MONBAZILLAC CÔTE RÔTIE HERMITAGE

Bordeaux• BERGERAC ARDÈCHE CÔTES DU RHÔNE

CLARET MARMANDAIS CLAIRETTE DE DIE

BARSAC CAHORS

SAUTERNES R. Garonne VENTOUX

BUZET GAILLAC LUBERON

TURSAN COSTIÈRES DE NÎMES AIX-EN-PROVENCE

JURANÇON MADIRAN BOUCHES-DU-RHÔNE

FRONTON HÉRAULT CÔTES DE PROVENCE

IROULEGUY CASSIS

LANGUEDOC BANDOL

MINERVOIS

AUDE FITOU

CORBIÈRES

ROUSSILLON

R. Rhône

| 0 | 100 | 200 |
kilometres

PROPERTY ——— CHÂTEAU **RAMAGE LA BATISSE**

HAUT-MÉDOC

WINE LAW GRADE ——— APPELLATION HAUT-MÉDOC CONTROLÉE ——— GROWING AREA

CRU BOURGEOIS

— 1983 — ——— VINTAGE

PRODUCER'S NAME AND ADDRESS ——— ——— COUNTRY OF ORIGIN

ESTATE/CHÂTEAU BOTTLED ——— MIS EN BOUTEILLES AU CHÂTEAU ——— BOTTLE SIZE

BOTTLE No. ——— ——— AWARDS (IF ANY)

While the world of wine is humming with new developments, new growing areas, new grape strains and new techniques, there is almost always one standard by which the results are judged – how does it compare with Bordeaux/Burgundy/Champagne/Alsace/Loire/Rhône or whatever area of France produces that particular archetypal wine style.

What has produced this apparently unrivalled position as the arbiter of the quality of the world's wine? As with so many quality criteria, it has been a combination of variables over the centuries, which together have produced the situation that is France today.

The Romans provided the impetus. They created vineyards on likely looking slopes near good sized towns with, preferably, adequate means of water transport. They first tried grapes from Italy but later adopted not only local wild vines but also vines from other nations under Roman domination and from these somewhat haphazard origins we now see their vinous descendants spreading around the world. 'French' varieties like Cabernet Sauvignon, Merlot, Syrah, Chardonnay, Sauvignon Blanc and Muscat are the most widely planted across the globe.

History did France a favour by ensuring that her southerly neighbour, Spain, spent much of the Middle Ages under Moslem influence with consequent restrictions on wine production, while her neighbours to the north were becoming ever more receptive as wine trading customers. In fact cognac production developed because wines exported to the Netherlands deteriorated in transit and that, together with a tax levied by volume, created a desire to concentrate the wine and reduce the volume. From which came distillation . . .

France also pioneered a system of wine laws which, with the exception of Germany, has been used (for better or for worse) by all other wine-producing nations as the basis for their own legislation. The system of Appellation d'Origine Contrôleé (AC or AOC) came into being in 1932 and is now split into four categories:

● full *AC* status where the area is clearly defined, permitted grape varieties are stipulated and outputs per hectare are controlled.
● below this classification is *VDQS*, standing for *Vin Délimité de Qualité Supérieure*. In effect it is simply a less stringent set of AC regulations and is generally applied to an area as a sort of probationary AC status.
● next comes the classification *Vin de Pays*. This worthwhile category was introduced in 1970 for sound regional wines which would probably never aspire to full AC status and yet deserve to have their better-than-Vin-de-Table quality signalled to potential customers. Continual amendments keep this category up to date and it is especially useful for individualists who perhaps want to experiment in a certain area with a grape variety or varieties other than those stipulated by the existing law. If Vin de Pays did not exist the only qualification available would be that of the rock-bottom *Vin de Consommation Courante* – the official name for Vin Ordinaire where price is simply based on the alcohol level.

France neither produces the most wine in the world, that honour falling to Italy, nor does it have the greatest area of cultivation, that honour going to Spain. France does, however, claim the title 'Producer of more quality wines' than any other source and, although in terms of absolute prestige there are now tiny areas of production in other countries with products to rival even the greatest that France can put forward, in overall terms France still has a very healthy lead in the volume of quality wines produced.

FRENCH WINE LAWS

We will look at the French wine laws in some detail, partly because France is such an important exporter to the UK and partly because these laws have been followed by other countries in setting out their own vinous legal systems – sometimes followed too closely!

The Institut National des Appellations d'Origine was set up in Paris in 1932 with nationwide staffing and offices. This organisation only dealt with superior wines, the vins ordinaires were administered by a separate organisation, the Office National Interprofessional des Vins de Table.

There are four quality classifications of French wine. In descending order these are: Appellation d'Origine Contrôleé (AC or AOC), Vin Délimité de Qualité Supérieure (VDQS), Vin de Pays and Vin de Consommation Courante.

Just under a quarter of all French wines now qualify under the two higher Appellation Contrôleé grades, AC and VDQS, a total of about two and a half billion bottles a year.

APPELLATION D'ORIGINE CONTRÔLEÉ (AC OR AOC)

A number of factors are considered and fixed when granting this superior status to a wine-growing area of which there are now over 450. These are:

- a clearly defined boundary
- stipulated approved grape varieties
- minimum alcohol level which, in most areas except the Rhône, allows chaptalisation
- maximum output in hectolitres per hectare. Fine in theory but subject to the most flagrant legalised abuses, in Burgundy especially
- methods, intended to control vineyard practices such as pruning and vine density. A major problem on the horizon is the advent of machine-picking which requires different planting patterns
- production: oversight and control of addition or extraction of acids and of general methods and equipment employed
- testing of the finished product. Since 1979 submission of wine to tough tasting panels has been required. Only two submissions are allowed. After that the AC for the property is lost

- bottling, only applies to a few areas, notably Champagne and Alsace

VIN DÉLIMITÉ DE QUALITÉ SUPÉRIEURE (VDQS)

Over 50 properties have this classification, in which there are really two types of wine:

- those wines that cannot become AC however good they are because they use grapes other than those stipulated for the region. The most often quoted example is that of the excellent Sauvignon de St Bris which, because it uses the Sauvignon Blanc grape in Burgundy, where only the Chardonnay and the Aligoté are allowed, is condemned to a sort of second grade limbo.
- those wines which are on their way up. An example is Haut-Poitou where the effectiveness of the co-operative has raised the quality of what was previously a below average area to a level now where full AC status is already overdue.

VIN DE PAYS

Introduced in 1970, this was one of the French authorities' smarter moves. Intended to reduce over-production and encourage regional pride and identity, it has been remarkably successful in many areas. Each area is geographically defined, but can be as vast as the Vins du Pays du Jardin de la France, which includes wine from practically anywhere in the Loire valley, or no bigger than two or three parishes.

Normal output is generally a respectable 80hl per ha, with a few exceptions; alcoholic strengths are normally 10.5% or 11%. Grape varieties are somewhat flexible, usually there must be a major proportion of recognised local species to maintain the local character but otherwise considerable freedom is allowed. In the comparatively short time since the introduction of this classification some Vins de Pays have been elevated to VDQS status and are obviously destined for even greater things.

VIN DE CONSOMMATION COURANTE

Vin de Table to you and me, Vin Ordinaire to a Frenchman. Normally just sold on alcoholic strength – hence the famous 'onze degrees' or 11° the usual strength of French red café wine.

BORDEAUX

More than a half of the fine wines of the world come from France – and about a half of these come from Bordeaux. It is the most important wine region of France and the annual production of about 75 million gallons dwarfs all of the other French fine wine areas put together.

Wine production in the Bordeaux area can be traced back to the Romans. Their arrival in about 56 BC brought the vine and by the 1st century AD the writer Pliny was reporting on the wines of Bordeaux, or Burdigala as it was then known.

The Romans left about AD 500 and were followed by the Visigoths who held this area until around AD 1000. During this time only the survival of Christianity protected the knowledge of viniculture. From 1150 to 1450 English kings held Bordeaux and the wines of this region were shipped to England in significant quantity.

However, for the last 500 years Bordeaux has been the standard by which other wines are judged and this has remained true irrespective of revolution, conquest, religion or any other factor.

The great glory of Bordeaux is, of course, the range of red wines produced from what is known as 'The Bordeaux Blend', a combination of the Cabernet Sauvignon, Merlot and Cabernet Franc grapes with, sometimes, some Petit Verdot. These varieties are all related and probably trace their ancestry back to the ancient Biturica grape. However, there are really two sides to red wine production in this area – the large volume mass-market red wine, produced without much fuss and designed to become drinkable within three or four years, and the output of the great, the greater and the greatest properties, the names of which are often known even to non-wine drinkers. These properties 'design' their wines for longevity – drunk too

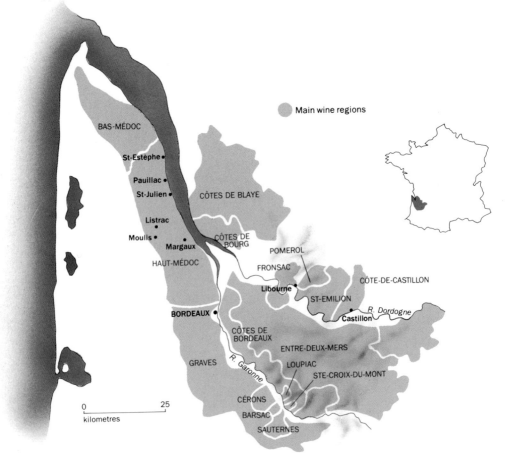

Main wine regions

BAS-MÉDOC
St-Estèphe
Pauillac
St-Julien
CÔTES DE BLAYE
Listrac
Moulis
CÔTES DE BOURG
Margaux
HAUT-MÉDOC
POMEROL
FRONSAC
CÔTE-DE-CASTILLON
Libourne
ST-EMILION
BORDEAUX
R. Dordogne
Castillon
CÔTES DE BORDEAUX
ENTRE-DEUX-MERS
GRAVES
R. Garonne
LOUPIAC
STE-CROIX-DU-MONT
CÉRONS
BARSAC
SAUTERNES

0   25
kilometres

young and they can be an unpleasant experience, being far too hard, sharp and acidic. In addition Bordeaux produces two other distinct types of wine. Large volumes of dry wine mainly of little character or consequence and sweet dessert wines which rank among the finest in the world.

VOLUME RED WINE PRODUCTION
We are talking of a wine volume of around two million hectolitres – just over 22 million cases of wine. These wines will be sold as branded lines or with the name of a château which will more often than not be a romantic invention to give marketing status to an otherwise unexciting product.

QUALITY RED WINE PRODUCTION
Roughly 14.5 million cases of quality wine are produced compared with the 22 million cases of the less prestigious wines.

DRY WHITE TABLE WINES
Although the production is, in the main, unexciting, the output is still staggering – around 10 million cases a year.

SWEET WHITE WINES
The lowest output of the four types of Bordeaux wine – but still an impressive 1.25 million cases, of which 200,000 are quality Barsac or Sauternes.

The total output in an average year in the 1980s was around 50 million cases of wine – more than the entire output of Bulgaria, Chile or Australia – and all from an area of roughly 160km by 100km. This concentrated area of production and seat of many of the world's greatest wines has been dealt with in very great detail in almost every book on wine. I do not therefore propose to discuss details of all the various properties, of the soils, the rainfall levels, etc, but to concentrate on some of the more interesting trends which have become discernible.

BORDEAUX – THE FUTURE THREATENED

The area around Bordeaux under vine is about 81,000 hectares and this total has remained fairly steady for the past decade and a half. But during this same period the number of property owners has more than halved – from around 55,000 to below 25,000. The average size of each ownership has therefore significantly increased, producing an increase in production efficiency due to economy of scale and to this has been added the startling advances in understanding wine-making techniques. Thus there has been a steady rise in average output per hectare, from below 30hl per hectare to almost 45hl – a 50% increase per unit of land under cultivation.

Moreover, technological improvements produce a more consistent quality, the day is fast approaching when there will still be 'highs' – good vintages in especially favoured years – but no balancing 'lows'. In poor years the quality of output will only descend to 'drinkable' rather than to the desperately undrinkable levels of times gone by.

These changes are already producing a glut of wine in Bordeaux and the artificially high prices being demanded for wines 'en primeur' – that is, sold while still in cask at the châteaux and destined to be held for two or three years before being bottled and available for shipping – can hardly be sustained. A minor groundswell of reaction is already apparent and soon the Bordelaise will be forced to realise that wine is, after all, a beverage and not an international brokerage commodity to be dealt in like stocks and shares.

A further problem for the Bordelaise comes from the 'new' growing areas of the world. Some of these are not new at all – northern Spain and Tuscany in Italy have centuries of wine-growing history – but these areas are 'new' to the growing of the Cabernet Sauvignon grape and when the products of these competitors are added to the excellent Cabernet Sauvignon wines from Australia, California, Chile and so on, then Bordeaux can no longer regard itself as the only source of good claret-style wines.

A very few of the more internationally minded growers see their situation against the world stage – the late Baron Philippe de Rothschild, for example, formed his liaison with the master of the Napa Valley, Robert Mondavi, to produce their much-hyped Opus One wine. In general, however, there has been much less enthusiasm to get out and about in the world than there has been, for example, in Champagne. Bollinger are active in Australia, Möet are producing in California and most of the larger 'houses' are buying land or have formed partnerships abroad.

BORDEAUX NÉGOCIANTS

By a tradition which stretches back to Roman times when there was a Negotiator Britannicus, the wine trade does not buy from the grower, instead it buys from a *négociant*. These middlemen have exercised a virtual stranglehold on Bordeaux for centuries by setting the prices for the various properties. Historically the justification for this system was simple – they knew the qualities of the properties and could save a buyer much time and money in research. But modern communications have removed the validity of that argument, so now they claim to exercise a benign influence by 'stabilising' prices and ironing out wild fluctuations. Naturally, the négociants have fought tooth and nail to protect their comfortable cocoon – none of the problems of growing the crop and none of the risks of holding unsold stocks, merely the fat percentage when the bills are paid. There are signs that their importance is declining. If so, this can only benefit claret lovers.

GEOGRAPHICAL LOCATION

It will sound heretical to suggest that Bordeaux is not ideally situated for the growing of vines! Much has been written of the analysis of the perfect conjunction of good drainage, gravelly soils, river mists and all the myriad factors that make for such excellence in years of good sunlight. However, the comparative lack of sunlight in average years tends to produce a poor ratio of sweet pulp to bitter skin and pips in the small-berried Cabernet Sauvignon. It is something of an oversimplification to suggest that the Merlot and Cabernet Franc content of the 'Bordeaux blend' is simply there to take the initial 'sting' out of under-ripe Cabernet Sauvignon, for their presence definitely adds to the complexity of the flavours. However, it must be noted how often international judges are awarding gold medals to 'foreign' wines containing mainly or exclusively Cabernet Sauvignon with little or no other varieties blended in, which suggests that perhaps riper Cabernet Sauvignon by itself is more acceptable in world markets.

If Bordeaux was two or three hundred miles further south it would be on latitudes which include the Duero, Lérida and Penedés in Spain, Tuscany in Italy as well as northern California – all homes of superlative reasonably priced Cabernet Sauvignon-based wines.

CLASSIFICATION OF CHÂTEAUX

The words Grand Crû (Great Growth), or literal translations thereof, may be found with varying degrees of accuracy on bottles from virtually every wine-growing country. In France the phrase is frequently used: grand crû champagnes indicating that the wine is produced only from the highest classification of vineyard, grand crû Alsace wines, grand crû burgundies and so on.

But how valid is this categorisation? Can a customer be assured of an international, or even a national, standard of excellence from a bottle so labelled?

As far as Bordeaux is concerned the answer is both simple and complex.

The original attempt at classifying and rating the quality of Bordeaux properties was carried out for the 1855 Paris Exhibition. However, due to snobbery on the part of the négociants who undertook the classification, Pomerol and St-Emilion were excluded together with the previously great area of Graves which had fallen behind in producing wines of quality. Thus only the wines of the Médoc and Sauternes were assessed. Properties were graded for quality, the highest being Château Yquem which was granted Premier Grand Crû (First Great Growth) status. After Yquem came four Premiers Crûs (First Growths) succeeded by Deuxième, Troisième, Quatrième and Cinquième Crûs (2nd, 3rd, 4th and 5th Growths). In all, out of more than 2000 properties, only 62 were granted crû classé, or classed growth, status. After these came properties accorded, in descending order of quality, Crû Exceptionnel (Exceptional Growth), Crû Bourgeois (Bourgeois Growth) and, finally, Crû Artisan (Artisan Growth).

Judgement was based on the prices historically obtained for each château going back, in some cases, for as much as a century. A consideration of the then current condition of the property was also included and this 1855 classification, unchanged but for one major exception, is still with us today. Despite the changes that have occurred in the intervening years this classification still represents a reasonable league table of Médoc quality.

Other major areas of Bordeaux have, with one exception, also been classified, but with gradings and assessments that carry somewhat less authority even than the 1855 scale for the Médoc. In 1953 a grading for Graves was

▼ *Since 1945, the label for each vintage of Mouton-Rothschild has an original work by a notable* *modern artist across the top strip. Artists have included Jean Cocteau (1947), Braque (1955),* *Dali (1958), Henry Moore (1964), Chagall (1970), Kandinsky (1971), Picasso (1973).*

produced which required revision in 1959 and a further correction in 1960. St-Emilion was classified in 1955 while classification of Pomerol has never been officially attempted.

There are, however, some generally accepted exceptions to the 1855 classification.

Perhaps the best known was the exclusion of

Château Mouton-Rothschild. In 1973, after a life-long fight for recognition by the late Baron Philippe de Rothschild, this outstanding property was granted premier crû status by an act of the French parliament. It finally joined the other three 'Greats' of the Médoc – Lafite-Rothschild, Latour and Margaux together with

Haut-Brion which, although in the Graves district, had been included as an exception in 1855, and Château Yquem of Sauternes.

Other important exclusions were the great properties of Pétrus in Pomerol together with Châteaux Ausone and Cheval-Blanc of St-Emilion all of which, it is generally agreed, are of premier crû status. Château Palmer languishes as a troisième crû while regularly commanding premier crû prices at auction and similarly situated is Château La Mission-Haut-Brion sited across the road from Haut-Brion proper and, again, requiring premier crû prices from auction bidders. An obvious danger of the sort of listing arrived at in 1855 by the courtiers – as the Bordeaux négociants were then known – is that it will be seen as too rigid or too elitist a structure. 'Oh! It's only a third growth . . .' is a nonsensical statement. All of the Bordeaux wines which enjoy a 'crû' rating, whether in the original 1855 table or in later listings, are superlative wines of their type.

BORDEAUX – COMMUNES AND PROPERTIES

The map shows that the most famous districts and communes, with the exception of St-Emilion, all lie on the west bank of the Gironde.

Other districts of Bordeaux produce an average mix of worthy and worthless – but it is the hallowed names of the Médoc starting in the north, in the Bas-Médoc, and reaching to the gates of the city of Bordeaux itself that spell the greatness that is truly claret.

BAS-MÉDOC

In spite of the name this area is 'higher', ie more northerly, than the rest of the Médoc. Previously thought to be of little consequence because the glacial deposits of large gravels, long believed to be the key to Bordeaux's greatness, finish south of this area. However, recent advances in production technology and understanding have lead to increasingly worthwhile wines. Leading names are:

Ch Loudenne – the pink château, owned by Gilbey Vintners/IDV and in English hands for more than a century

Ch Potensac – developed by the owners of Ch Léoville-Lascases

Ch Patache d'Aux

Ch La Tour de By
Ch La Tour St-Bonnet

HAUT-MÉDOC

An all-purpose appellation designed to catch those properties that do not fall neatly within the boundaries of the four famed communes listed below. Haut-Médoc on the label provides little guidance – individual property names and reputations being more important here than elsewhere in the Médoc. Best-known names include:

Ch La Lagune – very close to the advancing city boundaries of Bordeaux. Improved after acquisition by Ayala Champagne. Officially 3me crû

Ch Cantemerle – also very close to Bordeaux's residential areas. Again, acquisition, this time by Cordier, has resulted in investment and improvement. Officially 5me crû

Ch Belgrave – another property undergoing resuscitation. Too early yet for judgement but the signs are good. 5me crû

Non 1855 crû classé wines to look out for

Ch Caronne-Ste-Gemme – a big property producing typically hard wines

Ch Chasse-Spleen – well-made classic wine. Crû classé quality

Ch Citran – consistency coupled with constant improvement

Ch Coufran – everyone's favourite lesser known property. Softer wines than average due to higher Merlot content

Ch Fourcas-Hosten – the best in the Listrac commune

Ch Gressier Grand-Poujeaux – look-alike label to Fourcas-Hosten

Ch Malescasse – replanted by Americans and repurchased by the French

Ch Maucaillou – owned by French company Dourthe Frères

Ch Ramage La Batisse – new money, new methods, traditional style

Ch Larose-Trintaudon – created by Enrique Forner of Rioja's Marqués de Cáceres fame. Very modern methods

Ch Sociando-Mallet – ever increasing reputation. One to watch!

Ch Villegeorge – the ubiquitous Lurton family. 60% Merlot content

The four famous communes are:

● ST-ESTÈPHE

Most northerly of the four, this commune also has a heavier soil, with a higher clay content in the magic Médoc gravel.

Good crû classé properties
Ch Cos d'Estournel – an exotic 'chinoiserie' palace, it produces one of the best 2me crû

Ch Montrose – powerful, strong, hard wines for long ageing. 2me crû

Ch Calon-Ségur – most northerly of classed growths, the label shows a heart for an 18th-century owner, the Comte de Ségur, who claimed that, in spite of owning both Lafite and Latour, he had his heart in Calon. 3me crû

Ch Lafon-Rochet – had deteriorated, but Cognac money in the 1960s restored quality. Still improving. 4me crû

Ch Cos Labory – honest but not inspirational. 5me crû

Non crû classé wines to look out for
Ch Haut-Marbuzet – consistently reliable, if a little dull

Ch Meyney – Cordier money contributes consistency but little sparkle

Ch Les-Ormes-de-Pez – same owners as

Ch Lynch-Bages in Pauillac, well flavoured

Ch de Pez – should be crû classé. Quite outstanding.

Ch Phélan-Ségur – big property, same director as Ch Léoville-Poyferré in St-Julien

● PAUILLAC

This is the true heart of the Médoc. Here are three of the premier crû vineyards: Lafite, Latour and Mouton. These, in turn, are surrounded by a number of almost equally high quality producers although few are officially above 5me crû status.

Premier crû properties
Ch Lafite-Rothschild – almost in St-Estèphe yet wines more like those of St-Julien! 90 hectares produces only 1000 barrels – about 400 cases per hectare. Went through a patchy phase in the early 1970s

Ch Latour – British-owned by Harveys/Allied Lyons. Rock-solid wines of absolute integrity year after year. 'Second' wine, Les Forts de Latour, about 2me crû standard

Ch Mouton-Rothschild – elevated to 1re crû in 1973, although recognised as being of that standard for decades before. A tradition of the property is that each vintage the wine labels feature the work of a different prominent artist

▲ *The Grand Chai at Château Mouton-Rothschild. It holds wines maturing in traditional 225-litre Bordeaux barriques. Holding a nominal 300 bottles, each barrique of young wine is worth around £10,000.*

Other good crû classé properties

Ch Pichon-Longueville Baron – not inspired but showing signs of beginning to justify 2me crû

Ch Pichon-Longueville, Comtesse de Lalande – for obvious reasons the previous property is referred to as Pichon Baron and this as Pichon Lalande. This is definitely the better of the two although both are 'equal' at 2me crû

Ch Duhart-Milon-Rothschild – Rothschild money has enlarged and replanted the property. Young vines need to age yet, but the aim is high. 4me crû

The best 5me crû properties

Ch Grand-Puy-Lacoste – owned by M. Borie of Ducru-Beaucaillou in St-Julien

Ch Haut-Batailley – also owned by M. Borie. Sound and reliable

Ch Lynch-Bages – excellent property, same ownership as Ormes-de-Pez in St-Estèphe

Non crû classé wines to look out for

Ch La Couronne – wines of Haut-Batailley/Borie family standard!

Moulin des Carruades – the 'second' wine of Lafite-Rothschild

Ch La Rose – from the Pauillac growers' co-operative

● ST-JULIEN

Smallest of the four prestige communes, it nevertheless has the highest proportion of classed growths. There are no premier crû or 5me properties, and practically no non crû classé properties either! Léoville, which was once the largest of all estates in the Médoc, lies in this commune although it is now split up into three separate properties: Léoville-Barton, Léoville-Las Cases and Léoville Poyferré.

Good crû classé properties

Ch Ducru-Beaucaillou – Beaucaillou, or beautiful pebbles, refers to the Médoc gravel. 2me crû

Ch Gruaud-Larose – part of, and best of, the Cordier empire. 2me crû

Ch Langoa-Barton – family headquarters of the Barton family. 2me crû

Ch Léoville-Barton – smallest of the Léoville estate split. 2me crû

Ch Léoville-Las Cases – probably the best 2me crû!

Ch Branaire-Ducru – 4me crû

Watch out also for the effect of Japanese ownership on Ch Lagrange

Non crû classé wine to look out for:

Ch Gloria – probably the best non crû classé property

● MARGAUX

Most southerly of the prestige communes and bounded by the advancing boundary of Bordeaux's development.

Premier crû

Ch Margaux – revived by the fortune of the late André Mentzelopoulos and now supervised by his widow; also produces Pavillon Blanc from the Sauvignon Blanc.

Good crû classé properties

Ch Brane-Cantenac – Lurton family ownership. Best 2me crû

Ch Dufort-Vivens – sometimes a selection mixed with Brane-Cantenac

Ch Giscours – deserves a higher grading than 3me crû

Ch d'Issan – 3me crû. Accurate Margaux flavour, more oak recently

▼ *Château Lascombes, a 2me crû classé Margaux property, restored in the 1950s by Alexis Lichine and currently owned by the British Bass-Charrington group. At just under 100 hectares it is fairly large, and produces around 40,000 cases per year.*

Ch Malescot St-Exupéry – much improved during the 1970s. 3me crû

Ch Palmer – Dutch/British/French ownership and 1re crû quality despite classification as 3me crû

Ch Prieuré-Lichine – this property was assembled by the late Alexis Lichine in the 1950s. 4me crû

Ch du Tertre – two decades of steady improvement. 5me crû

Non crû classé wines to look out for

Ch d'Angludet – home of Peter Sichel, part-owner of Ch Palmer

Ch Labégorce-Zédé – good substantial wines

Ch Paveil de Luze – estate of Baron Geoffrey de Luze. One to watch

Ch Siran – run by a fanatic determined to raise the estate's status

Ch La Tour-de-Mons – three centuries in the same family. Good wines

BORDEAUX – SECOND WINES

More and more properties are finding it attractive to market their second wines – wines which are produced from young vines not yet mature enough to qualify for the top quality level of that particular vineyard or wine which for some other reason the property prefers to downgrade. In the past the honest sent these products off to be blended into generic 'bordeaux' and the less-than-honest were known to have sneaked these wines into their full-blown first-label wines to 'stretch' them.

These wines should not be under-estimated and can represent first-class value.

GRAVES

Historically this is where it all began. Graves, gravel in regional French, was producing fine wine during the three centuries in the Middle Ages when Bordeaux came under the English crown. At that time the Médoc was little more than an impassable swamp and the original

PROPERTY	AREA	SECOND WINE
PREMIERS CRÛS		
Ch Lafite	Pauillac	Le Moulin des Carruades
Ch Latour	Pauillac	Les Forts de Latour
Ch Margaux	Margaux	Pavillon Rouge
Ch Haut-Brion	Pessac	Ch Bahans Haut-Brion NV
DEUXIÈMES CRÛS		
Ch Léoville-Las Cases	St-Julien	Clos de Marquis
Ch Léoville-Poyferré	St-Julien	Ch Moulin Riche
Ch Dufort-Vivens	Margaux	Domaine de Curebourse
Ch Lascombes	Margaux	Ch le Gombaude 3rd wine: Ch Segonnes
Ch Brane-Cantenac	Cantenac Margaux	Ch Notton 3rd wine: Dom de Fontarney
Ch Pichon-Lalande	Pauillac	La Reserve de la Comtesse
Ch Pichon-Baron	Pauillac	Le Baronnet de Pichon
Ch Ducru-Beaucaillou	St-Julien	Ch la Croix
Ch Cos d'Estournel	St-Estèphe	goes to Ch de Marbuzet
TROISIEMES CRÛS		
Ch Lagrange	St-Julien	Les Fiefs de Lagrange
Ch Malescot St-Exupéry	Margaux	Ch de Loyac 3rd wine: Dom de Balardin
Ch La Lagune	Ludon	Ch Ludon, Pomies Agassac
Ch Desmirail	Margaux	Ch Daubry
Ch Calon-Ségur	St-Estèphe	Le Marquis de Segur 3rd wine: Moulin Decalon
Ch Boyd-Cantenac	Margaux	Goes to adjoining Ch Pouget

claret, or clairet as it was then known, of Bordeaux came from Graves.

In the 17th century Graves was exported to England, where Samuel Pepys enjoyed the wine of Haut-Brion, then, as now, one of the finest properties. In the Royal Oak, a tavern in Lombard Street, he drank 'a sort of French wine called Ho Bryen that hath a good and most particular taste'. Throughout the 18th century the wines of Graves were held in good repute but, by the mid 19th century, the area was in decline. Overtaken in quality by the Médoc and

slower to respond to the scourge of oïdium which struck hard in the early 1850s, the area was ignored by the Bordeaux courtiers when preparing the 1855 classification. Ignored, that is, except for Haut-Brion which was well managed and which, as it couldn't be ignored, was listed as a Médoc property!

Graves is also the foremost area producing both high quality red and white wines. Lying between the almost exclusively red areas of the Médoc and the almost exclusively white areas to the south – Sauternes and Barsac – the

PROPERTY	AREA	SECOND WINE
QUATRIÈMES CRÛS		
Ch St-Pierre Sevaistre	St-Julien	Ch St Louis le Bosq
Ch Talbot	St-Julien	Le Connetable de Talbot
Ch Duhart-Milon	Pauillac	Moulin de Duhart
Ch Pouget	Cantenac Margaux	see Ch Boyd-Cantenac
Ch La Tour-Carnet	St Laurent	Le Sire de Camin
Ch Beychevelle	St-Julien	Reserve de l'Amiral
Ch Prieuré-Lichine	Cantenac Margaux	Ch de Clairefont Haut Prieuré
Ch Marquis-de-Terme	Margaux	Domaine des Condats
CINQUIÈMES CRÛS		
Ch Pontet-Canet	Pauillac	Les Hauts de Pontet
Ch Grand-Puy-Lacoste	Pauillac	Ch Lacoste Borie
Ch Grand-Puy-Ducasse	Pauillac	Ch Artigues Arnaud
Ch Haut-Batailley	Pauillac	La Tour d'Aspic
Ch Lynch-Bages	Pauillac	Ch Haut Bages Averous
Ch Croizet-Bages	Pauillac	Enclos de Moncabon
Ch Cantemerle	Macau	Ch Villeneuve de-Cantenac
SAUTERNES PREMIERS CRÛS		
Ch Guiraud		Le Dauphin de Lalague
Ch La Tour Blanche		Crû St Marc
Ch Rieussec		Clos la Bere

official classifications carried out in 1953 and 1959 (page 48) recognised properties for their excellence in producing both types of wine. Even so Haut-Brion suffered by being listed only as a red wine producer even though it also produces one of the world's finest white wines: Château Haut-Brion Blanc. An amendment in 1960 rectified this.

Premier crû

Ch Haut-Brion – surrounded by urban
    development, this property is protected only
    by the high prices achieved by its wines.
    Good second wine, Bahans Haut-Brion, 2me
    crû. Exceptional white wine – Ch Haut-
    Brion Blanc.

Other good properties
(R = red wines; W = white wines):
Dom de Chevalier R+W – tiny estate. Solid
    reds but divine whites
Ch de Fieuzal R+W – another tiny property, an
    improving reputation
Ch Haut-Bailly R – one of the four top Graves
    properties
Ch Malartic-Lagravière R+W – interesting
    100% Sauvignon white
Ch La Mission-Haut-Brion R+W – previously a
    rival, now same owners as Haut-Brion.
    Superb wines. 'Second' red Ch La Tour
    Haut-Brion better than Bahans. White
    Laville Haut-Brion has astounding flavour
    concentration
Ch Pape-Clément R+W – in the 14th century
    owned by Clement V, the 'Pape' of
    Châteauneuf. High Merlot content reds

Other good properties to look out for
Ch Couhins-Lurton W
Ch Rahoul R+W
Ch La Tour-Martillac R
Ch La Louvière W

ST-EMILION

This is Merlot country. Most of the quality producers of this vast area (more than 5000 hectares) are concentrated around the ancient town of St-Emilion itself. Here, on the limestone and clay soil of the 'côtes' of St-Emilion, the Cabernet Sauvignon only manages a dull wine while the Merlot produces excellent quality. Further away to the north-west, practically on the borders of Pomerol, are 'graves' – gravelly soils with a highly sandy

character – which are better for Cabernet Sauvignon yet even here only one notable property, Ch Figeac, has any significant Médoc-like Cabernet Sauvignon content.

A further geological characteristic in St-Emilion occurs towards the banks of the river Dordogne where the pale sandy soil encourages plentiful quantities, but little by way of quality.

In St-Emilion the term 'grand crû' can, it seems, be applied to almost any wine. This is

the result of some remarkably inept legislation in 1954 which allowed four appellations – St-Emilion Premier Crû Classé which listed two category 'A' châteaux and four category 'B's. These were followed in the league table by over 70 properties entitled to the description St-Emilion Grand Crû Classé and, in turn, by around 200 estates entitled to St-Emilion Grand Crû by submitting wines for testing each year. Thus, of the 1000 or so St-Emilion growers around one-third could claim to be 'Grand Crû'

▼ *The vines of Les Vieilles Murailles grow right up to the remaining wall of the convent from which the vineyard gets its name. Nearby is the picturesque old town of St-Emilion itself.*

or better. Not a very useful scale of excellence!

In 1984 some degree of sanity was restored by changing to just two categories: St-Emilion Grand Crû, for which about 90 properties were eligible, and plain St-Emilion. The qualifications for the former were tightened and some properties were even demoted. The 1954 regulations called for reviews every decade and, indeed, reviews took place in 1969 and 1984 – the last of which produced these profound improvements. However, as the legislation changes did not come into effect until the growing season of 1986 these undoubted improvements are only now beginning to be seen on bottles of St-Emilion offered for sale.

Premier grand crû classé 'A' properties (1985):

Ch Ausone – 50:50 Merlot and Cabernet Franc from this most perfect of sites. Small 7 hectare vineyard and only just over 2000 cases a year

Ch Cheval Blanc – ⅔:⅓ Cabernet Franc to Merlot and a totally different soil highlights the differences between these two top properties. Huge wines

Best of the other grand crû classé properties

Ch Belair – close to Ausone in position and in style, same owner and manager but wines lack subtlety

Ch Canon – suitable name for the wine of this conservative property

Ch Figeac – close to Cheval Blanc and a part of the same original estate yet different wine-making with 35% Cabernet Sauvignon

Clos Fourtet – run by Lucien Lurton's brother Dominique

Ch Magdelaine – belongs to the Moueix, another influential Bordelaise family. Next door to Ch Ausone. Well balanced wines

Ch Pavie – biggest site on the prestigious 'côtes' of St-Emilion. Unusual (for this part of St-Emilion) 20% Cabernet Sauvignon

Best of the rest

Ch L'Arrosée
Ch Beau-Séjour-Bécot
Ch Canon-La-Gaffelière
Ch Curé-Bon-La-Madeleine
Ch Dassault
Ch Fombrauge
Ch Fonplégade
Ch Fonroque

Ch Laroque
Ch Moulin du Cadet
Ch Soutard
Ch la Tour-Figeac
Ch Troplong-Mondot

POMEROL

This is where the whole controversial subject of grand crû, premier crû and the like falls down completely. To purchase a case of mature 1970 claret at auction in 1990 would cost around £550 for Ch Margaux; £600 for Haut-Brion; £650 for Cheval Blanc or Palmer; £700–£800 for Lafite, Latour or Mouton – and £2000 for Pomerol's Ch Pétrus. Yet the label of Pétrus' wine merely states 'Grand Vin'.

Pomerol arrived quite recently on the fine wine scene. A century ago the name was virtually unknown outside the immediate area and even now there is a seeming lack of regional identity. It has no major town, no significant geological feature and almost no significant houses – certainly few that look at all like the popular image of a 'château'.

Another curiosity is that the area abounds in tiny vineyards, the average vineyard size for the whole area being 4 hectares and the biggest estate only 48 hectares. The diamond shape of Pomerol contains at its eastern point the old Dordogne river port of Libourne and from here, moving westwards, the soil changes from a predominantly sandy structure to a clay-dominated subsoil which, towards the centre of the region, lies only a few feet below the surface. Merlot and Cabernet Franc (as in St-Emilion, here called the Bouchet) are the grapes best suited and the results, as in much of St-Emilion, are early developing wines of rich softness that make friends easily. So easily in fact that, in spite of the large number of tiny vineyards, there is no co-operative, the wines finding a ready market in Belgium, the Low Countries and the UK.

The Greatest:

Ch Pétrus – the Moueix family influence is again present. This property is unique among the greats because it is a post-war creation. Originally the Loubat family were the architects of excellence, being joined through marriage in 1961 to the Moueixs. Limited volume, often less than 4000 cases, and the ruthless pursuit of absolute quality are the magic ingredients of greatness

Other good properties – Médoc 2me or 3me crû standard
Western Pomerol, close to Libourne and with sandier soil:
Ch L'Enclos
Clos René
Ch de Sales
Southern Pomerol bordering St-Emilion and with more gravelly soil:
Ch Beauregard
Ch La Conseillante
Ch Petit-Village
Central Pomerol, clay substrata with heavy iron deposits:
Ch Certan de May
Ch L'Evangile
Ch La Fleur-Pétrus
Ch La Grave Trigant de Boisset
Ch Lafleur
Ch Latour à Pomerol
Ch Trotanoy
Vieux Château Certan

THE REST OF BORDEAUX

When is a Bordeaux wine not a Bordeaux wine? Not, it seems, until it is produced many kilometres away. The official minor areas are:

PREMIÈRES CÔTES DE BLAYE
The most northerly of the red-wine producing areas on the right bank of the Gironde. Further north the production is exclusively of white grapes leading into Cognac country. White wines from the Côtes de Blaye are, in general, pretty dull – especially the medium-sweet versions. Reds are fairly Côtes de Bourg in style although possibly less gutsy.

CÔTES DE BOURG
When the Médoc was still marshland, the Côtes de Bourg on the right bank of the Gironde was already a substantial vineyard area. Here cultivation is intensive and the product consciously commercial. Merlot and Cabernet Franc help to produce reasonably easy-drinking reds. White wine output is increasing, but so far the wines have little interest or distinction.

FRONSAC AND CANON-FRONSAC
To the west of Libourne lies the jumble of hills, hillocks, little lanes and modest properties known as Fronsac and long regarded as an impenetrable area. The wines, which traditionally include a large proportion of the Malbec grape and so are high in colour, fruit and alcohol have for years been used as cutting wines to beef up other more anaemic Bordeaux products or have been recommended for their alleged medicinal benefits! Worthwhile wines can be found but careful selection is necessary.

PREMIÈRES CÔTES DE BORDEAUX
Squeezed along the north bank of the Garonne between the river itself and the hinterland of Entre-deux-Mers lies this rather anonymous area. Changing habits and fashions are dictating a move out of the sweet and sticky market, yet do the growers commit themselves to reds, and increase the tide of Bordeaux reds already available, or go for crisp white wines which, to be really successful, call for considerable investment in stainless steel and in technology? A few brave pioneers have appeared but more are needed.

ENTRE-DEUX-MERS
There are, of course, no 'mers' to be 'entre', the nearest open water being the Bay of Biscay at the mouth of the Gironde. In fact Entre-deux-Mers lies between the rivers Dordogne and Garonne. Traditionally its wines were in the sweet and sticky category, but, as the world has turned away from the medium-sweet market, so Entre-deux-Mers has turned with it. An image as the Muscadet of the south has been created, an ocean of reasonable crisp whites is produced and, while there are few wines from this area that would win medals, yet the average quality level is respectable. Any red wines produced do not enjoy the regional appellation – they are simply labelled Bordeaux AC or Bordeaux Supérieur depending on qualification.

STE-CROIX-DU-MONT AND LOUPIAC
These two areas are on the opposite side of the Garonne to the more illustrious Barsac and Sauternes, yet share the same type of micro climate that helps develop the noble rot so essential to the production of quality dessert wines. Ste-Croix-du-Mont is the more favoured of the two, and is capable, on occasion, of providing wines to rank almost alongside the greatest of Sauternes yet at a far more economic price. Some dry white and even some lightweight reds are also produced. Loupiac tends towards slightly less massive sweetness, although whether from choice or necessity is open to question.

SAUTERNES AND BARSAC

About 20 miles upstream of Bordeaux city centre, on the south bank of the Garonne and at the southern end of the Appellation 'Bordeaux' area, are the five communes which collectively produce the honeyed delights of Barsac and Sauternes. These communes split neatly into three producing the heavier style of Sauternes – Bommes, Fargues and Sauternes itself – and two producing a slightly lighter style – Preignac and Barsac. Of the five properties that make up the whole area called, collectively, Sauternes, only growers in the Barsac commune can use their own village name if they prefer, which is no more than another way of saying that all Barsac is Sauternes but not all Sauternes is Barsac!

▲ *Sauvignon Blanc grapes at Château Coutet infected with the benign* mould pourriture noble *or noble rot and destined to produce 1re crû Barsac.*

CHÂTEAU YQUEM

Château Yquem is the best-known property in this area and has belonged to descendants of the Lur-Saluces family since the Comte de Lur-Saluces married Josephine Sauvage d'Yquem in 1785. The d'Yquems had owned the château for the previous 200 years! Sweet wine was not produced here until 1847 following experiments by Herr Focke, the German owner of nearby Château La Tour Blanche who, in 1836, tried the method used for producing sweet wines on the Rhine. It therefore follows that the wines drunk at Yquem by the American President, Thomas Jefferson, during his celebrated visit to Bordeaux in 1787, would have been dry white wines and not the dessert wines we now associate with the property. Some of the bottles Jefferson ordered from his visits to the various Bordeaux properties have recently been auctioned for tens of thousands of dollars. A lot to pay for wine whose drinkability must be, shall we say, suspect.

The techniques employed to persuade sweetness from the grapes of this area are described on page 28, but it is worth emphasising that the effort that has to be put into the production of such wines inevitably makes them uneconomic to produce because, with the exception of Château d'Yquem, dessert wines have never commanded a price in any way related to the cost of production.

Apart from the high labour costs, production costs are raised by the very low output per hectare – the lowest of any wine-growing area in the world. All the quality producing châteaux drastically prune the vines to limit the number of bunches per plant, thus increasing the concentration of flavour before the dehydration due to noble rot concentrates it still further. Once produced, the wines are stored for three and a half years to mature, losing a further 20% from evaporation. At Château Yquem, the final production of saleable wine works out at 1 glass per vine. Even the slightly less prestigious properties only manage 4 glasses per vine.

DRY SWEET WHITE WINES

Some growers prune their grapes and leave them late on the vines to obtain the maximum sweetness in the berries, but then allow fermentation to carry through until a dry wine results. The resulting wines are a puzzle, they are so full of apparent sweetness, both on the nose and the palate that it is difficult to believe that the wines are, at least scientifically, dry.

Naturally these wines are great rarities. Putting the considerable effort into producing sweet grapes, only to ferment the sweetness out of the wine, involves much expense to produce only a tiny quantity. The outstanding example of these dry sweet wines is Yquem's Château Y pronounced Ygrec, French for the letter Y. Another, lesser, example is Château R, pronounced 'air' from neighbouring Château Rieussec.

RECOMMENDED PROPERTIES

Sauternes properties were included in the original 1855 classification and, like the Médoc, those ratings still hold remarkably true.

In the 1855 classification, however, there was one Sauternes property thought to be superior even to the 'greats' of the Médoc – Château Yquem – and, while Latour, Lafite, Haut-Brion and Margaux were awarded premier crû status, Yquem was out on its own as the only Premier Grand Crû. At that time it was followed by nine 1re crûs and a further nine 2me crûs but, nowadays, division of the old properties has increased the number to 11 1re crûs and 14 2me crûs.

The Greatest Property (in the world?)

Ch d'Yquem – tiny production equals expensive wine. Is it worth it? Unquestionably.

Premier crû properties

Ch Climens – close to Yquem cropping levels. The biggest Barsac

Ch Coutet – Barsac again. Marginally second to Climens

Ch Guiraud – Canadian money to the rescue. Produces dry 'G' and also Le Dauphin Château Guiraud red. Neighbour of Yquem

Ch Rieussec – (Lafite) Rothschild money and a lighter style of wine

Ch Suduiraut – new management producing poor man's d'Yquem

Deuxième crû properties

Ch Broustet – originally the home of the cooper who standardised the 225-litre Bordeaux barrique. Typically lighter Barsac

Ch Doisy-Daëne – modern technology comes to Barsac. Their dry white includes the Riesling grape!

Ch Doisy-Védrines – bigger Barsac in the Climens/Coutet style

Ch Filhot – largest 2me crû estate. Some dry white and a little red

Best of the rest

Ch Bastor-Lamontagne – bargain prices for a standard that's certainly 2me crû

Ch de Fargues – same owners and same standards as Yquem, *almost* the same wines

Ch Raymond-Lafon – owned by the manager of Yquem

OTHER AREAS

There are other appellations within the Bordeaux area. In general they are small and produce little wine of consequence.

Alphabetically these are:

Cerons
Côtes-de-Bordeaux-St-Macaire
Coutras
Cubzac
Graves de Vayre
Guitres
Ste-Foy-Bordeaux

BORDEAUX AND BORDEAUX SUPÉRIEUR

These are not geographically defined areas but catch-all appellations available to any grower in the vastness that is the Bordeaux wine-growing region. Any wine which does not qualify as something else automatically becomes Bordeaux or Bordeaux Supérieur provided the grape varieties are those prescribed and the cropping and alcohol levels are correct.
The regulations are quite simple, the statutory requirements are:

White wines
● *Bordeaux* – minimum 10.5° alcohol with maximum crop of 65hl per hectare
● *Bordeaux Supérieur* – minimum 11.5°, crop maximum of 40hl per hectare

Red wines
● *Bordeaux* – minimum 10° alcohol with maximum crop of 55hl per hectare
● *Bordeaux Supérieur* – minimum 10.5°, crop maximum of 40hl per hectare

Naturally, such a wide net catches all sorts of vinous fish. Some are pure gems of the highest quality, yet modestly priced as they do not carry a more prestigious title. Others are so worthless they need to be thrown back into the European wine lake.

THE SOUTH-WEST

BERGERAC AND MONBAZILLAC

Isolated inland, the area of Bergerac seems in the past to have been fated to be all too often just one step behind. Early legislation in favour of the Bordelaise prevented the growers of Bergerac using the large barrels of Bordeaux, thus their wine attracted a higher tax. For long they supplied the Dutch, who sailed up the Gironde and on up the Dordogne, who sought either sweet white wines or thin acidic white wines for distilling (as in Charente and Muscadet). More recently many growers switched from sweet whites and thin whites to reds – just as world taste moved towards crisp fruity whites. But now the area is coming good. Best known producer in the English market is Henry Ryman late of stationery fame and owner of Château de la Jaubertie since 1973. All here is modern and the quality is quite exceptional as his frequent medal successes in competition attest.

A forward-looking co-operative has also given the wines of Bergerac a lift and, as they also own the historic Château de Monbazillac where traditional sweeties are still produced, they are promoting the best of both worlds – crisp Sauvignon Blanc-based dry wines and rich, Sémillon-based, dessert wines.

All the best properties are producing red wines based on the Bordeaux blend of grapes and, in the main, they are very good value for money.

Good Bergerac names

Ch de la Jaubertie – Australia-in-France production methods, has Merlot-based red and Cabernet-based Reserve red. 100% Sauvignon white plus a 'Tradition' and a Reserve Semillon-based

Ch Belingard, Boudigand and du Chayne – three estates with maceration carbonique red, Sauvignon white, sweet Monbazillac-style white and a méthode champenoise sparkler too!

Ch de Monbazillac – see UNIDOR on the opposite page

Ch de Panisseau – inspiring whites, both Sauvignon and Sémillon

Ch Tiregand – biggest in Pecharmant at 33 hectares. Usual grapes

UNIDOR – Dordogne Co-operative of co-operatives, 4000 hectares produces 40% of the total output. Generally good quality, see also opposite

LESSER KNOWN AC AND VDQS AREAS

France is naturally littered with significant, if small, growing areas. Many of these are in the départements bordering the Mediterranean coast and these will be dealt with in the section on The South Coast (pages 80–89), the rest will be treated as satellites to whichever of the great growing areas they adjoin.

The following areas stretch in an arc from Bordeaux down to the eastern Pyrenees.

CÔTES DE DURAS
Some good value and quite substantial Sauvignon-based whites and reasonable Bordeaux-based, often macération carbonique, reds mainly from the co-operative founded in 1965. Co-op wines are actually marketed by UNIDOR (see top of page).

CÔTES DU MARMANDAIS
UNIDOR influences two co-operatives producing 'clarets' and Sauvignon/Sémillon whites. Vin de Pays l'Agenais also produced here. Improving all the time.

CÔTES DE BUZET
Historically a producer of thin whites destined for distillation, they now offer good Bordeaux-style reds assisted by strong identity style marketing. Virtually the work of one man, M. Jean Mermillo, ex-manager of Ch Lafite, who helped to create the fine co-operative Caves Reunis des Côtes de Buzet in 1954. Their perseverance was rewarded in 1973 with a very well merited elevation to AC status.

CAHORS
Unusual in producing only red wine based on the Malbec grape, also called Cot or Auxerrois, with additions of Gamay, Merlot and others. The dense coloured, highly tannic, 'black' wines of yesteryear are happily long gone. Nowadays the more modern outlook leads to more immediately drinkable wines of considerable character.

GAILLAC
Wine production dates back to the Romans. Gaillac was beloved of the English court in the Middle Ages. Today's wines are flat whites, sometimes with pétillance, and racy reds. Unusual grape varieties like l'En del'El, Loin de l'Oeil, Ondenc, Brocol and Ferservadou do not easily make friends.

CÔTES DE FRONTON
Long the captive supplier of the wine requirements of Toulouse, now better known and granted AC status in 1975 for their attractively drinkable reds.

MADIRAN
The white Pancherenc du Vic Bilh is normally a moelleux wine tending towards a rather flat, flaccid, taste. Rather uninspiring. The red, however, is well worth seeking out. The taste is primarily that of the Tannat and is completely individual to this recently-revived area.

BEARN
Almost unknown outside France and little known even in France. Most of the wines seem to go to local restaurants.

JURANÇON
A tiny area which hardly seems French at all. Most of the exclusively white production is nowadays dull. A few stalwarts still perpetuate the memory of the greatness of the sweet moelleux wines which are the true greatness of this appellation in the Pyrenean foothills.

IROULEGUY
A Basque bastion producing mountain wines. Mainly local grapes but Tannat also present. Local interest only.

Throughout this south-western area there is the beneficial presence of GIVISO or Groupement d'Intérêt Economique de Vignerons du Sud Ouest. It was set up in 1975 as a Co-operative of co-ops and the members are the seven leading co-operative groups in the south-west. Under the oversight of GIVISO they are devoted to improving standards – a target they are certainly achieving.

CHAMPAGNE

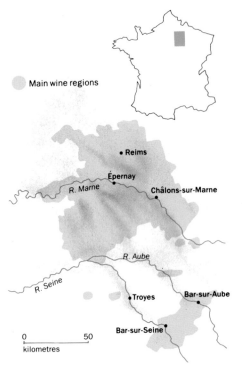

Main wine regions

Reims

Épernay

R. Marne

Châlons-sur-Marne

R. Aube

R. Seine

Troyes

Bar-sur-Aube

Bar-sur-Seine

0   50

kilometres

The vineyards of Champagne, 140km north-east of Paris, are the most northerly vineyards in France and it was this that led to the development of the local sparkling wine now regarded as the ultimate in luxury celebratory drinks.

These northern vineyards could only produce grapes low in sugar even though they were always picked as late in the year as possible. The highly acidic grapes were therefore being fermented in cold months and the process was inhibited by the low temperatures, to the extent that the wines were being bottled with the fermentation incomplete and thus a secondary fermentation would often begin in the spring when the rising temperature 'awakened' the yeasts still present in the wine.

This attractive characteristic, the mild fizz, was seized on by Dom Perignon, the blind master of the Abbey of Hautvillers who, probably together with another brother, Dom Ruinart, developed the method of increasing and capturing the secondary fermentation by re-bottling with a small amount of sugar and fresh yeast. His pioneering work included the use of stronger bottles to withstand the pressures generated and corks secured by

twine in place of the waxed rags used hitherto. Even so, his losses due to explosion were considerable – 6 atmospheres (that is six times normal atmospheric pressure) is the standard nowadays – however those bottles that remained intact more than justified the effort involved.

But Dom Perignon has a further and more significant claim to fame. It was he who pioneered the blending of wines from different local areas and vineyards to produce a wine of consistent taste. It may be that his palate was more acute than others, but he was determined to use the characteristics of wines from different sources to cancel out the usual seasonal variations.

It is amusing to note the low regard in which blended wines, Hirondelle, for example, are generally regarded by people who fail to realise that it is the blender's art that maintains the consistent taste of many of the world's most prestigious wines, such as sherries, ports and champagnes. Nowadays the blending of wines from the tightly controlled 24,500 hectares is fundamental to the production of champagne. The great 'houses', as the largest champagne-making companies are known, can use up to 30 or 40 wines from up to 10 different vintages to balance out and maintain the consistent flavour that they regard as their own particular house 'style'.

An elaborate system is used to grade the output of the vineyards of Champagne – under 15% of which are actually owned by the champagne houses. There are over 18,000 vineyard owners and, of these, nearly 10,000 own less than half a hectare. The area is controlled by the Comité Interprofessional du Vin de Champagne – the CIVC – which, having laid down a grading from 80% to 100% for the vineyards, fixes a price per kilo for grapes for the particular year. Growers are paid on a pro rata basis for their crop according to its fixed percentage rating.

In the decade 1970–80 the price paid for grapes rose from 5 francs per kilo to nearly 25 francs per kilo, and it takes 1.4 kilos of grapes to make a bottle of bubbly! With grapes so dear and with very high production and storage costs it is easy to see why prices for champagne shot up in the last decade.

The UK, the USA and Italy vie for the title of best export market and it is these overseas sales that have lead to many of the marketing

◀ Picking black grapes for Moët et Chandon in Champagne. This photograph was taken in an exceptional year, when the harvest was so late that the vine leaves had already fallen.

▲ The statue of Dom Perignon standing outside the headquarters of Moët et Chandon in the Avenue de Champagne, Épernay.

ideas that have resulted in subtle changes in the way we regard champagne. These include:

VINTAGE CHAMPAGNES

In theory, the exclusive product of one particularly favoured year. In practice, quite often modified or 'adjusted' by blending for exactly the reason that blending is such a cornerstone of champagne production – to ensure that a wine is neither too rich or too lean, that it possesses 'balance'. By law, however, the house may not sell more of a given vintage than it has actually made!

PRESTIGE CUVÉES

These are normally, but not invariably, super-duper vintage wines. Moët's Dom Perignon, created in 1921, was the first and now every house has its top wine.

BLANC DE BLANCS

An excellent marketing strategy. Being so far north the white Chardonnay grape tends to crop more satisfactorily than the red Pinots Noir and Meunier and thus the idea of persuading champagne lovers that wines made only from white grapes have a greater delicacy, more finesse and are more sophisticated has considerable commercial attractions! Sadly, it is most often the red grape content that maintains the balance of a champagne as evidenced by the high proportions of red grapes used by the great houses. There is also the danger that, drastically over-chilled as many champagnes are, it will have a taste more reminiscent of Perrier water than Perrier-Jouet!

VERY DRY WINES

The marketing men thought: if dry is chic, then very dry is very chic! When produced, champagne is bone dry but has an important addition (dosage) of still wine with either brandy or sugar to sweeten the final product. The scale of sweetness with the French definitions, is:

- *Brut* 0.5%–1.5% sugar added, very dry
- *Extra Dry* 1.5%–2.5% sugar added, dry
- *Sec* 2%–4% sugar added, slightly sweet
- *Demi-Sec* 4%–6% sugar added, quite sweet
- *Doux* over 6% sugar added, very sweet

but wines with no sweetness added are marketed as Brut Zero, Brut Nature, Zero Dosage etc. and, not surprisingly, are very, very dry. Whether they are also very, very chic is for the customer to decide!

CRÉMANT

A less sparkling wine, having had less yeast and sugar added for the secondary fermentation – normally about 3–4 atmospheres of pressure. One of the most popular is Mumm's Crémant de Cramant.

RD (RÉCEMMENT DÉGORGÉ)

This is champagne with the sediment left in the bottle for, in the case of the best known, Bollinger's RD, ten years. This is a similar principle to Muscadet-sur-lie, the lees giving greater flavour to the wine. After degorgement the wine naturally does not need the statutory period maturing in bottle. Most of the houses keep some of their old wines available for special occasions – I was lucky enough to have a 1911 RD at Moët: still youthful and fresh!

BLANC DE NOIRS

Champagne produced only from black grapes. Mme Bollinger was the first to do this with her seventieth birthday wine produced in 1969. She intended to do this only once and used grapes from two tiny plots which still grow ungrafted pre-phylloxera vines. (Some people said she only did it to show what little regard she had for the Blanc de Blancs school of thought.) On her death in 1977 Christian Bizot became head of the company and he has perpetuated the idea, although re-naming the wine Vielle Vignes Français. Naturally it is only produced as a vintage champagne.

COTEAUX CHAMPENOIS

This is a separate appellation for wines which qualify as a 'Vin nature de la Champagne' – in other words, still champagne. These are seldom of great interest, after all, they're using grapes which could otherwise be used to make the 'real stuff'. White Coteaux Champenois is the most common and several of the great houses produce a version but some red Coteaux Champenois is also produced – that from the village of Bouzy is called Bouzy Rouge! Apart from the amusing name, this wine is sometimes used to encourage the tint in what might otherwise be an anaemic rosé champagne.

Another wine from this area is the exclusive Rosé des Riceys – really only of academic interest for the price far outweighs the vinous merits. Good rosé certainly, but when you have to pay more for it than for a bottle of champagne – or, for that matter, a reasonable bottle of burgundy – is it really worth it?

BOBs

The grand marque houses all clearly boast their own name on their labels but, in terms of sheer volume, their wines represent a minority of the total output of the whole Champagne district. In the past the great houses controlled the whole of the champagne market but recently, with a series of small harvests and increasing world markets, the growers have found themselves in a stronger bargaining position. Gradually, apart from raising the prices demanded for their grapes, they began to make their own champagnes, often through co-operatives, and to market these products aggressively. This has led to an explosion in BOB or Buyer's Own Brand labelling.

Of course, throughout the 20th century, there have been labels printed on demand – if you are prepared to order, say, 50 cases, you can have more or less any name you like printed on the label – but with the increased demand from supermarkets and from high street chains for their own 'House Champagne' and with the greater power of the growers such labels have proliferated.

Champagnes – the Best of the Best (at a price!)

Bollinger Vielle Vignes Français – see above

Moët & Chandon Dom Perignon – in spite of the hype consistently good

Heidsieck Monopole Diamant Bleu – often under-rated

Krug – although non-vintage this champagne can make most other prestige champagnes look dull

Laurent Perrier Grand Siecle – excellent non-vintage blending

Roederer Cristal – originally exclusive to the Tsars. Clear bottles

Perrier-Jouet La Belle Epoque – excellent, in spite of hand-painted Christmas roses on the bottle!

Taittinger Comtes de Champagne – a blanc de blancs, but one that disproves the thinness theory. Rare Comtes de Champagnes Rosé also good.

Best of the Rest

Billion – buy if you can find it, especially 1979 vintage

Boizel – consistent small house, fifth generation owners

Granier – old-style toasty flavour, excellent value for money

Pol Roger – still family run, Cuvée Sir Winston Churchill top brand

Ruinart – oldest champagne house, founded by nephew of Dom Ruinart

Salon – buy now, since Robert Billion's death in 1984 standards have not seemed quite as high as they were

---

There is always a series of letters and numbers at the bottom of each champagne label, the letters indicating the type of producer while the numbers define the particular wine-maker.

Letter codes effective from 1989 are:

NM Négociant-Manipulant or 'Merchant-Handler'. The commonest category. Champagne produced from grapes or from wines purchased from anywhere in Champagne. All the big houses come into this category and the wines should be reliably good.

RM Recoltant-Manipulant or 'Harvester-Handler'. Mainly small growers' own champagnes produced from their own grapes. 'Grand Crû' wines will have used 100% rated grapes, while 'Premier Crû' indicates over 90% rated grapes were used.

CM Co-operative-Manipulant or 'Co-operative-Handler'. The wines have been made by a co-operative and are normally none the worse for that.

MA Marque Auxiliaire or Marque d'Acheteur, literally 'Mark of the Buyer'. This is found on all BOB wines but times may change for if champagne house X produces champagne Y for a supermarket chain and it scores a great success in a tasting, then the champagne house might like some of the glory to rub off on itself. In the future the letters MA and the producer's own number may be replaced by the actual name of the producer.

RC Recoltant Co-operateur or 'Cooperative-Harvester'. A grower selling champagne produced by a co-operative.

SR Société des Recoltants or 'Harvesters' Company'. Found on bottles produced by a company created by wine producers who are members of the same family.

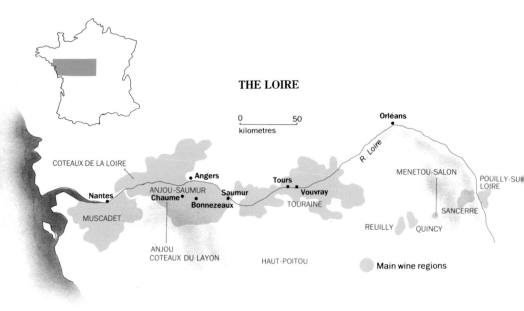

THE LOIRE

0 — 50
kilometres

Orléans

COTEAUX DE LA LOIRE

R. Loire

MENETOU-SALON

POUILLY-SUR LOIRE

Angers

Tours

ANJOU-SAUMUR

Nantes

Chaume

Saumur

Vouvray

Bonnezeaux

TOURAINE

SANCERRE

MUSCADET

REUILLY   QUINCY

ANJOU
COTEAUX DU LAYON

HAUT-POITOU

Main wine regions

The Loire is France's longest river. It rises only 160km from the Mediterranean and, for the first 160km of its journey to the Atlantic, it flows north while, 48km to the east, the Rhône flows south!

The two rivers offer an interesting contrast in that the Loire produces mainly white wines and the Rhône mainly red. The Loire having a northerly location produces light wines, the warmer location of the Rhône vineyards giving bigger wines with depth and substance. The Loire is mainly for aperitif, fish course and dessert wines, while the Rhône excels in the main course wines. A complementary situation.

Along some 400km of the Loire wine is serious business although, as one might expect, there are considerable differences of vine and of character. Fortunately it is relatively easy – and not too much of an over-simplification – to split the wine styles into four major categories:

1 At the mouth, the production of austere wines, long believed the perfect accompaniment for seafood, from the early ripening Muscadet grape or the more traditional Gros Plant.
2 Next main stop upstream is Anjou-Saumur where the rather bland Chenin Blanc produces mainly dull table wines, good sparklers and, if carefully cultivated and matured, brilliant dessert wines from the Coteaux du Layon. Some reasonable red is produced from the

▶ *Distinctive autumnal tints of Gamay vines in Anjou. The Gamay Tinturier vines, with dark foliage, produce berries with red flesh, while the lighter-leafed Gamay à Jus Blanc, the true Beaujolais Gamay, is white-fleshed.*

Gamay grape and some altogether more interesting red from the Cabernet Franc.

3 Touraine-Vouvray is the next major area/grouping. Here Sauvignon Blanc begins to creep into the picture alongside Chenin Blanc, and the Cabernet Franc starts to overwhelm the Gamay.

4 Finally, and at some distance from the other areas, are the Sauvignon Blanc white wine and the Pinot Noir red wine areas. Quality certainly but, unfortunately, fashionable quality – with 'fashionable' prices.

Let us look at these areas in greater detail.

MUSCADET

The name of the grape, the wine and the area. Grown around the seaport of Nantes, the grape actually originated, and is still grown to a limited extent, in Burgundy where it is called the Melon. Technically, when grown outside its native Burgundy the suffix 'de Bourgogne' is added, but it is better known simply as Muscadet. The original grape of this area is, however, the Folle Blanche which is still grown extensively in the area. Here again, we have a name given to a grape, its wine and the area in which it is grown – this time the name is Gros Plant and the wine is remarkably similar to Muscadet. The best version of each wine is the 'sur lie' variety where the fermented wine is allowed to mature through the winter in the fermentation barrels or vats on its lees, 'sur lie'. This increases the flavour and, by being bottled straight from the barrel, the wine contains traces of dissolved carbon dioxide which imparts a pleasant prickle to the tongue, so increasing its freshness and appeal.

Traditionally both Muscadet and Gros Plant wines are regarded as particularly suitable for drinking with seafood, especially shellfish. Although many feel that these wines are thin and lacking in flavour due to the northerly sea-shore environment of the vineyards, there must

of the influential Chereau family

Ch de Chasseloire MSMsl – another Chereau property

Donatien-Bahuaud & Cie MSMsl – négociants who have introduced a new wine, Le Master de Donatien, a jury-selected cuvée

Marquis de Goulaine MSMsl – 1000-year old property still in family hands, prestige Cuvée du Millenaire is definitive

Grand Fief de la Cormeraie MSMsl – especially Grand Reserve du Commandeur

Pierre Lusseaud MSMsl + GP – modern methods, classic flavours. Ch de la Jannière a fine brand

Louis Metaireau MSMsl + GP – leader of group of nine producers devoted to excellence

Sauvion et fils MSMsl + GP – reliable. Cardinal Richard, selected by a committee of restaurateurs and others is good

COTEAUX DU LAYON

Travelling upstream from Nantes and the Muscadet area, the next vinous milestone is the Layon, a southern tributory of the Loire. Along the banks of the Layon, Coteaux du Layon is the appellation, are produced some of the most delightful and delicate of all dessert wines – ideal for those who do not appreciate a massively sweet confection with their pud. The French expression for this degree of sweetness is 'moelleux', literally marrowy, but this hardly does them justice. The Chenin Blanc is the grape, and noble rot to produce sweet wines, perhaps surprisingly for this far north, occurs quite frequently in this region. Two historic appellations are Bonnezeaux and Quarts de Chaume. The latter quaintly named, legend has it, because the original vineyard was owned by one man who divided the vineyard into four dowries for his four daughters – hence the quarters of Chaume.

Another classic of this area, although without the status of its own appellation, is the famed Anjou Moulin Touchais. The Touchais family are wealthy industrialists who also have considerable vineyard holdings and wine-production facilities – but the old moelleux wines from their pre-phylloxera vines are gorgeously full and complex. Examples exist from the end of the last century and their longevity is amazing, the 1885 has a honey/toffee softness yet still retains a youthful freshness – quite remarkable.

also be many who would not agree with this description for the annual production of Muscadet runs to 3.5 million cases a year with a further 1.5 million of Gros Plant.

MUSCADET APPELLATIONS
There are three Muscadet appellations:

● *Muscadet* covers everything and that includes oceans of dull wine
● *Muscadet des Coteaux de la Loire* rarely seen and only academically interesting
● *Muscadet de Sevre et Maine* from the central area, biggest and best. If there is a choice, go for de Sevre et Maine sur lie and remember the rule of the Marquis de Goulaine, one of the most respected producers, 'two months, two years' indicating Muscadet should not be drunk younger than two months nor older than two years.

Best properties/growers/merchants
MSMsl = Muscadet de Sevre et Maine sur lie
GP = Gros Plant
Dom du Bois Bruley MSMsl + GP – a property

Top moelleux producers:
Dom des Baumard – produces other Loire
    wines as well as sweeties
Jacques Boivin – definitive Bonnezeaux in
    suitable vintages
A Laffourcade – owner of nearly half of Grand
    Crû Quarts de Chaume
Jacques Lalanne – owner of most of the other
    half
Dom de la Motte – look for Coteaux du Layon
    Rochefort
René Renou – Bonnezeaux producer – sixth
    son to bear the same name
Les Vins Touchais – massive stocks of
    venerable Coteaux du Layon

ANJOU-SAUMUR

The Chenin Blanc is also the grape of the
vineyards which follow the banks of the Loire
itself – but these produce dry table wines
rather than dessert wines. One outstanding
appellation of this region is Savennières
although the reputation of the legendary Joly
family wines of Coulée de Serrant no longer
seems to live up to past grandeurs. The rest
of the Chenin Blanc production is pretty
average, below average even, a sort of French
Liebfraumilch – medium-ish, bland-ish – a
generally -ish sort of wine. However, in poor
years when the acidity is high excellent
sparkling wines are made by the méthode
champenoise.

Good producers of table wines
Dom des Baumard – Savennières and some off-
    dry Coteaux du Layon
Claude Deheuiller – excellent red Cabernet-
    based Saumur-Champigny AC
Ch d'Epire – Savennières for ageing, also
    Cabernet-based rosé
Paul Filliatreau – 100-year old Cabernet vines
    for wood-aged reds
Mme J. de Jessey – wood-aged Savennières
    and some Cabernet Anjou
Mme A. Joly – a decreasing, but still
    substantial, reputation
Syvain Mainfray – old established quality
    négociants
Vins Mottron – modern outlook and a wide
    range of wines
Remy Pannier – biggest and best of the Loire
    négociants. Very reliable
Pierre & Yves Soulez – ultra-modern
    approach. Ch de Chamboureau

**Top producers of sparkling Saumur/
Vouvray**
Ackerman-Laurance – founded 1811 and
    introduced méthode champenoise
Bouvet-Ladubay – second oldest, now
    Taittinger owned. Vintage crémant
Gratien, Meyer, Seydoux – Seydoux family
    also own Champagne Gratien
Langlois-Château – Bollinger ownership since
    1973, also négociants
De Neuville – small but generally of good
    quality
Remy Pannier – see above. Also own most of
    Ackerman-Laurance

TOURAINE AND NON-SPARKLING
VOUVRAY

Touraine is the loose classification of the second
part of the middle Loire. Here red grapes begin
to come more into their own to stand alongside
the whites. Gamay and Cabernet Franc are the
grapes – the latter being used for the classic
wines of Chinon and Bourgeuil, while the former
has a bright commercial future producing simple
quaffing wines to rival the now over-priced
examples from Beaujolais. The Chenin Blanc
continues as the grape for white wine and some
sweet wines as well. Sparklers are produced
around Vouvray in particular. Outside the small
historic Appellation Contrôlée areas lies a larger
area producing millions of cases of Gamay reds
and some good, inexpensive Sauvignon Blanc
whites which provide a little relief from the
escalating prices obtained in Pouilly and
Sancerre (see page 72). In addition there is a
lake of Rosé d'Anjou, unexciting middle-of-the
road stuff, from the undemanding Groslot
grape.

Touraine producers of note
Audebert & Fils – one of the biggest modern-
    style red wine producers
Aimé Boucher – founded in 1900, one of the
    biggest négociants
Caslot-Galbrun – probably best Bourgeuil
    producer. Small volume
Couly-Dutheil – major Chinon producer and
    also big négociant
Gaston-Huet – sweet, dry, still and sparkling
    Vouvrays. Very high quality
Prince Poniatowski – grand crû vineyards
    produce classic Vouvray
Jean Maurice Raffault – old established (1693)
    but now expanding

Sparkling Vouvray specialists

Aimé Boucher – see page 71

Marc Brédif – range of styles. Vouvray Brédif
Pétillant excellent

Le Clos Baudoin – owned by Prince
Poniatowski. Exceptional wines

Gaston-Huet – see above. Can be variable but
when good, very good!

POUILLY-SUR-LOIRE AND SANCERRE

After Vouvray the Loire sweeps north-east to
the city of Orleans before curving south-east
towards the twin towns of Pouilly-sur-Loire and
Sancerre on either bank. At this point where the
river has carved out the chalky hills the
Sauvignon Blanc is supreme, the richness of the
smoky, grassy, gooseberry flavours –
sometimes also described as gun-flint – here
reaches heights difficult to match elsewhere in
the world. Two other wines are produced here,
a light red from the difficult Pinot Noir in
Sancerre and wines labelled Pouilly-sur-Loire
– as opposed to Pouilly Fumé – from the long
established Chasselas grape.

It seems amazing that the wines of these
small areas were almost unknown 25 years ago.
Only a small proportion of the output was
Sauvignon Blanc – but then Parisians
'discovered' the crisp delights available. In the
following decade the message that Sancerre
was chic and sophisticated spread far and wide,
and there were improvements not only in the
Sauvignon Blanc plantings but also in the Pinot
Noir-based reds and rosés. This was timely for,
by the end of the 1970s the lighter style of
cooking, Cuisine Nouvelle, was gaining a faithful
following and the light reds of Sancerre seemed
a perfect accompaniment and foil for the new
dishes. In truth, the reputation gained for red
Sancerre has never seemed completely justified
but it certainly swelled the coffers of the

growers of the upper Loire and has led to
continuing and increasing investment in the
fascinating whites.

Specialists in the upper Loire

Sancerre – best vineyard sites Monts-Damnés,
Clos du Chêne Marchand

Bernard Balland et Fils – Grand Chemarin, Le
Chêne Marchand and Clos d'Ervocs

Francis & Paul Cotat – perfectionist brothers
using old methods

Andre Dézat – archetypal Frenchman
producing fine wines

Paul Prieur – Les Monts-Damnés whites, good
rosé and even better red

Domaine Vacheron – comparatively large and
getting larger. Good wine

Pouilly – best vineyard sites Les Loges,
Les Bérthiers

Gerard Coulbois – good Pouilly and one of the
few Chasselas growers

Serge Dagueneau – full bodied and well-
flavoured Pouilly

J.M. Masson-Blondelet –'Les Bascoins' regular
Pouilly medal winner

Ch du Nozet – Baron Patrick de Ladoucette
major producer in the area – top label is
prestigious Pouilly Fumé Baron de L

Guy Saget – ever expanding area of vines. Also
Pouilly-sur-Loire

Such is the demand for Pouilly Fumé and
Sancerre, that the areas of Menetou-Salon,
Reuilly and Quincy are reviving after many
years of depression and, together with the
energetic co-operative of Haut-Poitou well to
the south on the main road to Poitiers, are all
producing crisp Sauvignon Blanc wines. In
Haut-Poitou these are joined by a successful
light Chardonnay and a flavoursome deep rosé
produced from Cabernet Franc.

Other significant AC areas around the Loire

Reuilly

Robert Cordier et Fils – Sauvignon for white and Pinot Noir for rosé Menetou-Salon

Georges Chavet et Fils – consistent medal winner, outstanding rosé

Jean-Paul Gilbert – old established producers of white, red and rosé

Quincy

Raymond Pipet – good quality and improving all the time

Haut-Poitou

Caves Co-op – the Caves Cooperatives founded in 1948, VDQS in 1970 – AC cannot be far away. Excellent inexpensive wines – the best of both worlds. Drink young

St-Pourçain-sur-Sioule

Union des Vignerons – local Tressalier grape gives way to 'modern' varieties. Cuvée Printanière 50:50 Sauvignon Blanc and Chardonnay

VDQS areas of the Loire

Little of interest here at present. However, Côtes de Forez, Côtes d'Auvergne and Côtes Roannaise should be watched for their grapes are 'classics' – Chardonnay, Gamay, Pinot Noir and Syrah – so the potential is there. Vin du Thouarsais from the Thouet valley using Gamay for reds and Chenin for whites has its adherents and Coteaux d'Ancenis also has potential for Cabernet-based reds and rosés.

▼ *Grubbed-up old vine roots and broken barrel staves at Le Champ-sur-Layon on the Coteaux du Layon, Anjou.*

THE RHÔNE

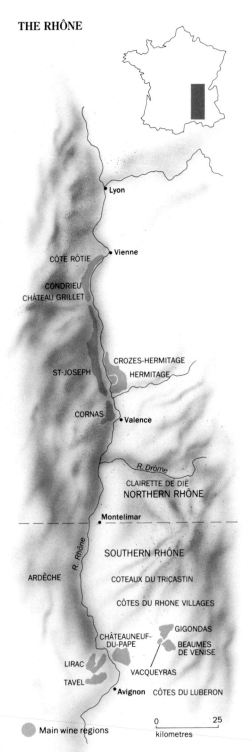

Lyon

Vienne

CÔTE RÔTIE

CONDRIEU
CHÂTEAU GRILLET

CROZES-HERMITAGE

ST-JOSEPH   HERMITAGE

CORNAS   **Valence**

R. Drôme

CLAIRETTE DE DIE
NORTHERN RHÔNE

Montelimar

R. Rhône

SOUTHERN RHÔNE

ARDÈCHE   COTEAUX DU TRICASTIN

CÔTES DU RHONE VILLAGES

GIGONDAS
CHÂTEAUNEUF-   BEAUMES
DU-PAPE   DE VENISE

LIRAC   VACQUEYRAS

TAVEL

Avignon   CÔTES DU LUBERON

Main wine regions

0   25
kilometres

The Rhône, like the Loire, flows for a considerable part of its length through wine-growing areas to which it has given its name. However, and again like the Loire, the river is their only common denominator. Just as Loire wines are mainly white and characterised by lightness – similarly all one can say about Rhône wines is that they are mainly red and are best described as 'gutsy'. This, of course is a generalisation, so we will discuss specific areas.

THE NORTHERN RHÔNE

Throughout the Rhône there is little by way of quality guidance. There are no formal classifications – no grand/premier crû rating as in Burgundy nor league table/pecking order system as in Bordeaux. This means the only quality assurance lies in the producer's name and reputation, although the 'producer' in many cases is a merchant who may own plots all along the Rhône and buy-in considerably too. Names to look out for on northern Rhône wines are Chapoutier and Delas Frères (now owned by Champagne Deutz) together with the ubiquitous Paul-Jaboulet Aîné who operates in both the northern and southern Rhône areas.

CÔTE RÔTIE

Some twenty miles south of Lyon the river swings in a south-westerly curve giving the steep northern banks a perfect south-eastern aspect for sunlight. The terraced hillsides are planted with the Syrah grape (sometimes called the Serine here and the Shiraz elsewhere in the world). Sadly, commercial cynicism has led to the AC area being expanded from the original 250 acres of hillside to include a further 750 acres of flat land behind the Côtes themselves. In my view this should have been differentiated with another name, for 'flatland' Côtes Rôtie are not as individual as 'Côtes' Rôtie itself.

Côte Rôtie specialist growers

Albert Derevieux-Thaize – La Garde (Côte Blonde), Côte Brune and Viaillére. Needs time to mature, 5–10 yrs

E. Guigal – Côte Rôtie specialists. Extremely long-lived wines

Robert Jasmin – traditionalist, adds Viognier to Syrah

J. Vidal-Fleury – largest property owner. Big wines need decades to mature past their initial toughness

CONDRIEU AND CHÂTEAU GRILLET

Condrieu is the next major appellation downstream. Like all the other quality production areas of the Rhône, it is surrounded by a vast area producing red wines to which are merely ascribed the appellation Côtes du Rhône and which use the softer, more prolific, Grenache grape with some Syrah to stiffen the backbone if one is lucky.

The short distance between Côte Rôtie and Condrieu, however, shows a marked change of production. In Condrieu only the white Viognier is allowed which is, unfortunately, a rather poor sort of variety. It is typified by a fruity, Germanic background, a light floral scent and an aftertaste slightly Gewürztraminer-like, very slightly spicy. The wines, however, are generally dull, and it is not until Château Grillet, that wine of real consequence is found. This property of 2.5 hectares up the steep, terraced, river bank, has the distinction of having its own appellation – the smallest in France. The tiny production of around 300 cases a year, after 18 months ageing in oak, commands an extraordinary price for its rarity value. A value not wholly matched by the wine.

Personally, I find most Château Grillet and Condrieu wines to be over-hyped. Others find

them 'Dreamy tasting rarities' with 'That apricot scent leaps out of the glass at you'. . . .

Condrieu and Château Grillet specialists
Pierre Dumazet – expensive and confined almost exclusively to France
Château Grillet – the Neyret-Gachet family for 150 years. Over-priced
Paul Multier – tiny production, under 600 cases. Barrel fermentation
Georges Vernay – biggest in Condrieu, has some Côte Rôtie vines too

ST-JOSEPH

One of the lesser known appellations. Almost the whole distance from Condrieu to Valence – about 45km – is appellation St-Joseph and in the main it is pretty undistinguished red wine. However, there are some high spots, Jaboulet's Grand Pompée is one.

St-Joseph specialists
Pierre Coursodon – benefits from being up on the slopes
Bernard Gripa – 80% red wines and 20% whites from the Marsanne grape
Jean-Louis Grippat – eighth generation Grippat, 5 hectares in St-Joseph

▲ *The twin hills of the Côte Rôtie, Côte Brune and Côte Blonde, get their names because the soil of one is dark, while the other is chalky.*

HERMITAGE

Downriver from this unpromising area is
Hermitage, one of the greatest of all red wine
appellations – indeed, one of the greatest red
wines of the world.

Well before Valence the river swings east
giving the steep hillside on the right bank a
southerly aspect. Above the town of Tain are
the terraced vineyards that once produced wine
to rank with the greatest of Bordeaux or
Burgundy. Hermitage wines are massive, dark
and closed-in when young with their great
concentration of fruit lurking behind a very
tannin-laden foretaste, but some white grape
content is allowed to alleviate a little of the
heaviness. At Hermitage the white Rousanne
and Marsanne grapes are used for this but, as
with the more northerly appellations, a white
wine is also produced. Like red Hermitage,
white Hermitage ages well – a decade in bottle
expanding on the almost citrus-like freshness.

If you can afford Hermitage, look for these
names:
J.L. Chave – 9 hectares and 500 years direct
descent. Superlative R & W
Desmeure Pere & Fils – Hermitage and
Crozes-Hermitage
Jules Fayolle et ses Fils – again both Hermitage
and Crozes-Hermitage
Jean-Louis Grippat – 1.6 hectares; little red,
mainly white

CROZES-HERMITAGE

The town of Crozes-Hermitage gives its name to
the appellation for wines grown around the hill
of Hermitage itself. The better wines, bearing
in mind the very high prices commanded for
both red and white Hermitage, may be as close
to classic Hermitage as one can afford to get.
But beware the indifferent wines sold simply on
the strength of the appellation, 'average' would
be a kind description for many of them.

Crozes-Hermitage growers and merchants
tend to be the same as for Hermitage itself.

Few in Crozes-Hermitage are not in the
superior appellation area. An exception is:
Mme Begot – under her late husband's
direction, organic before it became
fashionable. Reds and whites are produced
Otherwise Desmeure and Fayolle see above.

▼ *Above the Rhône, the
steep, south-facing
vineyards on the*

*Hermitage hillside produce
some great, long-lived
wines.*

CORNAS

Downstream and opposite Valence lies the appellation Cornas. Located on the eastern bank it has, for some years, been a declining area. Now, with the high prices for the appellations higher up river, it is again expanding and winning friends with its very Hermitage-style Syrah reds. Look out for it!

Cornas specialists
Guy de Barjac – labelled La Barjasse the property goes back to the 14th century
Auguste Clape – 4 hectares producing dense tannic wines needing years to mature
Marcel Juge – small grower, old-style methods giving cheerful wines
Robert Michel – La Geynole best wine from old vines. Others good too
Alain Voge – again, old family, old methods, traditional wines

OTHER SIGNIFICANT NORTHERN RHÔNE AREAS

CÔTES DU VIVARAIS VDQS
Reds are best although a pale Rhône-ish style is about all they manage to achieve. Ignore the rosés and whites.

PAYS DE L'ARDÈCHE VIN DE PAYS
A very different story to Vivarais. 'Only' Vin de Pays but gallons upon gallons of superb, honest, fruity, quaffing wines. Classic wine-planting programme now offers Cabernet Sauvignon or maceration carbonique Syrah as single varieties whereas in the past, before the new vineyards became fully productive, these varieties were normally blended with Grenache, Cinsault etc. Probably best of all is still luscious Gamay de l'Ardèche – at its best a real Beaujolais beater. Convincing whites too, Chardonnay is now fairly prevalent and Sauvignon Blanc could be exciting in the future.

CHATILLON-EN-DIOISE
Produced by the Clairette-en-Die Cave Co-operative. Aligoté and Chardonnay white and Gamay red should be good in theory. In practice they needn't have bothered! Best stick to the scrumptious Muscat-based sparkler. After Valence and the appellation Cornas,

except for some sparkling wines of which Muscat-based Clairette de Die is the best known, there is a vinous desert for about 12 km. But then, having left the steep, almost precipitous, hillsides along the route of the Rhône in its northern phase the countryside changes. The crags are replaced by smoother, rounder hills, the soil is pebbly rather than chalk or granite. This is the southern Rhône with its proliferation of appellations, styles of wine and grapes. We are in the cornucopia of Provence.

THE SOUTHERN RHÔNE

CHÂTEAUNEUF-DU-PAPE

Undoubtedly the best known of all southern Rhône wines is Châteauneuf-du-Pape. This wine, although normally listed with other Rhône reds, is a different wine. Similar in style perhaps, but owing its taste not to one predominant grape, but to a cocktail of no less than 13 permitted varieties. In practice only four or five of the permitted grapes are significant, the others forming an historic part of particular vineyards or supposedly providing an extra characteristic or dimension for an individual grower. The main varieties are Grenache, Cinsault, Syrah, Mourvèdre and the whites Clairette (producer of the sparkling wines further north) and Picpoule. Châteauneuf-du-Pape should be regarded as a Grenache wine for this is the variety which is included in the greatest quantity and gives the initial softness and warmth that is one of the attractions of this great wine. The Grenache is to the Syrah on the Rhône what the Merlot is to the Cabernet Sauvignon in Bordeaux. However, there is a downside to this attractive softness. The wines can lack character and personality – after all there are some 3000 hectares of vines in Châteauneuf-du-Pape and, like large growing areas all over the world, there is the average, the good and the excellent. Unfortunately, these are usually in the ratio 70%:25%:5%!

Names to look out for
Père Anselme – what Jaboulet is to the northern Rhône, Anselme is to the southern
Ch de Beaucastel – organic methods, some white as well as 'four-star' red
Dom Chante-Cigale – only reds, old-style vinification, long-lived wines in the area's 'top ten'

Ch de Vaudieu – reliable Gabriel Meffre property near Ch Rayas

Ch Fortia – good wines from descendants of Appellation Contrôlée originator

Dom de Mont-Redon – biggest vineyard in the area and biggest white wine producer. Long-lived wines need ageing

Louis Mousset – reliable wines from one of the biggest total estate holdings in the area

Clos des Papes – 300 years in the same family. Needs years in bottle

Ch Rayas – possibly the very best. Small estate, whites as well

Dom du Vieux Télégraphe – Brunier family go for concentration of taste with whole bunch fermentation

TAVEL AND LIRAC

In the countryside west of the Rhône are the towns of Lirac and Tavel, which each give their name to an appellation contrôlée production area. Historically, both are best known as producers of rosé wines but this, now, is more exclusively the production of Tavel while Lirac is concentrating more on fruity, full reds. Tavel rosé is marked by an orangey tint to the wine and is, unlike many rosés, quite full and flavoursome. It is generally regarded as being one of the best of all French rosé wines – although the competition could hardly be described as severe.

Tavel specialists

Ch d'Aqueria – Olivier family property, lightly aged Tavel

Dom Bernard – Dom de la Genestiere (T&L) and Dom de Longval (T)

Dom Maby – half their properties in Tavel, a quarter in Lirac

Ch de Manissy – religious order produce deep wood-aged rosé

Gabriel Roudil et Fils – 100-year-old estate producing big wines

Ch de Trinquevedel – mixture of old and new techniques

Tavel Co-operative – 130 members; over 400 hectares; drink young

Lirac specialists

Dom Assemat – Dom Les Garrigues and Dom des Causses et St-Eymes

Dom Bernard – see above

Dom de Castel Oualou – medal-winning reds plus whites and rosés

Dom Pelaquie – developing their Lirac wines

Gabriel Roudil et Fils – see above. Strong red Lirac's

Dom Louis Rousseau – 25 hectares, a lighter, non wood-aged style

Ch St-Roch – substantial reds and 'supple' rosés from 40 hectares

Ch de Segries – long-lived big reds, aged rosés, fresh whites

Dom de la Tour de Lirac – modern property, mainly reds

GIGONDAS AND CÔTES DU RHÔNE VILLAGES

This jumble of an area has a system of classification rather similar to Beaujolais. There is the basic simple Côtes du Rhône AC (often *very* simple Côtes du Rhône!), Côtes du Rhône Villages and Gigondas as the first individual village AC with others surely to follow. Qualifications for basic Côtes du Rhône wines are simple: reds must achieve 12.5° of alcohol, rosés and whites 12°.

Confusingly a complete mix of grapes is planted – all varieties familiar in the Rhône but mixed in whatever way the grower decides. Broadly, the wines are Grenache-based with stiffening added by other varieties. Some are a great success, some less so – and some are, frankly, horrendous, but then the area of Côtes du Rhônes Villages has some 3250 hectares of vines and they face price competition from wines labelled with the simpler Côtes du Rhône appellation produced from an area ten times that size.

Some producers of typical Gigondas

Pierre Amadieu – vineyards in Gigondas and Côtes du Ventoux, also important négociants

Arnoux et Fils – medal winning producer of range of Côtes du Rhônes

Bellicard d'Avignon – specialist Rhône négociant, Piat owned

Edmond Burle – old vines and mixture of ancient and modern methods

Dom du Grand Montmirail – owned by Denis Cheron, one of the most important names in Gigondas (see Pascal)

Gabriel Meffre – important family owning many Rhône and Provence properties, good wines (see Châteauneuf-du-Pape)

Pascal S.A. – négociant offering wines from all over southern Rhône, owned by Denis Cheron (see Grand Montmirail)

Les Fils de Hilarion Roux – specialist producer of long-ageing wines

Dom St-Gayan – father and son producing uncompromising wines

Ch du Trignon – lighter style, less tannic, more approachable

Gigondas Co-operative – 120 members, 18 month wood-aged wines

Best of the rest: Côtes du Rhône Villages and other areas

Dom des Anges – Englishman making attractively light wines

Arnoux et Fils – (see Gigondas) especially good Vacqueyras

Dom des Bernardins – Muscat de Beaumes de Venise and red wines

Romaine Bouchard – label says Dom du Val des Rois. Trying Gamay too

Maurice Charavin – Rasteau, traditional sweet red plus red and rosé

Dom du Devoy – 40 hectares for first class reds plus full rosés

Dom Durban – one of the best Beaumes de Venise plus some reds

Dom de Grangeneuve/Dom des Lones – Coteaux du Tricastin red, white and rosé

Pierre Labeye – Tricastin pioneer, Dom de la Tour d'Elyssas red and rosé

Ch St-Esteve – produce everything, sparkler and nouveau as well

Dom de Verquiere – Sablet, Vacqueyras and Rasteau red and sweet

La Vieille Ferme – organic light white from Luberon and Ventoux red

also co-operatives at Chusclan, La Courtoise, Rasteau and Valreas

BEAUMES DE VENISE

We cannot leave this lush area without mentioning the sweet Muscat wines of Beaumes de Venise. Little known 25 years ago, this wine has found deserved popularity as an inexpensive dessert wine often available by the glass in the more up-to-date restaurants. Using the superior strain of Muscat, the Muscat Blanc à Petits Grains, it has a soft honey-like flavour which contrasts with the bite of the high alcohol level from mild fortification with an almost unfermented grape juice sweetness as a further component. Often, and sensibly, offered in a bottle with a screw top to underline this wine's ability to last for some days, if not weeks, in a fridge after opening if the level is not too low.

Just as many wine drinkers seem to start with Mateus or Liebfraumilch and go on to greater things so, in the case of dessert wines, many start with an exploratory glass of B de V, as it is familiarly known, and move up to other, more complex, dessert wines once their interest has been excited. For producers see Best of the rest above.

SOUTHERN RHÔNE SATELLITE AREAS

The area from Montelimar in the north to Nîmes in the south, apart from the specific areas already discussed, is a sea of Côtes du Rhône production. Grapes are more or less up to the individual grower as there are so many to choose from and over 140 communes come within the net.

In this sea there are a few islands worthy of separate mention, often where ex-Algerian settlers, homeless after the bloody 1962 revolution, have brought a breath of fresh ideas to moribund or defunct properties.

COTEAUX DU TRICASTIN
Granted AC in 1974. Meffre-style planting by 'Pieds Noir' from Algeria in the 1950s and 60s now usually better than ordinary Côtes du Rhône. Good wines at cheap prices – great!

CÔTES DU VENTOUX
Somewhat lighter and fruitier than run-of-the-mill Rhône. Hardly a Rhône-ish Beaujolais, yet still fresh and fruity. Good red and rosé quaffing wines. Another 1974-awarded AC.

CÔTES DU LUBERON VDQS
For a change the white wines are more persuasive than the reds – and the rosés too have youthful charm. Some sparkling wines are also attempted with a degree or two of success. Various Vins de Pays are accredited in this productive area but all are, as yet, doing little more than trying to raise the aspirations of the growers above the all-too-easy level of 'By Appointment, suppliers of wines to the EEC wine lake'.

THE SOUTH COAST

This is a truly vast and complex area. All the other major regions of France have common denominators, although these may vary from the utter simplicity of a major area devoted to one basic product as in Champagne, to areas like the Loire or the Rhône where there are many products simply linked by a geographical feature.

The south coast is a honey-pot of wines. Everything from aged, oxidised whites called Rancios to Muscat dessert wines, from historic sparklers to the modernity of laboratory-like Listel. The sheer volume of output is staggering, the Midi alone produces one-third of all French wine and, although it is easy to lose sight of the fact in this wash of wine-lake wines, standards *are* improving and more producers are looking towards saleable quality rather than anonymous quantity. As recently as 1977 there were only two AC areas in the Midi, but now there are seven, with more than twenty in the whole coastal sweep.

Times they are a changin'. Out go the weary old methods and in comes New World modernity. Who would ever have thought that this would come to pass – the New World showing the Old World of traditionalist France how to avoid bankruptcy. Of course not everyone is convinced, but the signs are good, and especially good for drinkers, for the new-style vignerons of the Midi and Provence are unlikely to try to compete with the illustrious estates of the classic areas, there are few with that sort of money or backing. No, what we are seeing is more and more good honest wine, the sort it's a pleasure to put in your supermarket trolley. It's a market with rich pickings for the forward thinking few.

The easiest way to tackle the huge region is simply to go from the Pyrenees in the west to the Italian border in the east – with a final skip across to Corsica. The first third of the journey is through the Midi, sometimes referred to as Languedoc-Roussillon, starting in Banyuls. Because the area is so large and diverse, I will mention the worthwhile wines as we go. The date after the name of each area indicates the year in which it was granted AC status.

BANYULS VDN

This small area has an AC for its sweet red wines. These come in the vins doux naturel (or VDN) category, which is rather a misnomer. Regulations require these wines to achieve at least 15° naturally so, in a sense, they are naturally 'doux', but then an addition of 10% eau de vie is allowed (compared with, for example, 25% for port). In Banyuls and a few other areas

these wines are still produced from red grapes – mainly Grenache with some Mourvèdre. To Englishmen perhaps familiar with port, they certainly lose something in the translation.

Occasionally some are allowed to mature, sometimes in cask but more often in 30-litre glass carboy-shaped vessels called bonbonnes from the Spanish bombonas. The intensely oxidised wine that results is called Rancio and is definitely an acquired taste!

Banyuls borders:

COLLIOURE AC (1949)

The major growers of Banyuls are common to Collioure but this AC produces big red table wine. Mourvèdre, Syrah and Grenache Noir are the main constituents and the taste can only be described as mouth-filling. Sadly, little reaches the UK.

CÔTES DU ROUSSILLON (1977)

This is the second largest Midi AC in terms of area. Roussillon red wines were known in England in the 1700s and it is fitting that a region with historic claims to success should now be in the front rank of re-vitalised growing areas. The classification is similar to Beaujolais and Côtes du Rhône: a large area is graded simply Côtes du Roussillon, a superior area in the valley of the River Agly is graded Côtes du Roussillon Villages with the normal requirements of lower cropping and higher strength and, at a higher level, are villages that sell under their individual village name appellation. So far there are only two: Latour-de-France AC and Caramany AC, both 1977.

One property worthy of note is Château de Corneilla which can trace its history back to the 12th century. They use Merlot, Cabernet Sauvignon and Syrah in addition to Carignan and Grenache to produce a notable wine.

Grapes elsewhere are the usual southern cocktail of a base of Carignan with Grenache, Mourvèdre and Cinsault in varying percentages. Some sensible rosé is also produced and white wines from the Macabeo, the Viura grape of Rioja.

CORBIÈRES (1975)

A vast area of craggy hills and wild valleys. Originally the largest VDQS area in France, now the producer of 7½ million cases of wine a year. Dull Carignan-based wines have been the tradition but maceration carbonique is becoming more popular with resulting benefits by way of freshness and fruitiness.

Leading the way is the remarkable property of Château Lastours at Portel. Backed by the French government and a syndicat of banks, the property employs as its workforce mentally handicapped men and women who live in an award-winning village. One of the only four gold medals gained by France at the 1989 International Wine Challenge (two of the others were Château Cheval Blanc and the second wine of Château Margaux) was awarded to this property.

Most of the smaller growers are members of a co-operative. Within the area of Corbières, mainly in the southern corner of the appellation, is Fitou, an appellation within an appellation.

FITOU (1949)

Again, Carignan-based, but this time with definite aspirations to quality. Nine months in cask is a requirement and indicates the more 'serious' approach of the members of this

▲ *Jean-Marie Lignères, oenologist, doctor of psychiatry and the driving force behind Château Lastours with his winning wine (above).*

▶ *At Caves de Tuchan, the winery of Producteurs du Mont Tauche in Fitou, Michel Not, their director, has brightened-up the concrete vats with pictures by local artists.*

◄ Pickers filling a trailer with Carignan grapes for the co-operative winery of Mont Tauch, in Fitou.

◄ Mechanical picking in Corbiéres. The use of these machines is limited to fairly level vineyards .

appellation. The Co-operative 'Les Producteurs du Mont Tauch' is leading the way on quality and the widely-available branded Cuvée Mme Claude Parmentier from Val d'Orbieu co-operative marketing group has done much to popularise Fitou in the UK.

MINERVOIS (1985)

The river Aude and the Canal du Midi divide Corbières from inland Minervois, the area surrounding the tiny walled town of Minerve. The terrain includes flat gravelly soils along the northern bank of the Aude rising to a higher plateau behind.

The best wines come from the higher vineyards, again Carignan-based but without the flabbiness which often afflicts wines produced nearer the Mediterranean. A large proportion of the massive output is from the lower levels where a group of ten co-operatives produce for Chantovent, the French table wine giant, under the name Vin de Pays Peyriac.

ST-JEAN-EN-MINERVOIS

Tucked in the north-eastern corner of Minervois is a VDN AC for St-Jean-de-Minervois but with a mere 14,000-case output the wine is only of academic interest.

▲ *Carignan grapes being pumped from the arrival hopper into macération* *carbonique fermentation vats at Château Paraza, Corbiéres.*

THE REST OF THE LANGUEDOC

The serious wine producers in Languedoc are all inland on the 'Coteaux' rather than down on the plain around Béziers. This plain, from Narbonne in the west to Montpellier in the east, produces a tidal wave of reds for blending and it is here especially that the French government is trying to raise the aspirations of the growers. Hérault now has nearly 30 official Vins de Pays and there are already some signs of success. Cante-Cigale, a property on the coast near Cap d'Agde, is showing the way.

ST-CHINIAN (1983)
This AC enjoys an unusual soil of chalky clay and manganese-laden schist. This may be the reason for the excellence of the wines, or perhaps it is the more obvious reasons of careful tending of the vines and sensible wine-making techniques. The results are outstanding – mainly macération carbonique fermentation with Carignan being a compulsory 50% and the usual south coast mix of red grapes making up the rest.

FAUGÈRES (1983)
Has become something of a cult wine. Otherwise fairly indistinguishable from St-Chinian.

There is also a VDQS classification covering most of the foothills of the Massif Central. Outstanding, possibly unique, in this classification is Mas de Daumas Gassac at Aniane whose Cabernet Sauvignon wines some have likened to a first growth. That may be excessive praise but the wine is undoubtedly of star quality.

Another name to be reckoned with in the Coteaux du Languedoc is the unfortunately named La Clape VDQS. Here, south of Narbonne on the hills around the great limestone bluff of La Clape and cooled by the breezes from the Mediterranean, some worthwhile wines are produced. Whites are all too often from the neutral Clairette grape but sometimes, rewardingly, from the Malvasia (here called the Bourboulenc). Reds are unconvincing. White grape experimentation has led at least one grower to plant Chardonnay and similar exploration of other alternatives are under discussion. Could be exciting.

SICAREX
It is important to mention at this point the tremendous influence of the government-sponsored SICAREX operation. The full name is Société d'Intérêt Collectif Agricole de Recherches Experimentales (Pour l'Amelioration des Produits de la Vigne). The organisation functions as a co-operative for research into the best varieties and strains for particular vineyards and the best methods of production individuality. They are trying to lead the way into classic varieties for quality wine and into better, more scientific, methods of fermentation and bottling. Their 60-odd members are not confined to the Midi, indeed some are as far away as Ardéche up the Rhône valley or the Var north of Toulon, but they are all devoted to designing and producing wines fit for the 20th century that can meet the New World products head-on.

They have opponents steeped in French conservatism and traditionalism, yet Hugh Johnson's description of their research station as 'The Cape Canaveral of French viticulture' sums it up very neatly.

CLAIRETTE DU LANGUEDOC AND PICPOULE DE PINET
The Clairette is a neutral grape beloved of French vermouth manufacturers. Quite why growers in these two AC areas should want to try to convince the world that reasonable table wines can also be produced from this grape is beyond common sense. They certainly don't succeed.

MUSCAT DE FRONTIGNAN (1915) AND MUSCAT DE MIREVAL VDN (1961)
Both, as might be supposed from their titles, are Muscat based VDNs and very good they normally are. Perhaps lacking the subtlety or bite of the better known Beaumes de Venise from the Rhône, they go some way to balance this with a more obvious Muscat aroma and attack.

BLANQUETTE DE LIMOUX
Because it is so different, one other product has been bypassed in our journey west to east. In the hills beyond Corbières, along the upper reaches of the Aude beyond Carcassonne, is the area producing Blanquette de Limoux. There is some evidence – and much local conviction – that this area discovered how to make sparkling

wine at least a century before Champagne. The Mauzac grape is the dominant partner with Clairette in a subservient role. Originally produced in a petillant form with less fizz, most producers have eschewed that traditional méthode rurale for the higher fizz méthode champenoise and, to further ape the northern producers, there are experiments with Chenin Blanc and Chardonnay plantings.

At best a sprightly drink with a refreshingly appley hint, the majority, around 80%, is produced by the local co-operative whose output averages over a half a million cases a year. This co-operative is now linked with the co-operative at Tuchan in Fitou.

The first, and major, third of the journey around the south coast is now completed. Now a change in character and a shift in grape emphasis becomes apparent as we move towards the mouth of the Rhône.

BOUCHES-DU-RHÔNE

This area is somewhat sparse after the intensity of Languedoc-Roussillon, almost a pause before entering the cornucopia of Provence. Montpellier to Marseilles has a fascinating coastline including the magic of the Carmargue, but the alluvial soils washed down by the Rhône have created a flat fertile area better suited to crops other than the vine. Around Montpellier there are a sprinkling of the remnants of the Coteaux du Languedoc VDQS producers, but not until Lunel do things get at all serious.

LUNEL

Really one of a trio – a family relative of the Muscats of Frontignan and Mireval and almost as far east of Montpellier as they are west. Essentially the same wines and, again, mainly produced by a co-operative, this time founded in 1956. Its 69 members produce typical sweet Muscat-based vin doux naturelle.

COSTIÈRES DE NÎMES

A freak of geology provides a good basis for the vines of this area. Substantial reds vaguely Rhône-ish in style, less convincing rosés and totally uninspiring whites with their own appellation of Clairette de Bellegard AC.

LISTEL

The brand name of wine from the giant company, Salins du Midi, which has practically made this Vin de Pays classification area their own. The company, as its name suggests, produces salt and in the post-phylloxera years it started experimenting with vines planted in the sand dunes where, due to the saline soil, the phylloxera bugs were kept at bay. (Much the same thing happened at Colares in Portugal, where the established vines remained unscathed by phylloxera.) Their plantings have expanded to the point where they are now the largest single estate in the whole of France: 1600 hectares of vines are planted in what is, essentially, a neutral growing medium with sea water held at bay by dykes filled with fresh water. Noble varieties are planted and the processing is as high-tech as it is possible to imagine.

Commercially, Listel is as far in the lead as Salins du Midi are technologically. Their methods have long been 'organic' – and now they are reaping the benefits of being a part of the 'green' production movement. The public develops a taste for light wines with fruit flavours and in no time there is a range of Listel to fill the need.

As well as Listel wines, Salins du Midi sell Domaine de Jarras, du Bousquet and de Villeroy labels and they also have inland vineyards.

PROVENCE

If France possessed no vineyards except those around the majestic Mediterranean sweep of its south-eastern coast, it could still qualify for vinous greatness. To produce wines of complexity and elegance, finesse and subtlety, requires a happy conjunction of different soils, varying altitude and consistent, preferably dry, weather – and in all these Provence to the east of Marseilles is well endowed.

However, to be merely eligible for wine-making excellence by accident of geology and of latitude is not enough. There must also be critical demand and appreciation in the market place and a hardcore of committed producers prepared to look beyond the short-term exigencies of the balance sheet. In these respects the deep south has, in the past, been so overshadowed by the international acclaim awarded its illustrious neighbours to the north and so seduced by the ease of selling unremarkable wines to the summer hordes carpeting its beaches, that few have made the effort to realise the true potential for greatness. There are, however, a few who have.

COTEAUX DES BAUX EN PROVENCE
(1984)
Strictly speaking this area should have been included in the previous section but the name and the wine style suggested it would be more at home in this section on Provence. The wines are in many ways similar to those of Coteaux d'Aix en Provence but are generally a mite better. Consistency is the word and all examples, red, white and rosé, have given great pleasure. As with so many other southern areas, the planting of more noble varieties than those traditionally found works wonders and the arrival of Cabernet Sauvignon and Syrah has improved quality by a quantum leap.

COTEAUX D'AIX EN PROVENCE
(1984)
Predominantly red production area covering a large area north-east of Marseilles. Some first-rate properties exist – Château Vignelaure has a strong, classic, Cabernet Sauvignon-based wine with strong leanings towards the Médoc where the owner, Georges Brunet, had already transformed Château La Lagune. The two labels of the estates of the Marquis de Saporta, Château Fonscalombe (the 's' is silent) and Domaine de la Crémade are used for persuasive whites, characterful rosés and, as with Château Vignelaure, plantings of more noble varieties are giving backbone to the substantial reds. The Marquis is a major supporter of the work of SICAREX (see page 86).

Château de Beaulieu is another wine worth seeking out.

PALETTE
Completely within the greater Coteaux d'Aix en Provence AC area is the tiny appellation of Palette. Only Château Simone is at all well known and even this is only worthy of passing interest for the wines are strangely hard and piney, a sort of Provence retsina effect, doubtless due to the pine trees surrounding the property.

CASSIS
This has absolutely nothing to do with the blackcurrant syrup of the same name. It is a long-established AC area on the coast east of Marseille, which is where the majority of the predominantly white wine is sold. Grapes are Marsanne and Clairette, although more Sauvignon Blanc is being introduced. The wine is reasonable but the prices demanded are not. Tradition on the south coast demands Cassis with bouillabaisse, both of which should provide the ingredients for an inexpensive evening out. However, both have been hyped out of all reason and the traditional arm and a leg would be needed to pay the bill for this double act at most restaurants in the area.

BANDOL
Another expensive luxury. Undoubtedly good wines, the reds are mainly from Mourvèdre and firm with their minimum of 18 months cask ageing – but Riviera prices dilute the anticipation and prejudice the critical faculties. White and rosé are also produced, and some are the best in the area, yet once again overloaded prices remove the thrill.

BELLET
A small appellation just behind Nice producing wines for Nice at Nice – but not nice – prices.

CÔTES DE PROVENCE (1977)

This huge area, curving from Toulon almost to St Raphael, contains some excellent and some awful wines within its all-embracing coverage. The few who enjoyed a good reputation prior to elevation from VDQS to AC in 1977 are still producing good wines, the others, whom the elevation was supposed to have encouraged to greater efforts are, as yet, showing few signs of interest or activity. One of the area's driving forces are Domaines Ott founded in 1896 by a citizen of Alsace and now holding several substantial and reputable estates in its portfolio. Names like Clos Mireille, Ch de Selle, Ch Romasson all produce worthwhile wines. Domaine de Feraud use a proportion of Cabernet Sauvignon and Syrah along with the southern grape varieties and use Sauvignon Blanc for their whites.

Other than these, plus a few who are beginning to rise to the challenge and the co-operative Les Vignerons Provençaux, the rest of the wines are designed to go with the sun-tan oil.

CORSICA

Corsica has a history of good wine-making, wines from this island were enjoyed on mainland Europe for centuries until the arrival of phylloxera. Unlike the rest of France, the Corsicans never really recovered from the blight. It was not until Algerian independence in 1962 caused the flight of so many 'pieds noir' – the French colonials of Algeria – that vineyards were again established and an 'export' market for high strength cutting wines was created on the mainland. Today Corsica's main output,

about 90% of the production from the 32,000 hectares under vine, is in cutting wines. Our interests, though, lie in the other 10%!

Traditional grapes are the reds Sciacarello and Nielluccio and the white Vermentino – to which we must add the better known varieties Malvasia and Trebbiano.

Patrimonio AC uses the Nielluccio for its excellent rosés – this was the first Corsican AC granted back in 1968 and in addition to the first-class rosés they offer Rhône-style reds, some well-flavoured whites (hints of liquorice have been found) and a very good Muscat VDN.

Coteaux de Cap Corse AC boasts the Muscatellu from Rogliano on the northern tip of the island, thought by some to be a classier VDN Muscat even than Beaumes de Venise or Muscat de Frontignan – and that is praise indeed!

Porto Vecchio AC in the south-east is probably the best AC for all-round quality – certainly they have tamed local varieties and introduced mainland grapes which, allied to modern wine-making techniques, have led to the production, especially in white wines, of north European-style crisp, bright fruity wines.

There are five other ACs which fail to inspire – but mention should be made of the efforts of some of the growers to move out of dull volume tanker-load high strength cutting wine production and into something more worthwhile. A Vin de Pays, that first stepping stone out of the vinous rut, charmingly named de L'Ile de Beauté, has been approved and there are fledgling signs of worth on the horizon. SICA Uväl is one of the better co-operative names to look for and their plantings of Cabernet Sauvignon, Syrah and Chardonnay suggest serious intent.

BURGUNDY

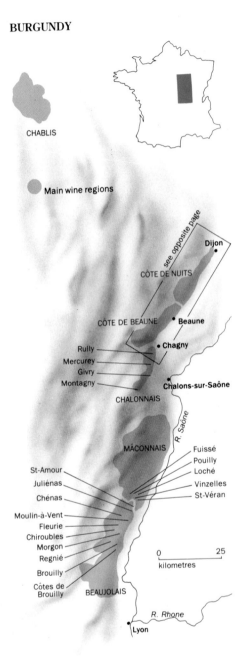

CHABLIS

● Main wine regions

see opposite page

Dijon

CÔTE DE NUITS

CÔTE DE BEAUNE ● Beaune

● Chagny

Rully —
Mercurey —
Givry —
Montagny —

● Chalons-sur-Saône

CHALONNAIS

R. Saône

MÂCONNAIS   Fuissé
              Pouilly
              Loché
St-Amour —   Vinzelles
Juliénas —   St-Véran
Chénas —

Moulin-à-Vent —
Fleurie —
Chiroubles —
Morgon —
Regnié —
Brouilly —
Côtes de —
Brouilly   BEAUJOLAIS

0   25
kilometres

R. Rhone

● Lyon

Geography and history have favoured the wine-growers of Burgundy. For centuries the easiest route from Paris, and much of northern Europe, to the south of France and Italy passed along the length of the Burgundian growing area. This highway through France has acted like a shop window for the wares of Burgundian growers, and it may well be that, had the area been away from this well-worn thoroughfare, Burgundian wines might now be of little more than historic interest, consigned, in practical terms, to a limbo of local purchase.

There are many who would say 'Would that it had been so!' for the continued reverence and regard for Burgundy is baffling on many counts. Most especially in that the average drinker's expectation from a bottle of red burgundy is still that it will contain a full, fat, soft, deeply coloured, velvety-tasting wine when, in fact, however good the wine is and assuming it has not cost more than £100, it will be none of those things.

Bear in mind that the central area – the true 'Burgundy' of Burgundy rather than the Chablis, the Mâcon or the Pouilly-Fuissé never mind the Beaujolais – produces rather less than 2 million cases a year. This is only a little more than Salins du Midi on the south coast or the output of classed growth Médocs taken together with the rated properties in Graves, St-Emilion and Pomerol. (Bordeaux taken as a whole produces over 40 million cases a year, greater Burgundy, even including the sea of Beaujolais only totals half of that.) At the lower price level, the products of almost any large French co-operative or big company with these sorts of production volumes are usually consistently good. At higher price levels the wines of the rated Bordeaux properties at least normally match reputation with price, in contrast to what you find in Burgundy. All of which leads me to believe that a disproportionate amount of time and space is allowed the wines of Burgundy in most wine books and I do not propose to fall into the same trap.

In its widest interpretation 'Burgundy' includes all the growing areas from Chablis in the north to the Côte Chalonnais and Beaujolais just above Lyon in the south – a distance of some 320km. However, there are such clear distinctions between the components of this great area that, for the purpose of this book, I shall use the term to refer only to the growing areas to the immediate north and south of Beaune – the so-called Côte d'Or (well named

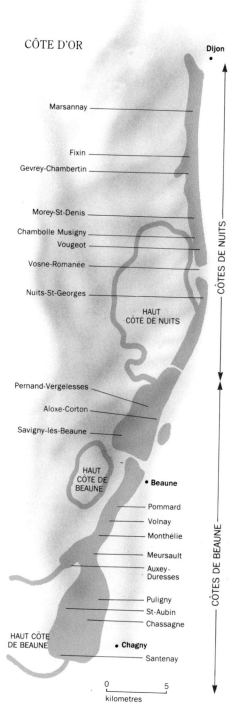

CÔTE D'OR

Dijon

Marsannay

Fixin

Gevrey-Chambertin

Morey-St-Denis

Chambolle Musigny

Vougeot

Vosne-Romanée

Nuits-St-Georges

HAUT
CÔTE DE NUITS

CÔTES DE NUITS

Pernand-Vergelesses

Aloxe-Corton

Savigny-lès-Beaune

HAUT
CÔTE DE
BEAUNE

Beaune

Pommard

Volnay

Monthélie

Meursault

Auxey-Duresses

CÔTES DE BEAUNE

Puligny

St-Aubin

Chassagne

HAUT CÔTE
DE BEAUNE

Chagny

Santenay

0   5
kilometres

considering the prices charged) which is the combined Côtes of de Nuits and de Beaune. Other areas, such as Chablis and Mâcon, will be treated separately.

Generic names are, in the main, standard throughout the greater Burgundy region and they are:
Bourgogne Whites in the main from Chardonnay, and reds and rosés from Pinot Noir, except in Beaujolais where the red grape is the Gamay. Minimum strength of 10.5° for whites and 10° for red and rosé wines.
Bourgogne Passe-Tout-Grains A two to one mix of Gamay to Pinot Noir. The grapes must be fermented together and not mixed afterwards. Minimum strength 9.5°.
Bourgogne Aligoté The only other white grape allowed is the supposedly inferior Aligoté, although Chardonnay can be included to any extent. Minimum strength 9.5°.
Bourgogne Grand Ordinaire or *Bourgogne Ordinaire* A catch-all appellation. Red, rosé or white wines from any of the grape varieties approved, minimum 9.5° for whites and 9° for reds and rosés.

CHAPTALISATION

The figures above are the minimum alcohol levels allowed for each appellation. However, look at the label on a typical bottle and it will show a level normally one or one and a half degrees above the minimum. Why is this? Or, more particularly, how is this? Many areas of France are blessed with less than the full amount of sunlight required to produce fully ripe grapes and, as the amount of grape sugar available for conversion to alcohol determines the final alcohol level, really ripe grapes equal more sugar and more sugar equals more alcohol. Alexis Lichine took the view that 'In regions where the sun is hot enough to generate the requisite amount of sugar in the grapes, it [the addition of sugar] is not necessary'. So true! but trying to produce full, flavoursome red wines with reasonable levels of alcohol in latitudes as far north as Burgundy (and in Germany for whites as well) requires a great deal of assistance and that assistance comes in the form of legalised sugar addition. Napoleon had as Minister of Agriculture a Dr Jean Chaptal, Comte de Canteloup (1756–1832) who, during a sugar-beet glut around the turn of the 18th century, authorised the addition of beet sugar to the grape must to raise the sugar level – and thus the alcohol level – after fermentation. This process continues its legalised existence as chaptalisation (except in Germany where it is called the Gall Process or gallation after one Dr Gall) and it is the salvation of many a grower from Auxerre to Lyon.

French growers claim that chaptalisation is much more than simply adding sugar to raise the alcohol level. They claim that the fermentation of sugar gives rise to side products such as glycerol, succinic acid and others whose presence are beneficial to the final balance of the wine. While probably true, this would also be the case if there was more natural grape sugar present at the outset. The regulations allow a maximum alcohol increase of 2°, so wine that would naturally ferment to a maximum of 10.5° if left to its own devices is allowed sufficient sugar to ferment out to 12.5°, and so on, pro rata. There is little doubt that this system is abused in many areas – commercial pressures with customers demanding wines (in the favoured regions anyway) and the sun not contributing the necessary warmth means that resort to sugars, in whatever form is available and cheap, must be an almost overpowering temptation. Oversoft, flaccid wines are the result.

Is Burgundy really too far north for successful wine production? The answer, I think, is a qualified 'Yes'. There is no doubt that in especially good years, with fierce pruning, the wines of the best estates are delightful, if impossibly expensive. Unfortunately, most years are far from optimum!

Before delving into the manifold complexities of Burgundy we have to set out the ground rules – for those are literally what they are! Bordeaux is bought on the status or repute of a particular property whose boundaries are clearly defined. In contrast, champagne is priced and bought entirely on the standing of the particular producer and wines from Alsace similarly depend on the repute of the producer and/or bottler. However, in both the last cases the area from whence the grapes came is not normally of importance to the customer – he or she will not look for a vineyard name on a champagne and would rarely find one on an Alsacian wine label.

Burgundy, however, is a battle of the names, both of terrain and of grower-négociant/bottler. Names have always meant a lot – to the extent that in the last century when certain vineyard names became famous they were tacked onto the less famous name of the village in which they were located. In this way the village could bask in the reflected glory of its prized vineyard and, by association, other wines from that village would (and did!) escalate in price. This explains the proliferation of hyphens in Burgundy. The name of the superior vineyard of Montrachet was added to the names of both its local villages to give Chassagne-Montrachet and Puligny-Montrachet, Chambertin was added to give Gevrey-Chambertin, Chambolle added Musigny, Aloxe-Corton, Volnay-Fremiets and so on.

In a perfect world the naming of a particularly favoured vineyard should establish confidence in the product. In Burgundy this is not necessarily so for two reasons.

First, being so far north, the micro-climates *within* one vineyard can change from beneficial to indifferent, altering the quality across that vineyard. That might not be so critical if the whole vineyard were under single ownership when the grapes would be all mixed up, good, bad and indifferent, in the fermentation vats. But, and second, due to the effect of French inheritance laws causing holdings to be subdivided between the heirs on the owner's death, and also due to the astronomical land values that pertain in Burgundy, famed vineyards almost always have a multiplicity of owners.

Thus, the care and attention devoted by one grower with a favoured plot can produce a superb wine whereas close by, in the next rows even, an absentee owner, a time-serving manager or an unfavourable aspect can produce a wine a mere shadow of what might reasonably be expected. But both wines will carry the same vineyard name. This problem was and still is, although to a lesser extent than hitherto, further compounded by the fact that a large proportion of growers simply sent their wines to négociants-eleveurs. On the face of it this is a sensible move, for a grower, however good, does not necessarily make a good cellarman and as the grower is likely to be either very small in terms of landholding or else have little bits of several vineyards scattered through the Côte d'Or, centralised maturing is not always easy or possible. Thus the role of the négociant-eleveur has become pivotal in Burgundy for it is he who will blend, mix and match the wines of the same appellation to produce a classic wine to lay down.

▼ *At the corner of En l'Ormeau vineyard, Puligny-Montrachet. Over the crest of the distant hill is the village of Gamay where the grape of that name allegedly originated.*

That, however, is the theory. The practice is somewhat different. Government inspectors with fairly draconian powers certainly exist, but given the apparently unlimited world demand for the products of this all-too-thin strip of land, the temptations towards demand-led compromises or, even worse, outright dishonesty, must be almost overpowering. Apparently 'twas always thus – there were consumer complaints about the region in Roman times.

RED BURGUNDY

Because the area does not have constant strong sunlight, grapes are normally lacking in colour and have a low sugar content. Inevitably this means the production of a light-bodied pale wine with a low alcohol content. Undoubtedly more substantial wines can be produced, but these gems are so hugely expensive that ordinary mortals are most unlikely to come into contact with them. So, for years the wine trade in both France and England has long endeavoured to 'help' the more normal products of Burgundy to be more like their exotic brethren and this 'help' took the form of adding 'cutting wine'. These cutting wines are full-bodied, well coloured, high alcohol content wines, preferably without much flavour, and were added either in France or England in judicious measure to make up for deficiencies of soil and/or sun.

Originally these wines came mainly from Algeria, but after independence in 1962 other sources were sought. As supplies from Spain, Italy or Portugal cost valuable foreign currency the French government supported the development of expanded vineyards from Marseilles to the Spanish border and these wines, together with those of Provence, flowed up the Rhône to aid the thin wines of Burgundy.

However, the EEC has now clamped down fairly heavily on the use of cutting wine and Burgundian reds are, more and more, becoming the real thing – pale, anaemic and often over-sweetened to produce an acceptable alcohol level. Fashion and social snobbery has raised the price of Burgundian wines to ridiculous levels – the Pinot Noir grape enjoying a privileged position among the world's grapes in that it is hardly successful anywhere else (many would doubt its success in Burgundy!) So the minds of Burgundian wine-makers are not concentrated by competition.

A review of growers and négociant-eleveurs appears after 'White burgundy'.

WHITE BURGUNDY

The delights of the wines produced from the Chardonnay grape in Burgundy are many and varied – from the steely smoky timbres of Chablis to the opulent colour and charisma of Corton – but the fashion for these wines is holding prices at an artificially high level. However, there is hope on the horizon, at least as far as export sales are concerned – the reds of Burgundy have little competition while the whites have a great deal!

If the value of the US dollar sinks and the excellence of many of the US grown Chardonnays (often unashamedly but inaccurately called 'Chablis') gradually dawns on the citizens of that country, then the magic of paying through the nose for French labels may lose its charm. In the UK, the second largest export market for white Burgundies, great inroads have already been made by the very fine New World Chardonnays now available in the shops and the more up-to-date restaurants.

Generally reliable producers

For the brave, here are some names to look out for, but while these are the most reliable no guarantees are offered!

Aloxe-Corton – Bouchard Père et Fils, Louis Jadot, Louis Latour, Tollot-Beaut, Michel Voarick

Auxey-Duresses – Duc de Magenta, Roland Thevenin

Beaune – Bouchard Père et Fils, Joseph Drouhin, Louis Jadot, Tollot-Beaut

Chambolle Musigny Bonne Mares – Louis Jadot

Chassagne-Montrachet – Duc de Magenta,

Albert Morey, Ramonet-Prudhon

Corton-Charlemagne – Bonneau de Martray, Louis Latour

Gevrey-Chambertin – Armand Rousseau, Clair Dau, Joseph Drouhin

Pommard – Ch de Pommard, Dom Parent, Dom de la Pousse d'Or

Rose de Marsannay – Clair Dau

Meursault – Robert Ampeau, Dom des Comtes Lafon, J & P Matrot, Dom Jacques Prieur

Monthélie – Henrie Potinet, Rene Thevenin-Monthélie

Nuits St-Georges – Jean Chauvenet, Laboure-Roi

Puligny-Montrachet – Bouchard Père et Fils, Louis Jadot, Dom Leflaive, Dom Sauzet

St-Aubin – Raoul Clerget, Dom Roux

St-Romain – both Thevenin's, Roland and Dom René Thevenin-Monthelie

Santenay – Dom de la Pousse d'Or, Dom Roux, Prosper Malfoux

Volnay – Dom de la Pousse d'Or, Dom Y Clerget, Marquis d'Angerville

Vosne-Romanée – Dom de la Romanée-Conti

Vougeot – Jacques Prieur, Dom Bertagna, Henri Lamarche

In general the names of Bouchard Père et Fils, Robert Drouhin, Louis Jadot and Louis Latour can be relied on throughout Burgundy.

CHABLIS

Recent history has not been kind to Chablis. As part of the huge département of Yonne which had traditionally supplied Paris with wine, it was hard hit by the coming of the railways that allowed vineyards from further south to compete successfully for the Paris trade. The decline was accelerated by the arrival of phylloxera which almost put paid to Chablis as a source of wine – thousands of acres of the Yonne having been converted to cereals or grazing, Chablis nearly suffered the same fate.

Chablis, however, enjoyed two priceless advantages. One is the soil. Kimmeridge is the technical description for this type of strata containing shells from what was previously ocean-bed and a perfect partner for the Chardonnay, here called the Beaunois – the grape of Beaune. The other great advantage is the steep south-west facing slopes of the valley cut by the river Serein – especially the slopes immediately overlooking the town of Chablis itself.

► *A tractor towing a chemical spray tank in Chablis. The hillside opposite has mixed strip planting including some vines – typical of the outer Chablis area.*

▼ *Chablis vineyards have piped water for frost protection spraying. A fine mist of water coats the newly-formed berries with an insulating layer of ice.*

▼ *Chablis town still retains its rustic charm with specialised vineyard equipment all around.*

Notice the sign to nearby St Bris famed for Sauvignon Blanc-based wines.

In Chablis the Chardonnay has 'bite'. A tougher, more austere, wine than the Chardonnay wine of further south, it has a sort of stoney, almost metallic overtone, the sort found in good Sauvignon Blanc wines, yet it retains the Chardonnay fatness. The buttery background taste so characteristic of the Chardonnay is always present. The popularity of Chablis, especially in the USA where the name is mightily mis-used in domestic production, has lead to a continual increase in the appellation contrôlée boundaries of the permitted area. From around 400 hectares in 1930 when the AC was established, the area has now grown to over 1600 hectares. As in other areas of large output, there is a three-tier quality structure. Here, simple Chablis AC corresponds to, say, Beaujolais AC, Premier Crû Chablis to Beaujolais Villages and the superior Grand Crû Chablis to the Crû Beaujolais. Of the 1600 hectares under vine only 100 are of Grand Crû status, 750 hectares are Premier Crû and 800 hectares are plain Chablis. Technically there is also a fourth grade,

Petit Chablis, below plain Chablis AC but this is becoming less and less common.

While the larger, general area has increased in the past ten years, and may well continue to do so, and the more prestigious premier crû area has also expanded somewhat, there seems little doubt that the area of the top grading of grand crû will remain as it has been since the introduction of the AC in 1930, so the very significant price differential between premier and grand crû wines will remain.

Strangely, in spite of the American-lead escalation in price for Chablis, the wine is still relatively under-valued when compared with the prices achieved for other white burgundies, especially those of the Côte d'Or. The particular blend of complex delicate flavours that characterises a great Chablis is not easily reproduced elsewhere in the world – the fat white wine tastes of the Côte d'Or being easier in this respect – and so it may be the very austerity of taste of Chablis that provides its protection from imitation and lower-priced competition.

Chablis producers of note

Paul Droin – over 100 years family experience. One of the best

Joseph Drouhin – the Beaune négociant, the same high quality

William Fevre – largest grand crû owner. Oak-aged wines

Dom Laroche – fifth generation owner, also Bacheroy-Josselin label

Louis Michel & Fils – good wine-making and concentrated wines

François Raveneau – traditionalist with mainly French sales

Dom Rottiers-Clotilde – new regrouping with good modern production standards

Caves Co-operative La Chablisienne – responsible for a quarter of the entire production of Chablis. Good, honest, wines

SAUVIGNON DE ST BRIS VDQS

One of the best VDQS wines in France. The effrontery of producing wine from the Sauvignon Blanc in Burgundy, fortress Chardonnay, has doubtless been a major factor in these wines never achieving the status they deserve. All the better for drinkers as the prices are lower than if the wines were full AC.

MÂCON AND THE CÔTE CHALONNAISE

These two areas have come to recent popularity and fame not just for the reasonable wines they produce, but for the realistic prices charged – so far.

Around Mâcon the Chardonnay is queen and the white wines, although no match for the whites of the Côte d'Or in Burgundy, are satisfying and flavoursome. Unfortunately, one area, Pouilly-Fuissé, having a lighter style than the greats of Burgundy, has attracted the Americans so that virtually all of it is now shipped across the Atlantic. The smaller subsidiary appellations of Pouilly-Vinzelles and Pouilly-Loché are rapidly pricing themselves on the same scale.

Not yet too far up the price ladder are St-Verán, where Duboeuf has a striking example, Mâcon-Viré and Mâcon-Lugny. Indeed, the lower appellation of Mâcon-Blanc-Villages has a very high reliability factor when weighed against cost.

Some 56km north of Mâcon is Chalons-sur-Saône which gives its name to the Côtes Chalonnaise – the nearest point of which is 8km to the west. Suggestions to call the area Region

de Mercurey after the town in its centre have come up against traditional usage. It is a strange sort of mish-mash of an area. Mercurey is famed for its Pinot Noir reds and the best are the Chante-Flûte selection; Givry also gives Pinot Noir reds, but somewhat lighter in style than Mercurey; Rully produces both red and white wines but, although the whites are certainly of consequence, the area is best known for its large quantities of sparkling Burgundy from a mixture of Chardonnay and Pinot Blanc grapes and, lastly, Montagny, an all white appellation with almost all their wines qualifying as 1re Crû – they only have to reach 11.5° to claim this distinction!

The town of Buxy is also worthy of note. Although their whites are similar to those of Montagny and represent good value for money, Buxy is best known as the home of the Caves des Vignerons de Buxy. Formed in 1931, but recently extensively re-equipped, they bottle reliable generic wines – Passe-tout-Grains; Bourgogne Rouge, Bourgogne Grand Ordinaire plus a very good Aligoté. In addition, and perhaps the best, is their excellent Montagny 1re Crû.

Mâcon and the Côte Chalonnaise, names to look for

Chanzy Frères – Rully Rouge specialist but other worthwhile wines

Joseph Corsin – amongst the best of Pouilly-Fuissé. Classic wines

Jean-François Delorme – total of 60 hectares across the region

Paul & Henri Jacquesson – still 'tread' the grapes' best is Rully

Dom Michel Juillot – regular medal-winner for their Mercureys

Noël-Bouton – excellent long-lived wines with maturing potential

Dom Roy-Thevenin – classic 'big' Montagnys with potential

Jean Thevenet – Mâcon specialist. Excellent Mâcon-Lugny

Caves des Vignerons de Buxy – mostly generic wines except for Montagny 1re Crû

The majority of the wines of Mâcon are from co-operatives. In this area the whole co-operative movement is organised to a higher degree and commands greater loyalty than anywhere else in France. 50% of Mâconnais production comes from the 18 groupings and several merchants buy from co-operatives as the co-op's bottlings are often safer!

BEAUJOLAIS

In contrast to the complexities of Burgundy to the north and the Rhône to the south, the area immediately north of Lyon is blissfully simple. A combination of the fruity red Gamay, and a production method, macération carbonique, brings out the full flavour of the grape and reduces the tannic taste that might otherwise mask the grapiness. In style, production and drinkability the wines of the Beaujolais are unmatched by any other reds, unfortunately, for the drinker, the price of success is just exactly that – increased prices charged for successful, popular wines. Instead of being a reasonably priced, readily drinkable wine without great pretensions, Beaujolais has become a wine for which the prices charged mean that it *should* have some pretensions! The growers are in danger of forgetting that other areas also produce drinkable Gamay wines.

The appellation requirements in Beaujolais are

Beaujolais AC Red wine from the Gamay with a minimum alcohol level of 9° – the lowest required for any red wine, but normally exceeded. Often exceeded by the addition of sugar.
Beaujolais Villages AC The area around a group of villages on steeper hills in the north where the soil, sandy clay over granite, produces a better wine, deeper and with more flavour than Beaujolais AC and with a degree more alcohol.
Crû Beaujolais Ten areas or separate villages use their own names for individual wines. Each has a different style and range from the lightest, Fleurie and Chiroubles, through to tougher Morgon and Moulin-a-Vent that can show some improvement after a year or two in bottle.
If sold with a vineyard name as well as the village appellation a minimum of 11° alcohol is required.
Beaujolais nouveau/Beaujolais primeur The interest in slurping jugfuls of the 'new' Beaujolais each year is declining. There is no doubt that in a good year, and from a good producer, the young purpley beverage is very satisfying and refreshing, but otherwise . . .
Beaujolais blanc Now almost unknown. A little Chardonnay is still grown in the northern fringes of the area where it borders Mâcon. Logically, white Beaujolais is very similar to an average Mâconnais white – Mâcon-Blanc-Villages for example.

The production of wine in Beaujolais is staggering: 21,500 hectares producing an average of 1¼ million hectolitres – that's over 14½ million cases a year!

It breaks down by category as follows:

Beaujolais	615,000hl
Beaujolais Superieur	21,000hl
Beaujolais Villages	335,000hl
TOTAL	971,000hl

(of which 55% is Beaujolais Nouveau)

Add to this Crû Beaujolais:

Brouilly	72,670hl
Morgon	60,800hl
Fleurie	42,010hl
Moulin-à-Vent	38,000hl
Regnie	35,090hl
Julienas	32,680hl
Chiroubles	18,310hl
Côte de Brouilly	17,750hl
Saint-Amour	16,400hl
Chenas	14,700hl
TOTAL	348,410hl

Beaujolais is a conundrum when it comes to recommending producers. The area is honeycombed with small growers – about 4000 have properties of under 8 hectares and many of these are less than one hectare. One or two significant properties can be regarded as quality leaders but their availability is seldom national. Apart from these the safest course is to go for the big reliable names – they have the clearest idea what their customers are looking for and they have the resources to achieve it.

In a way, making recommendations about anything or anyone in Beaujolais is almost to deny the very soul of the region. The wines are meant to be light, bright, flirtatious even. Only the ever upward price spiral makes us begin to have to be 'serious' about this most un-serious of wines.

Leading properties
Ch des Tours, Brouilly – consistently winning
    well-deserved awards

▼ *The Gamay covered hillsides of Brouilly. A view from the AD 1153 tower of Château des Tours towards the Côte de Brouilly in the distance.*

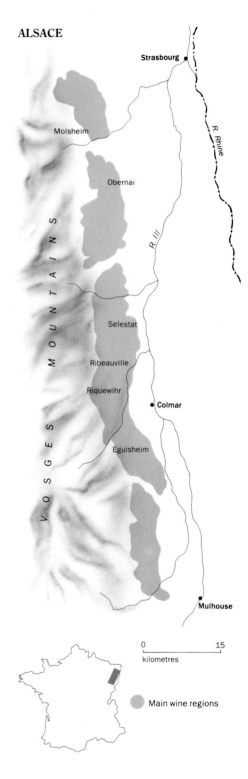

ALSACE

Ch de la Chaize, Brouilly – owned by the
Marquis de Roussy de Sales
Ch des Capitans, Julienas – individual wines
from the large Robert Sarrau empire
Dom de la Grosse Pierre, Chiroubles – Alain
Passot

The leading merchant is Georges Duboeuf,
the uncrowned king of Beaujolais. The presence
of this company is felt everywhere and, almost
single-handed, they persuaded the authorities
that a tenth Crû, Regnie, was needed and/or
deserved. Leading the way with light-hearted,
floral, labels too.

Best of the rest
Chanut Frères – expanding in the supermarket
sales sphere
Loron et Fils – have continued to improve for
the past decade
Mommessin – a big name in Burgundy as well
as Beaujolais
Pasquier-Desvignes – modern outlook, also
moving into supermarkets
Piat – forget Piat d'Or. IDV owned, deal in
some good Beaujolais
Robert Sarrau – growers as well as merchants.
Modern outlook
Thorin – very reliable. Property owners as well
as merchants

COTEAUX DU LYONNAIS (1984)
A bit of a Burgundian afterthought. The AC is
for red, white and rosé wines grown south of
Beaujolais down to the outskirts of Lyon. Most
wines are Gamay reds, the very few whites are
from Chardonnay, Aligoté and the Muscadet –
here in its Burgundian disguise as Melon de
Bourgogne. Regard them as cheap Beaujolais –
cheap in price, but not in quality.

Alsace, or the Rhineland to give it its historic name, is a region of back-to-front: of 'German' and 'dessert' grapes producing dry wines; of French controls in a German-speaking area; of varietal wines from an old-established European area; of tougher standards imposed by the growers themselves than required by the authorities; of producers more concerned with quality than quantity. Alsace stands alone.

The earliest records of vines planted in Alsace are of around AD 800 and since that time wine has been a major regional product. In the Middle Ages the wines of Aussay, or Osoy as Shakespeare spelled it, were shipped down the Rhine and across the North Sea to England. At that time the area was under German dominion, but that changed when France belatedly joined Sweden towards the end of the Thirty Years' War and, as a reward under the Peace Treaty of Westphalia in 1648, received the Rhineland from the defeated Emperor of Germany. A century later, with a flourishing export trade to Austria and Switzerland, the Alsacians introduced wine laws which, although primitive by today's standards, were effective in regulating the quality of production. They even had full-time wine inspectors to check on export shipments where documentation had to state the origin of the wine, the method of production and so on. Moreover, these laws also prohibited the planting of volume production wines – then, as now, quality was preferred to quantity.

The French Revolution broke up the larger estates into smaller parcels, and this effect is still seen today – 12000 hectares under vine and 9000 growers – an average of just over one hectare per grower. By 1850 the effect of the Revolution had been overcome and wine production was again in full swing when, in 1870, war again broke out between France and Germany. This time the Germans reclaimed the Rhineland and the border moved back again to the Vosges mountains. This, of course, meant that the wines of Alsace now had to compete with wines from the Moselle, the Rhine, Palatinate and so on for their national trade. Economic pressures forced the growers to lower their standards in order to compete and this sad state of affairs continued until the end of the First World War when, once again, the boundary moved and Alsace was again French! This again dealt a severe blow to the Alsacians for, having been forced to produce lower quality, higher volume wines to compete when a part of Germany, they now found that they were badly placed in the French market where many areas to the south were better able to accommodate the lower end of the market.

A momentous decision was made. The wines of Alsace would change – and change so radically that quality would become the sole criteria. This brave decision has brought Alsace to the position it holds today, unrivalled for the production of dry, yet lightly scented table wines, wines with possibly the very best balance of flavour in the whole world.

Of course the devastation of the Second World War left its mark on Alsace – but at least the boundaries remained unchanged!

So, today, we have one of the simplest and one of the most recent of French AC areas – for long Alsace has been so effective at self-regulation that other controls were thought unnecessary – the regulations simply call for a 100% unblended wine from one of the 'noble' Alsace varieties bottled in the traditional German shaped bottle. Some blends are allowed but these are easily explained and controlled:

NOBLE VARIETIES OF GRAPES USED IN ALSACE

Riesling The 'king' of Alsace and, perhaps, produced better here than anywhere else in the world. Fermented, as with all Alsace wines, through to dryness, yet still retaining the beautiful floral touch of this great grape.

Gewürztraminer The 'spicy'·(Gewürz) grape of Tramin in Austria. To many the best known variety of Alsace, occasionally flabby, but normally enjoying the full charm of a totally definitive taste.

Muscat d'Alsace The dessert grape still little used for dry wines anywhere else in the world with a contrast, almost a conflict, between the sweet bouquet and the dry flavoursome palate.

Pinot Gris or Tokay d'Alsace The original name, Tokay, is now giving way to the more correct terminology and removes confusion with the totally different Hungarian Tokay dessert wines.

Pinot Blanc Here called the Klevner and increasingly popular for the light wines it produces. Also used as a main ingredient in sparkling Crémant d'Alsace.

Pinot Noir Here used for rosé wines – or for reds so pale they are more rosé than red! Some fairly extreme methods are needed to obtain sufficient colour and, in most cases, the wines are undistinguished.

GRADES OF WINE IN ALSACE

Zwicker wines Blends from any of the approved Alsace varieties, these include such bulk producers as the Müller-Thurgau, the Chasselas, the Knipperle and others as well as the noble varieties.

Edelzwicker Edel, noble, zwicker wines may only be blended from the noble grape varieties of Alsace.

Alsace grand crû Normal cropping limits are 100hl per hectare of minimum 8.5° wines. For grand crû status the limits are 70hl and a minimum alcohol of 10° for Muscat and Riesling and 11° for Gewürztraminer and Pinot Gris. Where a vineyard name is added the grapes must come exclusively from that vineyard. Quality levels have now been agreed whereby the rather loose use of titles like Reserve or Reserve Personelle have been, to a degree, formalised.

The grading scale depends on a measurement based on the Oechsle scale devised by Ferdinand Oechsle (1774–1852) to measure specific gravity which can be used to measure the sugar content of a liquid because as the sugar content increases, so does the specific gravity. On the Oechsle scale 1° indicates 1 litre of grape juice that is heavier than 1 litre of pure water by 1 gram. Thus 3° Oechsle equal 3 grams of sugar per litre, 80° Oechsle equal 80 grams of sugar per litre and so on. Another useful characteristic of this scale is that dividing the Oechsle reading by eight gives the approximate alcohol level that will be achieved after fermentation, so an Oechsle reading of 80° indicates an alcohol potential of about 10% after fermentation.

In the case of Alsace Appellation Contrôlée laws require that grape juice shows a minimum of 68° Oechsle or 8.8% potential alcohol. Provided this minimum is achieved it may be legally boosted by the addition of sugar to the unfermented must so as to raise the Oechsle reading to a maximum of 88° – resulting in an alcohol content of 11% when fermented.

The minimum Oechsle figures permitted for the grape musts of two grape varieties before fermentation to qualify in different quality grades in Alsace are shown in this table.

	Standard	Réserve	Réserve Personelle	Vendage Tardive	Selection de Grains Noble
Riesling	70 – 75	76 – 85	80 – 95	95	110
Gewürztraminer	85	85 – 95	95 – 105	105	120

▲ *The church, the crucifix and the vine. Religion and wine have been pivotal influences throughout Alsace's stormy history of conquest and re-conquest.*

VENDAGE TARDIVE
To qualify, the grapes must not be picked before a certain date which is set by agreement each year. The wines may not be chaptalised and they have to be tested by a tasting panel. This would compare with a German spätlese quality wine.

SELECTION DE GRAINS NOBLE (SGN)
Restrictions similar to Vendage Tardive wines but grapes are 'selected' by hand to use only the ripest. German Beerenauslese corresponds to this grading and method. In 1989 some incredibly high Oechsle readings were achieved. Hugel recorded 204° (potential alcohol 27.6%)

in one cask of Pinot Gris SGN and 214° (potential alcohol 30.0%) in a cask of Gewürztraminer SGN. Those wines will be *really* sweet!

Wine-making techniques have changed little over the years – the Alsacians are nothing if not traditionalists! Most of the major producers still age their wines in wooden casks although, due to the age of the casks, these do not impart any flavour to the wines. Oxidation is kept to a minimum with as little exposure to the atmosphere as possible during filtering and by bottling with high wine levels and long corks. The wines are therefore as fresh-tasting as careful production will allow and this, together

◀ *View from one of the Louis Gisselbrecht Riesling vineyards down to Dambach-la-Ville, famed for its Riesling wines.*

major producers – the Grandes Maisons d'Alsace – are all totally reliable at all levels.

They are:
Leon Beyer, Dopff & Irion, Dopff au Moulin, Hugel et Fils, Quentz Bas, Gustave Lorentz, Preiss-Zimmer and F.E. Trimbach

Personal favourites
Louis Gisselbrecht – frequent medal winners, especially for Riesling

Theo Faller – late harvest for full maturity is the family policy

Willy Gisselbrecht – larger half of the family. Especially good medal-winning Gewürztraminers

Jos Meyer – some grand crû wines. Others extremely good, especially Riesling

Schlumberger – largest estate owners in Alsace with 140 hectares

JURA AND SAVOIE

Invariably these two Alpine growing areas get lumped together as no one knows what else to do with them. In fact they are very different from each other – and from the rest of France too.

JURA

Almost a separate world from mainstream French wines and wine-making, yet with one very significant claim to fame. It was in Arbois that Louis Pasteur (1822–95) made his discovery so important to the wine trade – that fermentation is a living process triggered off and maintained by living organisms and not, as had been previously supposed, a chemical reaction. From this came both pasteurisation, of considerable benefit to the health of the world, and a greater appreciation of the mechanisms and variables governing the making of good, stable, wines.

Jura wines can best be described as characterful. This may be because their very individual flavours are simply outside our normal range of experience, but it is possibly also a reflection of the rugged life of the Jura, mountainous certainly, yet with the greater majesty of the Alps always on the skyline to the east. Jura wines enjoyed fame and popularity in times past – the Romans certainly recorded wine production in this area. Grapes are a hotch-potch of local varieties which may or may

with attention to detail at every other stage in the cycle ensures consistent quality.

Unfortunately, this fact seems to have escaped the majority of the wine-buying public, but has certainly not escaped the notice of the wine-trade itself – hence the often-heard expression in wine circles 'the wine the wine trade drinks'.

Recommendations
It is almost unfair to select a list of recommended names in Alsace – the standards are so high throughout the region that it is near impossible to find a bottle of less than adequate quality. However, members of the 'union' of

not be related to classic grapes. Whites are Savagnin, originally thought to be a Traminer but now less certain, and the Melon d'Arbois or Gamay Blanc which has a firmer claim on really being a Chardonnay. Red wines are made from Poulsard and Trousseau with increasing use of Gros Noirien alias Pinot Noir. The Trousseau must have had a remarkable journey to end up in the Jura for it is none other than the Bastardo, the grape of port and Dão in Portugal and of Madeira. It is also the popular Cabernet Gros of cheap Australian dessert wines and 'ports'!

Red wines, due largely to the overpowering influence of the Trousseau, are pretty brutal in their approach. Rosés manage more sophistication, normally being Poulsard-based while whites are mainly made into méthode champenois sparklers – just as well too for the Savagnin, Chardonnay or not, is as savage as its name suggests. The most interesting wines are probably the rosés or *vins gris* as the locals call them.

A further claim to fame, or notoriety, is the Vin Jaune produced here. To simply call it a French sherry is unfair, yet the production method and the ensuing taste do lead one to that comparison. After fermentation, wine from the Savagnin is left in almost full barrels for six years and, as in Jerez, a flor, a skin of yeast, develops across the surface of the wine, limiting oxidation. Strangely, and unlike fino sherry which is best drunk young, Vin Jaune goes on improving with age. But don't get too excited. Only tiny amounts are produced, it is naturally expensive – and when you've tried it you do wonder why you bothered!

Another rarity is the Vin de Paille – straw wine. The name comes from the custom of drying grapes in the loft on straw mats as was the custom in Germany for trockenbeeren-auslen and throughout the Mediterranean for producing sweet wine by raisining the grapes.

JURA APPELLATIONS

Côtes du Jura is the general appellation for reds, rosés, whites, vins de paille, vins jaune, etc, etc, whilst Côtes du Jura Mousseux covers those sparklers not otherwise included.
The more specific Arbois appellation covers the best whites of the region while l'Etoile looks after other whites, jaune wines and, more importantly, the bulk of the good sparklers.
Château Chalon is the appellation, *not* a property, for one wine only, the very individual Vin Jaune de Garde.

SAVOIE

It may come from living too near the Swiss but Savoie, from a vinous point of view, is dullsville. Consumed mainly by winter holiday-makers who pay a high price for unsensational wines, only two are known to have escaped to the UK in any sort of quantity.

SAVOIE APPELLATIONS

Seyssel in the Rhône valley produces a very dry aperitif-style sparkling wine from the Altesse and the less interesting Molette.

Vin de Savoie is the appellation for white wines from the Jacquère, the predominant local grape. The characteristics, or lack of them, are best summed up by Jancis Robinson in *Vines, Grapes and Wines* '. . . Jacquère's usual strong suit is blameless neutrality'. Rousette de Savoie covers the decreasing production of white wines from the Altesse grape, which is a shame for this is a grape that should, by virtue of its history and of its taste, be destined for greater things. It came from Cyprus towards the end of the Middle Ages but it seems probable that it was taken to Cyprus from Hungary by the Knights Templar. The taste is cast in the Gewürztraminer mould, spicy scent and aromatic flavour, but this counts for little in today's commercial world, for a cropping level of under 25hl per hectare damns the vine to eventual oblivion. Crépy, just across the border from Switzerland, is really a Swiss wine from the Swiss Chasselas grape – also called the Fendant. The completely uninspiring wine provided by the Chasselas/Fendant is at variance with its fascinating history. Theories abound that this is the mother lode – the original grape!

Fresh crisp Chardonnays are now appearing under the Vin de Savoie banner as well – excellent value-for-money too!

Boring red skiing wines come, surprisingly, from the Gamay and the Pinot Noir, while less boring skiing wines are produced from the local Mondeuse (Refosco in Italy) in the appellations of St-Jean-de-la-Porte, Arbin and Montmelian.

Finally, there are wines from the appellation Bugey VDQS. Located well to the west on the way towards Lyon, the wines are a sort of logical step Beaujolais-wards.

GERMANY

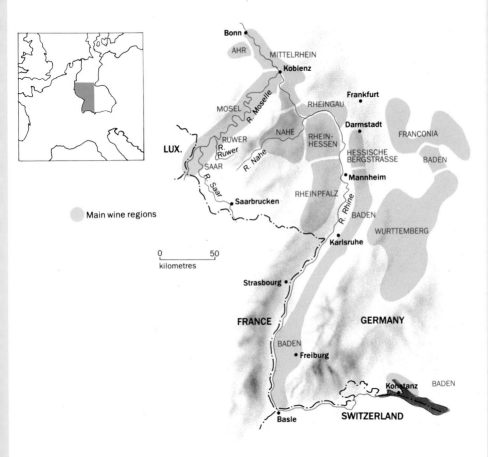

Bonn •

AHR

MITTELRHEIN

• Koblenz

Frankfurt •

MOSEL

R. Moselle

RHEINGAU

NAHE

RHEIN-
HESSEN

Darmstadt •

FRANCONIA

RUWER
R.
Rüwer

R. Nahe

HESSISCHE
BERGSTRASSE

BADEN

LUX.

SAAR

R. Saar

• Mannheim

RHEINPFALZ

R. Rhine

BADEN

• Saarbrücken

WURTTEMBERG

○ Main wine regions

Karlsruhe •

Strasbourg •

FRANCE

GERMANY

BADEN

0   50
kilometres

BADEN

• Freiburg

Konstanz

BADEN

• Basle

SWITZERLAND

GROWING AREA ——————— MOSEL SAAR RUWER

WINE LAW GRADE
VINEYARD

Qualitätswein mit Prädikat

BOTTLE SIZE ———————————

VINTAGE ——————— 1980er

ALCOHOLIC STRENGTH

VILLAGE ——————— 07l℮ ——————— Alkohol 8,4 Vol. %

Briedeler Herzchen Kabinett

QmP GRADE (IF ANY)

GRAPE VARIETY ——————— —Riesling—

COUNTRY OF ORIGIN

AP No. ——————— Amtliche Prüfungsnummer 1 920 165 18 81

Produce of
Germany

PRODUCER ——————— Erzeugerabfüllung — Estate bottled

PRODUCER'S ADDRESS

Winzermeister Wilfried Reis Briedel/Mosel
WEINGUT-WEINVERSAND

107

Discussion of German wine and German wine laws is a potentially boring subject.

The meticulous and methodical Germans have produced a sterile set of legislative rules that, in their detail and complexity, deter understanding and yet, at the same time, can ensure that the drinker is denied information useful or even essential in making a choice. The laws are dealt with below, here we will try to discover some individuality in what is mainly a sea of apparently chemically contrived commercial confections. The task is daunting due mainly to the fact that these extremely northern vineyards really only tolerate one grape, the Riesling, and even this hardy vine is seldom allowed to develop its full potential due to the German obsession for high crop levels at the expense of fruit quality. The efforts to 'improve' the Riesling are discussed on pages 13–14, but, sadly, the combination of commercial pressures to produce ever more bland, boring wines and the prima donna nature of the genuine article itself has lead to vast aeas of vineyards deliberately using inferior but higher cropping hybrids which, with suitable additives, will provide what the mass-market demands. Character, individuality and interest are the attributes that suffer. The little-known gems of

GERMAN WINE LAWS

German quality wines would benefit from a system which depended more on grape or geography for its standard of excellence. As it is, the laws are based almost solely on grape sugar levels at harvest time – and as long as this holds true customers have to accept that better equals sweeter. It also provides little incentive for growers to prune back to achieve better quality wine through more intense flavours. Rather, there is every incentive to produce the very maximum quantity of wine which will, inevitably, need the help of added sugar – süssreserve (page 28) is the legal way but many less-than-legal methods have been developed. However, in spite of, or perhaps because of, its failings, the laws are relatively straightforward.

There are four grades of wine: Tafelwein, Landwein, QbA and QmP, which have further subdivisions.

TAFELWEIN
Normally imported wine with some German wine and sweetening added.
● *Deutscher Tafelwein* Undistinguished German wine with added sweeteners.

LANDWEIN
Introduced in 1982, a Tafelwein that is from one of 20 designated areas and is either Trocken (dry) or Halb-trocken (half-dry). A sort of German Vin de Pays classification.

QbA (QUALITÄTSWEIN BESTIMMTER ANBAUGEBIETE)
Quality wine from a designated region. This is unblended wine from one of 11 Anbaugebiete areas using approved grapes which have to reach a certain level of sweetness before sugars are added. The wine is analysed and tasted and then issued with a certificate giving the AP number which will then be shown on the wine label.

QmP (QUALITÄTSWEIN MIT PRÄDIKAT)
Quality wine with special character. This group has six categories.
● *Kabinett* The highest quality of normal German sweetness.
● *Spätlese* Wines from late-gathered grapes, often considerably sweeter than Kabinett, but not necessarily so.
● *Auslese* Wine from grape bunches that are ripe or over-ripe, sometimes having a degree of 'noble rot' to enhance the natural sweetness.
● *Beerenauslese* Here the grapes are hand-picked and only the sweetest over-ripe berries are used. Intensely sweet wines.
● *Trockenbeerenauslese (TBA)* Wine from berries that have dried on the vine through the action of noble rot and/or berries which have been dried to a raisin-like state. Overpoweringly sweet.
● *Eiswein* A rarity produced from bunches left on the vine until, in the depths of winter, sufficiently low overnight temperatures will enable the grapes to be picked and pressed with the water content of the grape pulp remaining as ice crystals. A wine of very delicate, concentrated flavour normally of about Auslese sweetness level. An expensive rarity.

Germany are more difficult to find than equivalently unusual wines of other countries largely because although people accept that France, Italy, Spain and the like may well have low production specialist wines, the idea of Germany offering anything out of the ordinary seems most unlikely.

The origins of the few areas or properties with individuality go back to the beginnings of recorded vine-growing. The Romans introduced viniculture and their settlements along the Rhine and the Moselle provided the nucleus of the modern industry. After the departure of the Romans the activity survived in and around the monasteries and this heritage is still obvious at tourist spots like the monastery of Kloster Eberbach above Hattenheim on the Rhine, where the vast maturing halls and cellars still contain the huge wooden vats in use hundreds of years ago. Many Einzellage and Grosslage names begin 'Kloster . . .', German for monastery, and this, too, refers back to the huge land holdings of the religious institutions.

Land ownership was affected by retaining the Roman laws of inheritance which decreed that, on the death of the owner, land should not pass to the eldest son, or to any one person, but should be divided between the members of the

In addition to the system of wine quality grading there is a clearly defined system of geographical location information. The 11 specified areas are subdivided into 32 Bereichs or defined areas within a region: Bereich Bernkastel, Bereich Nierstein and so on. The Bereichs are further subdivided into Gemeinden or villages, and these are again subdivided into Einzellagen which are vineyards or groups of vineyards.

'Winkeler Jesuitengarten Riesling Spätlese' on a wine label tells you that the wine is made from late-gathered (Spätlese) grapes, exclusively from Riesling vines grown in the Jesuitengarten vineyard just outside of the village of Winkel on the Rhine.

For the very best vineyards the information is perfectly precise, but vineyards or even villages can be grouped into a Grosslage or larger grouping if considered of similar quality – and the Grosslage will normally take the name of the best-known vineyard in that larger group. Piesporter Michelsberg or Bernkastler Kurfurstlay are examples of areas of huge output labelled in this way. One of the most serious defects of the German wine laws is that growers are actually forbidden to specify whether the last, most specific, word on a label designating the locality/region/village is genuinely an individual vineyard or a collection of similar vineyards taking their name from the most famous. Bernkastel, for example, has only two Grosslage names, the infamous Kurfurstlay extending for miles down the Moselle and producing a flood of average or less than average wines, and the Badstube Grosslage, a very select little area containing only the five greatest vineyards in the area.

STATUTORY SUGAR LEVELS

Regions	Table wine	Quality wine	Kabinett	Spätlese	Auslese	Beeren- auslese	Trocken- beerenauslese
The first figure is degrees Oechsle (for Riesling); the second figure is potential percentage alcohol							
Ahr	5°/44	5.9°/50	8.6°/67	10°/76	11.1°/83	15.3°/110	21.5°/150
Rheingau	5°/44	7°/57	9.5°/73	11.4°/85	13°/95	17.7°/125	21.5°/150
Rheinhessen and Rheinpfalz	5°/44	7.5°/60	9.5°/73	11.4°/85	13°/95	16.9°/120	21.5°/150
Mosel-Saar- Ruwer	5°/44	5.9°/50	8.6°/67	10°/76	11.1°/83	15.3°/110	21.5°/150
Nahe	5°/44	7°/57	9.1°/70	10.3°/78	11.4°/85	16.9°/120	21.5°/150

▲ *Ornately carved 300-year-old barrel-end set into*   *the wall at Huesgen,*
Traben-Trarbach, Moselle.

family. Thus Germany became a network of postage-stamp sized holdings except for those held by the church – which tended to grow in size through religious bequest or outright purchase. In 1803 all the vineyards were secularised and so, with a few exceptions, the only evidence of the vital part the church played in the fostering and maintenance of wine production is in the traditional names of the vineyards which, in many cases, go back for centuries. In Germany 'chaptalisation' (page 91) is known as the Gall Process after a German doctor who advocated its use. This method of adding sugar to the unfermented grape juices was of even more benefit in Germany with its cooler summers and has been refined to a point where the bulk wine producers of Germany depend on it.

While on the subject of sweetness in wines, it is worth recounting the story which allegedly explains the origins of sweet German and, through them, sweet French wines. The story is that the Bishop of Fulda of Schloss Johannisberg, who was apparently quite lazy, forgot to give instructions to start the harvest at the correct time and, by the time the order was belatedly given, the grapes were found to be rotted and were therefore given to the servants. Having no choice in the matter, the servants fermented the rotted grapes and produced an amazingly sweet wine and the secret of noble rot was discovered. An alternative version is kinder to the Bishop, blaming his messenger for being late, but whoever was to blame, the year of 1775 is agreed as the first fermentation of a sweet wine from berries affected by what the Germans call Edelfäule – the noble rot. And from Germany the practice spread to France.

When selecting German wine it is worth remembering that due to the sweetness premise on which the wine laws are based (pages 108–109) each increase in quality beyond a certain point results in an increase in wine sweetness. Therefore, as a start, it is wise to look for 'Riesling Kabinett' on the label. This will ensure that the grape is the noble Riesling rather than one of its many descendants and that the must quality is between 65° and 75° Oechsle (page 102) rather than the 50° to 60° Oechsle range for QbA wines. Kabinett quality carries the highest Oechsle rating before sweetness increases.

MOSEL-SAAR-RUWER

The river Moselle follows a tortuous route of more than 480 kilometres from the Vosges mountains in France, through Luxembourg where extensive vineyards clothe the river valley, to Germany where its vinous greatness is fully realised. Soon after entering Germany it is joined by two tributaries, first the Saar and then the Ruwer, and the whole length of its journey to Koblenz, where it meets the Rhine, is through wine-growing areas. This is the Mosel-Saar-Ruwer region, or M-S-R for short. In fact, along the upper reaches of the Moselle the wines are markedly inferior to those from the two tributaries, it is only in the Mittelmosel that the quality of great Moselle wines shows through before fading from greatness as the meeting with the Rhine approaches.

In the Mittelmosel the Riesling is king. Apart from the 24 kilometres of Rhine river frontage called Rheingau this is the only area in Germany where the Riesling is still the most widely planted vine. In all other areas the prolific but dull Müller-Thurgau is the dominant vine, the commercial attractions of quantity having forced out the more difficult-to-sell delights of Riesling quality.

This far north every minute of sunshine is important and the precise inclination and aspect of a vineyard's slope can affect the quality of the end product. The slatey soil, too, has its part to play in reflecting and storing heat, so any soil washed down from the steep vineyard slopes is carefully collected and replaced. It is a labour-intensive operation to grow grapes under these conditions and labour costs in a society as affluent as Germany's can never be cheap. Add to this the late-ripening nature of the Riesling – harvesting in late November as sometimes happens is fraught with potential disaster – and one can see the attraction of a Müller-Thurgau vineyard, after all, Müller-Thurgau wines seem to sell just as well. . . .

The recommendations I give for German wines take a different form from those for other countries, reflecting what appears on German wine labels. First comes the name of the Einzellage, the vineyard, where applicable. This is followed by the producer. In some cases particularly good producers have numerous vineyards, in which case their entry starts 'Numerous Einzellagen'.

SAAR

Names to look out for

Scharzhofberg – one of the few vineyards in Germany to use only the vineyard name. Egon Muller's estate owns much of the vineyard

Wiltinger Braune Kupp – Le Gallais, French owner, but Egon Muller management

Ockfener Bockstein – Dr Fischer, other good Ockfen sites too

Saarburger and Ockfen – Forstmeister Geltz Zilliken, now run by the great-grandson of the original Forstmeister (Master Forester)

Oberemmeler and Scharzhofberg – von Hövel, fine, elegant wines

Numerous Einzellagen – Edmund Reverchon based at Konz but with vineyards throughout the Saar

Numerous Einzellagen – Herrenberg, owner Bert Simon. US market

RUWER

Names to look out for

Eitelsbacher – Gutsverwaltung Karthauserhof, very unusually only uses a neck label

Maximin Grunhaus – Carl von Schubert only uses the village name for his sensational wines. One of Germany's greatest

MITTELMOSEL

Names to look out for

Urziger and others – Josef Christoffel, with a century of experience

Graacher and others – Kies-Kieren, winners of many national awards

Bernkasteler – Lauerburg founded in 1700 produces wines for ageing

Numerous Einzellagen – Nicolay-Erben, oak-matured Riesling

Graacher and Bernkasteler – Otto Pauly, growers since 1620

Wehlener and others – J. J. Prüm, the most famous Moselle family

Wehlener and others – S. A. Prüm, another part of the famous Moselle family

Ockfener and others – Adolf Rheinart Erben, 20% new varieties

Numerous Einzellagen – Dr H. Thanisch, family estate goes back to 1650, 'made' the famous name of Bernkastler Doctor

Numerous Einzellagen – Wegeler-Deinhard, Dienhard wines well known in the UK

Companies operating throughout the M-S-R

Verwaltung der Bischöflichen Weinguter Trier

Stiftung Staatliches Friedrich-Wilhelm-Gymnasium

Weingut Reichsgraf von Kesselstatt

Verwaltung der Staatlichen Weinbaudomanen

MITTELRHEIN AND AHR

This most northerly of the Rhine regions extends from just south of Bonn to just north of Bingen. The Mittelrhein is seldom discussed in works of reference and the wines seldom drunk outside the immediate region – except for quantities of Sekt which can sometimes be found elsewhere in Germany, part of the region's annual output of a million cases of this one type of wine.

Ahr is famous for having the most northerly red grape vineyards in the world. Pinot Noir, here called Spätburgunder, was brought from Burgundy in the 17th century. As you would expect, the wine is quite pale although pleasant and delicate to the taste.

NAHE

In the middle of this region the rivers Nahe and Glan join before reaching the Rhine at Bingen. They provide the river banks for the vineyards for there is only a tiny strip of actual Rhine frontage for the *gebiet*, or region, of Nahe. The State Domaine at Niederhausen-Schloss-Bockelheim owns some of the best sites, including Kupfergrube and Felsenberg. Grape varieties are split almost equally: Müller-Thurgau 30%, Sylvaner 27% and Riesling 23%.

Names to look out for

Note Einzellagen names have been omitted because most Nahe growers have properties spread all around the best sites in the area

August E. Anheuser – the best of the Kreuznach vineyards and others

Paul Anheuser – started in 1888 by breaking away from family (see above) by the man who introduced Riesling to Ruwer

Hans Crusius & Sohn – probably the best in the Nahe

Diel auf Burg Layen – experiments with new varieties. Rosés too

Weinbaulehranstalt – excellent research station at Bad Kreuznach

Reichsgraf von Plettenberg – large family estate since 18th century

Verwaltung der Staatlichen Weinbaudomanen – the local 'state domaine'

RHEINGAU

South of Bingen the Rhine flows in an east-west curve, so the north bank has a southerly aspect for about 32 kilometres. The north bank, the Rheingau, produces the cream of German wines while the south bank, part of the Rheinhessen, has the less favourable aspect and produces vast floods of simple commercially-appealing wine.

In the Rheingau the plantings of Riesling represent 81% of the vineyard area with Müller-Thurgau a mere 9%! This area represents the essence of German excellence. Yet the region begins with an exception. Before the river assumes its favourable course, around the corner as it were, lies the area of Assmannhausen famous only for production of Pinot Noir reds. Pretty thin reds they are too, which is hardly surprising so far north, but worse is to come! The State Domaine (the German equivalent of the French co-operative) produces a strange, although valued in Germany, sweet rosé from late-picked grapes.

However, once around the river bend are the first true quality vineyards – those of Rudesheimer Berg, where each separate vineyard starts with the word Berg although the best-known name from Rudesheim itself is probably the Rosengarten vineyard close to the town. The next town is Geisenheim which, although producing good wines, is, nevertheless, more famous internationally for its wine school – Germany's equivalent of California's Davis campus. Like Davis, they create and test new hybrids and their vines such as Scheurebe and Kerner are now planted throughout the world.

Between Geisenheim and before Winkel, inland up the steep riverbank, is Schloss Johannisberg, one of the most prestigious vineyard names in Germany. Nearby is the almost equally impressive estate of Schloss Vollrads. Like Schloss Johannisberg it is an Ortsteile, an estate so grand that the town or village name does not appear on the labels, which is a shame for little-known Winkel for Winkel has another good vineyard called Hasensprung.

The wines of the two riverside villages, Mittelheim and Oestrich, are often said to lack 'breeding'. Perhaps this is due to having such illustrious neighbours, but I find this criticism unfair when levelled at Oestrich, whose Doosberg and Lenchen vineyards are capable of muted greatness. Inland is the village of Hallgarten, no connection with the famous wine shipping firm, and notable only for having the highest of the Rheingau vineyards – Hendelberg, 1000ft above sea level.

Now we reach the crême de la crême. The road inland from the next village, Hattenheim, winds up to the perfection that is the Cistercian monastery of Kloster Eberbach. Now owned by the Verwaltung der Staadsweinguter Eltville – the State Domaine for the Rheingau – it is a museum, the spiritual headquarters of the German wine industry and a wine academy. The whole atmosphere almost defies description, but if you are ever travelling along the Rhine be sure to visit Kloster Eberbach and share the concentration of six centuries of devotion to religion and to wine.

As a bonus, driving up to the old Cistercian monastery one passes possibly the greatest vineyard in Germany – Steinberg. Like Clos de Vougeot in Burgundy it was walled by the Cistercians and from within its boundaries come arguably the finest wines of the Rheingau and probably of Germany itself. Like the other great vineyards it is an Ortsteile – it can omit the Gemeinde (village) name from its label.

The next village, Erbach, is unusual in having its finest vineyard lying alongside and parallel to the river. At first sight this would seem to present problems of drainage and frost damage. However, neither seem to occur and the Marcobrunn vineyard has been famous for centuries. This vineyard is owned by several influential estates including that of Prince Frederick of Prussia whose family seat is at Schloss Rheinhartshausen in Erbach. The estate, which includes many other vineyard holdings and is experimenting with other grapes including Chardonnay, is now efficiently run by his son Prince Nicholas von Preussen.

Continuing upstream, the quality seems to fall away a little. After Erbach comes Eltville am Rhein – the 'capital' of the Rheingau if only by virtue of its size and having the headquarters of the State Domaine. After Eltville comes Ruenthal with several good vineyards, then Martinsthal, Walluf and Wiesbaden.

One area of interest remains, the town of Hochheim. Now almost separated from the rest of the Rheingau by the city of Weisbaden and by the knitting pattern of the autobahnen, it is the town which gave rise to the English term for Rhine wine: Hock. Apparently, this name arose as an abbreviation of Hockamore, itself an anglicised rendering of Hochheimer.

Names to look out for

Hochheim – Geheimrat Aschrott'sche Erben Weingutsverwaltung

Winkel – Baron von Brentano'sche Gutsverwaltung Winkel

Kiedrich and Rudesheim – Schloss Groenesteyn dates from 1400

several Einzellagen – Landgraflich Hessisches Weingut

Schloss Johannisberg – owned by Prince Furst von Metternich

Hochheim – Konigin Victoria Berg, so named after a visit by Queen Victoria who watched the vintage gathering in 1850

several Einzellagen – G.H. Mumm'sches Weingut, owned by Rudolf Oetker, who also controls Schloss Johannisberg

many Einzellagen – Schloss Schönborn, the biggest privately owned estate in the Rheingau based at Hattenheim

Scloss Vollrads – Graf Matuschka-Greiffenclau. Commercial links with Burklin-Wolf and Anheuser, and with Suntory the Japanese drinks giant

many Einzellagen – Weger-Deinhard, part of the high-quality Deinhard empire

Verwaltung der Staatsweinguter Eltville the State Domaine for Rheingau and owners of Kloster Eberbach – throughout the Rheingau

RHEINHESSEN

The home of Liebfraumilch. The grape ratios say it all – Müller-Thurgau 27%, Sylvaner 15%, Scheurebe 9%, Bacchus 8%, Faber 7%, Kerner 7%, Riesling 6% and Morio-Muskat 5%. Production is around 38 million cases a year from 24,000 hectares in an area bounded by the Nahe on the short eastern side, the Rhine on the northern and western sides and with the towns of Bingen, Mainz, Worms and Bad Kreuznach at the corners.

The definition of Liebfraumilch, which now legally carries a QbA classification, is that it shall be produced from *at least* 50% of Müller-Thurgau, Sylvaner or Riesling grapes (my italics) grown in Rheinpfalz, Rheinhessen, Nahe or Rheingau and that it shall be a wine 'with pleasant character' having a minimum Oechsle reading of 60°. That certainly leaves the door open very wide! The origin of this extensively used name which, literally, means 'milk of the beautiful wife' but really relates to Ôur Lady, derives from the name of the Liebfrauenstift vineyards surrounding the Liebfrauenkirch, Church of Our Lady, in the city of Worms. Nowadays, to distance themselves from the all too popular name, the producers of Liebfraumilch call their wines Liebfrauenmorgen.

Apart from the superabundance ot bottles ot Liebfraumilch, there is also a wash of wineş labelled Niersteiner or Bereich Nierstein. Another common name, Niersteiner Gutes Domtal, can be used by 15 villages, but not by Nierstein itself – except for one area which happens to be the least distinguished!

A few significant names

Nierstein – Anton Balbach Erben, 80% Riesling notifies good intent and improving wines

several Einzellagen – Louis Guntrum, masses of commercial wines but also some classic estate-bottled wines

Bornheim and Flondheim – Koehler-Weidmann, ninth generation but one of the leaders with new varieties

Alsheim and Guntersblum – Rappenhof, one of the best in the district

several Einzellagen – Heinrich Seip, pioneering new varieties

several Einzellagen – Carl Sittmann, biggest private estate

Nierstein – Eugen Wehrheim, established 1693, 24% 'other varieties'

Staatsweingut der Landes-Lehr-und Versuchsanstalt – with vineyards in Oppenheim, Nierstein and Dienheim, the wine school and wine museum of the region with a heavy commitment to experimentation.

RHEINPFALZ (PALATINATE)

At 56,000 acres the Rheinpfalz or Palatinate is marginally smaller than Rheinhessen, but frequently exceeds the output of that region due to better cropping from the protection afforded by the Haardt mountains – an extension of the Vosges that protect Alsace – and also to its more southerly location. Like Rheinhessen, a large producer of plonk Liebfraumilch with a few sparkling gems for the determined researcher.

The region has three distinct areas: the southern area, Oberhaardt, where anonymity abounds, the centre, or Mittelhaardt, which is a cradle of excellence and the Unterhaardt where, once again, commercial products rule the roost. The southern section has now officially become the Sudliche Weinstrasse, which is fair enough, but the middle *and* northern sections have been lumped together as Mittelhaardt-Deutsche Weinstrasse. Presumably this was done to give some reflected glory to the Palatinate's northern vineyards. In reality it only detracts from the reputation of the Mittelhaardt area where three of the greatest name in German viniculture are located.

Names to look out for – the big three

several Einzellagen – Dr von Bassermann-Jordan one of the great names of Germany. 99% of the 40 hectare estate is Riesling

several Einzellagen – von Buhl. One of the biggest German estates at 95 hectares. 80% Riesling but increasing to 90%

several Einzellagen – Dr Bürklin-Wolf. Modern ideas and 400-year-old history

and others

several Einzellagen – Dr Deinhard, part of the Deinhard empire

Burkweil – Rebholz, early pioneer in this area, no süssreserve used

Annaberg – Weingut Annaberg, perfect model estate of a single hectare

Deidesheim – Wegeler-Dienhard, another part of the Dienhard empire

Gebiets-Winzergenossenschaft Deutsches Weintor – one of the largest European co-operatives. 'Deutsches Weintor' refers to the stone gateway of that name which stands at the border with France. The co-operative itself has over 1,250 members, more than 11,300 hectares in 35 different communes and a wine storage capacity, although modest by California's Gallo standards, of over 30 million litres. That's almost a bottle of wine for every man, woman and child in the UK – which is probably where most of it will go anyway.

HESSISCHE BERGSTRASSE

After the size of the co-operative above, it seems silly to talk about a wine region of just 360 hectares. In fact it's so dull that we won't.

▲ *Kloster Eberbach, the 12th-century Cistercian abbey guardian of the*   *Steinberg vineyard and now the German Wine Academy.*   ▶ *The Liebfrauenkirche in the city of Worms. The name Liebfraumilch*   *originated from the Liebfrauenstift vineyards around the church.*

FRANCONIA

This area is of academic interest only, for you seldom encounter a Franken wine on UK shop shelves. If you do, then they are immediately recognisable for they will be in a bocksbeutel – a dumpy flagon best described as being like a Mateus Rosé bottle and allegedly based on the shape of a goat's scrotum full of wine, for these were, apparently, used as primitive wine-bags!

In this region the best wines are traditionally made from the Sylvaner rather than the Riesling grape although, as elsewhere, the march of the Müller-Thurgau is impossible to deny. The great wines of Franken are still Sylvaner-based for it is this grape that is most at home on the Muschelkalk, a soil relative of the Kimmeridge of Chablis.

The name Steinwein is used loosely for all Franken wines and 'Stein' was included in A. Jullien's famous 1866 listing of the best wines of Europe. There were only nine German wines on that list and seven are still regarded as truly great wines.

Proof of the longevity of Franken wines was given during the last decade when a bottle of the great vintage of 1540 was opened – it was just drinkable. In Würzburg at the palace of the Prince-Bishops, the vast vaults still hold massive casks of old vintages, including the legendary 1540. The wine museum at Pfalz has wine from the Lleste vineyard in Würzburg from the 17th century.

Names to look out for

Bürgerspital zum Heiligen Geist – a charity founded in 1319 and the fourth biggest wine estate in Germany

Fürstlich Castell'sches Domänenamt owned by Prince Albrecht zu Castell-Castell. Classic Sylvaners

Ernst Gebhardt – unusually extending their plantings of Riesling

Juliusspital-Weingut – a religious charity foundation dating back to 1576. The third largest German estate. All wines are cask matured in old oak

Staatlicher Hofkeller – the Bavarian state domain, previously the vineyards of the Prince-Bishops of Würzburg

Hans Wirsching – old 1630 cellars and completely modern ones as well

WÜRTTEMBERG

Another vast 'unknown' German wine region. Their best-known product is an uninteresting red from the Pinot Noir or Spätburgunder as they call it in Germany. They also produce white wines from the Trollinger, the Limberger and the Pinot Meunier of Champagne fame, here called Schwarzriesling. A number of the usual German grapes are planted in small quantities, Sylvaner, Müller-Thurgau, but, as elsewhere, the few good wines of this area use the Riesling.

BADEN

In this part of Germany the Rhine flows almost due north and its eastern bank from Basle in Switzerland almost to Frankfurt is one long thin vineyard. In the southern part it is squeezed between the river and the Black Forest but further north the constraints on the cultivated area are industrialisation – Karlsruhe, Mannheim and Darmstadt all continually encroach on the historic wine production areas.

In the south the vineyards lie just across the Rhine from Alsace – and the variety of vines echoes that area: Pinot Noir, Pinot Gris (here called Ruländer), Pinot Blanc, Sylvaner, Gewürztraminer and, for the real quality wines, Riesling. Naturally, the ubiquitous Müller-Thurgau has also made itself felt here too. In the far south there are even plantings of the favourite Swiss grape, the Chasselas, here called Gutedel.

The whole of Baden has been extensively modernised in the past decade, the vineyards have doubled in size and quadrupled in output and most good UK wine-merchants, supermarkets even, have at least one, normally dry, Baden example. It is a co-operative controlled area, there are more than 100 and they account for at least 90% of the crop and, of that, more than 50% ends up at the cellars of the Zentralkellerei Badischer Winzergenossen-schaften (ZBW for short) at Breisach. Here they bottle up to 500 different types of wine and the majority seen in Britain are from this dynamic organisation.

ITALY

1. Valtellina
2. Friuli
3. Carema
4. Gattinara
5. Bardolino
6. Valpolicella/Soave
7. Barbera
8. Asti Spumante
9. Barbaresco
10. Barolo
11. Lambrusco
12. Sangiovese di Romagna
13. Chianti
14. Verdicchio
15. Orvieto
16. Frascati
17. Lacryma Christi
18. Marsala
19. Moscato di Pantelleria
20. Trentino
21. Venegazzù
22. Sassicaia
23. Brunello di Montalcino
24. Vino Nobile di Montepulciano
25. Est!Est!!Est!!!
26. Rapitala & Regaleali

GROWING AREA — Vernaccia di S. Gimignano — GRAPE VARIETY

COUNTRY OF ORIGIN — DENOMINAZIONE DI ORIGINE CONTROLLATA — WINE LAW GRADE

ESTATE/PRODUCER BOTTLED — Proprietà Vecchione — VINTAGE

PRODUCER'S NAME AND ADDRESS —

0,750 litri   12% vol.

BOTTLE SIZE   ALCOHOLIC STRENGTH

While the problem with German wines is that they all tend to taste the same, the problem with Italy is the vast diversity of types and flavours. The attitude of the two countries to wine laws also provides a total contrast – the Germans being ponderously methodical and the Italians characteristically haphazard and, in general, preferring tradition to innovation. The easy-going Italian approach to wine has effectively denied them access to foreign markets for their quality wines and, tracing the export situation of Italian wines through the increased wine consumption of recent decades shows them, either through misfortune or inactivity, to be always one step behind.

The 1960s saw the great growth of interest in wine in the UK. Foreign travel had become easier and cheaper, Italy and Spain had become the holiday targets and the taste for the holiday wines returned with the travellers. Thus Chianti, Frascati, Soave and other undistinguished volume wines made their appearance and gained a foothold in the market. However, the 1960s also saw the introduction of the Italian wine laws, following pressure from the newly formed EEC, to control the flood of cheap Italian blending wines into France and Germany. Unfortunately, these laws were framed in such a way as to freeze the methods used historically in each area and to preserve these with little room for improvement or modification – and this at the very time when great strides were being made in analysing every aspect of wine-making. Through the 1970s the Californian-led technological revolution was watched by many but followed by few in Italy, either through indolence or through the legal constrictions. The few brave

souls who did make improvements were almost automatically required to 'downgrade' their wines to the lowest rating: Vino da Tavola. Sadly, this came at a time when the US dollar was undervalued and Californian wines were establishing themselves in the market place.

Then, as the 1980s dawned, it seemed that the age of Italian quality wines was upon us. At last, there seemed to be signs of market acceptance of the exciting ventures by the forward-thinking producers. Prominent were, and are, Antinori, Masi, Villa Banfi, Tedeschi in the historically well established areas and Lageder, Tiefenbrunner, Conte d'Almerita and others in the lesser-known but well chosen new areas. Sadly, the methanol additive scandal in Italy, following so closely on the Austrian di-ethylene glycol additives disgrace did great and disproportionate damage to the reputation of Italy. To add insult to injury, the Australian dollar was sliding downhill, making their excellent wines very cheap, and the commercially astute Bulgarian government was offering first-class state subsidised wines for silly prices. Wine drinkers had no need to look at suspect Italy with so many exciting choices from other countries which were, generally, clearly labelled as varietal wines (page 11).

And in the 1990s? With Spain and Portugal now both in the EEC there will be no shortage of attractively priced full-bodied reds or, to a lesser degree, crisp dry whites at basic prices. In the value-for-money stakes Italy has an uphill struggle.

From a wine point of view, if from no other, Italy is best dealt with in four regions: the north-east, the north-west, central Italy and southern Italy with Sicily.

ITALIAN WINE LAWS

There are really only two effective grades: Vino da Tavola (VdaT) and Denominazione di Origine Controllata (DOC), although officially there is a third grade: Denominazione di Origine Controllata Guarantita (DOCG).
Vino da Tavola, table wine, may be just that, or it may be something quite superb, a so-called Super Vino da Tavola (SVdaT) – a category without legal recognition. Only the price will tell

you which is which!
Denominazione di Origine Controllata (DOC) is the basic level of the quality grade, for which only 10% of Italy's wines qualify (it's 20% in France).
Denominazione di Origine Controllata Guarantita (DOCG) is DOC with Guarantita added, a category introduced in the early 1980s. The quality of the wines accorded this status is, to say the least, variable and is no guarantee of quality. Perhaps fortunately only six DOCGs

SWITZERLAND

AUSTRIA

THE NORTH-EAST

Merano • Bressanone

TERLANO

SANTA MADDALENA

LAGREIN

LAGO DI CALDARO • Bolzano

TRENTINO-ALTO ADIGE

FRIULI-VENEZIA-GIULIA

TEROLDEGO PINOT

MERLOT RIESLING

VIN SANTO • Trento

TRENTINO VERNACCIA

COLLI FRIULANI VERDUZZO

PICOLIT

REFOSCO Udine •

MERLOT

VALTELLINA

MARZEMINO

• Gorizia

BREGANZE

PROSECCO

TOCAI DI LISON

SAUVIGNON

VENETO Treviso

PIAVE

Trieste •

FRANCIACORTA

Brescia

VALPOLICELLA TORCOLATO

RECIOTO DI VALPOLICELLA

Vicenza

Verona • SOAVE

BARDOLINO

BIANCO DI CUSTOZA

COLLI EUGANEI

• Padua • Venice

YUGOSLAVIA

GAMBELLARA

COLLI BERICI

Cremona Mantova

MOSCATO

• Parma

LAMBRUSCO DI SORBARA

Modena •

EMILIA-ROMAGNA

LAMBRUSCO

Bologna •

ALBANA DI ROMAGNA

TREBBIANO

SANGIOVESE

ALBANA

Ravenna •

0 ____ 50
kilometres

ColBaraca
Possessioni in Monteforte d'Alpone

Soave classico (denominazione di origine controllata)
prodotto e vinificato dal viticultore a Monteforte.
Assistenza tecnica, imbottigliamento e distribuzione
a cura di
MASI

Zona storica di produzione del vino classico
Masi Agricola s.p.a. imbottigliatore in S. Ambrogio di Valpolicella - Italia
750 ml e Annata 1986 n. 13037 Alc. 12% by vol.

This region includes Trentino-Alto Adige, Friuli-Venezia-Giulia, Veneto and Emilia-Romagna.

In many ways it is the most exciting of the country's four subdivisions. Traditional wines are

Soave made from the Garganega grape with up to 30% Trebbiano and grown between Verona and Vicenza.

Bardolino and *Valpolicella* made north of the autostrada from the shores of Lake Garda to the outskirts of Vicenza and using a mixture of, in descending order of quantity, Corvina, Rondinella and Molinara with up to a further 10% made up from Sangiovese, Barbera, Rossignola and Negrara.

Barbera wines from the grape of the same name grown around Bologna.

Lambrusco beloved by the Americans, from the grape of the same name grown around Modena.

Sangiovese di Romagna together with *Trebbiano di Romagna* from a large area between Bologna and Ravenna.

All of these wines have been produced in these areas for centuries and they form the core of the region's wine trade. However, there are developments which deserve very special

have been granted: Barolo, Barbaresco, Brunello di Montalcino, minimum-aged Chiantis, Vino Nobile de Montepulciano and Albana di Romagna. The first three are fine, the fourth passable (just), but the fifth and sixth should be avoided.

The real problem with Italy's wine laws is that they have frozen wine-making in the mid 1960s. They make no allowance for the introduction of other grapes or of other, more modern,

techniques in wine-making. This had led to the proliferation of the so-called Super Vinos da Tavola (SVdaT) – wines condemned, on strictly legal grounds, to lowly VdaT status, although in many cases the recipients of international praise and competition medals. It is a ridiculous situation when some of the world's finest wines carry the status of Vino da Tavola, while some absolute nonentities carry the supposedly more prestigious DOCG title – exasperating for growers and consumers alike.

attention. For example, the efforts of Masi to improve on standard Valpolicella and Soave, firstly by bottling excellent small estate wines, such as the Serego Alighieri Valpolicella, the Col Baraca single estate Soave which does much to redeem that abused name and a single vineyard Bardolini, La Vegrona. Secondly by improving normally thin Valpolicella by maceration on the skins of Recioto grapes before pressing, thus giving more colour, alcohol and taste to this all too often insipid wine. Tedeschi, another forward thinking producer, also boost some Valpolicella in this way.

Two of the more individual of the wines produced in the north-east are Recioto and Recioto Amarone della Valpolicella. For these wines, selected Valpolicella grapes are air-dried before fermentation and the resulting wine is either semi-sweet Recioto, if fermentation is arrested at a reasonable 13%-14% alcohol, or if fermentation is allowed to continue to finality then the alcohol reaches a whopping 16% plus alcohol at which point the yeasts are completely stunned and fermentation ceases. The wine has a trace of sweetness, but this is balanced with natural acidity which is more obvious due to the lower sugar level. This is the Recioto Amarone, literally 'bitter' but more accurately translated as dry. Air drying is also applied to Soave for Recioto di Soave, a relatively delicate sweet wine.

In this region much credit is due to the pioneering exploits of Fausto Maculan and his sister Franca who inherited, and revolutionised, their family's long established wine business in the relatively unprepossessing area around Breganze due north of Vicenza. Their policy embraces the very best of the traditions of the area together with a refreshing, by Italian standards, refusal to be bound by convention. Their revival of the production of air-dried dessert wines is justified by their sumptuous Torcolato and is more than justified by the exotic Actinobile which is rarely exported. Traditional grapes go into the production of their basic white wines, Breganze di Breganze and Vespaiolo di Breganza, yet Chardonnay is also planted and is used for superior whites, while Cabernet Sauvignon is planted for production of their range of Cabernet reds culminating in Fratta, a great wine by any standards.

It is a pity that more Italian wine-makers do not follow Fausto Maculan's example and look beyond their country's borders to see what developments abroad could usefully be incorporated alongside local traditions to produce more 'internationally minded' wines.

More significant in the long term than the improvements to the quality of existing Italian wines or the individual efforts of inspired

growers, is the development and expansion of newer growing areas. The north-east has two such areas: Friuli-Venezia-Giulia and Trentino-Alto Adige.

Friuli-Venezia-Giulia has three DOCs: Colli Goriziano, Colli Orientali del Friuli and Grave del Friuli. These produce fresh, young varietal labelled wines from Pinot Gris (here given the old Alsacian name of Tocai), Pinot Blanc (sometimes either called Chardonnay or mixed with Chardonnay), Traminer, Malvasia and, most exciting of the whites, some Sauvignon Blanc. Red wines are also light-weight with Merlot and Cabernet (Franc not Sauvignon) being labels to look out for – growers are not quite as important here as in, say, France because only the best plant these grapes anyway.

Trentino-Alto Adige lies in the mountains north of Lake Garda, between Trento and Merano. This valley carries the Brenner Pass between Italy and Austria and hardly thinks of itself as Italian at all and both the wines and the dialect reflect this. The Süd-Tirol, as the locals prefer the area to be known, is at the forefront of Italian production of crisp, north European-style white wines. Grapes are many, but especially Pinot Blanc, Pinot Gris/Tocai, Müller-Thurgau (surprisingly good here), Sylvaner, Sauvignon Blanc and outstandingly good Goldmuskateller. Among the reds, naturally light at this altitude, are the Cabernets, Pinot Noir and Merlot. The area is the birthplace of the Gewürztraminer, being named after the town of Tramin, or Termeno as the Italians prefer to call it. Growers' names to look out for are Roberto Zeni, Alois Lageder, Herbert Tiefenbrunner and Ruggero de Tarczal whose Marzemino produced from the grape of that name is quite outstanding.

Further south, along the A1/A14 autostrada, lies the Emilia-Romagna, a large growing area producing unimaginative wines – the Lambrusco and the Trebbiano whites and Sangiovese reds. Only two producers are of interest and they show two opposing approaches to wine production. The Pasolini dall'Onda family have been wine-makers since the 16th century and own properties across Italy, from Ravenna across to south of Livorno encompassing Chianti as well as their good examples from Trebbiano/Sangiovese in this area. The other side of the coin is represented by Riunite, now one of the largest wine-producing complexes in the world. Devoted to Lambrusco for the American market, they export around 6 million cases a year of this pink froth through their agents Banfi (page 129).

We cannot leave the north-east without mentioning wines from the estate of Conte

◀ *The home of Pieralvise Alighieri, descendant of Dante Alighieri who wrote* The Divine Comedy *and lived here in the 14th century. The estate now produces excellent Serego Alighieri Valpolicella.*

▶ *Alois Lageder, who produces some of the finest wines in the Trentino-Alto Adige.*

Loredan-Gasparini, which was set up by Piero Loredan in 1940 and sold to Giancarlo Palla in 1974. Their Venegazzù, a méthode champenoise would be enough reason for special mention, but their international fame is for two other wines, one modestly called Della Casa, wine of the house or house wine, and the other, Etichetta Nera or Black Label. These wines use the traditional Bordeaux blend of Cabernets Sauvignon and Franc, Merlot and Malbec and are of outstanding quality. They can rank on a par with wines such as Torres Black Label from Spain, Sassicaia from Italy and the best of Australia and the USA.

Another wine of specialist interest is the Picolit, produced from the grape of the same name in Colli Orientali. In the 18th and 19th centuries this dessert wine was ranked with the great sweet wines of d'Yquem, the lost Constantia of Cape Province, the legendary Cotnari of Romania and Tokay Essencia from Hungary. Sweet wines would seem an unlikely product for this area, but the Picolit suffers from an hereditary defect in that floral abortion reduces the grape production per vine as surely as the severe pruning of vines that is carried out at Château Yquem. This, of course, concentrates the flavour but renders the tiny production per vineyard hardly economic except at very high prices indeed.

◄ *Vines grown under contract to Alois Lageder trained over pergolas in the traditional manner. In the distance is Lago di Caldaro.*

▼ *As in days of old, so still in Breganze! Vines growing up into and draping over trees as they have done since Roman times.*

Top wines of the north-east
All the wines of the following producers, listed alphabetically:
Lageder, Maculan, Masi, Venegazzu Estate, Zeni

White wines
Soave Classico, Pieropan – helps make clear what good Soave should be like

Schiava, Pojer & Sandri – a 'pale and pretty' wine says one expert

Chardonnay dell'Alto Adige, Portico dei Leoni – combined talents of Chianti wine-maker Maurizio Castelli, wine writer Burton Anderson and producer Alois Lageder

Pinot Bianco, Jermann – one of the best in Friuli-Venezia-Giulia

Soaves from Anselmi – also produces interesting Cabernet Sauvignon

Ramandolo di Verduzzo, either G.B. Comelli or Giovanni Dri – this sweet Verduzzo Amabile has to be tasted to be believed

Red wines
Valpolicella/Recioto Amarone, Fratelli Tedeschi – classic wines. Try also their Capitel San Rocco 'improved' Valpolicella

Marzemino Trentino, de Tarczal – smooth, dark ruby-violet, a delight

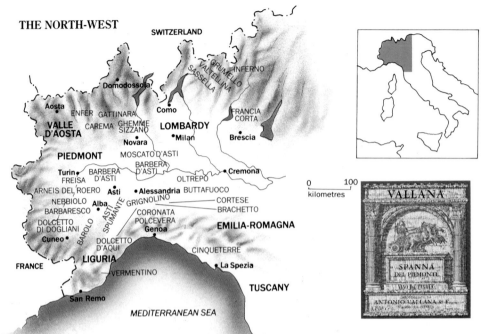

THE NORTH-WEST

Martini & Rossi, Fontanfredda, Cinzano, Riccadonna and so on.

Asti Spumante is often regarded as a sort of joke wine, something between a poor man's unsophisticated champagne and a white Lambrusco. This is a sad level of opinion as the quality controls exercised by the producers' consortium led by the famed Renato Ratti (producer of some of the very best Barolos and winner of awards for the artistic quality of his labels!) has ensured that, albeit in that medium-sweet taste bracket looked down on by wine snobs, these wines are an important part of the vinous spectrum.

This region includes the Valle d'Aosta, Lombardy, Piedmont and Liguria. It is the kingdom of the Nebbiolo. Wines from this red grape have won few friends in the UK, although interest in Barolo seems to be increasing. Produced south of the road connecting Alba with the upliftingly named town of Bra, these wines justify the word 'big'. All Barolos are aged in wood for two years followed by a year in bottle, riservas need four years and riserva speciales five, but even then another five years would be a sensible addition before opening. The firmness and tannic quality is uncompromising and it has been suggested that you open a Barolo when you send out the party invitations! Certainly the wine improves with double or even triple decanting – oxygen is definitely needed – and a riserva speciale from a good property, probably with the dialect word Bricco (ridge) in the title, can be one of the great events in anyone's wine drinking.

There is little still white wine of anything other than local interest except, perhaps, Gavi and Arneis. But the world famous Asti Spumante is produced in a large area of fairly dull hillside east of Alba and south of the town of Asti itself. Output is vast and the production method expensive although efficient, the volumes required to justify the millions of pounds of equipment that have to be installed are really only achieved by the giants, Gancia,

In addition to 'proper' Asti Spumante there is a vast amount of simpler sparkling Muscat-based wine produced outside the official Asti area. Labelled Moscato Spumante or Moscato Frizzante, the simple freshness of these inexpensive wines is often overlooked.

One tiny gem of a wine, Carema, is of interest alongside the vast production wines and the complicated Nebbiolo reds of the north-west. Production of this wine puts the Nebbiolo to its severest test, produced at around 760m above sea level alongside the main Turin-Mont Blanc autostrada in the foothills of the Alps. This can be a classic wine but it needs such an unlikely combination of good weather and good fortune to produce a good vintage that these are prized highly – and priced accordingly!

Interesting wines from the north-west

All the wines of the following producers listed alphabetically:

Ca' del Bosco, Ceretto, Fontanafredda, Gaja, Pio Cesare, Ratti

White wines

Arneis delle Langhe, Castello di Nieve – revival of the Arneis grape

Arneis di Canale, Cornarea – even better than above

Principessa Gavi, Banfi Strevi – cold fermentation, modern style, white

Gavi Vignavecchia, Marchese Paulo Spinola – expensive but worth it

Santo Stefano Asti – Ceretto owned, only vintage Asti produced

Red wines

Barolo Cannubi Riserva, Prunotto – needs nearly a decade of ageing

Barolo Riserva, Borgogno – major firm owned by the Boschis family

▼ *A bottling line at Ceretto, producers of good*

Barolo near Alba in north-west Italy.

Vigna Colonello, Aldo Conterno – another super vino da tavola red

Carema, Ferrando – almost the highest vineyards in Europe

Gagliassi Dolcetto d'Alba, Mascerello – surprisingly for Dolcetto, will probably age well

CENTRAL ITALY

This area comprising the regions of Tuscany, Marches, Umbria, Abruzzi, and Latium, is easier to understand than the north. Whereas there a minimum of 30 grape names need to be understood to begin to appreciate the wines of the area, in central Italy the Sangiovese is king of the red grapes and four names cover virtually the whole of red wine production, while three will do for whites.

CHIANTI

Chianti is the best-known wine of the area, possibly the best known of all Italian wines, and the success is due in a large part to the activities of Baron Ricasoll, the second prime minister of the then new nation of Italy. At his estate at Castle Brolio in the first part of the 19th century, he devised the basic formula or mix of grapes which is now enshrined in the DOC laws: Sangiovese 50%-80%, Red Canaiolo 10%-30%, and a mixture of white Trebbiano and red Malvasia also 10%-30%. However, apart from the obvious latitude within the formula, growers are allowed up to 15% by volume of 'corrective' wines which do not need to have been grown in the Chianti production area. The intention behind this very obvious loophole was to allow the mix to be strengthened in poorer years with wines from further south, traditionally, Apulia.

In addition, the regulations call for the wine to be held at least until 1 March after the harvest before being offered for sale; to be classed as Vecchio it must have a minimum of two years ageing and for Riserva, three. The upshot of the latitude in grape mix and in ageing is that Chianti can very between easy, young gulping wines, light ruby in colour through to darkly brooding violet-hued wine with oak overtones from the three years in wood. In addition to the areas of individual interpretation within the regulations for making the wine, the growing area is so vast, 100,000 hectares in Chianti Classico and another 300,000 hectares in the six surrounding Chianti districts for which Chianti Putto (Cherub) is the group name, that regional variations due to geography and geology are inevitable. To complicate the issue even further, the best modern producers are leaving out the white grape content (no longer necessary due to cooler fermentation) and are adding instead locally grown Cabernet Sauvignon and Merlot. In fact, the famed Tignanello from the forward-thinking Antinori family is now so far from the prescribed regulations that it has lost its DOC and has been 'demoted' to Vino da Tavola – a distinction it shares with many of Italy's other great red wines! Whatever the future for Chianti however, it will always have a place in history for it was here, in 1924 that the Chianti Classico consortium was formed, followed in 1927 by the Chianti Putto consortium. They were so appalled by the spread of pseudo-Chianti that they succeeded in having the growing areas defined by law in 1932 – a major step forward and the forerunner of the present DOC laws.

Recommended producers:
All the wines of the following producers, listed alphabetically:
Marchese Antinori, Badia a Coltibuono, Castellare di Castellina, Fattoria La Querce, Castello Vicchiomaggio and Capanelle – a

tiny production of superb wines from only 3 hectares
Riserva Ducale, Ruffino – best product from this giant producer
Riecine, Dunkley – an Englishman at work! Perfectionist wines
Castello di Volpaia – excellent Chianti, but see also Montepulciano
Castello Banfi – as well as their other regional wines
Rocca delle Macie – luckily widely available in shops and stores
Isole e Olena – tried and trusted true Chianti character
I Sodi di San Niccolo, Castellare – a non-Chianti Chianti, a super VdaT, superb!

BRUNELLO DI MONTALCINO

This most expensive of all Italian wines is the product of virtually one man. Ferruccio Biondi-Santi was that man, but the story begins with his maternal grandfather, Clemente Santi who, around 1850–70 was winning international prizes for his wines from Montalcino. He was intent on isolating the most suitable strain of the Sangiovese grape and to produce a wine from it alone, rather than the traditional Chianti 'mix' – Montalcino being in the southern part of the traditional Chianti area – but did not complete his work. This was left to the young Ferruccio who, at the age of 20, having fought with Garibaldi at the Battle of Bezzecca, returned and took up work with the vines on the estate at Greppo. He later added the Santi name to his own to continue the Santi tradition at Greppo and he was ruthless in his determination to produce not just a good, but an exceptional wine there.

Like most pioneers he was regarded with suspicion by neighbouring growers but, once he had completely isolated the strain of grape, which he called the Sangiovese Grosso, and once he had persuaded customers to pay prices which, for those days, were incredibly high, it took little time for the surrounding properties to want to charge similar prices. They quickly discovered, however, that the success of Biondi-Santi was not simply the growing of one grape variety, suitable though that variety might be. The success was due to a much deeper understanding of the many complex factors in growing, fermenting and maturing wines which we now take so much for granted but, for the Biondi-Santi family, was the result of a lifetime

of painstaking effort. Some of the rare pre-1900 vintages are occasionally drunk, a few are in the hands of collectors but most have been retained by the family. A bottle of 1945 Biondi-Santi Brunello di Montalcino costs around £300, while an 1891 fetched over £3500 at auction in the late 1970s.

As a footnote to the Montalcino story, Banfi, the biggest importer of Italian wine into the USA, decided to invest in property in Italy and called on Ezio Rivella, arguably Italy's greatest wine-maker, to prospect for suitable vineyards to purchase. His research showed that the best potential lay in the purchase of some 2800 hectares near Montalcino and there Villa Banfi created a vast modern winery. Huge by world, never mind by Italian standards, it is planting only about 10% of its holdings with the Brunello grape, 50% is Moscadello to make an inexpensive Asti Spumante competitor for export and the balance of 40% is Cabernet Sauvignon, Chardonnay, Sauvignon Blanc and Pinot Gris. Their products are being re-named Castello Banfi as they purchased the estate of Poggio alle Mura from the widow. This included a magnificent but dilapidated 14th-century castle on which Banfi have spent a fortune to convert

▲ *Large oak butts for maturing classic red wines at Castello Banfi, Sant' Angelo, Tuscany. Their total capacity in butts is 1.2 million litres!*

▼ *Inspecting and sampling maturing Brunello di Montalcino at Castello Banfi.*

▼ *Visible through the glass are two of the six enormous stainless steel* *storage vats at Castello Banfi. Each vat holds 60,000 litres.*

into a luxurious showpiece and entertainment centre for their estate.

To sum up the Banfi operation, Hugh Johnson put it thus 'Rivella, Italy's foremost oenologist, is using Montalcino as his base for leading Italian wine into the future.' The 21st century of wine-making is alive and well and living 17km from Montalcino in the San' Angelo valley!

The best producers, listed alphabetically
Altesino, Castello Banfi, Biondi-Santi, Castelgiocondo, Costanti, Fattoria dei Barbi, Tenuto Carparzo, Tenuta Il Poggione and Val di Suga whose reputation is growing.

VINO NOBILE DI MONTEPULCIANO

A few miles east of Montalcino is the ancient vine-growing area around the town of Montepulciano. Although now split into two sections by the canal and the autostrada this area has only one claim to vinous fame – for some strange reason it was one of the first four Italian areas to be granted the higher DOCG status. The 'G' is similar in concept to the mit Prädikat definition in Germany – 'with guarantee' is the literal translation. Quite why the authorities chose these wines to stand alongside Brunello, Barolo and Barbaresco is difficult to imagine. Anyway, as they have chosen the almost unknown Albana di Romagna as the likely fifth DOCG their credibility is sinking rapidly from sight.

There are no producers of Vino Nobile di Montepulciano about whom I am inclined to give an unconditional recommendation. The following, in alphabetical order, are probably safest:
Avignonesi, Fassati, Tenuta di Gracciano, Poderi Boscarelli and Polizano.

Other central Italian red wines of *supreme* interest are
Tignanello, Antinori – Sangiovese with 10% Cabernet keeping the SVdaT movement under way. Superb wine, relatively inexpensive
Sassicaia – see page 133

Other central Italian red wines of interest:
Morellino di Scansano Riserva DOC, Le Pupille – apart from Brunello this is the only other 100% Sangiovese Tuscan red
Coltassaia, Castello di Volpaia – a 'super' Vino

de tavola, oak-aged Sangiovese and Mammolo. Violets and blackcurrants!
Balifico, Castello di Volpaia – another superb SVdaT. This time a mixture of Italian grapes with Cabernet Sauvignon
La Corte, Castello di Querceto – 'SVdaT' again, this time a Chianti producer breaking the mould
Cumaro, Umani Ronchi – 'SVdaT' from the Marches on the Adriatic coast
Rosso Conero, Fazi-Battaglia – also own Fassati in Montepulciano
Rosso Conero, Umani Ronchi – one of the best Marches producers
Torre Ercolana, Bruno Colacicchi – Cabernet, Merlot and Cesanese, one of Italy's rarest and finest red wines. SVdaT of course
Rubesco di Torgiano Monticcio Riserva, Lungarotti – this DOC is the creation of just one man, Dr Giorgio Lungarotti, whose pioneering work includes Cabernet Sauvignon and Chardonnay
Carmignano, Villa di Capezzana – 'legal' Chianti-with-Cabernet due to introduction by Bonacossi family generations ago

FRASCATI

From the beautiful Alban hills to the south of Rome, Frascati is a completely different wine when drunk in the area of production. There the wines are slightly oxidised, the Malvasia and Trebbiano being treated more like a red wine than a white with the wine lying on the skins during fermentation. However, although storage in the chill cellars in the volcanic rock preserves the wine well enough, for travel it has to be made more like conventional white wine with cold fermentation off the skins to allow greater stability. Unfortunately, but logically, the character suffers.

From an ocean of ordinary (usually *very* ordinary!) Frascati, a few producers try to get away from the Bland de Blands approach. In front by a kilometre are Colli di Catone whose normal offering is unusually good and whose wine from the Colle Gaio vineyard, albeit expensive due to heavy pruning to reduce the crop by 80%, redefines the standards for Frascati.

The 'best bets'
Colli di Catone especially Colle Gaio
Fontana Candida especially Vigneti Santa Teresa

VERDICCHIO

Verdicchio dei Castelli di Jesi, to give it its full name, is grown around the town of Jesi about 16km inland from Ancona. This wine is characterised by the amphora-shaped bottles – and by little else! The bottle shape is a recently introduced marketing ploy, and the success is attested by the fact that more than a million cases of Verdicchio are consumed each year. The Verdicchio grape is not easy to grow as the vine only forms clusters at the growing points, necessitating careful pruning, and it is prone to mould and mildew. However, the active promotion and publicity carried out since the early 1950s by Fazi-Battaglia and the enormous investment in a huge modern winery has captured the American market.

Producers worth mentioning
Verdicchio dei Castelli di Jesi Classico, Fratelli Bucci, Co-operative Vinicola Produtti Verdicchio, Fazi-Battaglia Titulus – responsible for introducing the amphora-shaped bottle
M. Brunori & Figlio, Garofoli, Monteschiavo, Umani Ronchi.

EST! EST!! EST!!!

Some 80km north of Rome, between the sea and the Orvieto district is an area producing a wine famous only for its name. Est! Est!! Est!!! di Montefiascone (and the wine is a bit of a fiascone too!). The story of the name is worth attention though, even if the wine is not.
In AD 111, Bishop Johannes Fugger was travelling with his servant Martin from his Austrian bishopric of Augsburg to Rome for the coronation of the Emperor Henry V.
He enjoyed quality wine, so sent Martin ahead each day to find hostelries for overnight stops which served good wine, these he was to mark with the words 'Est' – 'here is'. On arriving in Montefiascone Martin was so impressed with the local wine that he is said to have repeated the Est three times complete with exclamation

marks. Bishop Fugger died in Montefiascone and is buried in the local church. Martin caused his epitaph to report that he died of a surfeit of Est! Est!! Est!!! In defence of their palates, the wines in those days were almost certainly from a branch of the Muscat family and would have been sweet. Today the ubiquitous Trebbiano together with Malvasia produces an indifferent, rather flaccid beverage.

Only two producers are worth their exclamation marks
Italo Mazziotti – from 25 hectares comes a well-made, distinctive , wine
Marchese Antinori – anywhere Piero Antinori goes, quality is sure to follow close behind, even in Est! Est!! Est!!!

ORVIETO

A few kilometres east of Montefiascone is the district of Orvieto in Umbria. This is another white wine that suffers from the vices of poor grapes, Trebbiano and Malvasia, and a region suffering from a history of big, medium sweet wines when the world has shifted to crisp dry whites.

One hope for the future is that Piero Antinori has taken an interest and, in addition to building a large winery, heads the growers' and producers' consortium, and he seldom involves his company in an operation without a successful future. However, the future is unlikely to be bright using the historic grape varieties and Antinori has already carried out tests with Pinot Blanc and Chardonnay grapes – that is probably what will bring the wines of this fertile area back into prominence in the future.

Notable wines
Castello della Sala, Antinori – Mr 20th-Century Italian Wine strikes again!
Le Cortone, Barberani – old family estate, recently modernised
Collicheva, Luigi Bigi & Figli – trying hard with other 'lesser' wines too, Vino Nobile di Montepulciano, Est!Est!!Est!!!
Decugnano dei Barbi – arguably the best Orvieto, but also a stunning noble rot sweet version

VERNACCIA DI SAN GIMIGNANO

One of Italy's wines of yesteryear, Michelangelo's favourite wine. Having been 'discovered' (mainly thanks to Sainsburys) and become popular for being different, it is now sadly changing to become more modern! The attraction lay in the uncompromising style produced by fermenting the Vernaccia grape on its skins to produce a rich golden, deeply flavoured, dry white wine, but it is now moving towards the cold fermentation light, bright, style shared by so many other white wines around the world.

Worthwhile producers

Azienda Agricola S. Quirico, Riccardo Falchini (Casale), Ponte a Rondolino

Other central Italian white wines of interest

Villa Antinori Bianco – an apparently modest wine but so well made

Chardonnay di Miraduolo, Lungarotti – SVdaT, un-wooded Chardonnay

Grattamacco, Cavallari – one of Tuscany's finest white wines

Pomino Bianco, Frescobaldi – Chardonnay, Pinots and Sauvignon grown at altitude. Pale golden, light and polished

SASSICAIA

Central Italy is also the home of Sassicaia, regarded by many as one of the five best red wines in the world, and regarded by some as simply the best!

In the 1940s the family of the Marchese Mario Incisa della Rocchetta acquired the Tenuta San Guido south of Livorno at Bolgheri and, although it was an area that had never produced wine of any interest or quality, the Marchese decided to plant Cabernet Sauvignon vines. This was a bold plan, to say the least – indeed many of his contemporaries in the area felt that the Marchese from Piedmont was completely mad. The soil of the area was reputed to give a salty taste to local wine, so to introduce one of the noblest of French grapes seemed totally without reason. Indeed, after planting a hectare of the vines at a site he hoped would be high enough to escape the salty breezes, the earliest products seemed to confirm what the local scoffers had predicted, the wine was awful! The Marchese lost interest and there the matter rested until years later, more from curiosity than for serious consideration, the Marchese tried a few of the older vintages and found that some held a hint

of potential greatness. This revived his interest and more serious work was carried out, although the wine was still thought of as their house wine and without commercial interest. However, he was keen enough to plant a further small vineyard called Sassicaia with Cabernet Sauvignon. This was at a lower altitude, but protected from the salty winds, and the wine of that vineyard showed even more potential. In the mid 1960s the Marchese's nephew, Piero Antinori of the great Antinori wine company, persuaded his uncle to release some of the 1968 vintage for sale outside the family. The wine proved a triumph and the total production of 7300 bottles was quickly sold. Moreover the foundation of the world-wide reputation had been laid. One of the supreme moments in the brief history of this wine came in 1978 when the prestigious magazine *Decanter* held a tasting of 34 Cabernet Sauvignon wines from 11 different countries (to many this was equivalent to a World Championship) and Sassicaia was voted unanimously 'the best wine of the entire tasting' and won an unprecedented score of 20 out of 20 from two of the five judges. This remarkable wine is aged in barrel for two years and in bottle for a further two years prior to sale, production is tiny, the 1000 case output of 1975 has risen to around 3500 cases a year, but this is the maximum that will be allowed from the 4.5 hectares now in crop.

Sadly this wine proves yet again that although historic wines may carry the highest DOCG classification, many of the greatest of Italy's wines only enjoy the humble status of Vino da Tavola.

TUSCANY SUPER VDaTs v DOCG

The Italian wine laws section (page 120) mentions the chaotic state of the laws in general and of DOCG – the comparatively recently introduced highest grading – in particular.

Of the six areas so far elevated to DOCG status three, Chianti, Brunello di Montalcino and Vino Nobile di Montepulciano are in Tuscany and this is the area most combative, most questioning of the whole legal structure. It is here that we find the greatest concentration of Super Vinos da Tavola, although they exist elsewhere. Other notable non-Tuscan wines are the superb 100% Cabernet Sauvignon 'Fratta' from Fausto Maculan in Breganza and, to a lesser extent, Venegazzù by Loredan Gasparini in Veneto.

Here are some of the best Tuscan SVdaTs with, wherever possible, the percentages of their grape varieties, although these may vary a little from year to year.

PN	=	Pinot Noir	M	= Merlot
S	=	Sangiovese	C	= Canaiolo
CS	=	Cabernet Sauvignon	MN	= Malvasia Nera
CF	=	Cabernet Franc	Numbers	= percentages

Alte d'Altesi	*Altesino*		70S	30CS
Balifico	*Castello de Volpaia*		70S	30CS
Brunesco di San Lorenzo	*Montagliara*			100S
Bruno di Rocca	*Vecchie Terre di Montefili*		70S	30CS
Ca' del Pazzo	*Caparzo*		50S	50CS
Cabernet di Miraduolo	*Lungarotti*			100CS
Castello Banfi	*Villa Banfi*	45CS	45S	10PN
Cepparello	*Isole e Olena*			100S
Cetinaia	*Castello di San Polo in Rosso*			100S
Coltassaia	*Castello de Volpaia*			100S
Concerto	*Castello di Fonterutoli*		80S	20CS
Elegia	*Poliziano*			100S
Flaccianello della Piave	*Tenuta Fontodi*			100S
Fontalloro	*Felsina Berardenga*			100S
Ghiaie della Furba	*Villa di Capezzana*	33CS	33CF	33M
Grifi	*Avignonesi*		85S	15CF
Grosso Senese	*Il Palazzino*			100S
Il Sodaccio	*Monte Vertini*		85S	15C
Il Sodi di San Niccolo	*Castellare*		90S	10MN
La Corte	*Castello di Querceto*			100S
Palazzo Altesi	*Altesino*			100S
Querciagrande	*Podere Capaccia*			100S
Sammarco	*Castello dei Rampolla*		25S	75CS
San Giorgio	*Lungarotti*		80S	20CS
Sangiovetto	*Badia a Coltibuono*			100S
Sangiovetto Grosso	*Monsanto*			100S
Sassicaia	*Marchese Incisa della Rochetta*			100CS
Solaia	*Antinori*			100CS
Solatio Basilica	*Villa Cafaggio*			100S
Tavernelle	*Villa Banfi*			100CS
Tignanello	*Antinori*		80S	20CS
Vigorello	*San Felice*		85S	15CS
Vinattieri Rosso	*Castelli/Anderson/Mascheroni*			100S

SOUTHERN ITALY

In this part of Italy – that is the regions of Campania, Molise, Apulia, Basilicata and Calabria – DOCs become less important. Those that exist tend to be for tiny production areas of purely local interest and much of the area is given over to producing a huge volume of wine for shipment to more northerly areas and even to other European countries, especially Germany. The wines have a strength and body that result from a sufficiency, sometimes even a surfeit, of sunshine.

Lacryma Christi del Vesuvio is a name quite well recognised, but, like Est! Est!! Est!!!, recognised more for the unusual name than for the quality of the wine. This non-DOC region produces both red, rosé and white with little uniform character. Mastrobernadino are serious producers of wine in the south and their red and white versions are probably the best examples

available – although barely worth the trouble to track down.

Behind the port of Taranto is a DOC called Primitivo di Manduria for the big, almost overpowering reds from the Primitivo grape, which is probably the ancestor of the Zinfandel – one of the most widely planted grapes in California. Otherwise the area is of little interest.

A quality red wine is produced in the Taurasi DOC mainly from the Aglianico grape. The best examples are from Mastrobernadino and the riserva, aged for four years in wood, probably still needs at least another two or three years before reaching its peak. Close by, although over the regional border in Basilicata, is Aglianico del Vulture another blockbuster from this powerful grape, but slightly lighter than Taurasi because it is grown at a greater altitude and on volcanic soil.

One producer can be recommended for the whole range of wines:

Mastrobernadino of Campania. The wines are
Greco di Tufa, an almondy white from the
  Greco, an ancient variety of grape
Fiano di Avellino, superlative very dry white
  from Fiano
Lacrimarosa d'Irpinia, Aglianico grapes
  producing delicate dry rosé
Lacryma Christi del Vesuvio, can be red, rosé
  or white, dry, sweet or spumante. Seldom
  exceptional
Taurasi, from the Aglianico grape, one of Italy's
  great red wines – especially from this
  producer

Other recommended wines

Locorotondo, Cantina Sociale di Locorotondo –
  probably the best white wine of Apulia.
  Beware of other producers though
Squinzano Riserva, Giuseppi Strippoli – good
  inexpensive wines from the Negroamoro
  (bitter black) grape
Aglianico del Vulture Riserva, Fratelli D'Angelo
  – the only wine of consequence from
  Basilicata from the Aglianico grape
Ciro Riserva, Antonio Librandi – Ciro can be
  red, white or rosé. This is the best of the
  reds
Ciro, Vincenzo Ippolito or Cantina Sociale
  Capara & Siciliani – of the whites these are
  the best. The grape is mainly the Greco
  Bianco which leads to confusion with
Greco di Bianco, CACIB – dry white version of
  Greco grape grown in the town of Bianco at
  the very toe of Italy
Mantonico, Umberto Ceratti – again the Greco
  Bianco but this time as the finest dessert
  wine of southern Italy

SICILY, SARDINIA AND PANTELLERIA

Sicily is proof that pumping money into
a depressed area sometimes produces results.
It may be inflationary economics but, in the case
of Sicily, the massive government grant-
assisted investments have shown amazing
results in what is, in vinous terms, a very short
period. The Salaparuta estate is internationally
famous for both Corvo white and Corvo red
wines. The estate of Giuseppe Tasca d'Almerita
produces excellent Regaleali red, a Regaleali
white containing Sauvignon Blanc and the
superb Rosso del Conte Riserva red, probably
the best Sicilian wine. The Gatinais winery

belonging to Adelkam SpA produces crisp but
full-bodied white Rapitala from the Alcamo
grape and well balanced, quaffable, Rapitala
red.

Heavy dessert wines from this area include,
of course, Marsala, and also Moscatos from
Sardinia, and Moscato Passito, a gem from the
tiny island of Pantelleria made from Zibibbo, the
Muscat clone.

Recommendations

The wines of the three Sicilian producers
  discussed in the text are all excellent
Corvo wines from Duca di Salaparuta
Rapitala wines by Comte Hugues de la Gatinais
Regaleali wines and, most especially, the Rosso
  del Conte from Tasca d'Almerita. In my
  opinion Rosso del Conte is one of Italy's best
  red wines

In addition the following are quite exciting,
especially the Pantellerians
Bukkuram, Moscato Passito di Pantelleria,
  Marco de Bartoli – deep, almost silky-rich
  unctuous sweetie. Muscat perfection
Cellaro Bianco delle Colline Sambucesi, VdaT –
  typically southern, slightly oxidised taste but
  interesting complex flavour
Terre Bianche, Sella & Mosca – a Sardinian
  VdaT from the Torbato grape grown around
  Alghero. Sound if a bit expensive
Cannonau, Sella & Mosca – another Sardinian
  VdaT, this time a red
Tanit Liquoroso, Agricoltori Associati di
  Pantelleria – wonderfully rich, pure, Muscat
  fortified (21.5%) dessert wine

SPAIN

GALICIA
Bilbao
FRANCE
RIBEIRO
R.Miño
VALDEORRAS
R. Sil
LEÓN
NAVARRA
AMPURDÁN
RIBERA
DEL DUERO
RIOJA
CAMPO DE BORJA
CATALONIA
TORO
R. Duero
Zaragoza
LÉRIDA
PRIORATO
PENEDÉS
ALELLA
RUEDA
CARIÑENA
R. Ebro
Barcelona
MENTRIDA
Madrid
TARRAGONA
PORTUGAL
UTIEL-REQUENA
R.Tajus
MANCHUELA
R. Guadiana
LA MANCHA
Valencia
R. Jucar
VALENCIA
ALMANSA
R. Segura
JUMILLA
ALICANTE
VALDEPEÑAS
YECLA
Alicante
CONDADO
DE HUELVA
R. Guadalquivir
MONTILLA-
MORILES
Seville
MEDITERRANEAN SEA
ATLANTIC OCEAN
JEREZ
(SHERRY)
MALAGA
Málaga

0   100   200
kilometres

Main wine regions

Label diagram

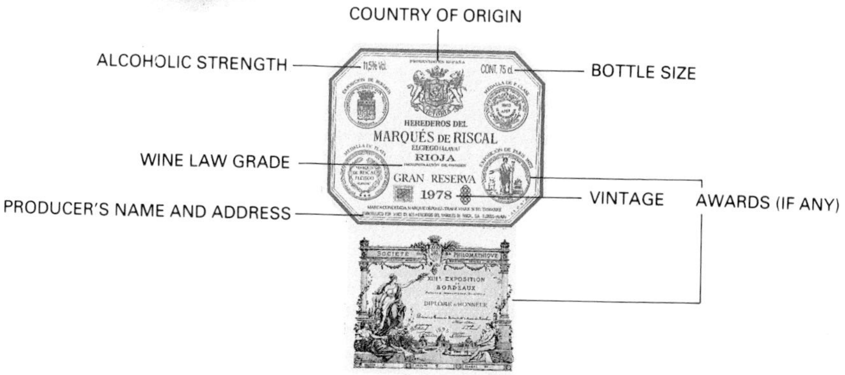

ALCOHOLIC STRENGTH — COUNTRY OF ORIGIN — BOTTLE SIZE

HEREDEROS DEL
MARQUÉS DE RISCAL
RIOJA
GRAN RESERVA
1978

WINE LAW GRADE

PRODUCER'S NAME AND ADDRESS — VINTAGE — AWARDS (IF ANY)

Spain claims to have the greatest area of land under vines – 1.5 million hectares – more than Italy, Russia or France which lie in second, third and fourth places respectively in comparison of vineyard area. However, it is symptomatic of many of Spain's difficulties in the production of wine that the output, averaging around 365 million cases a year, is fourth in total output and with an average of 20hl per hectare Spain is near the bottom of the production efficiency table. All major wine-producing countries achieve average figures between 35–70hl per hectare and even the less sophisticated producers (Cyprus, USSR etc) achieve around 25hl per hectare.

This can be explained by considering two important factors, both of which will have even greater effect now that Spain is a member of the EEC. First, agricultural methods are generally primitive, with a low degree of mechanisation. There has never been a shortage of suitable terrain for viniculture and so there has never been pressure to increase production from a given area, if more wine was required then more vines were planted. Compare this with the situation in Germany where the demands have resulted in intensive development and some areas now manage 10 times the output of Spain for a given area, 200hl per hectare versus an average of under 20!

Secondly, the generally poor soil and incorrect fertilisation combined with the growing of inferior strains of grape and hot sunny summers leads to the production of a huge volume of high strength, deeply coloured wines. These wines have hitherto found a ready market for blending in more northerly France and Germany and, to a very significant extent, the USSR. Unfortunately for Spain, times are changing and this demand for blending wines is falling each year.

The volume is still five times that of the export of bottled wines, but in terms of pesetas earned the two sections of the industry are now reaching parity. Moreover, the affluent middle-class which grew from the social structure of the Franco years is drinking less of the local wine bought in carafe from the cafe and drinking more bottled wines with pretensions to excellence.

Against this background and within the constraints of a fairly rigid system of wine legislation, some areas are taking great strides towards modernising their industry. They are concentrating on better, fresher, lighter wines, sometimes experimenting with newer grape varieties and looking towards an international market rather than the confines of the Iberian peninsula.

What of the historical background to this land of vines? Wine was certainly produced in Spain by the Romans but to what extent they brought vines or selected and improved on local varieties is impossible to guess. Sweet wines were being produced around Malaga at the time of the dawn of Christianity and it is probable that these wines were produced from the Muscat grape.

So great were the exports that some wine legislation became necessary to prevent Italian producers suffering from excessive imports – by AD 200 it is estimated that 20 million amphorae of Spanish wine had been taken to Rome and instructions were sent to the Spanish colonies foribidding the planting of new vineyards.

As elsewhere in Europe, there is no clue to what happened to the vineyards during the occupation by the Visigoths but, after AD 700, when the Moors captured the southern half of the country, many vineyards were rooted up or converted to the production of raisins, so it is reasonable to assume that these vines had been producing wine ever since the Romans left. Not all vineyards were destroyed during the Moorish occupation – they were enlightened conquerors and allowed the Spaniards to continue with both Christianity and wine drinking.

Gradually the northern Christians retook the peninsula and the place of wine in society was fostered by the activities of the Church – not least because wine is an essential part of the sacrament. In 1492 after the final defeat of the Moors at Granada all Jews were also expelled from Spain. Amongst the merchants and traders who flocked to fill the void left by the departing Jews were a number of Englishmen with an interest in the wine trade. Spanish wine had been exported to the British Isles for many years and the southern provinces especially attractive to the British traders who were to prove a major influence in the setting up of the sherry bodegas in the late 18th and early 19th centuries.

By the mid 19th century Spain already produced a significant volume of wine each year. Some of it would nowadays be regarded as, at best, poor, and most of it we would class as undrinkable. The heat of the Spanish summer

SPANISH WINE LAWS

Since 1979 the Consejo Reguladors (Regulation Councils) have been responsible to regional governments, although a central bureau – the INDO, Instituto de las Denominaciones de Origen – ensures that their activities conform to a national standard.

Basically, as in France, wine of a certain area must be from approved grapes grown within prescribed boundaries, there are controls on minimum alcohol levels – normally only 9° which would, in fact be difficult to get down to in Spain's abundant sunshine – and on Oeschle levels (page 102) for varying descriptions of sweetness. Conformity entitles the producer to DO status, the Denominacion de Origen, of which there are 40, including five provisionals, four specific denominations (one is for CAVA) and three provisional specific denominations.

The standards are rigorous although sometimes misplaced, as in the limitations on irrigation, but have, in the past, helped towards a raising of national standards of wine-making. The problem now is that with over 60% of the vineyards covered by the scheme it has become a statement of geography rather than of quality.

In each area wines can qualify for Reserva or Gran Reserva status. There is now a move towards national standardisation of the maturing periods needed for these titles although this is not yet complete, indeed, it seems somewhat pedantic to insist on similar periods of maturation throughout a country as large and variable as Spain.

The age of a wine is recorded from 1 January after the vintage, when it is regarded as becoming a second year wine. In effect wines are a year younger than they appear: a wine made in, say, September 1989 will become a three-year-old wine on 1 January 1991 – only 15 months after it was produced!

The following terms apply to red wines.
● *CVC* Contiene Varias Cosechas, wine produced from several vintages. Seldom exported.
● *Cosecha* normally followed by the year of the vintage, these are wines with little or no ageing
● *Vino de Crianza* these must be third-year wines (see above) with a minimum of one year in cask and a minimum of six months in bottle
● *Reserva* a selected wine with a minimum of three years ageing between cask and bottle, with a minimum of one year in cask. Cannot be sold until it is a fourth year wine.
● *Gran Reserva* a specially selected wine from a fine vintage. It must mature for a minimum of two years in cask and three years in bottle or vice versa. Cannot be sold until it is a sixth year wine.

Note
A some bodegas may mature their wines for longer if they feel it will benefit the wine.
B most of the essential information is carried on the back labels of Rioja wines, the rest are following suit slowly.

quickly causes oxidation of wine and the standard means of transportation, the skin of a pig turned inside-out and painted with pitch to make it watertight, could hardly have added a satisfying dimension to an already indifferent product.

Like most other wine-growing areas in Europe, Spain suffered the twin scourges of the 19th century: oïdium and phylloxera. Phylloxera had first been recorded in the Rhône valley in 1863 and was recognised in Bordeaux four years later. This caused an exodus of vineyard workers many of whom made their way south to the volume production area nearest to Bordeaux – the Rioja. Their arrival and the techniques they brought with them had a profound influence on wine production in the area and, although most returned to Bordeaux when production there was resumed and when phylloxera reached the Rioja, they left behind them methods of cultivation and especially of maturing that contributed significantly to the success of Rioja in international markets in the 1960s. Rioja wines were the first from Spain, apart from the wines of Jerez, to gain wide export acceptance and popularity.

In 1926 the Spaniards took their first steps towards controlling the growing areas and production standards by creating the first of the Consejo Reguladore systems of regional control in the Rioja. After Rioja came Jerez in 1933; Malaga followed in 1937 and so on right through to some of the smaller areas in the 1980s. These regulations control only the production of still table wines, all sparkling wines were controlled by a national standard set in 1972 but recently the authorities have altered this to a regional control system under a VDQS-type system that was introduced, as in Portugal, with a view to EEC membership.

There is one unfortunate regulation which has succeeded in holding Spain back in the production of quality wines – the almost universal banning of irrigation. This came about through copying too carefully AC laws applying in France where, for most of the growing areas, lack of water is the least of their worries. The Americans have shown the benefits to be gained from sensible water management and it is to be hoped that the Spaniards will modify this serious deterrent to good grape growth in arid areas.

When discussing the wine regions it is helpful to think of the near-square silhouette of Spain being divided into three horizontal strips and four angled vertical divisions.

The horizontal strips give us a northern third producing quality wines, some of which are among the best in the world; a central strip producing vast amounts of wines of very little merit except as cutting wine exports or for distillation; and a southern third of specialist wines: sherry, montilla, malaga and so on.

The vertical divisions leave Galicia out on a limb above Portugal. In some ways, the Galician wines duplicate those of northern Portugal and both come from areas with a similar Atlantic weather pattern. The next vertical division gives us Rueda and Ribera del Duero in the quality north – two areas already established, but with excitements yet to come; to the south is the central vinous desert of Estramadura followed by, in the southern third, the tiny and unimportant area of Huelva and the much more significant specialist area of sherry production around Jerez.

In the central vertical strip there are Rioja and Navarra in the quality north, then from the bulk-producing central region comes the ocean of production of La Mancha with tiny Valdepeñas as one exceptional outpost of quality and, in the south, the specialisations of Montilla and fortified dessert wines from Malaga. The last of our vertical divisions gives the excitement of Catalonia in general and Penedés in particular providing the signpost for the way ahead for Spanish wines. Below this northern quality area comes the lack of direction and identity of the six little known and less loved DOs inland from Alicante, followed by another vinous desert in the tourist-trap developments

around the coastline of the south-eastern corner.

In many areas the development of a particular region can often be traced to the activities of one particular company or group, for example Vega Sicilia in Ribera del Duero, and Torres in Penedés. This inevitably leads to more discussion of particular companies in the text than has been the case for other countries.

▲ *Horizontal presses being packed with grapes at Marqués de Riscal, Rueda. The grapes are pumped through the large overhead pipes to the presses (see also page 25).*

NORTHERN SPAIN

GALICIA AND LEÓN

The north-west province of Galicia has DOs for
Ribeiro and for Valdeorras and, due to their
similarities, includes the non-DO wines from
most of León as well. The climate and the
altitude of Galicia should allow for the
production of successful export wines especially
as the soils and the grapes are either identical,
or similar, to those across the border in
Portugal which earns a vast revenue. As with
the Minho, the red wines are an acquired taste
but the whites, especially those from the
Albarinho grape which produces Vinho Verde
just a few miles away, should have an excellent
potential. Sadly, this potential is unrealised.

Production levels in this corner of Spain are
very non-Spanish. They manage a much more
'European' level of 30–50hl per hectare, twice
the average for the rest of Spain. These levels
are also achieved in Valdeorras, the DO on the
eastern border of Galicia. Here the grapes are
the Palomino – the sherry producer in Jerez –
and the Garnacha, which is the Grenache of the
Rhône, and these two grapes, plus the
continental climate, are shared with the region
of León next door.

León does not have a DO for the majority of
the region, only the specialist area of Ribera del
Duero and the wines of León and of Valdeorras
DO which can be considered together as they
are so similar and are already making an impact
in the UK. The city of León is the home of the
unfortunately named, VILE private consortium
whose labels of Don Suero and Catedral de
León for their matured wines and Rey León for
the younger wines are already on shop shelves.
In Valdeorras the Co-operativa Barco de
Valdeorras are selling good quality simple red
and white wines from their bottling plant at
Orence under their El Barco label.

Few wines from Galicia are imported. Major
producers are Bodegas Campante and Bodegas
Chaves.

RIBERA DEL DUERO AND RUEDA

In the DO of Ribero del Duero the native grapes
are the reds Tinto Fino, a close relative of the
Tempranillo of Rioja; Garnacha and Albillo,
while Verdjo and Viura are used for white
wines. However, the greatness, both
historically and, potentially, lies in the approval

by the DO authorities of Cabernet Sauvignon,
Merlot and Malbec – the Bordeaux blend
constituents. This apparent laxity in the laws is
because Bodega Sicilia (page 146) was using these
grapes before the laws were promulgated.

In fact the developments which are taking
place seem to revolve around promoting the
Tinto Fino as a producer of classic wines –
the much hyped Pesquera for example – but it
seems very likely that growers will begin to
take fuller advantage of the potential of the
Bordeaux grapes before long.

At Valladolid is the Co-operativa de Ribera
del Duero Penafiel. Their reds are exported and
sometimes seen in specialist shops, the lightest
is simply called Ribera Duero, that labelled
Penafiel has a little oak-ageing while Protos
Gran Reserva is a huge, deep, wine best at
about ten years of age.

In Rueda, the DO south of Valladolid, is one
of the clearest pointers to the way things could,
or perhaps should, evolve in Spain. The
traditional white wines of Rueda, called Dorado
and Palido, were famed from the Middle Ages
but are reminiscent of sherry or the wines of
Montilla in that they are barrel-aged whites with
a covering of flor. These white wines can live
for 25 years and are undoubtedly interesting
historically, but that is of little use in an
international market demanding fresh, crisp,
young white wines.

Recently the Rioja bodega of Marqués de
Riscal has built a large, modern stainless steel
plant to produce modern-style whites from the
Verdejo grape with 10% Viura and these are
sold either with no barrel age or with just a
trace, quite a change from the old methods of
the area! Perhaps even more significant is that
Bodegas Marqués de Riscal are advised by the
eminent Emile Peynaud of Bordeaux and, with
his encouragement, they are producing wine
from 100% Sauvignon Blanc which is, the
Professor says, 'very good quality. Definitely
a pointer for the future. . . .'

Other modern excitements in Rueda are
attributable to the eminent Emile Peynaud of
Bordeaux. He advised on the well balanced
Rueda Superior, a 60% Verdelho wine from a
partnership between the local Sanz family and
the Marqués de Griñon who also grows
Cabernet Sauvignon grapes in sun-baked
Toledo and has them bottled by the Sanz'
Bodegas Castilla la Vieja. Definitely signs of
the times and rewarded with sixth place at a
tasting in the Wine Olympics in Paris in 1987.

▶ *Diagrammatic flow chart on the wall in the manager's office, Bodegas Farina, Toro.*

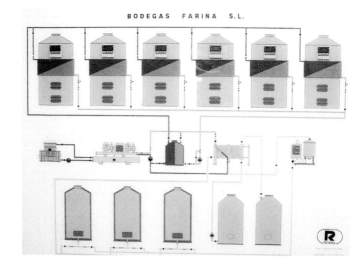

BODEGAS FARIÑA S.L.

▼ *A wine shop in Rueda. Notice the pyramid of plastic-covered 'take-away' bulk wine jars – the normal method of buying everyday drinking wine in Spain.*

◀ *The co-operative at Penafiel, Ribera del Duero. Their cellars are a labyrinth of tunnels in the limestone under the old hilltop castle.*

▲ *Maturing barrels of wine for the prestigious Protos label from the Penafiel co-operative.*

▶ *Lucia, daughter of Alejandro Fernandez who has worked such wonders at Pesquera, takes a days-old sample of the new vintage.*

145

BODEGAS VEGA SICILIA

In the Ribera del Duero is a property that stands alone in Spain, and possibly in the world, for the excellence of its wines: the Bodegas Vega Sicilia at Valbuena de Duero on the river Duero. Founded in 1864 by the family of Don Eloy Lecanda y Chaves, he planted the vineyards with imported Bordeaux varieties, Cabernet Sauvignon, Merlot and Malbec, in addition to Garnacha (Grenache) and a little Albillo. A mere 1000 cases a year come from the 300 acres and throughout the pressing and fermentation only the very best is good enough for this majestic wine. The unpressed, free-run juice is used alone and is fermented for about two weeks before maturing in Bordeaux barriques. A full ten years must pass before the sensational 'Unico' reserva is released for sale, but as storage space and barriques are limited, a junior member of the family, 'Valbuena' is released after a mere 3 to 5 years of ageing, depending on the speed of the wine's maturing. A comparatively recent development is the completion of cellarage under the vineyards which now allows a further two years of bottle ageing prior to sale.

The name of the property, incidentally, has nothing to do with the island of Sicily – these lands were described in an old census as 'pagos

de la Vega de Santa Cecilia' so the Sicilia is a corruption of Cecilia. Vega Sicilia's Unico and Valbuena point the way towards the production of great quality Spanish wines by others. Perhaps not as exotic but probably more economically priced, especially as the DO regulations for the Ribera del Duero, of necessity since Bodegas Vega Sicilia were there long before the regulations were drawn up, include Cabernet Sauvignon, Merlot and Malbec amongst the permitted grapes – the only DO in Spain so to do except for Penedés where red wines from these French varieties have swept all before them.

▼ *Arguably Spain's grandest bodega, Vega Sicilia in the Ribera del Duero – the valley of the river Duero – also produces some of the country's finest wines.*

▲ *The modest bodega of Pesquera contrasts with the grandeur of nearby Vega Sicilia. Both, however, have high reputations throughout the world.*

Recommendations

It goes without saying that Vega Sicilia wines are recommended as is Pesquera the overrated wine from Bodegas Alejandro Fernandez, sometimes called 'the Pétrus of Spain'.

Other good producers are

Bodegas Mauro
Bodegas Penalba Lopez – especially the
    Reserva Especial
Co-operativa Bodegas Ribera Duero – all
    wines, especially 'Protos' Gran Reserva

THE RIOJA

There is evidence that wines from this area were bought by the Cretans and, later, by the Phoenicians who navigated their small boats up the Ebro from the Mediterranean as far as Alfaro in the Rioja Baja. The Romans developed wine-making in the area and a large winery dating from about AD 175 to AD 225 has been excavated at Funes in Navarra. After the Romans left, here as elsewhere, it was the monasteries and other religious institutions that maintained the growth of vines for wine production to the end of the Middle Ages. In the 1500s the total production was of white wines, by the 1600s this had moved to six white wines to one red and on through the 1700s the ratio moved in favour of red wine. This shift was speeded by the preference of the French-born King Phillip V, the first of the Spanish Bourbons, and by the increasing export of wine to claret-loving Britain from the port of Bilbao.

Rioja, due to its geographical position had, for long, been difficult of access, but between 1790 and 1830 a road was built between Legrono and Haro bringing the sections of the Rioja into easier contact with each other and forging commercial links. It is only in recent times that a car journey to the Rioja has become less than exciting; before the construction of the motorway in the last decade the road was narrow and wound over mountain passes to reach the rgion.

In the 19th century several contacts were established with Bordeaux and at various times experts from Bordeaux came to the Rioja on a consultative basis. In 1868 Don Camilo Hurtado de Amezaga, Marqués de Riscal, availed himself of the services of one such expert whose contract had just been terminated due to a lack of interest on the part of Rioja growers and producers. Their lack of enthusiasm was the

Marqués' good fortune for the expert, Jean Pineau, designed a revolutionary new-style bodega at El Ciego which became the model for several others.

Following the Marqués de Riscal, the Marqués de Murrieta built his famous bodega on his estate, Ygay, near Legrono. This bodego still follows the precepts of the Marqués who advised his workers: 'Only three qualities are required to produce good wine – care, care and more care!' The caring Marqués had his bodega built on a hillside so that wine is not pumped, but falls under gravity from grape arrival at the top of the slope to bottling at the lowest level. The

bottling line is surely the slowest in Europe for the pressure on the liquid is only the height difference between the two floors!

The end of the 19th century was a time of rapid expansion for the Rioja and the methods of vinification and ageing were modelled on Bordeaux and the new-style Rioja bodegas. This froze these methods in a sort of time capsule for, after the ravages of odium and phylloxera had been overcome in Bordeaux they developed and amended their methods but in the Rioja, virtually cut off from the rest of the world, things remained unchanged.

By 1900 ten large bodegas had been

constructed, including that of Bodegas Riojanas at the railhead at Haro. Interestingly, Bodegas Riojanas still retain a small fermentation activity using the old Spanish and Portuguese system of lightly treading the grapes in 'lagos' or small tanks, running off the first fermentation, forking over the mass so as to maintain fermentation and running off the second wine which is then kept separate. The first wine is the most tannin-concentrated, while the second is considered best for alcoholic strength and colour. By careful blending of the two wines the optimum balance of all the required characteristics is controlled. This incompletely fermented wine

▲ *Early morning view of the plain of Rioja from the 1100m Portillo de la Herrera.*

is stored in cask through the winter months and carries on a slow fermentation throughout – producing what is thought to be the very optimum 'style'.

Legalisation, by royal decree, protecting the wines of the Rioja had been in operation since 1902, but 1926 saw the establishment of the first Consejo Regulador in Spain. Fairly inefficient at first, it was reorganised in 1944 and again in 1953 and now completely controls wine-making in the region. Although, for the first half of the 20th century, the wines of Rioja were almost unknown outside Spain, the boom in tourism and the increase in international interest in wine came at an ideal time for Rioja, with its soft fruity reds with warm oakey overtones at attractive, indeed cheap, prices. Indeed, it is greatly to the credit of the Consejo Regulador that there has been no slackening of quality or lessening of pride in the product even though giant conglomerates and international finance houses have built or bought huge bodegas. The only concessions that have been made have been those that, wisely, reduced the required periods of oak ageing in favour of bottle ageing to achieve a less hysterically woody wine.

White riojas are a mess. Not through poor quality but through not knowing where to go! The world is demanding every increasing quantities of fresh whites while the traditional white rioja is just the opposite – heavy, well oaked and slighted oxidised. This has resulted in a whole spectrum of new white wine interpretations being available from the excellent, youthful, 'European' commercial taste of the Marqués de Cáceres bodega, Enrique Forner's Cape Canaveral-like plant, right through to the uncompromising old-style majestic golden white from the Marqués de Murrieta. Experiments by some bodegas with medium-sweet blendings to compete with the German-dominated part of the wine market are best left unexplored and undiscussed.

Recommendations

Selecting Rioja bodegas to recommend is extremely difficult. To be fair, if one was to use the sort of quality criteria used for other regions, then virtually every producer would be included and the list would cover several pages. Yet to use tougher standards seems unfair. . . . I personally enjoy the wines of the following bodegas which are in alphabetical order, but I've added a few stars as well!

★	Bodegas Alavesas
★★★★	Bodegas Berberana
★	Bodegas Beronia
★★	Bodegas Bilbainas
★★★	Bodegas Campo Viejo
★★★★	Bodegas El Coto
★★★★	Compañía Vinícola del Norte de España
★★	Domecq
★★★	Bodegas Faustino
★★★	Bodegas Franco-Espanolas
★	Bodegas Lagunilla
★★	Bodegas Lan
★★★	Sociedad Vinicola Laserna
★★★★	Bodegas Lopez de Heredia
★★★	Bodegas Marqués de Cáceres
★★★★★	Bodegas Marqués de Murrieta
★★★	Marqués de Riscal – *improving*
★★	Bodegas Montecillo
★★★	Bodegas Muga
★★★★	Bodegas Ollara
★★★	Bodegas Federico Paternina
★★★★	Remélluri
★★★★★	Bodegas La Rioja Alta
★★★★	Bodegas Riojanas
★	Bodegas Santiago

Look out also for Don Darias, introduced by Tesco and now on other winelists – accurate taste and rock-bottom price.

NAVARRA

Lying between the Rioja and the Pyrenees, Navarra has a high volume output of wine using the same mix of grapes as Rioja but without their charm – or their export success! About 40% of the wines are rosé, and with reds over 55% of the production little white is produced. Vinícola Navarra at Las Campanas produce a very good 'Castillo de Tiebas' matured in French oak casks, well worth seeking out at its modest price. Bodegas Chivite export a large volume of wine, labels are Gran Feudo for the 4-years-old red, Cibonero for the 5-years-old and Parador for the big 10-years-old wine. However, the most prestigious producer in this area is Señorio de Sarría. The property dates back to the Middle Ages and has centuries of wine-making history, but it was re-modelled and re-planted in the second half of the 1950s by the construction magnate Snr Huarte. The matured wine of this estate, Vina del Perdon, is well balanced and oakey while the taste of their reservas owes something to Bordeaux in that they contain a small amount of Cabernet Sauvignon in addition to the usual Rioja mix of red grapes. The government-backed research station EVENA at Olite has done a great deal to up-grade the image of Navarra wines and the region's Department of Agriculture provides partial backing for the large, modern, CENALSA co-operative whose Agramont and Campo Nuevo labels are sold in the UK.

This is an area to watch closely. There is a considerable replanting programme, the Garnarcha is being replaced by Tempranillo and Viura, and some Cabernet Sauvignon as well.

Major producers
Bodegas Bardon, CENALSA, Julián Chivite, Bodegas Irache, Bodegas Ochoa, Bodegas de Sarría, Bodegas Villafranca de Navarra.

PENEDÉS

This area is really only half-Spanish. Self-assured in their Catalan identity, the area is showing the way with sparkling wines and quality table wines. It is an affluent area – the concrete jungle of the Costa Brava brings tourists in their season by the thousands; industrial Barcelona is rich enough to hold the Olympic games, while to the south is the up-market retirement area around Sitges. Legend has it that the vine was brought to this area by Gerion, the three-headed giant and enemy of Hercules but, legend aside, it is firmly recorded that there was a significant wine trade with Rome during the years of occupation, and that these wines were sweet – probably therefore from the Greek Malvoisie grape. After the departure of the Romans, in common with most of the rest of Europe, the vine and the production of the wine was maintained around monasteries. By the 19th century the area had a significant wine industry and was exporting around a million hectolitres by 1860. This, however, increased when the phylloxera bug blighted France and by 1880 had reached 7.5 million hectolitres. The affluence that resulted from this windfall allowed the huge financial investments necessary to create the sparkling wine industry in this area – now second only to Champagne in terms of quantity (and, some would say, quality) of output.

Twenty years ago the growers were happy enough with the standard range of Spanish grapes ratified by the DO: Parellada, the interestingly named Xarel-lo, Malvasia and Macabeo for the white grapes and Ull de Llebre (Tempranillo elsewhere), Garnacha Tinto, Monastrelle and Carinena for red grapes. In addition, outside the actual DO limits, Moscato grapes produced a great deal of dessert wine. The custom is to plant for sweet wines along the hot coast – Malvasia and Moscato – higher up, at around 200 metres, Macabeo and Xarel-lo are planted for sparkling wine production and higher again, up at about 700 metres, Parellada makes good crisp still table white wines. Nowadays the output is an average of about 1.5 million hectolitres or 165 million cases out of which 60% is of sparkling wine, about 20% bulk or bottled table wines and the balance is wine destined for distillation into Spanish brandy.

THE TORRES FAMILY
There have been momentous changes in Penedés in the last 20 years with many north European grape varieties planted alongside local ones. Spearheading this development has been the Torres family who now have Riesling, Gewürztraminer, Sauvignon Blanc, Muscat d'Alsace and Chardonnay for white wines and Cabernets Sauvignon and Franc, Pinot Noir, and Petite Syrah for the reds. These grapes complement the local white Parellada, Xarel-lo, Malvasia and Macabeo varieties and the red Ull de Llebre, Garnacha Tinto, Monastrelle and Carinena. The new varieties fit into the Torres range of wines in the following way:

White wines
● *Vina Sol* Parellada 100%
● *Gran Vina Sol* Parellada with Chardonnay
● *Gran Vina Sol Green Label* Parellada with Sauvignon Blanc and slightly oak-aged

To these has now been added Milmanda, a super 100% Chardonnay, oak-cask fermented and matured. Although barely out of the experimental stage, it did well at the Second Gault et Millaud Wine Olympics in Paris in 1987.

Red wines
● *Tres Torres* Garnacha and Carinena
● *Gran Sangre de Toro* a matured, reserva version of Tres Torres
● *Vina Magdala* Pinot Noir
● *Coronas* Monastrelle and Ull de Llebre
● *Gran Coronas* Monastrelle, Ull de Llebre and Cabernet Sauvignon
● *Gran Coronas Black Label* Cabernets Sauvignon and Franc and Monastrelle

◀ *Not good after a tasting! Looking down from the top of one of the Torres' 100-foot high giant stainless steel vats, Villafranca del Penedés.*

▶ *Cabernet Sauvignon maturing in barricas under the old winery at Raimat, Costers del Sagre.*

They also produce two rather less successful wines, Vina Esmeralda which blends Gewürztraminer with Muscat d'Alsace and Waltraud, named after Miguel Torres' German wife, using Riesling.

Undoubtedly the vindication of the Torres family's work was at the first Wine Olympics held in Paris in 1979 when Gran Coronas Black Label beat Ch Latour 1970 into second place. Seven years later, at the 1987 event, this wine came second in one session ahead of wines like Mondavi's Reserve and Stags Leap from Napa Valley in eighth and ninth places respectively.

Where the Torres family pioneered, others follow. For example, Jean Leon, a Los Angeles restaurant owner, has 112 hectares of Cabernet Sauvignon and 11 hectares of Chardonnay in Penedés. Little is seen in the UK as most goes to the USA.

Another first-rate property is Masía Bach. It was recently bought by Codorníu but continues with its excellent range of wines including the four-years oak-aged dessert wine 'Extrisimo' which some love and others hate.

Of the still wine producers of Penedés the following are the most reliable:
Rene Barbier, Ferret i Mateu, Jean León, Marqués de Monistrol, Masía Bach, Jaime Serra, Bodegas Torres.

SPARKLING WINES

These are a major product of the area – over 90% of all Spanish sparkling wines being produced in Penedés. When the true méthode champenoise is used these are called 'Cava' wines. Cava means a cave or cellar and refers to the fact that such wines have to be matured in a 'cava' for the sediment to settle out onto the cork for removal. The Raventos family, who had been making wine in Penedés since 1550, started the industry when, in 1872, Don José Raventos produced his first sparkling wine after a visit to Champagne. His lead was followed by Freixenet who are now second in output and, in third place, Segura Viudas – previously owned by Rumasa, but now, after their financial collapse, owned by a consortium of banks, and Marqués de Monistrol, recently bought by Martini and Rossi. All producers use differing mixes of Xarel-lo, Viura and Parellada, while some black content for added depth and longer life is usually supplied by Monastrelle. In rosés Carinena or Garnacha provide the colour.

The scale of operation of the sparkling wine producers is vast. Codorníu, for example, process more than a million kilos of grapes a day for the seven weeks from mid-September to end October. They have sales of three million cases a year, reserves of more than two years' stock and export a third of a million cases a year. The Spaniards therefore drink three and two-third million cases of Codorníu 'bubbly' each year – a ratio of 11:1 homes sales to exports! And Codorníu is not the only producer . . . !

Ever watchful of competitors, the champagne houses not only sue to prevent anyone else using the word 'champagne', they have now managed to obtain an EEC ruling protecting even the description 'méthode champenoise'. However, it is extremely difficult to differentiate between a good quality Cava and a normal NV from a 'genuine' champagne house – apart, of course, from the price!

Cava producers of repute
The Freixenet group – Conde de Caralt, Castellblanch, Segura Viudas, Canals & Nubiola and Rene Barbier; Codorníu; Masía

Vallformosa; Marqués de Monistrol. All these are in Penedés DO. In addition Vinas Jaime Serra of Alella DO and Raimat in Costers del Sagre DO are also good.

TARRAGONA

Amazingly, considering the world-wide fame of Penedés, the largest DO in Catalonia is actually Tarragona. In Victorian times 'Tarragona Classico' was a common tipple for those with a sweet tooth, and for centuries wines have been a major export of the ancient port of Tarragona. Today, however, with land under threat from hazelnut growers, this area is best known as a supplier of unassuming wines to supermarkets.

Two particular traditions do still exist though. One is the production of Rancio, the well-oxidised fortified sweet sherry-like wine often with extra sweetening supplied by adding

mistela. The other is the production of altar or sacramental wines. De Muller are prominent in this field and have held a sort of 'By Appointment' to successive popes since the 19th century.

LÉRIDA OR COSTERS DEL SAGRE

Near Lérida the Raventos family who were the first to produce Cava wines in Spain and are still the owners of the largest company, Codorníu, have replanted the vines around their estate of Raimat with classic international varieties.

▼ *The Rancio farm, Torres, Penedés. This unusual oxidised fortified wine is produced in north-eastern Spain and through to Narbonne in France.*

▶ *Two appropriate symbols: a bunch of grapes, 'raim' in Catalan, and a hand, 'mat', carved into the keystone of the castle doorway at Raimat.*

▼ *The mirror-glass wall of the grass-covered semi-underground bottling plant and maturation cellar at Raimat reflects the older buildings – equally revolutionary when constructed in 1919 – across the yard.*

In charge of operations is Daniel Pages Raventos, the great-great-grandson of the founder of Codorníu, Don Manuel Raventos Domenech. Daniel has enjoyed the now recognised training route for the sons and daughters of prominent European wine-makers: a degree at the Davis Campus of University of California, which, in his case, was followed by a Masters degree at Fresno.

Raimat has an almost ideal conjunction of climate, soil, money and technology. The wines reflect this, not only by their undisputed excellence but by their remarkably modest prices. Raimat Abadia Reserva set the wine world alight when, as an almost unknown wine, it won a Gold Medal in both the Cabernet Sauvignon class and in the Spanish Wines class at an important competitive tasting organised in London in late 1985 by *Wine* magazine. In both classes it beat Gran Coronas Black Label – the wine that beat the best of France including Château Latour 1970 on their own home ground (page 155).

The Abadia blend is 50% Cabernet Sauvignon

with 40% Ull de Llebre and 10% Grenache while their Chardonnay and Cabernet Sauvignon labelled wines have 80% of their respective varieties. In addition there is a sensational sparkling wine called, simply, Sparkling Chardonnay, which again sets standards of excellence few can match and, again, at a silly price. Drinking it blind with prestige and vintage champagnes tends to confirm suspicions that the prices for the champagnes are pretty ridiculous.

Daniel Raventos claims they have no need to look towards higher prices to damp down demand in the future. The estate is of 3200 hectares and only 1000 are planted with vines, they have no problem obtaining new vine stocks for they operate their own clonal selection and duplication and, best of all, owing Codorníu, they are not short of money.

They have recently received the ultimate accolade. The Spanish authorities have created a new DO area called Costers del Sagre which effectively has only one property – Raimat. Although this puts it in a special category like, for example, Château Grillet in France which is a single property having its own appellation, the parallel is probably closer to Italy where excellent wines – the Super Vino da Tavola's – simply don't need the protection of the wine laws around them. They are so good they sell in their own right. That's certainly been true for Raimat!

ALELLA

One other tiny DO area just north of Penedés and behind the Costa del Lager Louts is Alella. Of interest only due to the considerable improvements made by two companies and one co-operative. The outward movement of Barcelona and the attractiveness of the hillsides overlooking the sea has meant the loss of about a thousand hectares to bricks and concrete, but the remaining 400 hectares produce sound wines, especially whites. Parxet are the company and their Marqués de Alella wine has enjoyed several well-earned successes in international competitions.

The producers are – Alella Vinicola S Co-op, Parxet and Vinas Jaime Serra SA.

CENTRAL SPAIN

Returning to our mental map of Spain divided horizontally into thirds, we now come to the central strip: the land of bulk production of unremarkable wines. Plumb centre and to the south of Madrid is the vast area of La Mancha with the smaller area of Valdepeñas nestling to the south. Westwards, to the north-west of Toledo, is the DO of Mentrida while to the east, between La Mancha and the coast, there are six unremarkable DOs: Valencia, Utiel-Requena, Almansa, Jumilla, Yecla and Alicante.

Of the 15 million hectolitres produced – 165 million cases, there is little to be said, few

worthy or worthwhile products relieve the uniform averageness of this vast area. Only in Valdepeñas are there a few tiny pockets of interest.

In 1840, the traveller Richard Ford singled out just four wines of the Iberian peninsula as worthy of an Englishman's interest: Xeres, Oporto, Manzanilla and Valdepeñas. Of these only Valdepeñas is a table wine so, in those days, it was regarded as the best area of production. The name Val de Peñas means, literally, valley of stones and the sub-soil is conducive to good vine growth. The best vineyards are Los Llanos and Las Aberturas and the local expertise in fermenting was such that, in times past, grapes were brought from all over the vastness of La Mancha to this select area which seemed to hold the key to successful vinification.

The main red grape planted here, the Cencibel or Tempranillo as it is called elsewhere in Spain, is believed to descend from the Pinot Noir. Of the Valdepeñas wines most widely available Senhorio de Los Llanos Reservas and Gran Reservas have won many friends. Unusually it is a 100% Cencibel wine, for the custom in Valdepeñas is to blend Cencibel with a large proportion of the white Airen grape – often as high as 50:50 – to lighten a wine that might otherwise be too massively full. Even so, in spite of the 100% Cencibel content, this wine through the use of modern fermentation techniques is light in colour and surprisingly fresh after maturing for seven years. It has a deep, perfumed nose and a fine spread of taste.

With one exception only Valdepeñas produces wines of sufficient quality to be worth recommending – and of the 36 firms in Valdepeñas town itself and the three based in nearby Santa Cruz de Mudela only one has made any impact internationally: Bodegas Los Llanos – in addition to the excellent Reservas

and Gran Reservas already mentioned, in 1987 they released a white wine, Armonioso, made from the first pressing of Airen grapes.

The exceptions to the rule in La Mancha are the white and red wines labelled Castillo de Alhambra, both are good quality, simple, wines and *very* inexpensive.

THE CO-OPERATIVES

These are a feature of Spanish wine production, especially in the anonymous central areas. The normal system is for a central winery to be built with government funds or grants and for local farmers to be contracted to supply fruit. They are then paid on delivery and will receive a further share of the profits after expenses have been deducted. The system is far from perfect as there is little incentive for farmers to improve their crop quality, but, with over 450 of these co-operatives working in the central area alone, they are a feature of Spanish wine production that cannot be ignored. The worth of each co-operative is, to a great extent, dependent on the wisdom and enthusiasm of the president of the association – normally a grower himself but also a man of substance and local standing – some are keen to be up-to-date but others are merely time-serving office holders. Moves are being made to find systems that reward quality rather than quantity but changes are slow. However, the real benefit of this arrangement is that without centralised modern equipment for vinification the methods would be primitive and would lack the essential ingredient for these warm latitudes: temperature-controlled fermentation.

Wine from this area is known in the UK – Bodegas Schenk market the Don Cortez brand red and white wines which are the best known ones from this area.

Another interesting development in this region is the experimentation with maceration carbonique for red wines. This could, indeed should, have a very significant benefit in the production of lighter, fruitier, red wines from the rich and heavy local grapes.

Finally, we must mention the Marqués de Griñon (page 142) who is growing Cabernet Sauvignon at his Toledo estate. Vinification takes place further north, but, with advice from the great Professor Emile Peynaud of Bordeaux, he is producing very fine wine. Perhaps de Griñon could become the Torres of the central area!

THE SOUTH OF SPAIN

Apart from sherries which are discussed next, no significant table wines are produced except for a tiny DO, Condado de Huelva, which is mainly of historic interest. The first Spanish wines to be mentioned in English literature are those of Lepe on the coast west of Huelva. Chaucer's Pardoner in *The Canterbury Tales* says

Now keep ye from the white and from the red
And namely from the white wine of Lepe
That is to sell in Fish Street or in Chepe
This wine of Spain creepeth subtilly.

SHERRY

Sherry has had an image problem. For too long it has suffered a devalued reputation through confusion with non-sherry sherries and with its sweet-sticky old-maid associations. There was too much cheap sherry around for the quality products to shine through. Although times are changing and sales are improving it must still infuriate producers of the 'real thing' that British companies, some of whom are themselves large producers in Jerez (the centre of the Spanish sherry industry), can import grape must from Cyprus which, by adding water and fermenting, they can still call 'sherry'. This situation will probably be resolved in 1995 when the use of the name comes up for review by the EEC Commissioners but, until then, these lowest common denominator products can continue to masquerade as the genuine article.

Sherry comes only from Jerez – the very name is an anglicisation of Jerez – although originally in the 16th century it was known as 'sack' probably from the Spanish word 'secco' for 'dry'. As with the production of other fortified wines the English were instrumental in developing both the product and the international trade and names like Croft, Duff-Gordon, Harvey, Sandeman, Williams & Humbert, Wisdom & Warter, are all testimony to the British presence in Jerez in the 17th and 18th centuries.

Jerez de la Frontera, the central town of the region, lies inland about 15km north-east of Cadiz and 15km south-east of the coastal town of Sanlucar de Barrameda. The fertile headland which forms the major part of the triangular growing area is a mixture of three soil types. The best is the chalky *albariza*, also used are the clay-based *barro* areas, while the inferior sandy *arena* soils are being returned to vegetable production. The Palomino grape accounts for 95% of the vines and on the albariza produces, in spite of high temperatures, a stylish, crisp wine well suited to development into austere fino sherry – the ultimate aperitif! The remainder of the plantings are of Pedro Ximenez (PX) or Moscato, both sweet grapes and both used as additives to provide sweeter styles of sherry.

After picking and pressing, which used to be carried out in the vineyards but is now done in modern, purpose-built vinification centres, the first-run juices are fermented in stainless steel. The rest of the wines go for distillation – into brandy for the fortification process which comes later. The wines are pumped into American oak casks (called butts) of 500 litre capacity for their slow secondary fermentation and ageing which exhausts all the remaining sugar. This process is accelerated by leaving over 15cm of air space and a loose bung so as to promote oxidation.

In these butts there occurs the remarkable event to which sherry owes its individuality, the development of flor. This is a naturally occurring skin of yeast which, infuriatingly, appears in profusion on the surface of some butts while being meagre on others. As this skin limits the amount of oxygen available to the wine, it follows that after some months there will be butts of light-coloured, barely oxidised wine while those with a sparse covering of flor will be darker and more oxidised. There is no logic to the development of flor, the same grapes picked from the same vineyard on the same day and vinified together can give totally different results. For this reason the butts are assessed after about six months by the capataz, the cellar-master. Those butts with darker-hued, more strongly oxidised wine have sufficient fortifying brandy added to kill off any further flor development and become olorosos. The butts with the lighter wines are given less brandy and are destined to become finos and amontillados.

The classification is, however, more complex than simply dividing finos from olorosos for each butt is marked according to potential quality. Finos are marked with a palm symbol, the more 'palmas' the higher the quality, while olorosos are awarded 'rayas' – a single stroke of chalk on the end of the butt – and the fewer rayas the better the wine.

At this point the wines are ready, depending on their quality, to be introduced into one of the company's solera systems. This method of ageing wines and brandies is particular to Jerez and consists of a series of tiers of butts of increasing age. Wine for bottling is drawn from the oldest, the 'solera', with only about a third of the quantity being removed from any one butt. This is then replaced by an equal quantity from the next oldest tier in the 'criadera' (nursery) and the replacement goes on until the youngest wines are brought into the system. However, over a period of time it is possible to detect marginal changes in the overall quality of an individual solera – which may contain as many as 50 butts – and if there is a slight deterioration this can be corrected by 'boosting', by adding a small quantity of very fine old sherry. Alternatively, the wines used for bottling may be 'improved' with old sherry and the solera left to continue its own evolution.

The source of these old, high quality, sherries are the almacenistas, the stockholders, who age these top quality products, sometimes from single vineyards and often in individual soleras, for this express purpose. Rarely are these available for retail sale and, if seen, should be snapped up for they represent the pinnacle of sherry quality.

At this stage all sherry is bone-dry. To produce sweeter styles of wine various combinations of invert sugar and three different dulces – sweet wines from the PX and Moscato grapes – can be added. The complete spectrum of sherry styles, from driest and lightest to fullest and sweetest, is:

● *Manzanilla* fino which has been matured at Sanlucar de Barrameda. Strangely, the sea-salt air *does* seem to add a salty tang to the resulting wine. The palest and most delicate style of all.
● *Fino* best drunk chilled to savour the complex yeasty/nutty nuances. Only rivalled by champagne as the ultimate aperitif.
● *Manzanilla Pasada* a rarity. This is manzanilla which has been left in its individual cask until the flor has died off. Darker in colour, it has a greater concentration and pungency of taste. Sometimes left to mature into a manzanilla amontillado.
● *Fino Viejo* a fino corresponding to Manzanilla Pasada. This, too, can develop into a fino amontillado given time.

These four wines are invariably sold bone-dry and with an alcohol level of 15.5–17%.
● *Amontillado* literally a-montilla-do, in the

▼ *An illuminated cask of maturing sherry with a glass end to show the skin of flor across the surface of the fino and the air space over the wine to promote oxidation.*

▼ *The 'first sample' room at Gonzales Byass. The 'bird-table' has a candle so the cellar master can see the wine's colour without other light interfering.*

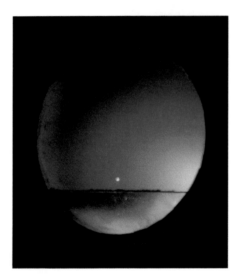

style of Montilla. Amber coloured with more body than the fino family. True amontillado will be dry, but most commercial blends are sweetened to provide a sort of medium-sweet level between fino and cream. For the real thing look for dry or secco on the label. 16–18% alcohol.

● *Palo Cortado* an unusually 'mixed-up' sherry. One which started by developing a flor and progressed towards fino/amontillado but somewhere along the road changed direction towards oloroso style. Normally kept separate from the solera, it is dark gold in colour with a luscious 'bite'. 18–20% alcohol.

● *Oloroso* some dry old olorosos can be found which will be full of richness and flavour to balance the dryness, but most are sweetened into amorosos by the addition of PX. 18–20% alcohol.

● *Pedro Ximenez* rarely, some sherry is made solely from sun-dried PX grapes. Intensely sweet and very dark. Up to 20% alcohol.

162

◀ 'La Constancia
Bodega' at Gonzales
Byass, with sherry butts
dedicated to the Spanish
royal family.

All these styles are, with the exception of the sweetened amontillados, traditional and natural products of Jerez. Now we come to the 'manufactured' styles.

● *Pale Cream* marketing hype. The salesmen said 'Pale dry sherry is sophisticated, nut-brown sweet sherry is auntie's tipple, so let's make a sweet *pale* sherry – sweet yet sophisticated-looking.' Produced by sweetening pale fino with young wine and invert sugar. Croft's Original was the first in the 1970s.

● *Cream* a British invention for the sweet British palate. Developed and popularised by Harveys with their branded Bristol Cream, others quickly climbed aboard the bandwagon. Oloroso with intensely sweet and dark dulce wine from sun-dried PX and Moscato grapes.

● *East India* takes the name from the Madeira-like habit of sending the sherry on a long, hot, journey to accelerate ageing, now seldom seen.

After the over production of the 1970s, producers embraced Plan Jerez in 1982 which set about reducing the area under vine, reducing the volume exported from a maximum of 40% of stock to around 30% and, finally, establishing minimum prices so as to provide a sensible cash return to attract fresh investment. After all, there is no logic in the price of an exceptional fino being a quarter of the price of good white burgundy or of a superb oloroso costing a fraction of the price of a good Madeira. Plan Jerez has been so successful that, although the four-year plan period ended in 1986, it is still effectively in action through the continuing voluntary agreement of the major producers.

It is now easier to isolate the imitations and the cheap blends and to provide quality drinks with a tale to tell, but those quality drinks must be treated fairly and presented correctly. Just as it is fundamental not to shake a good claret and not to serve white wine at room temperature, so with sherry there are very clear Do's and Don'ts.

● DO ensure that all sherries, but most especially finos, are fresh. Producers should long ago have ceased using reusable corks. Fino must be young and freshly opened. If ever a wine needed a sell-by or an open-by date, fino is it! Half bottles are becoming more available and vacuum-sealers also help solve the problem – which is tending to increase rather than diminish as the strength of finos' protective alcohol has reduced from the 20% current just 10 years ago to nearer 15% nowadays in the drive for lighter wines. And don't discount the spread of drink-by dating. Some supermarkets, so far Tesco and Safeway, are using dated labels and the movement will probably spread.

● DO chill finos. Mild fridge temperatures will be quite suitable – and a lump of ice in the sherry is no substitute for proper chilling as it dilutes the taste!

● DO look for special sherries. Explore almacenista sherries, single vineyard fino, dry old olorosos, manzanillas, palo cortados – the range is wide.

● DON'T serve sherries in unsuitable glasses. Copita-shaped glasses no more than half full are correct. There is no excuse for still using those dreadful concave-sided Elgin glasses and schooners filled to the brim, they are as inappropriate and as detrimental to wine enjoyment as are the awful saucer-shaped glasses still sadly used for champagnes and sparkling wines.

● DON'T go for cheap sherries. Sherry is already cheap in relation to the effort involved in production and the considerable quality improvement you will get for spending a little more is well worthwhile.

Recommendations

This list of 25 recommended quality sherries and their producers is by no means exhaustive.

Manzanilla – Barbadillo, La Gitana by Hidalgo, Valdespino

Manzanilla Pasada – Principe or Solear by Barbadillo, Herederos Argueso

Fino – Don Zoilo by Diez-Merito, Tio Pepe by Gonzales Byass, Puerto by Burdon, San Patricio by Garvey, Tio Mateo by Marqués de Real Tesoro, La Ina by Domecq and Inocente single vineyard fino by Valdespino

Amontillado – Amontillado del Duque Seco by Gonzales Byass, Fino Viejo Amontillado by Findlater

Palo Cortado – Harveys, Sibarita by Domecq, Dry Old Palo Cortado by Sandeman, De Soto, Croft

Oloroso (dry) – Apostoles Abbacado by Gonzales Byass, Dry Old Oloroso by Garvey, Rio Viejo by Domecq, Ochavico by Garvey

Oloroso (sweet)/Amoroso – Matusalem by Gonzales Byass

Pedro Ximenez – Venerable by Domecq

Almacenista sherries – Emilio Lustau

PORTUGAL

VINHO VERDE

TRAS OS MONTES

MINHO

UPPER DOURO

Oporto

R. Douro

BEIRA ALTA

DÃO

BAIRRADA

BEIRA LITORAL

BEIRA BAIXA

ESTREMADURA

RIBATEJO

COLARES

BUCELAS

MOSCATO DE SETUBAL

ALTO ALENTEJO

Lisbon

Setubal

CARCAVELOS

BAIXA ALENTJO

RD wine regions

ALGARVE

Faro

0   50

kilometres

A wine-producing country at the crossroads. In area, by far the smallest of the 'top ten' wine countries, yet sixth in the output league table with an annual production of some 10 million hectolitres or 1,330 million bottles, of which the home market takes around 75%. Of the 25% exported, almost all is accounted for by port and semi-sparkling rosé wines which sell well in less sophisticated markets, of which the UK is one. Any future expansion in exports, and wine is the single most valuable commodity in the Portuguese economy, must come from an increase in sales of 'fine' wines, which presents two problems.

The first is that Portuguese revere age in a wine and this seems to be more important to them than taste or flavour. The majority of the red grapes they use have a very high acid content, so producing very astringent wines when young. Ageing mellows the wines and they certainly become smoother, but there is little grapiness left, a distinct lack of fruit. To try to capture a reasonable share of the international market for quality table wines would require a replanting and restructuring programme as radical as that undertaken by the Bulgarians in the late 1960s.

The second problem facing the Portuguese is their entry into the Common Market. Falling in line with EEC regulations on wine production is forcing significant changes in their traditional methods. They have never been committed to the rigid system of regional types of grape in defined permitted areas. Those areas that have been defined have been either small, specialist areas or regions so huge that regional variations in style and quality were normally overcome by blending. This led wine companies to buy from a large number of sources, some not even in the area, and to ensure consistency of taste by skilfully blending the components into a regular house style – their interpretation of what the regional taste should be like.

In the Minho area, where vinho verde is produced, producers are starting to emphasise that their best wines are estate bottled – but the rest of Portugal has few named properties and the majority of these are recent developments. For this reason, it is important to know the good producers in any area rather than the good properties. Such companies as have gained an international reputation for quality will be mentioned in the geographical review which follows rather that listed separately.

Portugal has long had a system of defining the boundaries of established production areas – they were well ahead of the French in this respect – but the conservatism of the industry, together with industrial and commercial development in some areas, means that the older growing areas no longer present a full picture of Portuguese wine production. The ten Região Demarcada areas are, from north to south: Minho, Dão, Douro, Bairrada, Bucelas, Colares, Carcavelos, Setúbal, Algarve and the island of Madeira.

In addition, with entry to the Common Market requiring defined areas for all wines with quality aspirations, five new regions have been created in a sort of embryonic VDQS arrangement. These new regions will not have local official bodies controlling the quality of the wines and will not use a paper cork seal as do the other Demarcadas. They will, nevertheless, ensure that the areas are defined and the grape varieties are controlled so as to raise production standards and the international status of the wines. These new areas cover the whole of Portugal and include all wines that are not already part of a Região Demarcada. They are, from north to south, Região de Tras os Montes, Região das Beiras, Região de Estremadura, Região do Ribatejo and Região do Alentejo. We will now look at the regions in detail, travelling from north to south.

THE WINE REGIONS OF PORTUGAL

MINHO RD

The land of green wines – the 'green' referring to the youth of the wines, not the colour. This is the most export-oriented region but surprisingly, more red than white wines are produced. The reds are of a mouth-numbing acidity with a pronounced Rhône-earthy taste – wines seldom drunk twice. However, the local red grapes from which these wines are made have produced commercial success in the form of Mateus rosé and Lancers rosé. Development of white vinho verde, however, has been so rapid that now Mateus and Lancers are both produced outside these northern growing areas.

At the cheaper end of the vinho verde market wines are fermented through to stability and then mildly sweetened and carbonated and this is the method used by the mass-market rosés as well. Producers of better-quality vinho verdes ensure that the 'spritz', the columns of tiny

PORTUGUESE WINE LAWS

Almost non-existent. There are ten Demarcated Regions but, of these, three near Lisbon have almost disappeared and three others only apply to fortified wines.

EEC membership is forcing Portugal to accept the standardised European format based on Appellation Contrôlée but it will probably take years to organise, especially in some of the remoter rural districts.

bubbles of carbon dioxide, result from a genuine malolactic fermentation in the bottle, while the best wines of the region are now estate bottled in the main using the single most prestigious grape of the area, the Alvarinho.

One tiny area of individual non-vinho verde fizzy wines is around the town of Monção where the Alvarinho and then aged in wood to produce dry white table wines named after the grape – Palácio de Brejoeira is the best.

When selecting vinho verdes try to avoid the branded wines which tend to be sweetened, carbonated wines. Look for individual estate-bottled wines with names starting with Solar, Quinta, Casa or Casal, Paco or Paxo, as these will probably be from members of the APEVV – the producers' and bottlers' association devoted to improving the international image by marketing 'genuine' vinho verdes.

Interesting Vinhos Verdes
Paço do Cardido – owned by forward-thinking ultra modern João Pires
Paço do Teixeiro – owned by the excellent Champalimaud company
Palácio da Brejoeira – rare Alvarinho white (see text)
Quinta da Avelada – estate wine of popular Avelada branded version
Solar das Bouças – founder member of vinho verde producers' association

REGIÃO DE TRAS OS MONTES

This region is only of historical interest because Mateus Rosé was originally produced by the Sogrape giant outside the city of Vila Real. Production has now moved to Bairrada and uses grapes indigenous to Dão and Douro, although mainly grown north of the Douro.

DOURO RD

Best known as the home of port, yet also producing a quantity of both red and white table wines. The whites have a tendency to flabbiness, but some of the reds are outstanding. Two properties are worthy of note: Quinta de Pecheca and Quinta do Vale de Meao. At the former, 'foreign' varieties like Riesling, Cabernet Sauvignon, Sauvignon Blanc and Gewürztraminer are planted alongside local varieties and the red, combining Cabernet Sauvignon with local grapes, has a soft and flavoursome character. Since 1952 Quinta do Vale de Meao has produced the now legendary Barca Velha red in especially favoured years. This has been described as Portugal's Vega Sicilia and production rarely exceeds 4,000 cases, marketed by A. A. Ferreira, the largest seller of bottled port and owners of the estate.

Good Douro wines
Barca Velha – from Quinta do Vale de Meao (see text), but also –
Esteva – a sort of 'second label' Barca Velha. Excellent value – and
Casa Ferreirinha, Reserva Especial – all from Ferreira Port producers who market Barca Velha, this another 'second wine'!
Evel Garrafeira – Real Companhia Vinicola do Norte de Portugal. . . .
Quinta do Côtto, Grande Escolha – the Champalimaud company again

REGIÃO DAS BEIRAS

This encompasses three separate regions in Beiras. Beira Litoral runs down the coast from south of Oporto and encircles the important RD area of Bairrada while the more extensive RD area of Dão is in both the Beiras, Alta and Baixa.

BAIRRADA RD

Only granted full RD status in 1979, although a producer of quality white and red wines for centuries. The reds from the Baga grape have a lighter texture and more fruit on the palate than other Portuguese reds, but they, too, repay long ageing to fulfil their considerable potential.

This area also contains the remarkable Bucaco Palace Hotel where both red and white wines from the 15-hectare vineyard are aged in barrel in the cellars under the Disneyland style hotel. At their best, after decades, they are necessarily expensive!

For well matured Bairradas it is important to look for the wine companies' name, because before 1979 the word 'Bairrada' was normally missing from the label. Alianca, Imperio, São João and, especially, Caves do Barrocão are names to look out for, whilst there is one important estate, Quinta do Riberinho where excellent reds are produced as well as a fine méthode champenoise sparkler. Caves Alianca are the largest of the several other sparkling wine producers.

Bairrada bargains

Bairrada Reserva, Caves Acacio – normally sold after 5 years' ageing

Bairrada Mealhada – from the reliable Adega Co-operativa de Mealhada

other wines from producers mentioned in the text

DÃO RD

Named after a small river which more or less bisects this large growing area on its way to Coimbra and the sea, and confusingly similar in pronunciation to Dow as in port. The best known growing area outside the Minho, 20,000 hectares under vine are mainly of red grapes – the Douro varieties of Touriga Nacional, Alvarelhao and Bastardo, and the Jaen and Preto, particular to the Dão, produce the typically earthy, astringent wine which softens with age but gains nothing in taste. The Federacão do Dão supervises the production of all Dão wines, even those transported and matured outside the region. White wines are rather flat and one-dimensional – a characteristic of hot-country wines produced by unsophisticated methods and equipment. Typically whites are also cask aged which does little to improve their freshness or fruitiness.

Red wines must be held in cask for a minimum of 18 months prior to bottling, but more often they are held for a period of years and are sold when they qualify as Reservas or Garrafeiras – 15 years would be a good period of ageing for a top-quality Dão.

Dão delights

Conde de Santar – from Carvalho, Ribeiro & Ferreira, the only single estate Dão produced

Terras Atlas – good (by Dão standards) wines from J. M. da Fonseca

Caves Velhas – well-made Dão from the Bucelas wine specialists

Alexandre Magno – inexpensive examples from Caves do Casalinho

REGIÃO DO ESTREMADURA

This new region stretches from halfway between Oporto and the Tagus right around the Tagus estuary and inland along the course of the river. Although the largest wine-producing region of Portugal there is little of note, the wines being mainly used for blending. One exception is Quinta da Folgorosa, one of the few single estate wines in this area but Dom Teodosio's Casaleiro and Antonio Bernardino's Garrafeira Reserva Particular are fine wines in their own right even though a product of the blender's art. There are no other wines from this region worth mentioning.

CARCAVELOS RD

Sadly this has almost disappeared, swallowed by the commercial and residential development between Lisbon and Estoril.

BUCELAS RD

In the hills north of Lisbon. Known for its matured white wine from the Arinto grape. Bright yellow in colour with the slightly maderised overtones of a cask-matured white, they are somewhat unexciting, although Caves Velhas (who, confusingly, label their wine with the old spelling Bucellas) have a wide reputation.

COLARES RD

One of the few places in Europe supporting non-grafted vines. The phylloxera bug could not tolerate the salty sand in which the Ramisco red grape is planted – often in trenches three metres deep to start with – and protected by trees or wattle fences from the stinging winds blowing off the Atlantic.

The wine is a deep, dark, cherry-ink colour yet, unusually for Portugal, with a fruity aromatic nose and taste. Colares Chitas from Paulo da Silva and Real (Royal) Companhia Vinicola are the only two examples exported from this area.

Carcavelos, Bucelas and Colares rarities

Carcavelos – Raul Ferreira & Filho, Quinta do Barao. The very last
Bucelas Garrafeira – Adegas Camilo Alves, sole remaining producers
Colares – see text. Real Companhia Vinicola and Colares Chitas only examples

SETÚBAL RD

Around the old port of Setúbal are the Muscat vineyards, old pre-phylloxera vines many of them, but bearing the crop which is mainly bought by J. M. Fonseca (no relation to the port Fonsecas) to produce Moscatel do Setúbal, one of the gems of the wine world. Fermentation is stopped, as with all fortified wines, by the addition of spirit, but here the spirit has had Muscat grape skins macerated and steeped in it to add a heightened fruitiness to the resulting wine. Aged in cask it used to be released as either '6-year' or '25-year' matured wines; the younger wine is a deep orange colour with a surprisingly light, fresh taste for a matured fortified wine, while the older is a dark brown mouth-filling jewel, complex and subtle, yet still with a light freshness of taste that defies the years of maturing. Today the younger of the two has a vintage date, although it is not sold until it has matured for five years, while the 25-years old has become '20-years old' due to commercial pressures, but without any discernable decrease in quality.

The Soares Franco family market Camarate from their family quinta of that name; the red is from the excellent local Periquita grape with some Cabernet and Merlot content and is vinified by a young Australian Peter Bright who also, in the best Australian tradition, produces a tiny amount of Late Harvest dessert wine from the local Muscats.

Setúbal specials

Moscatel de Setúbal – J. M. da Fonseca
  virtually the only producers
Periquita – J. M. da Fonseca again. From the local Periquita red grape
Camarate – J. M. da Fonseca's blending of Cabernet Sauvignon, Merlot and Periquita plus other Fonseca/João Pires reds – Pasmados, Tinto da Anfora and Cabernet Sauvignon-based Quinta da Bacalhoa and whites, especially Palmela Dry Muscat

REGIÃO DO RIBATEJO

Up the Tagus from Lisbon is the area known as Ribatejo. Traditionally the source of wines sold in Lisbon's restaurants and bars, it has a high average quality level and many of Portugal's better blended brands originate here. Cavalho Ribeiro and Ferreira based in Vila Franca produce Serradayres – the romantically named 'Mountain Breeze'. Caves Dom Teodosio in Rio Maior produce the well known 'Teobar', other names to look out for include Caves Velhas 'Romeiro' and Dom Teodosio's Garrafeira Particular. There are no other wines worth mentioning.

REGIÃO DO ALENTEJO

From Lisbon and the Ribatejo south to the Algarve is the Região de Alentejo. This area covers nearly a third of Portugal and suffered extensively during the revolution of 1974. However, as Portugal comes into line with EEC directives about wine production there are signs of improvement. One is that the João Pires branch of the Fonseca operation buy extensively in this region for their good quality Tinta da Anfora branded wine. Serradayres, already mentioned, is also blended from wines of the Alentejo, together with Ribatejo wines and Cavalho Ribeiro and Ferreira are both expanding southwards.

Alentejo attractions

Reguengos de Monsaraz – José de Sousa Rosada Fernandes estate now owned by J. M. da Fonseca
Reguengos de Monsaraz – good regional Co-operativa - Agricola CRL

ALGARVE RD

Along Portugal's south coast is the Algarve. Better known for tourism than for wine, the area is being rapidly eroded by building. It is no great loss to the wine-drinking world.

PORT

There have been close links between Britain and Portugal since the Middle Ages. But it was not until the Treaty of Methuen in 1703 gave Portuguese wine a tax advantage over French wines that much Portuguese wine reached Britain.

However, the wines of Portugal at that time were unfortified beverages and were doubtless not improved by the long sea journey. The English merchants whose customers were used to claret from Bordeaux were seeking a claret-like replacement and they chose a most unlikely area, inhospitable and extraordinarily difficult to reach – the Upper Douro. Here, the apparently thin, arid soil composed of granite schist proved wonderfully fertile and the wines, strong dry reds, were made stronger to withstand the journey to England by the addition of 'a bucket or two of local brandie'. At what point the brandy became added before fermentation was complete, retaining the sweet fruitiness of the grapes, is unclear, but the fortified version of Douro wine proved extremely popular. Under Portuguese and British law port is now defined as wine from a 1250 square mile area of the Upper Douro fortified by the addition of 20% by volume of Portuguese grape brandy. For over 100 years the British have retained their pre-eminent position in the port trade, although, as a nation, we have lost our position of the biggest consumers of port to the French – who drink it as an aperitif – and to the Scandinavians.

The industry is controlled by the port 'houses'. These companies have their own estates, called quintas, in the Upper Douro where they grow their own grapes and to which they bring grapes purchased from neighbouring properties. Wine is created by pressing and fermenting but, at a certain crucial point, normally when fermentation is half completed, the wine is run off into casks containing brandy, the yeasts are stunned and fermentation ceases. The following spring these casks are shipped by river or rail to the port lodges in Vila Nova de Gaia opposite Oporto itself.

Here we see a similarity with champagne and sherry. The wines are carefully assessed for their quality and for their potential as a blending agent, for blending is the common denominator. All sherries, non-vintage port and champagnes are a product of the blender's art – the objective being a consistent taste in the predetermined house 'style' which can only be

maintained over the years by balancing the many variables through careful mixing of the different flavours available in different casks from different sources.

In an effort to combat a falling market, the port houses now offer a considerable range of port styles, involving names like LBV, Crusted, Single Quinta, Vintage Character and Colheita. Here, briefly, are the major varieties normally listed.

WOOD PORTS

These are ports aged entirely in cask and ready for immediate drinking for they throw no sediment in bottle and therefore do not need decanting.

● *White Port* not often seen, and not seen often enough. Naturally, only white grapes are used and it is usual for fermentation to be allowed to proceed further before running-off into the brandy so as to produce a wine slightly dryer and lower in alcohol than ruby port. Cask maturation is minimal at 2–3 years. An interesting aperitif drunk chilled.

● *Ruby Port* a poor description, for all port that is neither tawny nor white is officially ruby! However, this description has come to apply to the basic level of port offered by any of the producers. Average quality grapes will be used and the wines will be aged for around 3 years.

● *Tawny Port* again an over-simplified title. Officially, tawny is port from higher quality grapes which have had a longer maturation than the basic ruby style, 5 years being the normal minimum. However, as most port shippers offer a ruby and a tawny at exactly the same price it is difficult to see how the economics work.

● *Old Tawny Ports* these are what drinkers seeking prestige ports should go for. Agreed the colour is dark-golden brown rather than the ruby-red normally expected, but at around half the price asked for vintage ports of the same age and with no sedimentation to worry about these wines deserve to be better known. The colour comes from the long cask-ageing (as compared with long bottle-ageing in the case of vintage) and the frequent 'racking' – drawing the wines off the sediment by transferring from one cask to another – which promotes oxidation and thus accelerates maturation. Sold with the designations '10-years-old', '20-years-old' and so on, which indicate the age of the youngest wine in the blend. Tawny ports of 30 and 40 years of age are very rare old wines, the culmination of years of effort for, unlike vintage ports, they are contantly monitored throughout their maturation period.

● *Colheita Ports* these are dated tawny ports from one individual vintage, unlike the previous ports which are blended from various storage vats.

● *Vintage Character Ports* a logical step from ruby to vintage. Again a class of ports worthy of a long look. These blends are chosen from high-quality wines and are normally matured for 5 years before filtering and bottling.

● *LBV Ports* Late Bottled Vintage. Broadly the same as Vintage Character except for the (expensive) cachet of having a date on the label.

BOTTLE PORTS

These have a minimum cask ageing period followed by a much longer maturation period in bottle. As less oxygen is available slower maturation results and the rich ruby colour is preserved, but the wine throws a heavy sediment or crust that needs careful decanting before serving.

● *Vintage Ports* from the outset the very finest wines it is possible to produce and, naturally, from a single vintage. Bottled after only 2 years in cask, they are expected to spend at least 15 years in bottle before being fully mature. Apart from the snobbism implied in drinking a

▲ *One of the traditional barcos rabelos used to transport new port wine* *down the Douro to Vila Nova de Gaia before the river was dammed and* *there was reliable road and rail access to the upper Douro.*

Vintage Port there is little point in offering one which is too young.

● *Single Quinta Ports* when a company feels that the quality of the grapes picked on their own property is sufficiently high, yet not so exceptional as to declare a vintage, they produce what is in effect, a junior vintage port just from that one property.

● *Crusted Ports* wines which are, at the same time, increasingly rare and increasingly sought-after. These are quality blends from casks of a high standard which, after an initial 2–3 years in wood, are bottled and stored for a further 3–4 years. After the years in bottle a deposit is thrown just as in any port bottled young and unfiltered – the 'crust' referred to in the name.

MADEIRA

The story of Madeira reads more like a novel than a work of vinous appreciation. The island of Madeira, some 15 miles by 35 miles, together with its neighbours Porto-Santos and the Desertas, lies in the Atlantic off the coast of North Africa about 350 miles from Morocco, the nearest point on the mainland. Known as the 'Enchanted Isles' by the Phoenicians and the Genoese, it was not until 1418 that the Portuguese claimed the islands. The islands were so densely wooded that a landing was virtually impossible, so the first arrivals set fire to the trees. The fire allegedly burnt for seven years and resulted in an incredibly fertile soil. This bonfire of centuries old leaf-mould and humus combined with the naturally rich volcanic soil to produce the most fertile growing conditions in the world.

The island was gradually settled by immigrants from southern Europe who brought with them one of the original European grapes, the Malvoisie or Malvasia. The wines produced from these vines, encouraged by the favourable trade relationship between Portugal and England, became popular in the British Isles and the taste for madeira – still unfortified table wine at this stage – was taken by the English colonists to the eastern seaboard of the USA.

Far from being harmed by the long, hot sea journeys, the wine was found to improve, so much so that madeiras were shipped as ballast out to India and back to England where they became a highly prized, and highly priced, wine after their months at sea. During the 18th century it became more common to add a quantity of brandy to the wine to stabilise it and this, plus a shortage of shipping to meet the demand, led to changes that altered the wine to something nearer to the madeira of today.

To reproduce on land the conditions that occurred at sea hot stores (*estufas* in Portuguese) were set up in which a number of vats of madeira were slowly heated over a five-month period to around 42°C and, in the sixth month, allowed to return to island temperature. After this, the wine rested for 18 months before being blended for sale.

The mid 18th century to the mid 19th century was the high point for madeira production. The boom continued until, in 1852, the odium fungus blighted the vines and, no sooner had this problem been overcome, than the dreaded bug phylloxera arrived. This wiped out all the vines and the majority of growers and shippers left the island. The few who remained followed a blind alley for many years by planting native American vines, which took a long time to come into full production and, when they did, produced an inferior wine.

Even fewer growers remained after the American vine fiasco, but those that did finally got things right. Like the rest of the wine-producing countries they cut off the American vines at ground level and grafted on desirable European varieties. The four used for the best madeiras are, in ascending order of sweetness:

● *Sercial* also grown in Portugal to produce white Dão and white Bairrada
● *Verdelho* the most widely planted variety on the island
● *Bual* which also produces an undistinguished white table wine
● *Malmsey* the Malvoisie or Malvasia grape. Widely planted in Italy and also used for white port production in the Douro

Sadly, much of the output of Madeira these days is destined to be used in sauce madère – and 80% of the vines planted on the island are the obliging vine Tinta Nega Mole, which translates as 'Big Black Grape' and whose wine was called 'Tent' and can be cheaply modified to approximate to Sercial, Verdelho, Bual and Malmsey. Only 9% of the island is planted with the genuine quality vines, although things are already changing. The entry of Portugal to the Common Market means that madeira must now conform to EEC regulations – a wine labelled as a variety must contain at least 85% of the product of the named vine.

THE REST OF EUROPE

ENGLAND

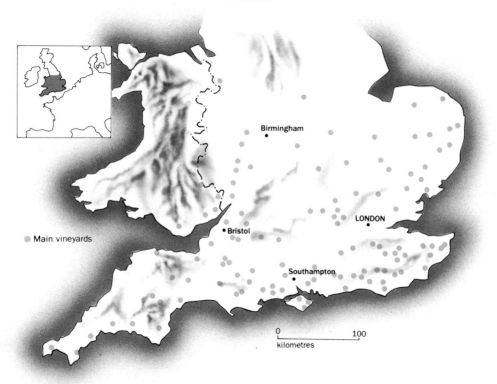

Birmingham

LONDON

● Bristol

● Main vineyards

Southampton

0   100
kilometres

The dedication needed to become a successful vigneron in the British Isles is awe-inspiring. Some countries can easily produce wine but have difficulty selling it, Algeria for example, other areas can easily sell wines but have difficulties in producing it, take Champagne, but in the UK the production problems are massive and the market for the finished product almost non-existent except for the few really well recognised wines.

It seems such a romantic dream to so many people, the plot of land, the rows of marching vines, the fun of the vendage with friends all gathering to help with the picking, quiet work through the winter until the spring pruning, the pride of living on one's own products, all so delightful.

The reality is far from this. The capital investment is large, very large for true efficiency, the weather is far from ideal and has a wayward habit of doing exactly the wrong thing at the wrong time, bright sun when rain is

173

needed and heavy rain when sunshine would be worth pounds – in weight of fruit and in cash terms!

There are between 700 and 800 vineyards of more than a 'playing at it' standard in England (and Wales) and 650 of these are full or associate members of the English Vineyards Association. The total area of vines is over 800 hectares and is increasing by an average of about 10% per year. This hectarage was divided among the following range of grapes: Müller-Thurgau 146, Reichensteiner 62, Seyval Blanc 53, Schonberger 34, Bacchus, Huxelrebe 30, Madeleine Angevine 24, Pinot Noir 20, Kerner 17, Ortega 16, others 110.

Was it the Romans who brought the vine to these shores? It seems likely but is, in fact, unproven. There are references to vines in the documents of the occupying forces, Emperor Domitian (AD 81–96) passed an edict prohibiting the growing of the vine in Britain, presumably to favour imports from Italy, but he would hardly have needed to pass the edict if vines were not already here! This law was not repealed until about AD 280 by Probus and, presumably, wine production restarted from that date.

Certainly the Venerable Bede mentions flourishing vineyards in AD 631, Kings Alfred (871–901) and Edgar (957–975) referred to vineyards in their laws and the *Domesday Book* gives details of no fewer than 38 vineyards, most of which were attached to monasteries. They were so numerous around Ely that the district was known as the 'Isle of Vines'.

The attraction of home-produced wines continued until, on his marriage to Eleanor of Aquitaine in 1152, Henry II gained the lands around Bordeaux. Suddenly it didn't seem such a good idea to produce wine in Britain and, excepting the monasteries still producing sacramental wines, the British drinker transferred his attention and allegiance largely to wines from abroad. From then until the 1950s the cultivation of vines for wine production was left to individual eccentrics, while drinking wine was all too often regarded as a beverage only for grand folk and very special occasions.

In some ways it is difficult to justify the basic premise that growing vines for wine is a worthwhile activity in the UK. Of course, enthusiasts argue that vines flourished or at least, grew, from Roman times until the English conquests in France made imports easier than home production and, had these conquests not

taken place, then vineyards would probably still be a part of our heritage. But that is exactly the point. If, in the Middle Ages, with their difficulties in transportation, it was better to import rather than produce here, then nowadays, with excellent wines from the other side of the world on our shelves at rock bottom prices, what is the point in fighting the elements? Yet some first-class wines are produced. Modern hybrids and modern production techniques allow good wines to be produced under the most disadvantageous conditions, but whether it is commercially viable is a very relevant question.

The restart of British viniculture came in the 1950s when the late Sir Guy Salisbury-Jones planted his Hambledon estate with vines. Real growth came in the 1970s when unemployment affected both the relatively wealthy and the less well off, and some decided to take their redundancy money and set up a small vineyard. The vogue grapes at that time were the dull Müller-Thurgau and the marginally more interesting Seyval hybrid. Naturally enough, wine from two uninspiring grapes grown in less than ideal conditions did little for the reputation of the fledgling industry. However, by the 1970s newer German-inspired crossings were introduced such as: Bacchus, Huxelrebe, Schonburger, Ortega, Reichensteiner, and even Madeline Angevine.

There is now no disputing the excellence of many of the best English wines. What is needed now is the economy of scale of larger production areas. Of our quality vineyards the largest by far is Denbies at Dorking with 85 hectares, followed by New Hall in Essex and Wellow in Hampshire with 35, Lamberhurst in Kent with 21 and The Isle of Wight Co. with 17 and a further 15 to plant. All other vineyards are under 15 hectares, many of them with under a hectare. The 25 largest producers represent 50% of the planted area and many hundreds farm the balance. It is difficult to produce enough profit from areas like these to cover the high capital investments in land, stock and machinery and produce a satisfactory living as well.

If there is to be a viable UK wine industry it is important that English vineyards plant vines quickly – it may soon be too late! At present the British Isles are defined for viniculture under EEC law as 'experimental' which means that the current EEC prohibitions on the planting of new vineyards are waived. These restrictions are part of the campaign to reduce the EEC wine lake – and large inducements are offered to vignerons throughout Europe to grub-up their vineyards. If the EEC decides that Britain is out of the 'experimental' stage then it will be impossible to extend the area under vine to improve financial viability.

The following vineyards (in alphabetical order) offer wines of both quality and interest, and produce enough to sell through retail outlets – although not always very widely: Adgestone, Isle of Wight; Barton Manor, Isle of Wight; Biddenden, Kent; Bruisyard, Suffolk; Carr-Taylor, Sussex; Cavendish Manor, Suffolk; Chilford Hundred, Cambridgeshire; Chilsdown, Sussex; Ditchling, Sussex; Elmham Park, Norfolk; Hambledon, Hampshire; Ightham, Kent; Lamberhurst, Kent; Moorlynch, Somerset; Pilton Manor, Somerset; St George's, Sussex; Spots Farm, Kent; Staple St James, Kent; Three Choirs, Gloucestershire; Wootton Vines, Somerset.

▲ *New vines growing at Pilton Manor Vineyard near Shepton Mallet,* *Somerset. In the distance is historic Glastonbury Tor.*

'I believe elder wine can be made less deleterious by putting an equal quantity of brandy in it. But why not drink the brandy by itself?'
George Saintsbury,
Notes on a Cellar-Book, 1920

SWITZERLAND

Main wine regions

Though it is rare to find Swiss wines on sale or on restaurant wine lists, that does not mean that Switzerland has no wine industry. It has a small thriving one, but the high cost of land and labour in Switzerland makes the wines expensive and few are exported.

Just as the country has three primary languages, so the country has three primary wine-growing regions and styles: French, German and Italian.

The French-speaking Swiss cantons lie around Lake Geneva and this is the most concentrated area with extensions from Lake Geneva up to Neuchâtel in the Jura parallel to the Franco-Swiss border and down into Valais and Vaud. On the lake-side slopes from Geneva round to Lausanne, vineyards have had to give way to housing development, but this is still the most significant Swiss wine region. The chief grape is the white Chasselas, confusingly called Fendant in Valais, Dorin in Vaud and Perlan in Geneva. In the Valais and Neuchâtel the red grapes Pinot Noir and Gamay are grown to produce home-made burgundy. The best reds in Valais are a combination of both these red varieties – a sort of Swiss Passe-Tout-Grains – which they call Dôle. Sylvaner is also widely planted in Valais (although confusingly called Johannisberg) along with Reisling, Muscat and Pinot Gris which, with little regard for the rest of the world, they call Malvoisie!

The best wines from around Zurich are from the Pinot Noir, here known by its German name of Blauburgunder.

The Italian-speaking canton of Ticino can produce reasonable wines from the Merlot – especially if the maker ignores his Italian wine heritage and allows the mellow flavours of fresh wine to come through rather than be stripped of fruit by over-long wood ageing.

The only sensible place to go to buy Swiss wines is, logically, the Swiss Centre in London, they have a wide selection.

LUXEMBOURG

The biggest production here is of sparkling wine but, with a few exceptions, they are best ignored. The major exceptions to this rule are the products of the Bernard-Massard company and of the powerful Wormeldange co-operative.

Still wines are much more interesting. The extension of the Moselle provides excellent growing conditions and the output is tightly monitored by a system which requires all wines to be submitted to an ajudication panel for assessment, chemical testing and allocation of status. This tough and thorough procedure is a part of a system which has been in place since 1935.

Grapes are the Rivaner, a Riesling/Sylvaner cross, Elbling, probably the original German grape that pre-dates the Romans, Auxerrois, so popular in Alsace, together with smaller plots of Gewürztraminer, Pinot Gris and Pinot Blanc.

The Luxembourg authorities are enthusiastically promoting their vinous products and prices are attractively competitive. Well worth seeking out – especially for German wine enthusiasts wanting to broaden their horizons.

Wines to look for
Sparklers from Caves Co-operative de Wormeldange (le Comte de Wormeldange) or Bernard-Massard (Charles le Roi)
Moselle Gewürztraminer 1re Crû, Caves Co-operative de Wormeldange
Pinot Blanc 1re Crû, Caves Co-operative de Wormeldange

AUSTRIA

In Austria the vine growing areas are all in the east and seem more like an extension of other countries' vineyards than Austria's own. North of Vienna the wine growing region abuts and continues into Czechoslovakia; south-east of Vienna the vineyards march on over the border with Hungary and in the south the vines cross into Yugoslavia.

Until recent years Austrian wine was almost all consumed domestically and little attention was paid to exports and, to make matters worse, those wines that were exported were almost all re-processed or re-labelled wines from the countries to the east en route to Italy and Germany. However, after the Germans introduced their wine laws in 1971 Austria introduced legislation along broadly similar lines a year later and this increase in national control of quality wines was followed by a healthy and steady growth in export trade. The two main areas for which Austrian wines competed were the large volume German style of easy-drinking white wines, for which the Schluck label became synonymous, and the more specialised dessert wine market.

Of the volume market there is little to be said. The grape is the Grüner Veltliner, an unexciting and undemanding grape tasting a little like Gewürztraminer well watered down with Müller-Thurgau, and the main growing area is the Wachau stretching from around Krems on the Danube to the Czech border. Most of the activities here are carried out by large co-operatives, some with thousands of committee members. The products taste pretty much like committee wines too.

Austrian efforts with dessert wines deserved more success than they achieved, for the delights of the Burgenland were extremely competitively priced. The vineyards for these dessert wines lie around the strange Neusiedler See, a lake about 30km long and an average one metre deep. The regular mist which this lake causes in late autuman makes noble rot a regular occurrence rather than a lucky chance. Hence the competitive prices for wines even up to trockenbeerenauslese standard.

The di-ethylene glycol additive scandal of

BOUVIER
Trockenbeerenauslese
Apetlon — Neusiedler See
1983

177

AUSTRIAN WINE LAWS

These are now, after the tightening-up which followed the di-ethylene glycol additive scandal, among the toughest in the world. The laws date from 1 November 1985 with amendments dated 3 July 1986.

The quality grades are:

TAFELWEIN
Sometimes called Tischwein. Grape maturity must produce a minimum of 63° Oechsle.

LANDWEIN
No grape maturity figures are set but the finished alcohol level may not exceed 11.5% and the residual sugar must not exceed 6.5g per litre. The grapes may only originate from one growing area.

QUALITATSWEIN
The grapes may only come from one growing area. Thre is a maximum yield per hectare which may not be exceeded.
There is a minimum Oechsle reading of 73° which may be boosted by no more than 4.5kg of sugar per hectolitre to result in no more than 94° Oechsle.
   There are a number of fixed minimum levels, extract, acidity, alcohol etc. which have been government-tested since July 1986.
● *Kabinettwein* a Qualitatswein with a minimum of 83.5° and a maximum of 94° Oechsle, no additional sweetening and no more than 9g residual sugar per litre.
● *Pradikatswein* these are Qualitatswein of exceptional maturity or vintage.

Any residual sugar shall be due to ceased fermentation, no added sugars are permitted. The vintage must be stated.
If the wine is made from late-gathered grapes then the grape variety must be stated.
No mechanical harvesting permitted.
By 9.00 am on the day of picking the 'community controller' must be advised of the day's projected harvest and the total harvest must be taken to the Mostwager (must-weigher) at the official grape weighing station. Pradikatswein cannot be sold until 1 May after the harvest (see Spatlese below).

SPATLESE
Grapes must be left until all other grapes have ripened and been picked. Mechanical picking may be used. Minimum must weight is 94° Oechsle. Can be sold from March after the vintage.

AUSLESE
Carefully selected grapes of Spatlese standard with unripe, bad or diseased grapes rejected. Minimum 105° Oechsle.

BEERENAUSLESE
Made only from selected late-picked grapes with a degree of noble rot and a minimum of 127° Oechsle.

EISWEIN
Produced from grapes picked frozen and still frozen when pressed. Mechanical picking permitted. Minimum must weight of 127° Oechsle.

1984 has effectively, but unfairly, killed off any serious interest in buying quality Austrian wines. It may take a decade before the shock waves subside and their export market recovers. The scale of the knock-on effect of this scandal is amazing: in 1984 Austria exported just under 500,000 hectolitres of wine, in 1986 the figure was just over 40,000 hectolitres! Eventually the very stiff wine laws that were introduced after the scandal will begin to reassure drinkers and help to revive the export market, but international competition is now so fierce that a market, once lost to another sources, is mighty difficult to retrieve.

Moreover, a series of poor harvests and an ever-stronger Austrian schilling makes bargains a thing of the past.
   Look out for the great Austrian dessert wines – eisweins even! Perhaps they lack the delicate balancing acidity of the finest German examples but, at a price a fraction of Germany's, the best way to impress your wine-enthusiast friends is with a bottle of trockenbeerenauslese to go with the pud.
   Dessert wines from Lenz-Moser, A. Unger or Sepp Hold are all good. Dry Grüner Veltliner wines from H. Augustin, Metternich Weinguter and Fritz Saloman can be trusted.

AUSBRUCH
Made from naturally dried late-harvested grapes with noble rot to which fresh grape juice or wine of similar quality can be added. 138° Oechsle is minimum must weight.

TROCKENBEERENAUSLESE
Is produced from withered Beerenauslese-quality grapes having a minimum of 150° Oechsle.

Compulsory information on all labels:
1 The place of production. The following marks of origin may also be specified – wine-growing area, district, location, vineyard or community
2 The official label giving the government inspection number (wine of Qualitatswein standard)
3 The name and location of the producer, bottler or manufacturer
4 The alcohol content
5 The revenue stamp with the registration number on a Banderolkapsel – a paper band across the top of the cork
6 'Austria', 'Austrian Wine' or 'Wine from Austria', if the wine is produced exclusively from Austrian grapes
7 If the grape variety or the vintage is stated then at least 85% of the contents must qualify
8 The category of the wine: eg Landwein, Qualitatswein
9 The sugar content as follows: Trocken (dry) or 'suitable for diabetics' if the sugar content is below 4g per litre, Halb-trocken (medium-dry) up to 9g per litre of residual sugar, Halbsuss or Lieblich (sweet) up to 18g per litre residual sugar and Suss (very sweet) if the residual sugar is over 18g per litre.

BULGARIA

In 1949 the Bulgarians set out with determination and single-mindedness to create a major industry and a substantial foreign currency earner from their national wine industry. Not that they had much of one, the Second World War having decimated what little had grown after Moslem occupation ceased in the late 1800s. Now, however, Bulgaria is the fifth biggest exporter of wine behind France, Italy, Spain and Portugal. The statistics are remarkable, and could hardly have happened without the benign influence of their state control system. But what makes the Bulgarians stand out from the other east European countries is their amazing prescience, or extreme good fortune, in anticipating the world move towards varietal labelling and the consequent acceptance of bottles clearly labelled Merlot, Chardonnay and so on. They have retained many of their indigenous grapes – Mavrud, Melnik, Gamza, Dimiat (thought to be related to the Chasselas) and Red Misket.

The regions of Bulgaria are of little more than academic interest. The country has been split into three major and two minor areas, the northern area is bounded by the Danube along the border with Romania and, to the south, the central mountain spine. This area specialises in reds, Cabernet Sauvignon and Gamza especially. The central ridge forms one of the smaller areas and grows whites, in particular Muscat and Riesling. To the south is a vast area with, again, concentration on reds but with fuller-bodied wines than from the north. Merlot and Cabernet Sauvignon succeed well especially around Orihovitza. The east of the country along the shores of the Black Sea and for many miles inland is the third major area, this time specialising in white wines, Chardonnay from Novi Pazar being especially good – light in a Chablis style rather than massive in the Australian manner. On the other hand, Khan Krum, next to Novi Pazar, produces oak-aged Chardonnays which do provide contrast and competition to the big, buttery, Australian wines. Riesling and some very accurate Sauvignon Blanc also comes from this area. Tucked away in the south-western corner alongside the Greek border is a tiny area specialising in the Melnik grape. This well-balanced and fruity red wine is unfairly overshadowed by the volume of 'European' varietal wines.

There are five quality bands to look out for:
1 The Mehana range of table wines made from blendings of native Bulgarian grapes.
2 'Country Wines', newly introduced blends of two varieties:
White wines
Bourgas Muscat and Ugni Blanc
Russe Riesling and local Misket
Red wines
Suhindol Merlot with local Gamza
Pavlikeni Cabernet Sauvignon and Merlot
3 The varietal range, the wines on which the reputation of Bulgaria has been founded. The

full range is: Chardonnay, Sauvignon Blanc, Riesling, Cabernet Sauvignon and Merlot.

4 The 'Reserve' range. Almost tailor-made for the UK after the Controliran range (see next) introduction showed initial failings by being either too under- or too over-stated.

The wines, which show the benefit of ageing in smaller, more Bordeaux barrique-sized oak barrels, are: Khan Krum Chardonnay, Orihovitza Cabernet Sauvignon and, from a local grape, Melnik from Damianitza.

5 Controliran wines. These come from newly designated areas and include two red wines which, at their introduction, were somewhat fat and full and lacking in length, but have since improved in these respects somewhat.

The white, again at introduction, was altogether too light and delicate to stand up to the then newly-arrived Australian competition. These wines are Novi Pazar Chardonnay, Svishtov Cabernet Sauvignon and Orihovitza Cabernet Sauvignon/Merlot.

Since 1980 the Sakar Mountain Cabernet which was initially (in 1976) quite sensational has faded disastrously. There also used to be a delightfully victoria-plummy Mavrud which disappeared but is due to reappear as the Controliran range expands.

Ultimately there will be a Controliran Reserve range, but prices are expected to be very non-Bulgarian.

Wines to look out for
Khan Krum Reserve Chardonnay
Bulgarian Chardonnay
Bulgarian Riesling – what a lesson to German wine producers!
Orihovitza Cabernet Sauvignon Reserve
Damianitza Melnik Reserve
Asenovgrad Mavrud

Previous pages
A Bulgarian vineyard.
The success of their wine
abroad has been a
significant factor in
Bulgaria's post-war
economy.

HUNGARY

Hungary provides a dramatic contrast with Bulgaria: the Hungarians, with the notable exception of Tokay, do not export their best wines. What the export market is offered is a range of anaemic versions of wines of true character.

Most of Hungary's wines are white and the largest volume is from the Italian Riesling, Olasz Riesling they call it, and using this grape is sufficient to condemn most wines to a dull blandness although a few producers manage distinction. Basic red wines use the Kadarka grape and most of the wines are again dull with just a few bright spots.

The Kadarka is used for one of the best-known red wines from Eastern Europe, Bulls Blood or Egers Bikaver. Produced around the town of Eger in the north-east of the country these wines once had substance and subtlety but in recent years have become more blandly commercial. Better-quality red wines come from the Kefrankos, called the Blaufrankisch in Austria and related to the Gamay, this grape is increasingly in use, often blended with Pinot Noir, called Nagyburgundi in Hungary, which tends to grow best in the south of the country. Merlot, called Médoc Noir, is improving and has its Hungarian home near Eger, the Bulls Blood town.

It should go without saying that the world's most compulsory red grape, the Cabernet Sauvignon, is being tried. Its junior brother, the Cabernet Franc, has also been widely planted, especially in the south-west where the wines of Hajos have a good reputation.

One white Hungarian grape deserves a special place in history: the Furmint. This grape is also used in other central European countries, but its glory is Tokay. The town of Tokay, 40 miles from the Russian border, gives its name to this historic wine and here Furmint and Harslevelu (Lime-leaf) grapes ripen and are fermented into a distinctive white wine. Sold as it is, the name is Tokay Szamorodni – which literally means 'as it comes'. This wine may be dry or sweetish depending on that year's climatic conditions but the great wines of Tokay only use this wine as the base. Other, well-ripened grapes that have sustained noble rot are picked, hand selected and destalked and left for about a week before being pulped into a puttony, a tub containing 30 litres. A number of puttonyos are added to base Tokay which is

stored in gonci – casks of 140 litres. The norm is either three, four or five puttonyos, although sometimes six may be used per gonci. The quantity is not necessarily an absolute measure of final sweetness for some years are more favoured than others and it is said by the Hungarians that the amount they use is altered from year to year. They suggest that, for example, one year's four puttonyos may be equivalent to a three puttonyos in a better year, but few back-to-back tests have been carried out!

After the addition of the sweet pulp the wine is again fermented, filtered and bottled in the traditional 50cl bottles and stored for a minimum of three years before being released. Unusually, the Hungarians store Tokay in their dark cellars under the town in a vertical position and replace the corks as necessary every 15 to 20 years.

Beyond Tokay Aszu, as the sweet wine is called, is Tokay Aszu Essencia. This is a rarity, and commands a rarity price. The wine is entirely produced from Aszu berries in only the finest years and there is no puttonyos rating for the whole wine is made from the pulped berries. The sugar level is so high that, like some trockenbeerenauslesen in Germany, fermentation is difficult. Over the years the Hungarians have developed their own strain of yeast called Tokay 22 and, even with this specalised yeast, fermentation takes several years. Further, the wines are aged for a minimum of ten years before sale.

As if this were not enough there is a wine more exotic still. The wine the Tsars had bottled in cut glass decanters and which possessed such restorative powers that a decanter was always close by the bed of an ageing Tsar. The wine is simply Tokay Essence, hardly a wine at all for it is the juice that exudes from Aszu berries as they spend their week waiting to be pulped. One puttony normally only produces 19mm of juice. This juice is collected into oak barrels where fermentation is attempted with the hardy Tokay 22, but after many years of gradual fermentation perhaps 5° of alcohol may have been achieved. The state cellars at Tallya have 60 barrels of Essence but none is bottled – if it were to be bottled and auctioned in the west it would probably finance the entire national debt of Hungary.

Strangely, when it comes to recommend-ations, there is one bright star right at the very bottom of the wine price scale. One of the cheapest wines available anywhere, yet a

Gold Medal winner at the International Wine Challenge in London in 1989 – Hungarian Merlot selling in Safeways and elsewhere at about £1.80. And the company it kept? Château Cheval Blanc, retail price around £50.00, Campo dei Fiori Cabernet Sauvignon from Chile at a modest £2.50 and Ch Margaux, Pavillion Rouge, at around £20.00!

Now if Hungary could produce more wines like that – in other words, do a Bulgaria – then the following list would be much longer.

Recommendations

White wine from the Furmint grape produced in Somlo, around Lake Balaton (Austria's Neusiedler See), called, logically Somlo Furmint

Tokay 5 puttonyos – sold only in the traditional half-litre bottles

Sopron Pinot Noir – called Nagyburgundi in Hungarian

Hungarian Merlot

Szekszard Nemes Kadarka

ROMANIA

An unbelievably boring country with wines entirely in character. A few brave wine importers have made half-hearted attempts to introduce British drinkers to the doubtful delights of Romanian wine, but without success. The wines are Russian oriented, being over sweet and unsubtle. The only glimmer of interest is Cotnari – one of the world's great dessert wines. Once called Perle de la Moldavie on Parisian restaurant lists it has now faded into semi-obscurity. Officially Cotnari is still produced in Moldavia, on the slopes of the Carpathians, but one suspects that the interesting, but hardly great, dessert wines they now offer bear only a passing resemblance to the Cotnaris of old.

For the curious, the following are bearable: Dealul Mare Merlot; Feteasca, a local grape with an interesting, somewhat Germanic flavour; Riesling de Banat and two dessert wines which show some character, Frankincense Edelbeerenlese and Ottonel Muscat.

USSR

A country of big numbers. In 1950 there were just under 400,000 hectares of vineyards. Now, following the efforts to reduce dependence upon

vodka, there are 3 million hectares growing grapes – 10% of the world's vineyards. Russia is second only to Spain in area of vineyard but, in spite of this, Russia imports huge quantities of wine each year: around 77 million cases. Their taste is towards the sweet and sticky, and dessert wines or so-called ports, sherries and madeiras are produced in enormous quantities. With her domestic demand and the national style of wine being so sweet there is little chance of meeting Russian wine, and, if one did, of enjoying it! Doubtless some of the dessert wines have character and interest, but there is a natural deterrent to visiting the vineyards as they must be amongst the most inaccessible in the world, being mostly beyond the eastern shores of the Black Sea. They do, however, show signs of wanting to export.

YUGOSLAVIA

The bulk of Yugoslavia's exports are branded white wines. The most popular in Britain is made with that commercial favourite, the Italian Riesling, here called the Laski Riesling. Mainly grown in the north of the country around the town of Lutomer it suffers the same fate as much of Portugal's Vinho Verde – in the country of origin it can be interestingly crisp and fresh, but when exported it is mildly sweetened for the unsophisticated, Liebfraumilch market and loses much of its charm and character.

The other great export success, and Yugoslavia is 10th in the international league table of wine exporters, is a sort of red Liebfraumilch, in fact, a slightly sweetened Pinot Noir called Amselfeld. Hardly seen (yet) in the British Isles, it is enormously popular in Germany where more than 30 million bottles a year are consumed.

The rest of the export volume is built up of bulk wines used for a variety of purposes – to Italy for Vermouth, to Japan for blending and bottling, to Switzerland and Germany to help beef up the anaemic local sunless red wine products.

Undoubtedly there must be wines of interest in a country so polyglot, but few are available to try. Moreover one suspects that varietal labelling controls are not all that they could be. A 'Cabernet from Kosovo', as the label proclaimed, had little resemblance to any of the Cabernets from anywhere else in the world – it could easily have been from another variety entirely or some blending may have crept in along the way. Similarly, a Sauvignon Blanc from Fruska Gora just north of Belgrade had little resemblance to any Sauvignon Blanc previously tasted – and was rather unpleasant to boot.

So far only red wines, specifically a Merlot and a Cabernet Sauvignon (alleged to come from the royal Serbian cellars) have filled me with any enthusiasm:

Milion Merlot
Milion Cabernet Sauvignon
Vranac from Montenegro has been enjoyed by
    others whose opinions I respect

GREECE

This is a wine nation that has virtually stood still for 3000 years. Fragments of ancient amphorae have been analysed and found to hold traces of resinated wines – and retsina today represents more than a half of the wine output of this nation. In the past there may have been good reasons to add pine resin to fermenting wine – either the wines were bad or the food was bad and the flavours needed masking – but nowadays the custom can only be maintained by tradition rather than by desire!

Other, non-resinated wines of any interest are few. Achaia Clauss, a company originally founded by Gustav Clauss, a Bavarian, but long since wholly Greek owned, produce reasonable large volume wines under their Demestica label and they also produce some of the celebrated Mavrodaphne, a sort of Greek Recioto, a sweet heavy red wine.

The most significant development of recent years has been the huge investments made by the late John Carras who planted, with advice from the ubiquitous Professor Emile Peynaud of Bordeaux, vineyards in the north with a high proportion of Cabernet Sauvignon. They produce virtually the only Greek wine with pretensions to grandeur, Chateau Carras, although his fears of a wine lacking in tannin have, unfortunately, turned out to be completely unfounded. Just when the world is looking for faster-drinking quality wines from warmer regions, these are still closed in after several years in bottle. As more recent vintages have shown signs of increasing softness perhaps the message is sinking in. Chateau Carras also has a white wine produced from the Sauvignon Blanc about which the less said the better.

If Greece really wanted to boost wine exports then the authorities could do worse than give some financial assistance and encouragement to the activities of their sweet wine producers. Samos Muscat is reasonably widely available and charms many with its very open, unsophisticated approach. This naturally sweet dessert wine is remarkably inexpensive and fully capable of putting many more prestigious European Muscat dessert wines to shame.

CRETE

Crete produces a well regarded sweet Malvasia from a long-established vinicultural heritage that seems to have remained unchanged for millennia. Crete's largest co-operative, the Peza Growers Association, produce a whopping red called Mantiko that is so full and flavoursome it practically needs a knife and fork!

CEPHALONIA

On the island of Cephalonia is a spark of enthusiasm. John Calliga produces two red wines from native Greek grapes – Monte Nero and Calliga Ruby – which are flavoursome and reasonably well made. Worth trying a bottle if you meet one if only for the interest.

PELOPONNESE

The Nemea of the Peloponnese is made from Agiogiorgitiko grapes and can be a fine red wine, although this region is perhaps better known for sweet red Mavrodaphne.

Otherwise, Greece's entry into the Common Market in 1981, which long promised to revolutionise their wine controls and increase their enthusiasm for quality wines rather than bulk wine products, has had no visible result. Indeed, since 1981 Greek wine exports have actually fallen.

Apart from the dessert wines, only red wines can be commended – and, even then, more as wines to try for the experience than for absolute enjoyment!

Wines to try

Muscat from Samos
Malvasia from Crete
Chateau Carras from the Khalkidhiki peninsula,
    Carras Wines
Calliga Ruby and Monte Nero from Cephalonia,
    John Calliga
Nemea from the Peloponnese if you can find it
Demestica Red, Achaia Clauss

THE EASTERN MEDITERRANEAN AND NORTH AFRICA

ALGERIA

TUNISIA

MOROCCO

● Main wine regions

TURKEY

If Noah did indeed plant a vineyard on the slopes of Mount Ararat then Turkey can reasonably claim to be the true cradle of viniculture. Indeed this claim seems borne out by the evidence of Hittite art of around 4000 BC showing wine being used as a civilised beverage.

However, as in all countries that enjoyed Moslem domination, the activities of wine-makers were slight, but Kemal Ataturk, as a part of his modernisation programme, re-introduced wine-making by building a winery in 1927. Unfortunately, with 99% of the country devout Moslems there was, and is, a negligible home market for wines and the Turks certainly lack the sophistication to take on, say, the Bulgarians or the Australians in international markets. Exports today are mainly the wines produced by the 21 state wineries and of the wines on offer (normally only in Turkish restaurants) the dry white Trakya Beyaz made from Sémillon has some class and Buzbag is good value for money. This wine is made from the Bogazkarasi grape and is deep and powerful, heavy yet flavoursome.

Over 100 private wineries exist and of these

the Villa Doluca vineyards on the Sea of Marmara produce good-quality wines. They offer Doluca, which is the local Papazkarasi grape with Cinsault, and Villa Doluca which is the same local grape with Gamay and Cabernet Sauvignon. Their whites are from Sémillon, either with or without oak-ageing and a Johannisberg Riesling – although how effective that grape is so far south is open to question.

CYPRUS

Over 10% of the cultivable land in Cyprus is given over to grapes – 50,000 hectares with the slopes of the Troodos Mountains as the best growing areas. The vast majority of the grapes go to make Cyprus 'sherries', which are usually of quite a good standard, but more and more go to the production of competitively priced bulk or bottom end of the market table wines.

Although the growing conditions are excellent, there is little incentive for change or improvement because the vines are protected from phylloxera, so the three native grapes are still grown: the black Mavron, the white Xynisteri and the Muscat of Alexandria. Some

efforts with other grapes have been attempted.
Palomino has been brought in to try to improve
the 'sherries' and a few plantings of Cabernet
Sauvignon have been experimented with on the
Troodos slopes with encouraging results –
although the Cypriots themselves seem less
than enthusiastic! There is, however, one truly
legendary wine produced, one that is frequently
overlooked when considering the world's
greatest wines: Commanderia.

In classical Greece Hesiod told of a Cypriot
wine called Nama which was made from sun-
dried grapes. In 1191 when Richard I gave the
island to the Knights Templar, the Commanders
of the order took control of the sale of this
exquisite wine and renamed it Commanderia.
Records throughout the Middle Ages refer to
this wine and it so attracted the attention of the
wine-loving Turkish Sultan Selim II that he
ordered his commander-in-chief to capture the
island for, he is recorded as saying, 'Within the
island there is a treasure which only the King of
Kings is worthy of possessing.' 'King of Kings'
was, of course, a modest reference to himself!
However, under Turkish Moslem rule,
notwithstanding the King of Kings' thoughts on
the subject, wine production virtually stopped

and it was not until the British took over the
administration of the island in 1878 that the
industry began to grow. As one might suppose
for a wine that has been in production for over
2000 years, there are no hard and fast rules.
Basically, the already very sweet grapes,
normally white Xynisteri but often with some
Mavron added, are dried on mats in the sun for
about 10 days, then pressed and fermented.
No fortification is needed and the wines ferment
out to 15° to 16° of alcohol before the yeast
enzymes are stunned by the alcohol level and
fermentation ceases. The wines are then
matured for long periods in conditions which
encourage concentration. Traditionally, the
wine is put in huge earthenware amphorae
coated with a mixture of pitch, goat-hair and
vine-ash to which are ascribed near magical
properties but which probably merely serve as
a waterproofing layer. Then the amphorae are
buried and left for years. True Commanderia
matured for years is one of the wonders of the
vinous world, but there are wines available
labelled Commanderia which are merely
commercially produced high-speed expediency
wines, sweet, luscious even, but not the stuff
that battles were fought over.

LEBANON

◄ *Maturing wines in the cellars under Chateau Musar, Serge Hochar's highly regarded property in the war-torn Bekaa Valley, Lebanon. Sadly, the cellars also serve as a shelter for local inhabitants during bomb and rocket attacks.*

Historically, the Middle East has a long tradition of wine production – the Shiraz (or Syrah), one of the oldest grapes in general use, is reputed to have originated in the city of that name in Iran and stories of Syria making wines 'the quality of Bordeaux' came back with travellers in the early 1800s.

In the late 1970s a wine appeared on the London market which proved history to be correct – Chateau Musar, a wine indeed to rival Bordeaux. This product of the Hochar family, father Gaston establishing the vineyards in the Bekaa Valley (the ancient land of Canaan) in the 1930s and son Serge, after training in

Bordeaux, becoming the wine-maker in 1959, set the wine world alight. Almost overnight the great round wines of this family of enthusiasts became accepted as being on a par with the other great wine families, the Torres, the Mondavis, the Antinoris who are proving that the frontiers of France are not the boundaries of great wine production.

Sadly, the continuing warfare in Lebanon has taken its toll. By a miracle of effort and bravery vintages were produced in 1982 and 1983 – even though the vineyards were on one side of the battlefield and the castle of Mzar where the Hochars have their winery was on the other –

but 1984 saw their almost suicidal efforts to produce a vintage come to naught.

1985 was only just possible through a mixture of bravery and good fortune and somehow every year since then they have managed a vintage, although tasters sometimes swear they can discern hints of gelignite or cordite in the wine!

As long as this once glorious country is sadly torn by war, then the future of the exceptional Chateau Musar Cabernet Sauvignon/Cinsault/Syrah blend must be under continual threat. There are two other producers, although their day-to-day existance is hardly more secure than Serge Hochar's, Domaine de Tournelles and Ksara use Cabernet Sauvignon, Carignan and other southern French red varieties.

ISRAEL

Wine is constantly referred to in pre- and post-biblical writings about Israel. In 1800 BC a writer says that 'the children of Israel sit each beneath his vine and his fig' and went on to say that vineyards were producing wine in greater quantity than water. Three hundred years later another correspondent refers to Palestine and says 'and the wine flowed from her cellars like waterfalls'. The peak period for wine production seems to have been in the first four centuries AD when wine was exported all over the Roman world including to England. Moslem conquest removed almost all the vineyards although Crusaders found a few still producing wine and expanded the production somewhat.

However, it was not until 1870 that wine production became viable again. Baron Edmond de Rothschild financed the laying out of the vineyards and the construction of two wineries, one outside Tel Aviv and the other near Haifa on the slopes of Mount Carmel. By 1890 3150 hectares were planted but production received a setback with the arrival of phylloxera. Once grafted vines had replaced the old stocks the industry regained momentum. It became, and remains, a small but nevertheless important part of the country's economy. Vineyard area is still as it was in 1890 and the main red grapes are red Carignan and Grenache with Muscat, Sémillon and Clairette for white wines. Recently, there has been interest in varietal wine labelling and production and some tentative plantings of Cabernet Sauvignon, Petit Syrah (Durif) and Sauvignon Blanc have shown promise.

One particularly forward looking development has taken place on the Golan Heights. The site was originally recommended by Dr Cornelius Ough of Davis University and the site is now mainly under the direction of Shimson Welner. Originally brought in to supervise the building of the Hatzor winery itself, he now directs operations. A Davis graduate, Andrew Starr, supervises the wine-making, but, although Jewish, he is not a practising Jew and therefore cannot help directly in the wine-making itself (see below) – his is strictly a 'hands-off' operation. Sauvignon Blanc and Chardonnay are planted for white wines and Cabernet Sauvignon and Pinot Noir for reds in the 180-hectare vineyards. Experimental plantings have also been made with Riesling, Colombard and Muscat, together with two Californian refugees: Zinfandel and Emerald Riesling. Production has risen to 85,000 cases a year from a mere 10,000 in 1984.

The most modern techniques are employed at Golan, mechanical picking – and mechanical pruning soon – drip-feed irrigation with trace elements contained in the feed water, night picking of the lower, and therefore hotter, vineyards, cooling of the cropped and de-stalked grapes immediately on arrival at the winery and so on. After cooling the grapes the wine-maker can choose between immediately pressing the grapes and chilling the must prior to adding selected yeasts for slow, low-temperature, fermentation or he may decide to return the

KOSHER WINE

For wine to be officially accepted as Kosher the following rules apply:

● Vines must be four years old before their grapes qualify as Kosher.
● Every seventh year the vineyard shall lie fallow.
● Only Orthodox Jews may work in the vineyards or the winery, and the Sabbath must be observed.
● Cultured yeasts, if used, must be declared Kosher.
● The grapes, vines and the wine produced must be blessed by a rabbi.
● No non-Orthodox Jew may touch any part of the produce or the equipment used.

must to the skins for a period of hours to extract more flavour before pressing begins.

Throughout the whole process, from picking to bottling, great care is taken to exclude oxygen to limit oxidation and equal attention is given to maintaining beneficially low working temperatures.

One interesting and practical compromise has had to be reached. Under Jewish law, to be Kosher, the vines must 'lie fallow' every seventh year. In vinous terms this would be damaging to the vines so, every seventh year, the vineyards are sold to a non-Orthodox Jew who merely carries out basic or essential work necessary to maintain the health of the plants. Thus their wine still qualifies as Kosher.

The Golan vineyards have had repeated medal-winning successes for their premium varietal wines under the Yarden (Hebrew for Jordan) label. These successes culminated in a gold medal for the Yarden Cabernet Sauvignon at both the International Wine Challenge in London in 1989 (when only 30 golds were awarded out of a total of 3200 wines entered) and at Vinexpo, the International Exhibition held each year in Bordeaux, an excellent place to win a Gold Medal for a Cabernet Sauvignon wine!

Recommendations

All the wines of the Hatzor winery, whether carrying the superior Yarden label or the 'second label' Golan name, are recommended, especially
Yarden Sauvignon Blanc
Yarden Muscat (Gold Medal at Vinexpo 1989)
Golan Mount Hermon White
Yarden Cabernet Sauvignon
Golan Cabernet Sauvignon

EGYPT

At Abu Hummus, inland from Alexandria, lie the Gianaclis vineyards mainly producing grapes for distillation, but also producing wine. The names of the wines enjoy a certain simple naivety – the whites being Cru des Ptolemees and Reine Cleopatra while one of the more successful is Muscat-based, you've guessed it, Omar Khayyam!

TUNISIA

Mainly consumed by tourists visiting this charming country, the wines have the same sort of haphazard simplicity that enfolds the whole

nation. The dry Muscat wines are at the same time interesting yet dull, the majority of the reds are deep, soft wines of little character and breeding. Good names, relatively speaking, are Royal Tardi (the red, not the rosé) which has more than a hint of Pinot Noir in its full textured palate, not unlike some of the false 'Burgundies' that appeared on British shelves before tightened regulations; Chateau Mornag (again, the red not the rosé) from the hills of the same name east of Tunis and Magon, a Cinsault/ Mourvèdre blend from east of the capital city. Only one European-style white is currently available simply, accurately and uninformatively called 'Blanc de Blancs'.

When visiting in May 1987 I was treated to a 1987 vintage red wine from Caves Lamblot in the Region de Bizerte – and when surprise was expressed at a 1987 red vintage wine being available so early it was promptly followed by a 1988. . . .

ALGERIA

Previously the producer of cutting wines for France, to boost both the ordinary onze degree to make sure it really was 11° wine, and, more especially, to make up for the very obvious deficiencies of Burgundy. Since independence in 1962 I have drunk many Algerian wines but found nothing of charm or interest – a sad comment on a country that has just under a quarter of a million hectares of vineyard.
Red Infuriator (yes really!) is stocked by one of the national high street chains and is not at all bad, in spite of its name.

MOROCCO

A small hectareage but some worthwhile wines. The best quality growing area is in the foothills of the Atlas range where the altitude of between 450 and 600 metres moderates the high ambient temperatures. Good wines result from mixtures of Carignan, Grenache and Cinsault. Look out for Tarik which is fairly freely available at good wine merchants.

Wines from Beni M'Tir are especially interesting and worthwhile. Sincomar, based south of Casablanca, produce one of the more unlikely wines of the world: a Kosher wine called Rabbi Jacob and produced in an Arab country. Mainly Grenache, it is soft, supple and very palatable, and quite a surprise to wine enthusiasts!

SOUTHERN AFRICA

SOUTH AFRICA

As with other former colonial territories, the history of wine-making in South Africa goes back to the earliest settlers. In 1955 they celebrated the tercentenary of the wine industry for it was in 1654 that the first Dutch cuttings came to the Cape, probably as short, 7 centimetre long slips of young vines from the Rhineland. The next year another consignment was sent from Holland and these were probably Muscat, Muscatelle, Sémillon and Chenin Blanc – or Green Grape and Steen to give the last two their South African names.

On 2 February 1659 wine was pressed for the first time at the Cape, and from that day to this an exact record of events has been kept. In 1688 French Huguenots arrived and extended and improved the quality of Cape wines, they mainly settled in Paarl and Stelenbosch in what is now a vast wine and spirit production area.

By the end of the 18th century South Africa was able to offer a popular range of wines and, thanks to the Napoleonic wars cutting off the supply of wine from France, the export of South African wines to Britain increased to the point that an official British taster, Sir John Craddock, was appointed in 1811.

At the end of the 19th century phylloxera decimated the South African vineyards, and the subsequent re-planting, together with improved techniques of viticulture, led to considerable over-production. This, in turn, led to the creation of a wine growers' co-operative association – the KWV – in 1917 and this organisation still controls the annual crop prices and, through this, the whole industry.

Sadly, their influence over the past two decades has proved counter-productive in that, whilst the rest of the world has forged ahead, South Africa has virtually stood still – isolated vinously as well as politically.

The KWV, as with most protectionist organisations, is a fortress of conservatism. Licences to plant more vines are only given to long-time members and, even then, they virtually prevent the introduction of fresh varieties by extremely onerous quarantine regulations. All this has conspired to leave South Africa stagnating while other countries have improved. This is particularly sad as the favoured areas of South Africa are among the very finest growing areas and conditions in the world.

In 1972 well formulated wine legislation based on a 'Wines of Origin' structure of 14 specified areas was introduced. All wines making claims as to provenance, grape type, superiority of quality and so on have to be certified and carry the corresponding government seal on the neck of the bottle. This seal has a system of bands for the various claims made for the wine. A blue band shows that the wine is from the stated region; a red band indicates the vintage; a green band guarantees that the wine contains 85% of the stated grape variety. These bands are applied to a white label for ordinary quality wines, while superior quality wines carry the bands on a gold label, in which case the wine will be 100% of the named grape variety. If 'Estate' is also printed, then the wine will have come from one of the 70 properties permitted to bottle only the wine from their own grapes.

The major white grape, almost to the exclusion of all others, is the Steen or Chenin Blanc. Over 30,000 hectares are planted and the grape is persuaded to produce everything from reasonably interesting off-dry table wine, to sparkling wine and 'sherries'. Some 'Riesling' is grown, but it is not the grape of the Rhine, rather it is the dull Crouchen, a little used French grape which also crops up in South Australia as the Clare Valley Riesling. Some true Riesling has been introduced in the last few years and, not surprisingly, has proved far superior! Chardonnay and Sauvignon Blanc were actually banned until quite recently so the only other quality white grape seen is the unexciting Sylvaner, although there are some plantings of the equally unexciting Müller-Thurgau – which the South Africans are inclined to call Sylvaner as well!

Red grapes offer a greater variety. The most widely planted is Cinsault which in Europe does not produce inspired wine, but does rather better in South Africa. They have produced the Pinotage by crossing the Cinsault, often here called the Hermitage, with Pinot Noir, but the outcome of this unlikely marriage is far from interesting. There are 2500 hectares of Pinotage compared with 18,000 hectares of Cinsault – and 2000 hectares of Cabernet Sauvignon which, again, is proving its versatility and is producing quality wines in yet another corner of the world. Shiraz is planted with Pinot Noir, Gamay, Zinfandel and Merlot in semi-experimental vineyards.

South Africa produces an outstanding dessert wine, Edelkeur, a special late-harvest Steen produced by the KWV, but even this is clearly only a shadow of Constantia, one of the famed and fabled great dessert wines of past centuries and now sadly no more than a legend.

Of the modern wines available, most of the KWV products are good value for money, if a little undramatic compared with Australian or Californian wines. Some private estates' wines are sold and a Hamilton-Russel vineyard Hemel-en-Aard NV white fully justified the rather high price asked.

ZIMBABWE

It is convenient that Zimbabwe produces wine, for it allows writers to claim that they cover the subject of wine from A – Z. There's never been a shortage of As (Argentina, Austria, Australia) but Zs have definitely been in short supply!

The news that this country is capable of producing respectable wine will come as no surprise to ex-colonials from the days when this was Southern Rhodesia, but to other people it seems most unlikely and these wines, along with those of China, India and so on, cause no end of fun at blind tastings!

Philips Central Cellars of Harare produce a limited range under their exotic Flame Lily brand name. On offer are Premium White, Dry White, Medium White and Red. Quality is far from being in the sensational category as yet, mainly due to using some pretty indifferent varieties in perhaps less than ideally suited terrain. But they are learning, and it will be interesting to see what comes of their experimental plantings of Sauvignon Blanc and Chardonnay. Two wines from Monis – their Mukuyu Cabernet and their VAT 10 Colombard have earned medals in competition in London so quality possibilities are certainly there!

NORTH AMERICA

BRITISH COLUMBIA

ALBERTA

CANADA

QUEBEC

NOVA SCOTIA

WASHINGTON

MINNESOTA

ONTARIO

NEW HAMPSHIRE

MONTANA

NEW YORK STATE

MASSACHUSETTS

OREGON

IDAHO

MICHIGAN

RHODE ISLAND

IOWA

PENNSYLVANIA

CONNECTICUT

NEW JERSEY

USA

OHIO

DELAWARE

UTAH

ILLINOIS

INDIANA

WEST VIRGINIA

MARYLAND

COLORADO

KANSAS

VIRGINIA

MISSOURI

KENTUCKY

NORTH CAROLINA

CALIFORNIA

NEW MEXICO

OKLAHOMA

ARKANSAS

TENNESSEE

SOUTH CAROLINA

ARIZONA

MISSISSIPPI

GEORGIA

HAWAII

TEXAS

LOUISIANA

ALABAMA

FLORIDA

MEXICO

Main wine regions

0 — 500
kilometres

THE UNITED STATES OF AMERICA

As far as wine is concerned the USA is truly a New World. A new world of production, of techniques, of experimentation and of consumption. However, in spite of its newness, the effect on the production methods in traditional areas of Europe has been profound.

American technological developments allied to extensive research into absolutely every single aspect of wine production, from plant sap to glass content, has endowed growers with detailed understanding of the controllable factors to such an extent that it is no longer necessary to 'write-off' a European vintage. Better wine of higher quality has been the result of the American-led technological revolution. Had it not been for the set-back of Prohibition between the two world wars the industry would be much more advanced than it is.

Wine production with European grape varieties began on the west coast when Father Junipo Serra founded a mission north of San Diego in 1769, thus extending the chain of missions that stretched through Mexico from the original Spanish landings and colonies around the Gulf of Mexico. This was the first time that there had been an alternative vine to the uninspiring indigenous varieties – *Vitis labrusca* and *Vitis rotundifolia*. The former grows on the eastern seaboard, and has a flavour described politely as 'foxy' and less so as 'cat's pee'. The latter is no better.

Vines clearly flourished in the climate of the western USA, and much pioneering work was done by the suitably-named Jean-Louis Vignes and the larger-than-life figure of Count (or General, all his titles were self-bestowed) Agoston Haraszthy who brought from Europe over 100,000 vine cuttings in 1840. Sadly some of the labels became lost and the ancestry of one of the most successful vines, which he called the Zinfandel, was unknown before modern research decided it was probably the Primitivo of southern Italy.

Sonoma became the cradle of the Californian wine industry in the 19th century when Count Haraszthy set up his winery at Buena Vista. However, came Prohibition and the fledgling industry was almost completely killed off. A few wineries survived by making 'sacramental wines' – even sparkling sacramental wines! – and by selling grape-juice with the stern caution that adding yeast might cause fermentation. Prohibition set the industry back for decades and, as repeal of this legislation came close to US involvement in the Second World War, it was not until the affluent 1960s that conditions were right for the wine-producing explosion.

Now we accept the place of the USA in the world of wine. They have the largest production plant for wine in the world at the unsuitably named town of Modesto in San Joaquin Valley and they have the focal point of the world's vinous research at Davis, the University of California's Department of Viticulture Campus just outside Sacramento. Here, during the 1970s, it was said that more than half of the students were from Europe – the sons and daughters of the vineyard owners learning how it really should be done!

An indication of the country's serious approach to wine and wine making was the introduction on 1 January 1990 of Appellation Napa Valley. Now, by law, the labels on all bottles of wine from the Napa Valley must clearly state this.

CALIFORNIA

WEATHER v SOIL

One of the major differences between France and California with regard to vine selection is that the French carry out extensive and exacting soil analysis and assume that the weather will be generally constant across one region, whereas the Californians pay less attention to the soil, but carry out detailed analysis of weather and temperatures.

In France the boundaries of areas of vinous legislation are largely determined by soil similarity, whereas in California the wine regions are categorised and, grape variety recommendations based on 'Climate Regions', which are determined by a degree-day scale. The scale was devised by Davis – the shorthand name for the Department of Agriculture and Enology of the University of California (Davis Campus) based at the town of the same name just west of Sacramento. They assume that a temperature of 50°F is required before a vine will become active and each day's average temperature between 1 April and 31 October above 50°F is multiplied by the number of days the minimum temperature is exceeded.

For example, for a seven day period we will assume for simplicity that there are four days with an average of 70°F and three days with an average of 80°F. That week would score:

$$(70–50) \times 4 + (80–50) \times 3 = 80 + 90$$
$$= 170 \text{ degree days}$$

Taking the total degree-days for an area over the seven month qualifying period will put the area in one of five Regions:

Region I	*less than 2500 d-d*	
similar to Champagne, Germany		
Region II	*2500–3000 d-d*	
similar to Bordeaux, northern Rhône		
Region III	*3000–3500 d-d*	
similar to southern Rhône, Provence		
Region IV	*3500–4000 d-d*	
similar to central Spain		
Region V	*over 4000 d-d*	
similar to North Africa		

In the past fairly rigid recommendations were laid down (see table page 196) but in recent years there has been a gradual realisation that there are still factors which lie beyond even the analytical powers of Davis. Nowadays some of the best of California's wines are being produced from varieties growing outside their prescribed Davis Degree Day/Climate Zone recommendations.

Throughout the growing areas of California the factor determining the Climate Region classification of any given valley is due almost entirely to the proximity, or otherwise, of cooling mists and breezes from the Pacific or from San Francisco Bay. The clearest example of this is in the Napa Valley where the southern end, which you might expect to be the hottest, is, in fact, the coolest, being rated as Region I, whereas the northern end of the valley is hotter, qualifying for a Region III rating. This back-to-front effect is caused by the southern end of the valley opening onto San Francisco Bay whereas the head of the valley is effectively sealed from it. Anywhere there is an east-west break in the coastal mountains and there is the possibility of cooling breezes coming through into the warmer terrain behind the mountains is where the prospectors for new growing areas will look. Soil is, of course, important and the damaging effect of frost is also a consideration, but both of these natural effects can be modified and moderated by irrigation, fertilisation, wind fans, gas burners, and so on, but so far no-one has managed to control the whole climate, which is why so much attention is paid to this one variable that cannot be influenced.

CENTRAL VALLEY

It is all too easy to pass off the Central Valley as an area only producing vast amounts of simple 'jug' wines – the US equivalent of plonk. This long valley, the valley of the San Joaquin, running from Sacramento in the north to Bakersfield in the south, has temperatures more akin to Bahrain than to Bordeaux and the flat river base with rich soils encourages huge crops of both dessert and wine grapes. Indeed over 70% of all the USA's wines come from this valley.

But the real interest of the Central Valley lies in the fact that this area demonstrates that technology can make the production of good wines under unlikely conditions possible. The area enjoys no cooling currents from the Pacific

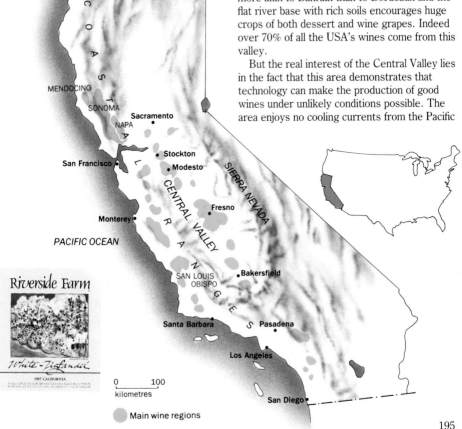

195

MAJOR VARIETIES AND THEIR DAVIS RECOMMENDED REGIONS:

Region I	Region II	Region III	Region IV	Region V
Chardonnay	Sauvignon Blanc	Barbera	Barbera	Palomino
Riesling	Cabernet Sauvignon	Carignan	Emerald Riesling	Malvasia
Sauvignon Blanc	Chardonnay	Colombard	Colombard	Mission
Cabernet Sauvignon	Chenin Blanc	Muscat	Malvasia	Souzao
Chenin Blanc	Grenache	Ruby Cabernet	Mission	Verdelho
'Gamay'	Riesling	(Chenin Blanc)	Ruby Cabernet	
Gewürztraminer	Muscat	(Chardonnay)	Zinfandel	
Pinot Noir	Petit Sirah	(Grenache)	(Muscat)	
Zinfandel	Sauvignon Blanc	(Malvasia)		
(Sémillon)	Sémillon	(Sauvignon Blanc)		
(Merlot)	Sylvaner	Sémillon		
(Sylvaner)	Syrah	Sylvaner		
	Zinfandel	Syrah		
		Zinfandel		

Notes
1 ( ) indicates varieties not recommended but doing well
2 The Emerald Riesling (Riesling × Muscat) and Ruby Cabernet (Cabernet Sauvignon × Carignan) are two popular Davis-developed crossed grape varieties.
3 Petit Sirah has nothing to do with the Syrah. It is, instead, a dull old French grape, the Durif.

Misnomers

Great confusion unfortunately exists in this state over the question of grape names. In Region I the Gamay appears in quotes, because two grapes have that name in California and neither are the true Gamay of Beaujolais! One is a clone of Pinot Noir and the other is the undistinguished Valdiguie of the Midi and south-west France which, although declining in popularity in its home country, still enjoys more than 1200 hectares of plantings in California. A few other classic misnomers are

Californian name	True identity
White grapes	
Pinot Blanc	Melon de Bourgogne/ Muscadet
Sauvignon Vert	Muscadelle
Savagnin Musque	Sauvignon Blanc
Gray Riesling	Nothing at all to do with the Riesling. Called Grey Riesling in New Zealand it is a mutation of the Jura's Trousseau
Red grapes	
Gamay Beaujolais	Pinot Noir clone
Napa Gamay	Valdiguie
Gros Manseng	Petit Verdot of Bordeaux
Valdepeñas	Probably but not definitely Tempranillo

▶ *Autumn tints creeping into the Carmenet Vineyard in Sonoma. Beyond the winery is* *Sonoma Valley and, in the distance, the Sonoma Mountains giving protection from the Pacific.* *Close by is Agoston Haraszthy's vineyard, Buena Vista.*

and the Region V degree-day rating has meant that for years it merely produced quantities of fortified wines or over-strong blousy reds and whites. Then, 25 years ago, plantings of the Davis-developed heat-resistant varieties like Ruby Cabernet and Emerald Riesling (nowadays more modern Davis hybrids like Carnelian, Centurian and Carmine are popular), together with methods of cooling the vines by high trellising to ensure good, shadey leaf-cover and of mist sprays for use on the hottest days, meant that more sophisticated, better balanced wines became possible. However, these changes in the vineyards would not have been enough without corresponding changes and developments in picking, pressing, fermenting and storing. Thus mechanical pickers now work at night when the temperature is lower, the whole system of transport and storage ensures an oxygen-free environment and, above all, cooled musts undergo temperature-controlled fermentation to produce crisp, fresh, wines in the modern style.

And, in all of these developments, the lead has repeatedly been taken by the Gallo Brothers.

E & J GALLO

Biggest of the big in this region, and therefore in the whole world, are E & J Gallo. They started in Modesto, in the very centre of the Central Valley, in 1933 with Ernest selling the wines produced by his brother Julio. By 1935 they had built their first winery on the site of the present one and by 1940 they were realising the basic truth that good wines come from good grapes. They were experimenting with better grapes and had even started to buy-in from the Napa and Sonoma valleys. Today they purchase about a third of all wine grapes grown in California.

In the mid 1960s they launched Hearty Burgundy, actually more Italian in style than Burgundian, and Chablis Blanc, again with scant regard for the origins of the name they used.

It is easy to joke about this apparently simplistic approach but Gallos have made very few mistakes. By the mid 1970s they correctly divined that Americans had become more sophisticated in their wine-drinking habits and they were ready with varietal wines. Initially fairly clumsy grapes, such as Barbera, Colombard and Ruby Cabernet were used, but now the accent is on wood-aged Chardonnays and Cabernet Sauvignons. Wood-ageing obviously needed barrel capacity and a place to

store the maturing wines so, in typical style, the Gallo brothers constructed a 2-acre cellarage area to hold 2 million gallons in oak casks. You can't think small with an output nudging a million cases a week!

All the size numbers are awe-inspiring. Production is around 50 million cases a year; they can hold up to 175 million gallons in their tank farm; their warehouse covers 25 acres yet holds only four weeks' stock and the bottling line starts in their glass factory – the biggest west of the Mississippi.

Amazingly there are other huge producers in the Central Valley:

J.F.J. Bronco Winery – 2 million cases a year, also in Modesto but Franzia-owned
Franzia Brothers Winery – 5 million cases a year
Guild Wineries – 3 million cases a year
all of whom are capable of good quality inexpensive wines

SOUTH OF THE BAY AND THE CENTRAL COAST

All around San Francisco Bay the land is developed. To the south is the city of San Jose and the natural spread of conurbation coupled with the rapid development of industry in Silicon Valley has put vine-growing land at a premium. As a result many of the older companies have retained their wineries, but have sold off their vineyards to developers and replanted further south. This move began in the early 1960s and several growers made the same mistake: seeking a warm environment but with access to the cooling mists and breezes off the Pacific, they planted in Salinas Valley which had long been famed for salads and fruits. Unfortunately the growers found that the exposed vines were being damaged by the very breezes they had sought. The valley acted as a funnel, especially on hot days, and the velocity of the winds was too much for the plants. Re-planting on a massive scale followed and now the large fields providing fruit for giants like Paul Masson, Almaden and Taylor California Cellars are further down the valley at Paso Robles. A few growers remain in the Livermore Valley just north of Alameda and San Jose. Here Concannon and Wente Brothers, both founded in 1883 to make altar wines, produce excellent, reliable wines. Stoney Ridge Winery and Livermore Valley Cellars are two newcomers to the area. Concannon, incidentally, produce a rare wine from the Russian Rkatsiteli grape which is an invigoratingly crisp white wine. They must be the only exponent of this grape outside Mother Russia!

To the south is the prestigious Jekel Vineyard with, by Californian standards, small plantings of Chardonnay, Riesling, Pinot Noir and Cabernet Sauvignon. Their quality makes up for their small size and they have a firm international following. Further south is another example of the by-now regular pattern. An opening in the mountains of the Coastal Range allows cooling sea breezes and mists to penetrate into a fertile inland valley and vines take over from grazing or dessert fruit production.

The next wine-growing area is Paso Robles. This receives less of the Pacific's cooling effect and so the Zinfandel is widely grown here for jug wines for home consumption. However, just south of Paso Robles and just outside the town of San Luis Obispo is the tiny area of Edna Valley. The outstanding winery here is the Edna Valley Vineyard, which produces, among other wines, a Chardonnay which is one of the very finest examples of wine from this grape in the world.

South of the developing area of the Santa Maria Valley is the Santa Ynez Valley, where the association between Brooks Firestone of the Firestone tyre family and the Japanese Suntory whisky company has created a showpiece estate. Here some of the most consistent and, for the price, best value-for-money wines are made, all from traditional European grapes: Gewürztraminer, Riesling, Chardonnay, Cabernet Sauvignon, Sauvignon Blanc and Pinot Noir.

Brander and Zaca Mesa also produce high-quality wines in the Santa Ynez Valley, although difficult to obtain in the UK.

SIGNIFICANT PRODUCERS IN THIS SOUTH OF THE BAY AREA

Livermore Valley
Concannon, Distillers-Somerset Group – revived by acquisition in 1982
Wente Brothers, the Wente family – now fourth generation. Best known for Cabernet Sauvignon in the UK but whites are probably best

San Jose
Almaden, Grand Met – 8.5 million cases a year, bulk wines only

Mirassou Vineyards, the Mirassou family – fifth generation. Victims of increasing urban expansion
Mount Eden Vineyards – part of old Martin Ray vineyard. Small but good, especially Chardonnay
Ridge Vineyards, Otsuka Co – highly prized vineyard bought by the Japanese in 1987

Salinas Valley
Calera Wine Company, Josh and Jeanne Jensen – well inland and off most wine maps of California. Good Pinot Noir and Zinfandel
Chalone, Richard Graff, wine-makers Michael Michaud and Richard Graff – closest to the Pinot Noir Holy Grail. See also Acacia (Napa), Carmenet (Sonoma) and Edna Valley vineyards
Paul Masson Vineyards – change of ownership and an uncertain future, but still 8 million cases a year
Taylor Californian Cellars, Seagram – 'Californian' to differentiate from their New York State operation, 7 million cases a year

Arroyo Seco
Jekel Vineyard, the Jekel family – great Cabernet Sauvignon but, surprisingly, even better whites

Paso Robles
Martin Brothers, the Martin family – one of the best Zinfandel exponents from near Templeton, the Zinfandel capital of the west

Edna Valley
Edna Valley Vineyard, owned by Chalone Vineyard of Soledad in the Salinas Valley who also own Acacia Vineyard in the Napa and Carmenet in Sonoma. Sensational Chardonnay and also, like all Chalone-owned vineyards, Pinot Noir

Santa Ynez Valley
Firestone Vineyard, the Firestone family/ Suntory – exceptional wines from a range of classic varietals. 100% Pinot Noir sparkler soon
Sanford Wines, Richard and Thekla Sanford – newly created, but already their floral Sauvignon Blanc has attracted attention
Zaca Mesa, Marshall Ream – phylloxera-free ungrafted vines in Santa Maria Valley plus a vineyard near their winery produces good quality wines

NAPA VALLEY

▲ *A typical view of neat
and orderly Napa Valley:
Monticello Cellars, Oak
Knoll Avenue, on the
outskirts of the township of
Napa.*

Those who know a little about Californian wines know at least one name – Napa Valley. And with good reason, for although Sonoma Valley was where California's wine industry began, the Napa was where the application of up-to-the-minute methods were first applied to quality wine. Many fine vineyards existed in the Napa before the 1960s – Beaulieu, Martini, Mayacamas and Christian Brothers among many others – but it is Robert Mondavi whose name is most usually linked to the leap into the 21st century. In 1966 he left his family winery of Charles Krug at St Helena in the hands of his brother Peter and set up just outside Oakville, six miles down the road. His was the first of the new wineries to combine the very best of technology with an architectural design of quality and interest in its own right. There are now just under 100 wineries in the Napa Valley on either side of US 29 which runs from the town of Napa, through Oakville and St Helena on to Calistoga, a distance of only 25 miles. In this short distance the Davis scale of degree-days (see page 194) splits the Napa into three different climate regions and their layout points up the importance of the modifying influence of the Pacific Ocean. The southern end of the valley, where it joins Sonoma Valley and abuts the shores of San Pablo Bay is Region I – the coolest. Then, going northwards up the valley through Napa itself we enter Region II at Oakville and a few miles further north, just beyond St Helena, is a Region III environment. To use a European analogy the climate changes from Champagne in the south, through Bordeaux to Provence in the north!

Recommendations

Classifying the wineries of Napa in order of merit would be impossible. In alphabetical order the following are the most significant:

Acacia – also own Chalone, Carmenet and Eden Valley vineyards. Closest to the Pinot Noir Holy Grail. Trying in other areas too

Atlas Peak, Whitbread/Antinori/Bollinger – an almost holy (in vinous terms) trinity of ownership. First sparkling wine vintage expected 1988

Beaulieu Vineyard, owned by Heublin Inc which is part of Grand Met – André Tchelistcheff, the 'father' of Napa wine-makers, worked here from 1940 to 1970

Beringer Vineyard, Nestlé Ltd – was declining before acquisition by Nestlé. Now on an upward path

Carneros Creek Winery, owner Balfour Gibson – located where Napa and Sonoma join in a Region I cool area which helps produce sophisticated classic wines

Christian Brothers, the Catholic Order of la Salle – vast land holdings, huge range of wines and an unassuming wine-maker, Brother Timothy, owned by Grand Met

Clos du Val Wine Co, John Golet – managed by one of the two Portet brothers, sons of ex-Lafite manager. Other brother runs Taltarni in Australia

Conn Creek, W.D. Collins – one of the partners here owns Ch La Mission Haut-Brion in France

Cuvaison, Swiss-owned – austere style of original Swiss wine-maker now softening. Calistoga Cellars is their second label

Diamond Creek Vineyards, Al Brounstein – *very* French influence and style. Pure Bordeaux blend and experimenting with different soils

Domaine Chandon, Moët-Hennessy – first of the French/European invasion forces. Followed by Deutz, Codorníu, Langguth etc

Dominus – the mighty Mouiex company of Bordeaux trying for a Pétrus

Far Niente Winery – old, pre-Prohibition winery revived and selling highly priced but highly prized Chardonnay and Cabernet Sauvignon

Freemark Abbey, Charles Carpy – old established (1895), newly reborn (1967). Brilliant wines. Pioneering team and no quality compromises

Grgich-Hills Cellars, Austin Hills and Mike Grgich – Hills grows the grapes, Grgich trained by André Tchelistcheff makes the wine

Heitz Wine Cellars, Joe and Alice Heitz – son David is wine-maker, trained under André Tchelistcheff

Inglenook Vineyards, Heublin Inc, part of Grand Met – old pre-Prohibition property. Improved under Heublin ownership

Charles Krug Winery, Peter Mondavi – brother of Robert Mondavi (see below), both sons of Cesare Mondavi, the Napa's oldest winery

Louis M. Martini, Louis P. Martini – another family dynasty, classic wines since the 1920s

Mayacamus, Bob and Nonie Travers – up the valley sides. One of the first to see the potential of the 'higher ground'

Robert Mondavi Winery, Robert Mondavi –

▼ *As in Champagne, so in Napa. 'Pupitres' holding bottles which have*

▼ *As in Champagne, so in Napa. 'Pupitres' holding bottles which have* *undergone secondary fermentation at Schramsberg in the Napa* *Valley. As the bottles are gradually turned and tilted the sediment spirals* *down until it is in contact with the cork.*

son Tim is the wine-maker. Famed for much-hyped joint enterprise with de Rothschild, Opus One

Mount Veeder, owner Henry Matheson – near Mayacamus in Pickle Canyon, well up off the floor of the valley on rocky ground

Joseph Phelps Vineyards, Joseph Phelps – mid 1970s arrival. A builder with a sense of vinous vocation. A mini-Mondavi

Rutherford Hill Winery, owners Chuck Carpy and Bill Jaeger – sold to the partners by Souverain. Connections with Freemark Abbey Winery

Saintsbury, Richard Ward and David Graves – Carneros Region I location gives quality

Pinot Noir and fine Chardonnay

Schramsberg Vineyards, Jack and Jamie Davies – Robert Louis Stevenson drank wine here. One of the best Californian sparklers

Stags Leap Wine Cellars, Warren and Barbara Winiarski – Warren, ex-Professor of Greek, trained under André Tchelistcheff. Possibly the best in the Napa. Second label is Hawk Crest

Sterling Vineyard, Seagram – built with British money in the 1960s, Coca Cola owned it in the 1970s, now belongs to Seagram

Trefethen Vineyards, John and Janet Trefethen – bought the old 'Eshcol' (see Numbers XIII v.23) in 1968, now outstanding wines

SONOMA VALLEY, RUSSIAN RIVER AND ALEXANDER VALLEY

The wines of Sonoma have been overshadowed by those of the Napa Valley. Honest, workmanlike wines rather than championship gold medal wines are produced. Old-established vineyards, many revived after the Depression and Prohibition, are finding a ready market for their products with Kenwood and Chateau St Jean in the forefront. There seems a more relaxed approach in Sonoma – so different to the frenetic activity just over the pass on the other side of the mountains! However, at the head of the Sonoma Valley is a larger area loosely called Russian River after an old Russian trading post that was here in years gone by, and in this area, especially in the Alexander Valley, are some of the most exciting new wines of California. Vineyards are not new to the area, but it mainly produced good quality bulk grapes for jug wines processed at wineries elsewhere. In the last ten years 'prospectors' from the Napa looking for cooler growing conditions than the Region III temperatures at the head of their valley came into this area and were well rewarded. They struck a rich vein in the perfect conjunction of weather and soil and have set to with typical American endeavour and enthusiasm.

The standard bearer for this new territory is Jordan Vineyard. The property is straight out of the Médoc – a French château in California – and the Cabernet Sauvignon/Merlot red wines, aged in oak barrels from Ch Lafite, are a fine example of what the Médoc would do if it could. Since the 1978 vintage, the wine is aged for five years before release and a glass of 1978 that I had the pleasure of drinking in 1987 proved to be possibly the finest glass of red wine that I have ever encountered.

MENDOCINO

North of the Russian River is the Mendocino. Protected from the Pacific by the coastal hills, the valley is relatively warm – warm enough to qualify as Region III, even, in places, as Region IV. Parducci are a long-established name, for their winery was built in 1931, a brave act during Prohibition. More important, and several rungs up the quality ladder is Fetzer with an output of mainly Cabernet Sauvignon, Sauvignon Blanc and Sémillon.

SIGNIFICANT PRODUCERS

Sonoma

Alexander Valley Vineyards, the Wetzel family – one of the earliest vineyards to recognise the excellence of Alexander Valley conditions

Buena Vista, A Racke – new (1979) German owners have moved from the historic site (see text) down to Carneros where Napa and Sonoma join

Carmenet, see Chalone (Salinas Valley) – this time the team seem to be looking to Bordeaux and not to Burgundy for their inspiration

Chateau St Jean, Suntory – heavy Japanese investments (they also own Ch Lagrange in the Médoc and part-own Firestone). Serious sparkling wines are the latest development

Dry Creek, David Stare – wine-maker Larry Levin produces some of this area's greatest wines expecially Sauvignon Blanc and Cabernet Sauvignon

Glen Ellen, the Benziger family – another revival of historic winery, this time to produce volumes of low-cost/high-quality wines

▲ *David Stare, owner of Dry Creek, about to start pressing Chardonnay grapes for the 1980 vintage.*

▶ *The main barrel room at Dry Creek.*

◄ *Barry Sterling of Iron Horse Vineyards in the Sonoma Valley, one of a number of producers who have done much to improve the area's reputation.*

Iron Horse, Audrey Sterling – almost on the Russian River border, their still wines are good but their sparklers even better

Matanzas Creek Winery, Sandra MacIver – small producer of excellent wines

Simi Winery, Moët-Hennessy – excellent Chardonnay from old established (1876) but frequently changing ownership. Other wines good too – oak-aged Zinfandel; Alexander Valley Cabernet Sauvignon

Mendocino

Fetzer, John Fetzer – a big operation well to the north of the Sonoma Valley extension in Mendocino

Parducci Wine Cellars, John Parducci – the first vineyard in Mendocino, now in the hands of the fourth generation

Alexander Valley

Clos du Bois, Frank Woods – 405 hectares of vineyards all in Dry Creek and Alexander Valleys. Wine-making by John Hawley

Jordan Vineyard, Thomas Jordan – Bordeaux-in-California. Complete with a château and oak barrels from Lafite. Outstanding reputation

THE PACIFIC NORTH-WEST

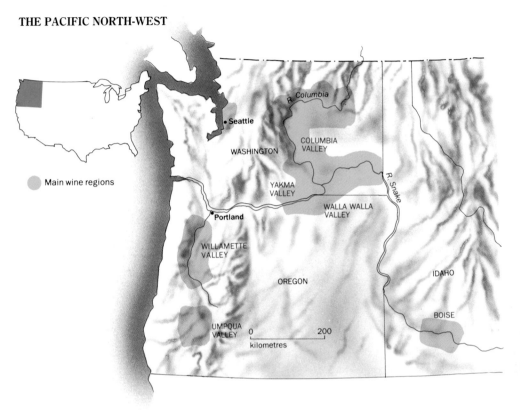

North of California lie the states of Oregon and Washington and here the weather is more European in style. The Pacific Ocean still has a moderating effect, but, whereas further south the breezes and mists from the sea cool what might otherwise be unsuitably hot growing conditions, here the sea has the reverse effect. Conditions that might otherwise be too cool are moderated by warm rains off the sea. Sometimes there is too much rain, especially at harvest time, but the cooler conditions give a complementary set of growing conditions to California where the danger exists of too much flavour and overstated wines.

Oregon gives the chance to produce lighter Chardonnays, more Germanic Rieslings and, above all, Pinot Noirs with sufficient sugar yet restrained enough to show the subtlety of the grape in the wine. Best exponents that are marketed in the UK are Knudsen Erath and Erie Vineyards although both, like all the vineyards in this area, have very small outputs.

Douglas Henn-Macrae, the specialist importer of wines from lesser-known US States, tells of a tasting held in New York in

1985, in which ten 1983 Oregon Pinot Noirs challenged seven 1983 French Burgundies; 25 professional wine-tasters took part. The Oregonians took 1st, 2nd and 3rd places; the top scorer was wrongly identified as French by 11 tasters, and the second prize-winner by 13; the most expensive wine shown (Chambolle-Musigny, $37 a bottle) got *no votes* and was wrongly identified as American by 12 tasters, and the cheapest (Alpine Vineyards, $9) also got no votes and nine judges thought it was French. The average price of the Burgundies was $24 a bottle, and the Oregon Pinot Noirs $13.

In 1987 at a tasting of Oregon and Burgundian Chardonnays the winner was a Puligny-Montrachet at $59 a bottle, but second was an Adelsheim's Oregon Chardonnay at $12, beating various Chassagne- and Chevalier-Montrachets, Meursaults etc. The average prices for the Burgundian Chardonnays was $40 and for the Oregonian Chardonnays $12.

This sort of story is hardly unusual these days. What is unusual is how little effect it has on the drinking habits of the buying public who, especially in the US seem to want to buy labels not wine. But perhaps the most eloquent evidence of the area's quality is that Robert Drouhin, one of the greatest producers of Burgundies, now owns land in Oregon!

Further north, in Washington State, Associated Vintners did pioneering work in the 1960s. Their Sémillon-based, simply named, Valley White is still a fine example of the refreshing wines this under-rated grape can produce. Now known as Columbia Winery, their wines are made by David Lake from the UK, who worked closely with David Lett at Erie before moving north. The largest winery in this developing area is Chateau Sainte Michelle north of Seattle.

Apart from the ten or so wineries around Seattle there is a further group of about ten inland around the Yakima and Columbia rivers that is showing well and has great prospects for future development.

The natural extension of the inland Washington State group of vineyards is the Snake River area. As yet small, it holds promise of good things to come, while further south in Idaho, around the capital Boise, there is a revival of some of the old pre-Prohibition wineries which show promise.

NOTEWORTHY PRODUCERS

Oregon

Adelsheim Vineyard, David and Virginia Adelsheim – only started in the Willamette Valley in 1978. All great wines with new Pinot Gris especially interesting

Alpine Vineyards – again in the Willamette Valley. Small, family-run, but perfectionist attitudes prevail

Amity Vineyards, Myron and Ione Redford and Janis Checchia – blend grapes from Washington and Oregon, especially Pinot Noir

Elk Cove Vineyards, Joe and Pat Campbell – Pinot Noir specialists, but also an interesting botrytis Riesling

The Eyrie Vineyards, David and Diana Lett – medal-winner in France and Oregon Pinot Noir pioneer. Looking at Pinot Gris too

Hillcrest Vineyard, Richard Sommer – in Umpqua Valley. Founded 1961

Knudsen Erath Winery, Calvert Knudsen and Richard Erath – apart from 'standard' Oregon Pinot Noir, now making sparkling wine too

Sokol Blosser Winery, Sokol and Blosser families – at just over 20,000 cases second only to Knudsen Erath. Wide range of varieties

Tualatin Vineyard, Bill Malkmus and William Fuller – almost equal second in output, buy in from Washington State as well as own vines

Washington State

Arbor Crest, the Mielke family – big, by north-western standards, producer of wide range of wines. Late-harvest specialist too

Chateau Ste Michelle, US Tobacco – vast output, 1 million cases a year, excellent quality to go with the size. Buy-in extensively

Columbia (formerly Associated Vintners), now well-established private company, with a well deserved reputation

F.W. Langguth – as the name suggests, a significant German investment by the Langguth company. 60,000 cases and growing

Staton Hills – Yakima Valley winery, new but growing at an amazing rate, now 100,000 cases a year! Includes pink Riesling!

Stewart Vineyards, George Stewart – ex-orthopaedic specialist turned wine-maker in possibly the 'best' area: Yakima Valley. Fine quality

Idaho

Ste Chapelle, the Symms family – significant output around 130,000 cases from 110 hectares plus bought-in grapes

Covey Rise – not well known but good Chardonnay. Do not confuse with Covey Run (formerly Quail Run) in Yakima, Washington

Rose Creek, Jamie Mertin – small producer on the Snake River who also buys-in. Cabernet Sauvignon and Chardonnays are good

THE FINGER LAKES

Historically important but of little interest to the European drinker, are the wines of upper New York State. Development of a wine industry began in this area in the mid 1800s in parallel to the activities on the western seaboard. Although the wines were crude, even unpleasant, they were what was there and so they were drunk – and gradually residents of the eastern seaboard came to accept that that was how wine tasted. The fault lies with the species *Vitis labrusca* with its 'foxy' taste, and the hardiest and best cropping hybrids and crosses of the region all contained at least a part of Labrusca. Vine names here are unfamiliar to us – Concord, a 100% Labrusca red grape is the most widely planted; Catawba, a pale red grape which makes red, rosé and even white wine; Delaware is another very pale red grape.

Until Prohibition, vineyards and wineries extended from the Canadian border down to Tallahassee on the Mexican Gulf and a great proportion of the wines produced were sparkling. Sparkling wine tends to mask the potentially unpleasant flavour of the Labrusca grape and the man who first realised this, and so made a fortune, was Nicholas Longworth whose Sparkling Catawba was produced from his 485 hectares around Cincinnati between 1830 and 1863. The industry was wiped out by Longworth's death, the Civil War, and diseased vines. The production of sparkling wine then moved up to the Finger Lakes area, where it has been for 100 years. However, the really interesting development in New York State and in neighbouring Ohio has been the gradual introduction of *Vitis vinifera* grapes. Few wineries have been prepared to uproot their vineyards and completely replant – there is little reason that they should as they still have an active market for their wines, but gradually tastes on the east coast are changing and the wineries are changing with them. The size of the existing Labrusca market can be judged by the outputs of the largest producers – six million cases a year by Canandaigua Wine Company (one of their popular brand names is 'Wild Irish Rose'!), whilst Taylor/Great Western/Pleasant Valley are a consortium of producers all owned by Coca Cola and are in the multiples of millions of cases a year category. However, another large producer, Gold Seal Vineyards, owned by Seagram but, under its former President Charles Fournier, a pioneer of Vinifera wines, produces sparkling wine from Vinifera grapes for its prestige label and from Labrusca for the cheaper products. They are uncompromising about the labelling too, the labels say simply 'Henri Marchant Labrusca'. Another pioneer of Vinifera grapes is Dr Konstantin Frank who, again, feels the direct approach is the best – the company is called Vinifera Wine Cellars. His son now produces reds from Pinot Noir and Gamay with indifferent results, but some Chardonnay and some late-

gathered Riesling have been great wines. One member of the Taylor family which sold out to Coca Cola continues with both Labrusca and hybrids at Bully Hill Vineyards, but their greatest claim to 'fame' must be the appalling label for their 'Love Goat' red wine.

On a more positive note, exciting developments are taking place on Long Island. Here the climate is better than around the Finger Lakes and all planting has been with European varieties. Hargrave Vineyard were the pioneers and they have been joined by more than a dozen others since they began in 1973 including the giant Banfi organisation.

Just one other state needs consideration – the Lone Star state of Texas. Here, in true Texan style, they're thinking big and they claim they will be second to California in only a decade.

French involvement, which in other areas has tended to be belated – they arrived when reputations were already established and the best sites had gone – is, in the case of Texas, immediate. Cordier, the Bordeaux giant, has taken control of an operation which has a $15 million winery near Fort Stockton and their wines are already being sold successfully by at least two UK chain retail outlets. Excellent Sauvignon.

Medal winning wines abound. Fall Creek is probably the leader for quality but Llano Estacado are also in the medal hunt and scored a notable success with a rare double gold in San Francisco in 1986.

Most easily obtainable are the Cordier Texas wines, but the

Best names are
Fall Creek, Llano Estacado, Pheasant Ridge and Sanchez Creek.

Alphabetically, the following US states produce wine commercially:
Alabama, Arizona, Arkansas, North Carolina, South Carolina, California, Colorado, Connecticut, Delaware, Florida, Georgia, Hawaii, Idaho, Illinois, Indiana, Iowa, Kentucky, Louisiana, Maryland, Massachusetts, Michigan, Minnesota, Mississippi, Missouri, Montana, New Hampshire, New Jersey, New Mexico, New York State, Ohio, Oklahoma, Oregon, Pennsylvania, Rhode Island, Tennessee, Texas, Utah, Virginia, West Virginia, Washington – 40 out of the 50 states.

THE REST OF NORTH AMERICA

CANADA

THE WEST COAST

Not surprisingly the conditions that are good for wines in Washington State apply across the border into Canada, where *Vitis vinifera* plantings are progressing. Some vineyards are barely out of the experimental stage but there are signs that we shall see some excellent Riesling, Chardonnay and Gewürztraminer in the future. The main centre is the Okanagan Valley to the east of Vancouver in British Columbia, a growing area which is on the same latitude as the Rhine and, until recently, specialised in producing wine from the incorrectly named Okanagan Riesling, a variety whose origins are unknown but may well be an American/Hungarian hybrid. Some 1600 hectares are planted in this district and the best producers seem to be the smaller companies like Claremont at Peachland who have the local hybrid Marechal Foch alongside Chenin Blanc, Gewürztraminer, Pinot Blanc and Pinot Noir. The largest company is the Jordan Ste Michelle – which has nothing to do with either the Alexander Valley Jordan or the Washington winery of Chateau Sainte Michelle.

EASTERN CANADA

In the east of Canada, on the Ontario peninsula between Toronto and Detroit, lie the country's other vineyards. *Vitis vinifera* is being more widely planted in place of local hybrids, Foch and de Chaunac and, although the latitude is the same as that of Rome, north European grapes are being planted – Riesling, Chardonnay and,

interestingly, Aligoté, with some examples of Seyval Blanc, a Labrusca/Vinifera crossing. Best-known producer is Inniskillin with 28 hectares at Niagara. Quality wines also come from Charal at Blenheim. Ontario introduced an AC system from the 1988 vintage.

Only one Canadian producer currently has wines available in the UK – Inniskillin, based in Ontario but using Vinifera grapes as well as Labrusca. Both their Chardonnay and Riesling are adequate, if expensive, and their red Marechal Foch and sweet Vidal are useful as examples of rarely available hybrids.

MEXICO

The Mexican wine industry pre-dates that of the USA by about 300 years, but, as it has stood still for the whole of its existence and is still using the inferior Mission grape, the only developments worthy of note are the plantings of European grapes first at Ensenada just over the border from California and, subsequently, north of Mexico City where the altitude theoretically counteracts the high temperatures. The most dramatic endorsement of the potential in Mexico has been the heavy financial investment made by Pedro Domecq of Spain who have over 1300 hectares planted near Tijuana with Cabernet Sauvignon and Zinfandel for varietal wines as well as for their Los Reyes branded wines. Another landmark was the arrival of Dimitri, the son of André Tchelistcheff, who has planted Bodegas de Santo Tomas at Ensenada with Chenin Blanc, Grenache and Carignan and is experimenting with Chardonnay, Pinot Noir and Cabernet Sauvignon as well.

SOUTH
AMERICA

ACONCAGUA

• Mendoza
MENDOZA

Santiago

TUPUNGATO

SANTIAGO

SAN CARLOS

CHILE

O'HIGGINS

ARGENTINA

COLCHAGUA

SAN RAFAEL

• Curico

PACIFIC OCEAN

ALVEAR

CURICO

0   100
kilometres

Main wine regions

ARGENTINA

Before the troubles over the Falkland Isles
Argentinian wines were appearing in the UK but
that conflict, together with the horrendous state
of Argentinian finances, has stopped exports to
Europe. Their wines carry a clear Italian
influence (probably due to extensive Italian
emigration there early this century) and grape
varieties like Bonarda, Barbera, Sangiovese and
Nebbiolo are common. Large foreign companies
control much of the industry with Moët-
Hennessy's subsidiary Proviar selling their
excellent méthode champenoise sparkling wine
unashamedly as 'champagne'. Seagram own the

Bianchi and Crillon labels but the star performer
must be Penaflor, an Argentinian-owned
company in the biggest of the vine-growing
states, Mendoza, tucked under the Andes in the
east of the country. Mendoza has 70% of
Argentina's vineyards and thus over 50% of all
of South America's vineyards. To put this into
perspective, Argentina has two-thirds of the
output of the USSR from under one-third of
the area. Ungrafted vines, liberal irrigation
and a remarkably stable climate on a southerly
latitude that compares with Morocco in the
northern hemisphere all combine to give
huge yields. As yet, little finds its way to
Europe.

CHILE

The geography of Chile allows vine growers a
generous choice of micro-climates, although
experience has proved the Central Valley from
Santiago in the north to Talca in the south to be
the best for quality wines. Probably the most
favoured region of this valley is around Maipo
and it is here that Undurraga, one of the
foremost exporters of Chilean wines have their
winery. They produce nearly 250,000 cases
a year and their top wines are Viejo Roble
or 'Old Oak' wines – whites as well as reds.
They are the last to use the traditional Chilean
bottle which, like Mateus Rosé, is based on the
old German bocksbeutel shape.

Another producer whose wines are exported
to the UK and are worth seeking out is
Cousiño Macul, one of only two producers to
grow all their own grapes, whose Antiguas
Reserva Cabernet Sauvignon wines, aged for
three years in cask and two years in bottle,
stand high in the international value-for-money
league.

The other producer to grow their own grapes
and whose wines are found without too much
difficulty is Concha y Toro. Their products have
been impressively flavoursome but without the
necessary finesse to match. A new winery
in Maipu run by the German Goetz von
Gerzdorf should change that. Last of the
producers whose products have been obtainable
here for some time is Santa Rita. Founded in
1880, they have only 100 hectares of their own,
so buy-in extensively. Their best-known
branded wine is '120' – named after the one
hundred and twenty soldiers of the liberator of
Chile, Bernardo O'Higgins who hid in the Santa
Rita cellars after the Battle of Rancagua.

Each country on the American continent
seems to have a major European wine
producer making large investments. Chile is no
exception, having the leading wine family of
Europe – Torres from Penedés in Spain. His
influence will be especially felt in the production
of cold-fermented white wines, much more to
international taste and fashion, and a few
excellent examples have already been shipped
to Europe. The attractions of Chile should
eventually bring in other Europeans for labour
costs are minimal, foreign currency has a high
exchange rate and, above all, planting is easy.
No risk of phylloxera in this area with the Pacific
on one side and the Andes on the other, so
vines are planted by simply pushing canes into

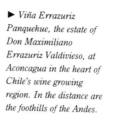

► *Viña Errazuriz
Panquehue, the estate of
Don Maximiliano
Errazuriz Valdivieso, at
Aconcagua in the heart of
Chile's wine growing
region. In the distance are
the foothills of the Andes.*

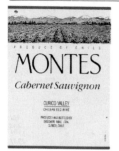

the fertile soil at six foot intervals and waiting for the first fruits after three years – even fertile Catalonia must seem difficult by comparison.

In recent years, however, the pioneering work by the aforementioned companies has established a significant foothold and now other Chilean exporters are crowding on to the scene. A well-known UK chain have long featured Campo dei Fiori Cabernet Sauvignon from the Maipo Valley at under £2.50 which won one of only 30 Gold Medals awarded out of 3,200 wines at the prestigious International Wine Challenge in London in 1989. Miguel Torres is now making his Chilean wines available in increasing quantities and they show all the flair one comes to expect of this great Catalan wine family. Other names, too, are making a great impression, among them Viña Santa Helena, Montes, Viña Linderos and Errazuriz Panquehue.

Names to look for
José Canepa, Maipu – reliable old-fashioned wines

Bodegas Centenarias, Maipo – excellent inexpensive Cabernet Sauvignon

Concha y Toro, Pirque, south of Santiago – the biggest and well on the way to redeeming their reputation

Cousino Macul, Santiago – good, somewhat 'green' white wines but excellent reds, especially Antiguas Reservas with three years in wood and two years in bottle before release

Errazuriz Panquehue (pronounced Pankayway) – Don Maximiliano Errazuriz Valdivieso's Panquehue estate vinifies Chardonnay and Sauvignon Blanc from the Maule region and Cabernet Sauvignon from the Aconcagua Valley to very good effect

Santa Rita, Buin – Casa Real and Medalla Real are the names given to their best wines but 'standard' varietals are good value. Most famous brand is '120'

Miguel Torres, Curico – interesting non-French style of Sauvignon Blanc plus other

substantial varietals. As usual collecting medals in international competitions

Viña Undurraga, Santiago – beginning to lose the limelight as others take the stage. Traditional and reliable rather than exciting

Viña San Pedro, Lontue – Castillo de Molina Cabernet Sauvignon

Note: Maipu and Maipo
Great confusion exists because there is a town in the northern growing area around Mendoza called Maipu, there is a large town south-west of Santiago in *that* particular growing area also called Maipu – and, to the south of that same growing region south of Santiago is an area called Maipo!

BRAZIL, URUGUAY AND PERU

Both Brazil and Uruguay have large wine industries but produce solely for national consumption. In Brazil, with the population explosion, large companies like Domecq, Moët-Hennessy, Cinzano and National Distillers are investing in the rapidly expanding market and vineyards extend right up the Atlantic coast from the boundary with Uruguay to north of Brasilia. Cinzano even have a vineyard at Recife and that is only 10° south of the Equator!

Greatest surprise on the South American continent has been the strides made in Peru. Here the Pacific has a moderating influence on the climate in a similar way to California and plantings, especially in the Tacama vineyards in Ica province south of Lima where the advice of the great Emile Peynaud of Bordeaux has been sought, are producing revelatory wines from Cabernet Sauvignon and Sauvignon Blanc – and also a surprisingly sophisticated méthode champenoise sparkling wine. With modern techniques it is becoming possible to select suitable vines and produce good wines almost anywhere in the world within the suitable latitudes – and sometimes even close to the Equator – provided the temperature is moderated by sea breezes or by altitude.

AUSTRALIA

NORTHERN TERRITORY

QUEENSLAND

WESTERN AUSTRALIA

SOUTH AUSTRALIA

NEW SOUTH WALES

Brisbane

Perth

Adelaide

Sydney

Canberra

VICTORIA

Melbourne

Main wine regions

0 ——————— 1000
kilometres

TASMANIA

Hobart

Australian wines are undoubtedly the wines of the 1980s. This old-established industry has gone though a complete change in direction and, so far, seems to need no control systems such as are found in most other countries.

In Australia there is only the year-long round of Regional and National Shows, in which wines are matched against each other in competitive tastings rather like athletes continually proving themselves against each other in competition. For this reason the wine-drinking world owes a considerable debt to the Australian show judges who have done so much to set the standards for an industry that has improved dramatically in a very short time.

Although Australia may seem to us in the UK to have come from nowhere at all to almost overnight prominence on the shelves of our wine retailers, in fact the industry there is as old as the colony itself. February 1788 is accepted as the date of the first plantings of vines at Farm Cove, now the Sydney Botanical Gardens. These vines fell prey to fungus attack, doubtless due to the very humid conditions, so a vineyard was established further inland on the Parramatta River where, by 1791, four acres of vines existed.

The next landmark was when Captain John

*Previous pages 'Toasting'
the oak of new barrels to
give a further dimension of
flavour to the wine.
Yalumba Cooperage,
Barossa Valley.*

Macarthur, who had pioneered the Merino sheep in Australia and who had made a number of enemies, felt it expedient to return to Europe. In 1815/16, together with his two sons, William and James, he toured Spain and France looking at vines, vineyards and wines. They took back a number of vines and, together with nephew Hannibal who had meanwhile bought the Parramatta vineyard, they set up what they felt was a European-style vineyard operation. William became the member of the family most directly involved in the wine production and he was instrumental in bringing out some German vineyard workers as colonists to provide a fresh injection of expertise. This must have had some good result as his wines and his brandies won prizes in London in the 1840s.

Another important figure in the early days was James Busby. He had experimented successfully with a small vineyard in the grounds of the orphanage where he ran the school farm and, later, had planted vines on a part of the 800 hectares he had been granted in the Hunter River district. He became enthusiastic and travelled to Europe, and in particular, France and Spain where he studied, learnt the methods, and collected some 600 cuttings. These, except for the vines he used at his Hunter River farm, were held at Farm Cove but were regrettably destroyed after Busby's later appointment as Governor of New Zealand. His vineyard, Kirkton, which continued sporadically after Busby's departure, was finally closed some time after the First World War and now only lives as the name of a wine produced by the Lindeman wine-making giant – owned by the Penfolds conglomerate.

By 1850 the New South Wales vineyards alone were producing 5000 hectolitres of wine and 68 hectolitres of brandy a year from the 400 hectares planted with vines – and by then most states had equally impressive outputs. Australia is a huge landmass but with a small population, nearly 90% of which live in and around the twelve major cities. As almost every one of these cities is close to land suitable for viniculture the industry developed with regional tastes supplied with regional wines – there was little point in shipping wine from Sydney to Adelaide when they could produce it in Adelaide just as well.

But, around 1960, the whole picture began to alter. First to change were the white wines. No longer very dry, high strength wines with little fruit, the wines became what the Australians call Moselles – just as bland as the cheap wines of Moselle or Liebfraumilch in Europe, but a revelation to Australian drinkers. And they took to these new, lighter, wines in a big way.

Fortified wine sales dropped, red wine sales dropped, even beer sales were affected. In 1975 dessert and heavy white wines represented nearly 42% of the annual production of 2.3 million hectolitres or 25 million cases. By 1984 dessert wines were a mere 6% of the annual output which had increased to nearly 40 million cases a year.

From this change in drinking habits came the enthusiasm and the finance to expand and to develop more sophisticated wines, an opportunity Australian wine-makers seized with both hands – to the great benefit of the wine-drinking public in the UK as well as in Australia itself.

To describe the growers, the areas and the wines of Australia is probably more difficult than for any other country. The regional or district names mean little to us geographically, they frequently mis-use grape names and there is virtually no wine control legislation to take as a quality yardstick. We have an old industry with many long-established companies producing vast amounts of bag-in-the-box wines, yet also having a limited output of quality wine; there are new arrivals successfully prospecting and developing new growing areas and there are companies producing good wine at their winery from grapes grown perhaps a thousand miles away – and therefore not at all representative of the location of the winery. Moreover, the number of Australian names appearing on retailers' shelves is growing, literally by the day.

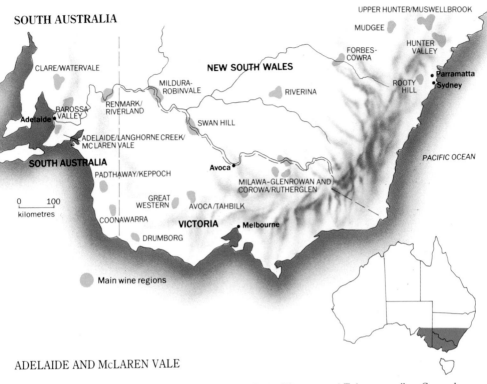

SOUTH AUSTRALIA

UPPER HUNTER/MUSWELLBROOK

MUDGEE

FORBES-
COWRA

HUNTER
VALLEY

CLARE/WATERVALE

MILDURA-
ROBINVALE

NEW SOUTH WALES

RIVERINA

ROOTY
HILL

Parramatta
Sydney

BAROSSA
VALLEY

RENMARK/
RIVERLAND

Adelaide

SWAN HILL

ADELAIDE/LANGHORNE CREEK/
MC LAREN VALE

PACIFIC OCEAN

SOUTH AUSTRALIA

PADTHAWAY/KEPPOCH

Avoca

MILAWA-GLENROWAN AND
COROWA/RUTHERGLEN

0   100
kilometres

GREAT
WESTERN

AVOCA/TAHBILK

COONAWARRA

VICTORIA   Melbourne

DRUMBORG

Main wine regions

ADELAIDE AND McLAREN VALE

This, historically, is the right place to start. Here vineyards go back to 1838 when John Reynell planted vines at Chateau Reynella. This site is now the headquarters of the equally old company of Thomas Hardy & Sons who bought the property in 1982, a sentimental purchase for the original Tom Hardy had had his first job at Ch Reynella five generations back.

The McLaren Vale is a triangle of land between the 'V' of the Pacific and the Southern Mount Lofty range of hills. Unfortunately, the other side of the triangle is Adelaide, and building development has encroached on many of the famous old vineyards, most notably Penfolds' Magill property. This historic site is where Christopher Rawson Penfold and his wife Mary, having arrived in 1840, set up a vineyard in 1844, then about four miles from Adelaide city centre. He planted Grenache cuttings he had brought from France and they moved into a cottage they expanded and called The Grange. Due to her husband's business commitments Mary became the successful wine-maker at this property and, on the death of her husband at 59, brought in her son-in-law, T.F. Hyland, as a partner. In the span of 10 years they expanded, growing Mataro,

Pedro Ximenez and Tokay as well as Grenache and buying in hundreds of tons of grapes from other growers. On Mary's death in 1892 the Penfold winery was one of the largest in Australia, but after the turn of the century the property was gradually swallowed up by the expansion of Adelaide until the last vintage was produced at the old estate in 1972. However, by this time Max Schubert was established in the company. Starting at a low position in the business, his enthusiasm persuaded the company to send him to college to study chemistry and they employed him as laboratory attendant. From here he progressed to wine-maker and was sent to tour France in 1949/50 and on his return he resolved to produce, alongside the vast output of Penfolds, the best red wine of the continent. He replanted the remains of the Grange vineyard with Shiraz, or Hermitage as the Australians sometimes call it, and started small barrel maturing in new oak to dampen some of the initial tannin which is a normal characteristic of this grape. The fame of this wine spread world-wide and it is now hailed as the Australian red coming closest to the finesse and complexity of first growths of the Médoc. In truth Grange Hermitage is not by any

◀ *'Plugs' or 'slips' of vine stems to be used for grafting developing in a neutral growing medium at Smith & Son's nursery at Yalumba.*

▲ *Bench grafting at Smiths, Yalumba. This device cuts the short lengths called 'plugs' or 'slips' that will be used for grafting.*

means from grapes grown exclusively at Grange vineyard. Penfolds have several prestige plantings of Shiraz in other districts and the best of these are mixed with a proportion, normally around 40%, from the historic site to produce not only the famed Grange Hermitage, but also two of their other top Shiraz wines, St Henri and Bin 389.

Adelaide producers to look for

A. Norman & Sons – over 125 years in the same family. Cool climate grapes, Gewürztraminer, Riesling and Pinot Noir especially

Thomas Hardy – huge company, 2.5 million cases. They own Houghton in Western Australia and Ch Reynella in McLaren Vale (below).

Penfolds – largest wine producer in Australia, own property in many sites and buy-in extensively. Uniformly high quality reds throughout the range. Own Kaiser Stuhl in the Barossa, Wynn's in Coonawarra (page 225) and Lindemans as well as their own extensive vineyards. Brand: Seaview

Petaluma – important names abound. Partners include Brian Croser, wine judge Len Evans and Bollinger. Grapes come in from the best areas for processing. Watch out for sparkling wines!

Tolley's Pedare – established in 1892 and still family owned. Now improving with advice from Tony Jordan and Brian Croser

McLaren Vale

Geoff Merrill – Hardy's (above) wine-maker here doing his own thing. Only two wines, Cabernet and Sémillon, but superb quality

Wirra Wirra – nearly a century old but overhauled in 1969 to good effect. Church Block is interesting Cabernet Sauvignon/Merlot/Shiraz blend

Ch Reynella – since 1982 owned by Hardy's and gradually redeeming its name for quality

CLARE VALLEY AND BAROSSA VALLEY

Clare Valley lies about 100 miles due north of Adelaide and the Barossa about half that distance to the north-east of the city.
Clare Valley is a tiny area best known for the excellence of its white Riesling wines. Stanley (Leasingham) is the largest and best-known producer. Under wine-maker Tim Knappstein, who now has his own company,

Enterprise Wines just outside the town of Clare, they lifted their quality by a considerable degree and are now among the leaders for excellence as well as for volume of production. The company is now owned by H.J. Heinz.

Another old company taken over by foreign investors is Quelltaler, here the quality of wine has improved greatly since they were bought by Remy-Martin who have even started maceration carbonique experiments.

The Barossa Valley is an area with a very Germanic heritage and, fittingly, the region is best known for its Riesling wines. Most of the larger wine companies of this continent have a presence here and the 7,000 hectares, the largest area in Australia given over to quality wine production, is able to accommodate them all. Old-established companies have estates alongside new arrivals and this has produced an environment where experience and the understanding of modern technology have found a harmonious balance. One of the older companies with a fine reputation, Leo Buring, is owned by Lindemans and, through them, by Penfolds who are also present, as well as Seppelt and Hardy. Newcomers seeking the best areas of the Barossa for fresh white wines have tended to plant in the eastern hills around Pewsey Vale and the Eden Valley, companies such as Hamiltons Ewell Vineyards and Wynns. Wolf Blass, one of the most expert of blenders, opened his winery at Nuriootpa at the northern end of the Barossa Valley in 1973 and buys grapes from whichever area or region will provide the particular taste characteristic he is looking for at the time. He has an enviable record in competition and often seems to be making wines to taste exactly the way the judges expect them to taste – anticipating desirable trends rather than following them.

Barossa Valley

Wolf Blass – owns few vineyards but wins most of the medals. Wolf is an amazing self-publicist who fully lives up to his hype

Hill-Smith Estate – gifted family now in their sixth generation of wine-makers. Whites better than reds, Rieslings especially

Kaiser Stuhl – now owned by Penfolds. This co-operative has a two-decade reputation for excellent Rieslings. Reds good too

Krondorf – now owned by Mildara. Style was set by original partners who, like Wolf Blass, sought good grapes from any region

Orlando – controlled by Pernod/Ricard.

▼ *The gentle slopes of the*
Barossa Range. This is
Pewsey Vale across the

range from the vineyards
in the Barossa Valley
itself. Valley wines are

mainly red but the higher
ground produces fine
Rhine Riesling.

3 million cases a year and terrific value for money. Brands, Jacobs Creek and RF, (merged with Wyndham in Hunter Valley)

Saltram – Seagram's owned. Mamre Brook Chardonnay a result of Brian Croser's advice. Best wines labelled Pinnacle

Seppelt – another important name. Vineyards in all the best sites, they dominate the sparkling wine market and they win many top prizes in the important Australian National Shows

Clare Valley/Watervale

Tim Adams – new style winery producing individual style wines, would be called 'boutique' in California. Unexpectedly good Cabernet Franc

Lindemans – third largest company with around 400 different labels. Owned by Penfolds, other names are Leo Buring (bought 1962) and Rouge Homme (bought 1965)

Quelltaler – was, briefly, Remy-Martin owned, now a part of Wolf Blass. White wines are best, Sémillon especially

Stanley – brand name Leasingham for their best wines. Most important of the Clare Valley wineries, with a good reputation, very good Rieslings

COONAWARRA

The most southerly of the major Australian growing areas, this tiny rectangle of land, only 32 km by 1.6 km has a soil structure and a

▼ *A stormy May sky in Australia: in the northern hemisphere vines would be sprouting, but here they are resting after picking and await their winter pruning.*

geographical location that is perfect for vines. Originally planted with Shiraz and Riesling, it now has mainly the fashionable Chardonnay and Cabernet Sauvignon grapes, so not surprisingly it produces wines with a more 'European' feel of lightness and subtlety, rather than the over-fruitiness that sometimes afflicts Australian wines grown in hotter areas. Wynns have the largest holding, while other big names are Mildara, Penfolds/Lindeman and Hungerford Hill.

Rosemount Estate and Petaluma are wineries in other areas which not only buy grapes in Coonawarra, but bottle them separately and advertise the wines as Coonawarra, although made many miles away. Rosemount Show Reserve Cabernet Sauvignon is probably the best known of these wines.

As Coonawarra is so clearly defined and incapable of expansion, other areas have been prospected and the favourite seems to be Padthaway/Keppoch where Lindemans, Seppelt and Hardys have all produced good results.

Wines to look for

Brand's Laira – family-owned 'boutique' style winery. One of the best Coonawarra Cabernets and good Cabernet Sauvignon/ Shiraz blending

Mildara Wines – better here than wines from their original Mildura vineyards. Improving all the time, especially the Cabernets

Wynns – part of Penfolds since 1985. Reds are good but whites are better

THE RIVERLAND

On the Murray River near the border with Victoria and New South Wales is an area which is very similar to the irrigated area around Riverina in New South Wales (page 229). These are the lands of the big volume producers, mainly co-operatives, who produce the amazingly good value-for-money simple wines of Australia. In many ways this is the great strength of Australia – their prestige wines can equal or even exceed the quality of their peers elsewhere, but are too expensive to drink regularly, whereas the good, honest, full-flavoured wines from the irrigated areas are more sophisticated than corresponding products from the Central Valley in California and come at everyday prices.

The most notable producers are
Berri Estates/Renmano – two vast
  co-operatives producing good-quality wine.
  Box wines as well as medal-winning oak-
  aged Cabernets

VICTORIA

At the beginning of the 20th century Victoria had more vineyards than New South Wales and South Australia together – over 1200 of them scattered over the State. Then phylloxera took its toll and many of the old properties converted to agriculture and were never replanted. What wine production was left concentrated on sweet wines, both dessert and fortified 'sherry' and 'port' types, the Australians like the Americans, never being bashful about using other people's names to indicate a style of wine.

Very active relics of the past glories of Victoria are Brown Bros of Milawa where four sons of the fourth generation of Browns continue the family traditions of excellence. Superb Muscat-based dessert wines are one of their great strengths but they also produce first-class modern-style white wines from vineyards recently planted on hillside sites, some as high as 750 metres, and their Estate Selection Cabernet Sauvignon is one of the ten best red wines of Australia.

The area is also known for sparkling wine production and 150 miles to the west of Melbourne lies the old district of Great Western. It is here that Seppelt, one of the most dynamic of the 'old' companies produce their Great Western Champagne from their 500 acres. They also have vineyards at Keppoch, in the Barossa Valley, at Drumborg in Victoria, two at Rutherglen on the border with New South Wales, one at Renmark on the Murray River in South Australia and another in the Adelaide Hills. This spread of growing sites is typical of the largest of the Australian companies and allows them to produce every type of wine the market requires. It would be like a European company producing wine in Champagne, Bordeaux, the Loire, the Rhône, Rioja, the Rhine and so on being able to use a single label name for a complete range of styles.

One old estate that has hardly changed with the times is Chateau Tahbilk confusingly sited at Tabilk. The English-born Purbrick family produce a succulent aged white wine from the Marsanne grape, best known for Hermitage white in France, a Riesling that will mature for nearly a decade and a massive Cabernet Sauvignon that probably needs 20 years before being opened.

In complete contrast Dominique Portet, brother of the Clos du Val Portet in the Napa Valley and son of the ex-Château Lafite manager, where Dominique was brought up, has established Taltarni Vineyards in the Avoca area and is producing from a completely modern winery the same sort of massive wines as Chateau Tahbilk. Taltarni wines are available in the UK and have the benefit of some excellent Ronald Searle cartoons to help with publicity – not that the wines need much help for they are first rate examples of Shiraz, Cabernet Sauvignon and Merlot with some good white from Riesling, Chardonnay and Sauvignon Blanc.

Just down the road, also in the Avoca area, is Chateau Remy which, as its name suggests, is partly owned by Remy Martin and partly by Krug who are providing their expertise for the production of good sparkling wines.

Central Victoria

Balgownie – owned by Mildara (page 225) since
  1986. Cool wine-growing area produces
  well-balanced wines
Taltarni – John Goelet also owns Clos du Val in
  the Napa and here the 'other' Portet brother
  is joint wine-maker. Reds are best from this
  ultra-modern winery
Yellowglen – now merged with Mildara
  (page 225). Determined to produce the best
  sparkling Australian wine. Petaluma
  competitor!

Geelong

Anakie Vineyards – mainly interesting because they buy cool-climate Cabernet grapes in Tasmania, ship them to Geelong and ferment them there with impressive results. Other wines less interesting

Goulburn Valley

Ch Tahbilk – traditional production of austere red wines which are only released for sale after more than five years and repay long ageing. Interesting white Marsanne too

Michelton – 750,000 cases of good value wines. Another Marsanne producer and their other whites are generally better than the reds

MURRAY RIVER

Small areas of wine production are scattered along most of the Murray River. After rising in the Australian Alps the first major area downstream is Rutherglen, followed by Echuca where the up and coming Tisdale company have 80 hectares of their Rosbercon vineyard planted with European quality varieties. A good Merlot is pointing the way forward and their wines from Mount Helen in central Victoria, where 40 hectares are planted with the same varieties, is also commanding attention. All its quality wines are sold under the Mt Helen label. The next quality production area is Mildura-Robinvale where Mildara Wines have been produced since 1891.

The river now crosses the state boundary of South Australia to reach the towns of Renmark, Beri and Morgan. Throughout this area the vineyards, for long producers of grapes for brandies and fortified wines, are now beginning to produce good quality grapes for table wines from the irrigated riverside vineyard plantations.

Murray Valley

Tisdall – two vineyards and two wine styles. Merlot best from Murray valley grapes and excellent Mount Helen labelled Chardonnay, other varieties from cool Strathbogie Hills grapes

Yarra Valley

Saint Huberts – largest in this new, high quality, area. Full range of varietals plus dessert wines

Yarra Burn – 'boutique' style winery as befits this area

Yarra Yering – owned by Dr Bailey Carrodus, the pioneer of the Yarra Valley. No sentimentalist, his wines are labelled Dry Red No 1 for Bordeaux-style, No 2 for Rhône-style. Well respected

North-east Victoria/Rutherglen

All Saints – one of many Liqueur Muscat specialists in this area

Brown Bros – the Mondavis of Australia? A full range of varietal wines plus gems like Orange Muscat and Flora, Late Harvest Riesling and Liqueur Muscats so traditional in this area

Campbells of Rutherglen – expanding away from dependence on sweet wines, but they're still their best!

W.H. Chambers – simply one of the very best Liqueur Muscat producers

Morris – Reckitt & Colman ownership. Superb Muscat and Tokay wines are now complemented by convincing Sémillon and Chardonnay

Stanton and Killeen – some of the finest reds, Shiraz and Cabernets, of Victoria as well as Rutherglen Liqueur Muscat

NEW SOUTH WALES

HUNTER VALLEY

On the face of it, this is an unlikely growing area, being so far north the temperatures expected at these latitudes should shrivel the grapes on the vine. But there are moderating local influences: extensive summer cloud cover for the older area, the Hunter Valley itself, and altitude in the newer Upper Hunter Valley area.

Traditional grapes here are the Shiraz and what the growers call Hunter Riesling, but is really the under-rated Sémillon. Modern trends are now pushing these varieties out in favour of Cabernet Sauvignon and Chardonnay. In fact, a certain amount of Chardonnay was grown on the Tyrrell estate and blended with Sémillon to produce a wine with the awful name Pinot Riesling – nothing, in fact, to do with any Pinot or Riesling. However, in the early 1970s Murray Tyrrell bottled his Chardonnay individually and the world took notice. Indeed it is the companies based here: Rothbury, Rosemount, McWilliams, Wyndham and Tyrrells, who have done so much to win foreign friends for Australian quality wines.

Recommended producers

Lake's Folly – creation of Sydney surgeon Max Lake, one of the first to recognise the potential of Hunter Valley for fine wines. Only two wines are produced – simply the best Chardonnay and the best Cabernet Sauvignon

McWilliams – extensive holdings elsewhere but best wines are from the Hunter. 'Royal' labels on their premium wines are Mount Pleasant Phillip Hermitage and Elizabeth Riesling

Rosemount – probably the best balance of quality and price. One of the most influential companies in bringing the UK drinker face to face with the excellence of Australian wines. The new Diamond Label wines are perhaps not so impressive. Premium label is Show Reserve – they are still outstanding!

Rothbury – shareholders own the winery and can buy their wines by post. Len Evans was the instigator. Premium labels are Individual Paddock in black

Saxonvale – much was expected from this technologically expert company. Has not yet met expectations, Chardonnay and Sémillon best

Tulloch – Allied Vintners owned. Premium label Private Bin

Tyrells – one of the Hunter Valley pioneers. Whites better than reds and house wine

▲ *Berri Estates in the Riverland. One of the largest wineries in South Australia, each year they crush around 50,000 tons of grapes to produce about 3 million cases of wine.*

level very good with quaintly named Short Flat White and Long Flat Red. Beware their 'Pinot Riesling' which is actually 50:50 Sémillon/Chardonnay!

Wyndham Estate – oldest winery still operating, opened in 1828. Like Rosemount, excellent quality/price relationship. Use the Australian liking for bin numbers, hence Bin 444 Cabernet Sauvignon, Bin TR2 Gewürztraminer, Bin 555 Shiraz, now control Orlando in Barossa. But remember their practice of using names like Sauternes, Moselle, Chablis, Graves and so on for wines which do not remotely resemble the European originals

MUDGEE AND MURRUMBIDGEE

Aside from the Hunter Valley, New South
Wales has few other regions of interest.
Mudgee is an historic area 160 kilometres west
of the Hunter and 360 metres higher. Apart
from Montrose, few of the wines reach the UK.

We do, however, see many of the wines of
Murrumbidgee or, to use its more attractive
name, Riverina. Like the Riverland area of
South Australia it has many big wineries
producing masses of good, honest wines at
attractively low prices.

McWilliams are the pioneers of the Riverina
area. Their prestige vineyard is Mount Pleasant
on the slopes of the Broken Back Range in
Hunter Valley but they achieved the difficult feat
of producing a range of slightly lower quality
wines at a very much lower price by planting
80 hectares near Griffith in the irrigated
area called Riverina using water from the
Murrumbidgee River brought by canal.
Here there are three wineries to process their

own and bought-in grapes, one of these
wineries, Hanwood, giving its name to the
first-class range of wines from this area
available in the UK.

Mudgee

Montrose – excellent quality with the medals to
prove it. Italian leanings with Barbera,
Nebbiolo, Sangiovese planted – also seems
to come through in their other reds which
incline to earthiness. Outstanding
Chardonnay

Riverina

de Bortoli – the master of the sweeties! Most
of the output is of average wines but botrytis
Sémillon and sweet Gewürztraminer and
Rieslings are stunning. They are now
working on their sparkling wines

▼ *New World wine-*
producers usually pick
when it is cool. Dawn at

Rosemount Estate, Upper
Hunter Valley, and
picking has begun.

WESTERN AUSTRALIA

The history of wine-making here goes back almost as far as that of Adelaide or Sydney. The first vines were planted in 1834 but the conditions, blistering heat and hot, dry winds, meant that, with a few small exceptions, dessert wines were all that could be profitably managed.

The 1960s revolution – seeking cooler growing areas – showed the growers of Western Australia there were two suitable sites, the Margaret River region and the Mount Barker/Frankland River region. Gradually these new areas took over from the old area of Swan Valley now included in the greater Perth conurbation.

The most exciting of the new properties is undoubtedly Leeuwin on the Margaret River. Here, since 1974 and with copious advice from Robert Mondavi of the Napa, they have produced some absolute blockbuster wines: Chardonnay to rival the very best of either Australia or the Napa, exquisite Rieslings including sensational Auslese, Gewürztraminer to rival Alsace, excellent Hermitage and, most surprising of all, a Pinot Noir of real charm and quality. Cabernets are well structured but, given the quality of the other varietal wines, it is asking much to look for a perfect Cabernet Sauvignon as well! Time will tell. That first-rate Cabernets are indeed possible here is proved by the example from Cape Mentelle winery. Established in 1969 and now with over 45 hectares under vine they are also famous for an excellent Zinfandel, a grape that could well find a second home in Australia.

Margaret River

Cape Mentelle – also own the legendary Cloudy Bay winery in New Zealand. This is California-in-Western Australia. Big wines

Cullen's – another escapee from the professional classes. Dr Kevin Cullen with wife Diana as wine-maker. Reds need ageing but Fumé-Cabernet, a rosé, and Sauvignon Blanc are very good

Leeuwin – unforgettable wines from ultra-modern surroundings built with advice from Robert Mondavi. Expensive but excellent

Moss Wood – one of the first to establish the reputation for Margaret River. Cabernet Sauvignon fine but needs ageing

Vasse Felix – Margaret River pioneer. Small output but fine quality

Mount Barker

Conti-Forest Hill – was Contiville, then Paul Conti (the owner's name), now re-named again. Boutique-style wines which are very elegant. Vinify for Forest Hill (below)

Ch Barker – specialise in strange names. Quondyp Riesling and Gewürztraminer, Pyramup blended red for example

Forest Hill – first in Mount Barker area. Government-established for research. Riesling, Gewürztraminer and Cabernet Sauvignon all excellent. Vinification carried out at Conti-Forest Hill

Swan River

Houghton – 50-year-old Western Australian pioneer. Now, since 1976 a part of Hardy's, it is coming out of a rut. Cabernets good

Mandurah

Peel Estate – part owned by an English syndicate. Produces Zinfandel and Cabernets as if in the Napa Valley. Shiraz less good

TASMANIA

The search for cooler growing areas naturally led to Australia's southernmost state. In Tasmania the whole environment is much more central European but with the benefit of never being far from the moderating influence of water. Best-known estate here is Moorilla with 8 hectares of Riesling, Pinot Noir and Cabernet Sauvignon, neither of the two reds yet have much character, the Pinot Noir especially being a bit ghostly, but the Riesling shows promise. It may be that the quest for cooler conditions has finally reached a limit with Tasmania actually having problems of under-ripeness in the same way as many of the classic areas of Europe.

Recommended producers

Heemskerk – using cool climate conditions which replicate France to produce Bordeaux-style Cabernets and, in collaboration with Louis Roederer, sparklers from Pinot Noir and Chardonnay

Moorilla – Bordeaux-style Cabernets and Moselle-style Rieslings. Pinot Noirs to watch

Pipers Brook – Riesling, Chardonnay, Pinot Noir and Cabernet all made in cool European styles

see also Anakie in Geelong, Victoria

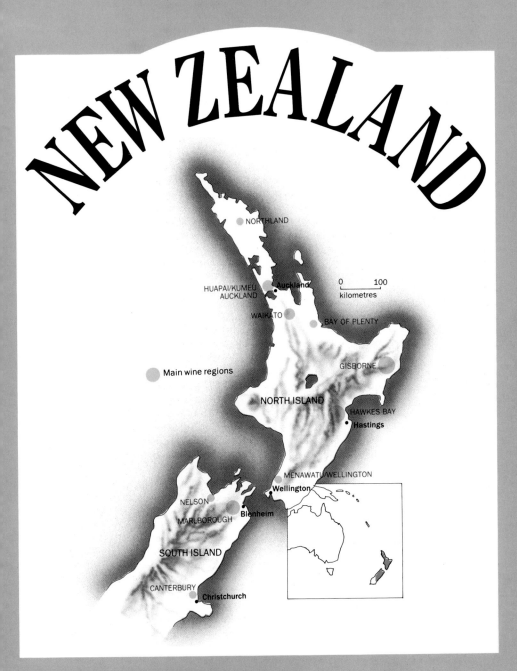

NEW ZEALAND

NORTHLAND

HUAPAI/KUMEU
AUCKLAND

Auckland

0   100
kilometres

WAIKATO

BAY OF PLENTY

GISBORNE

Main wine regions

NORTH ISLAND

HAWKES BAY

Hastings

MENAWATU/WELLINGTON

Wellington

NELSON

Blenheim

MARLBOROUGH

SOUTH ISLAND

CANTERBURY

Christchurch

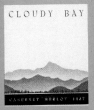

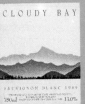

231

The rather strait-laced Victorian attitude to life in these islands seemed to dampen any enthusiasm for the vine until the 1960s. By then some of the Central European workers had started a sort of do-it-yourself wine-making activity but, luckily, they kept their rather crude products to themselves. Auckland was the main area for growing vines, and pretty unsuitable it was too. In 1960 the acreage under vine in New Zealand amounted to under 404 hectares and over half of that was around Auckland. By 1981 there were 5500 hectares and planting had spread to South Island down as far as Christchurch. In European terms the Auckland vineyards are on a similar latitude to Morocco and the Christchurch vineyards similar to the Rhône. However, the proximity of the ocean makes these comparisons fairly meaningless and, in general, all areas of New Zealand are much damper than their comparative European

vineyards. Indeed, damp, rot, fungus and vintage-time rain are all conditions the New Zealanders have learnt to live with.

One of the first companies to export wine to the UK was Cooks New Zealand Wine Company. Founded in 1968 they have vineyards in most of the main areas and grow twelve of the major European grape varieties including, sadly, the dull old Müller-Thurgau, which is accurately called the Riesling Sylvaner in New Zealand. Their best examples are a rich oak-aged Chardonnay, a delightfully spicy Gewürztraminer, a Coteaux du Layon-style Chenin Blanc and a crisp Sauvignon Blanc.

McWilliams of Australia are represented here, indeed they are the second largest company in the islands. Actually founded in 1944 they really only became serious when Tom McDonald was wine-maker in the 1960s. A whole spectrum of varieties are planted

including unlikely vines such as Pedro Ximenez, Palomino and Chasselas. Best is their Chardonnay but others are less convincing.

Montana wines, on the other hand, seem only to produce convincing wines, their Sauvignon Blanc is an inexpensive world benchmark for many drinkers and the unaged Chardonnay from the Gisborne area is a delight. Possibly the greatest of the world's Sauvignon Blanc wines comes from Cloudy Bay – so named by Captain Cook – in Marlborough County. Here David Hohnen of Western Australia's Cape Mentelle is the wine-making genius. Elsewhere surprisingly full and fruity Cabernet Sauvignons are available and interesting Pinotage (a South African Pinot Noir/Cinsault cross) wines, full of interest and relatively cheap.

Nick Nobilo is the wine-maker at the family owned winery in the Huapai Valley outside Auckland. They set up shop in 1943 and, being

▲ *Part of Montana Estate's Marlborough vineyard near Blenheim* *on the northern coast of New Zealand's South Island.*

Dalmatian in origin, represent a carry-over from the first central European beginnings of the industry. Red grapes come from their vineyards in Auckland but whites are bought in Gisborne. Pinot Noir is exciting in that he brings out the best flavour by macèration carbonique fermentation and then ages it for two years in oak. Burgundy could well look at this technique and the flavours that result. More impressive still is his Private Bin Cabernet Sauvignon which contains some Pinotage. A big, flavoursome wine of great depth and excellent balance.

Apart from the descendants of the original Central European pioneers – the Selaks,

Nobilos, Babitchs, the Brajkovich family of
Kumeu River Wines and so on – and apart from
the larger enterprises like Montana and Cooks,
the most exciting developments in the past five
years have been the number of smaller
'boutique' producers that have started up. Their
wines now widen the spectrum of flavours and
interpretations available and seem likely to
overtake the more established names as medal-
winners in European competitions.

Both Australia and the UK now look to New
Zealand for benchmark Sauvignon Blancs and
for flavoursome yet subtle Chardonnays – and
Pinot Noir also looks to be a likely success
story for the future as well. The increase in
exports – Australia's imports of quality New
Zealand wines increased by 600% in 1984 alone
– and in home consumption, which increased
from 1¾ litres per head in 1970 to nearly 14
litres in 1985, has left a shortfall in production.
All too often UK importers have to suffer the
indignity of quotas and all too often UK
drinkers, having read good reports of a
particular wine, find it is sold out, necessitating
a wait until the next vintage! But what a success
story. . . .

The future in New Zealand is bright. Many
businessmen are looking to vineyards as a
worthwhile investment and the plantings
furthest south in the Canterbury area outside
Christchurch are showing up well. National
pride in the wine industry has received a great
charge from the international successes of
wines like the Montana and Cloudy Bay
Sauvignon Blancs and the old-established
Babitch Wines who have a fine record of medal
winning. The success of Air New Zealand in
winning the 'Winelist of the Air' award two
years running has also received good publicity.

Names to look out for
Babitch – regular competition winners yet
    tending towards lighter tastes. Sémillon/
    Chardonnay (70%:30%) blend is popular
Cloudy Bay – normally sold out before it lands
    in the UK, the Chardonnay is now attracting
    almost as much acclaim as the world
    benchmark-standard Sauvignon Blanc
Collard – Bordeaux-style reds and German
    Riesling and Gewürztraminer styles less
    convincing than their big, open,
    Chardonnays
Cooks – everybody's New Zealand starting
    point. Widely available. Now premium

Stonleigh Abbey label is the one to look for
Delegats – use contract growers extensively.
    Hawkes Bay Sauvignon and Gisborne
    Chardonnay outstanding but Proprietors
    Reserve Chardonnay promises even greater
    delights
Hunters Wines – their Marlborough Sauvignon
    Blanc is good, the Oak-Aged version is great
    and their Pinot Noir thought-provoking
Matua Valley – excellence from California-
    inspired winery. 'Usual' varietals
    exceptional, more exceptional still are state-
    of-the-art wines like freeze-concentrated
    late-harvest Muscat
Mission Vineyard – like Christian Brothers in
    California, this is a winery run by a religious
    foundation. Whites are best and many
    unusual varieties are planted – Pinot Gris,
    Chasselas – but best is their exceptional
    Sémillon/Sauvignon Blanc
Montana Wines – South Island pioneers,
    Marlborough Vineyard Sauvignon Blanc
    deservedly 'White Wine of the Year' in 1987.
    Not only brilliant, but cheap as well! Botrytis
    Late-Picked Rhine Riesling looks promising
Morton Estate – Chardonnays star here. Style
    is more Australian than New Zealand
    although wine-maker is ex-Delegats.
    Sparklers using Pinot Noir and Chardonnay
    are looked forward to
Nobilo – the red wine specialists of New
    Zealand. White grapes are bought-in from
    Gisborne while reds come from their own
    vineyards: Cabernet Sauvignon, Pinotage,
    Pinot Noir, Merlot and Malbec. Aged
    Cabernets are amazingly deep and rich
Selaks Wines – long established but modern,
    export-oriented outlook. Very high standard
    Sauvignon Blanc, Sémillon and Chardonnay
Te Mata – established 1898 but revived
    recently. Red wine specialists with brilliant
    Cabernet Sauvignon/Merlot blend
Villa Maria – little known but fourth largest
    winery. Expensive yet classically full
    Chardonnay and less expensive yet more
    exceptional Cabernet Sauvignon Reserve.
    Both Cabernet Sauvignon Reserve and
    Cabernet Sauvignon/Merlot Reserve are Air
    New Zealand Gold Medal winners

Other names
Brookfield, Cellier Le Brun, Collards,
Esk Valley, Matawhero, Neudorf, St Nesbit,
and Vidal

THE REST OF THE WORLD

INDIA

The temperature in this vast country would hardly seem likely to produce table wines, especially sparkling table wines of good quality from French grapes and by méthode champenoise. However, thanks to the investments made by Shyam Chougule, a Bombay millionaire, and the expertise of ex-Piper Heidsieck adviser Raphael Brisbois, there is a thriving vineyard and winery directly inland from Bombay and about 50 miles north of Poona. The grapes are Chardonnay and Ugni Blanc – the Chardonnay grown in the winery vineyard and the Ugni Blanc grown under contract by local farmers. The Lenz-Moser high wire system is used to give leaf cover to the grapes and the altitude of nearly 2500 feet also moderates what would otherwise be furnace-like conditions, for the site is on latitude 18°N – the same as Jeddah in Saudi Arabia!

The production target is for a million bottles a year and that certainly seems achievable. Only one of their wines is at all widely available in the UK, the unimaginatively named but perfectly respectably flavoured Omar Khayyam. Others produced are Royal Mousseux, a Cuvée Close product and Marquise de Pompadour, a demi-sec méthode champenoise. Vintage wines are planned, as is a rosé using Cabernet Sauvignon and Pinot Noir for colouring.

Not outrageously priced for the quality is: Omar Khayyam Brut Méthode Champenoise

CHINA AND JAPAN

The grape began its voyage to encircle the globe in Mesopotamia and its use and cultivation spread ever westwards, to Greece, on to Rome and on across Europe to the USA and to Australia.

Not surprisingly its use and cultivation also spread eastwards along the trade route to India, China and, finally Japan. All of these countries have extensive historical reference to wine, in Japan it was used at the court of Nara in the 8th century AD; in 1186 a vine named Koshu was selected from the vineyards near Mount Fuji, and still, today, produces reasonable wines. In 1596 Oda Nobunaga held a wine tasting for his Samurai warriors – the tasting notes, sadly, have not survived! In China second century gardeners called a certain type of vine 'vegetable dragon pearls' and they made wine from the grapes.

If these are historical facts, then why is there no wine industry today? The answer seems to be that wine did not fit in with Oriental culture, in some way it is not attractive to their lifestyle, habits or attitudes. In the last 20 years, however, as the Orient has become more western in its aspirations there have been signs of a fledgling industry. It is now possible to purchase wines from Japan and, especially, from China where Remy Martin are co-operating with the Chinese in the production of wines from local grapes and with Muscat from vines brought from Bulgaria.

These oriental wines are not great, not really interesting in taste, but they do provide a clear sign that in the future we can expect more to follow.

AND THE REST . . .

Just for the record, in addition to the countries discussed, the following countries also produce wines commercially:
Bolivia, Columbia, Czechoslovakia, Ethiopia (before the internal conflict), Iran (before the overthrow of the Shah), Jordan, Korea, Libya, Liechtenstein, Macau, Madagascar, Malta, Nepal (allegedly), Poland, Syria and Tanzania.

These 16 together with the 38 dealt with previously total 54 wine-producing countries – or 55 if you include Ireland as a separate country!

It's a popular pastime. . . .

FIGURES AND FACTS

Metric equivalents

AREA

1 acre = 0.405 hectare (ha)
1 hectare = 2.471 acres (roughly 2.5)
Thus a 1000-hectare property is roughly 2,500 acres

LIQUID VOLUME

1 gallon = 4.546 litres
1 litre = 0.22 gallon or 1.76 pints
1 hectolitre (hl) = 22 gallons
So 5000 hectolitres production per annum = 110,000 gallons per annum
1000 millilitres (ml) = 100 centilitres (cl) = 1 litre (l or ltr)
A 75cl bottle contains 1.32 pints
1 case of 75cl bottles contains 15.84 pints or 1.98 gallons
So production of 50,000 cases a year is roughly 100,000 gallons (99,000).
The Bordeaux barrique holds 225 litres.

TEMPERATURE

°C	100	95	90	85	80	75	70	65	60	55	50
°F	212	203	194	185	176	167	158	149	140	131	122
°C	45	40	35	30	25	20	15	10	5	0	−5	−10
°F	113	104	95	86	77	68	59	50	41	32	23	14

ALCOHOLIC CONTENT

After years struggling with the British Sikes measurement, the French Gay-Lussac system and the American Proof method we are now, thanks to the EEC, more or less completely standardised on percentage alcohol (which was what Gay-Lussac was anyway . . .)

In case you meet any old bottles – especially spirits – the conversion from Gay-Lussac to American was simply to double the number, 10% GL = 20% American etc. British Proof is converted to GL by multiplying by 4 and dividing by 7: 100% British Proof times 4 divide by 7 = 57%

CASE WEIGHT

A bottle of wine normally weighs 2lb 10oz or 1.2 kg – and a bottle of champagne or sparkling wine 3lb 12 oz or 1.7 kg.
A case of wine weighs-in at about 32lb or 15kg and a case of champagne at just over 45lb or 21kg.

PRODUCTION VOLUMES

Normally expressed in hectolitres (hl) per hectare (ha). The lower the figure, the better quality the wine should be for, with each vine pruned to produce fewer bunches, the concentration of flavour is raised. Minimum quantities probably occur at Château d'Yquem where it is calculated that it takes one vine to produce one glass of finished wine.

Maximum cropping is achieved in the hot irrigated areas of central Australia or California's Central Valley. Prolific varieties like the Pedro Ximenez can yield up to 650 hl per ha – 20 tons of grapes per acre!

In Europe yields vary from the low national average of 20 hl per ha in Spain to about 100 hl per ha in Germany. The Germans, with high labour and land costs, have dramatically intensified their production, largely through improvements in vine quality by extensive use of clonal selection.
The mid 1950s saw a German average of about 45 hl per ha but by the mid 1970s this had risen to almost 100 hl per ha.

Yield per hectare is also obviously affected by the density of vines planted and this will be affected in turn by factors such as mechanical harvesting (which limits density to around 3000 vines per ha), moisture availability, retention of moisture by the soil, land values and so on.

Central Spain, where land is cheap, is planted at about 1000 vines per hectare while well watered and extremely expensive Burgundy plants at around 10 times that figure.

BOTTLE SIZES

CHAMPAGNE

Magnum	2 bottles
Jeroboam	4 bottles
Rehoboam	6 bottles
Methusalah	8 bottles
Salmanazar	12 bottles
Balthazar	16 bottles
Nebuchadnezzar	20 bottles

BORDEAUX

Magnum	2 bottles
Marie-Jeanne	approx 3 bottles
Double Magnum	4 bottles
Jeroboam	6 bottles
Imperial	8 bottles

GRAPE NAMES AROUND THE WORLD

Usual name followed by most common synonyms

MAJOR WHITE VARIETIES

Chardonnay *France* Beaunois (Chablis); Melon Blanc, Rousseau, Arnoison, Melon d'Arbois, even Gamay Blanc (elsewhere). *Germany* Weisser Klevner. *Italy* Gelber Weissburgunder
Muscat two major varieties exist:
1 Muscat Blanc à Petit Grains *France* Muscat de Frontignan, Muscat d'Alsace, Frontignac. *Germany* Muskateller. *Italy* Moscato d'Asti, Moscato di Canelli, Moscato Bianco. *Spain* Moscatel Dorado, Moscatel de Grano Menudo. *Portugal* Muscatel Branco. *Austria* Muskateller, Schmeckende. *California* White Muscat, Muscat Canelli, Muscat Frontignan, Muscat Blanc. *South Africa* Muskadel. *Australia* Brown Muscat, Frontignac, White Frontignan
2 Muscat of Alexandria *France* Muscat Roumain, Panse Musquée. *Italy* Zibibbo. *Spain* Moscatel, Moscatel de Malaga, Moscatel Gordo Blanco, Moscatel Romano. *Portugal* Moscatel de Setúbal. *Australia* Muscatel Gordo Blanco, Leixa. *South Africa* Hanepoot
Riesling *France* Gentil-Aromatique. *Germany* Johannisberger, Rheinriesling, Moselriesling, Rheingauer among many others. *Italy* Riesling Renano. *Austria and New Zealand* Rhine Riesling. *Yugoslavia and Bulgaria* Rizling. *USA* White Riesling. *Switzerland* Johannisberger
Sauvignon Blanc *France* Surin, Sauvignon Jaune, Gentil à Romarintin. *Germany* Muscat Sylvaner. *Australia, New Zealand, South Africa, California* Fumé Blanc. *California* also called Savagnin Musque

OTHER IMPORTANT WHITE VARIETIES

Aligoté *France* Only in Burgundy are alternative names used: Plant Gris (Meursault), Grislet Blanc (Beaune), Chaudenet Gras (Côte Chalonnaise), Troyen Blanc (Yonne), Giboudot Blanc (Rully)
Chenin Blanc *France* Pineau d'Anjou, Pineau de la Loire and other variations on the Pineau theme. *South Africa* Steen
Gewürztraminer *France* Traminer, Rotclevner (Alsace); Savagnin Rosé, Gentil Aromatique, Traminer Parfumé, Gris Rouge (elsewhere). *Germany* Clevner, Klavner, Rotfranke, Roter Traminer. *Italy* Traminer Aromatico, Traminer Rosé. *Central Europe* Many variations on the Traminac/Traminer theme
Malvasia *France* Malvoisie. *Germany* Malvasier. *Italy* Uva Greca, Malvasia del Lazio and other Malvasia suffixes. *Spain* Rojal, Subirat, Blancarroga, Tobia, Cagazal, Blanca-Roja. *Canaries* Malvasia Candida – the wine is Malmsey
Müller-Thurgau *Switzerland & New Zealand* Riesling-Sylvaner. *Luxembourg & Yugoslavia* Rivaner. *Hungary* Rizlingszilvani
Muscadet *France* Melon, Melon de Bourgogne (Loire); Melon (Burgundy); Gros Auxerrois, Gamay Blanc à Feuilles Rondes, Lyonnais Blanche (elsewhere). *Germany* Weisser Burgunder. *California* Pinot Blanc
Palomino *France* Listan. *Spain* Tempranilla, Temprana, Alban, Listan. *Portugal* Perrum. *South Africa* Fransdruif, White French. *Australia* Sweetwater, Paulo
Pinot Blanc *Germany* Combinations of Weisser, Klevner, Burgunder and Rulander. *Italy* Pinot Bianco, Pineau Blanc, Chasselas Dorato. *Yugoslavia* Beli Pinot. *Hungary* Feherburgundi. *Czechoslovakia* Rouci Bile
Pinot Gris *France* Pinot Beurot (Burgundy); Malvoisie (Loire and Savoie); Tokay d'Alsace, Auxerrois Gris (Alsace); Fauvet, Petit Gris,

Pinot Bennot (elsewhere). *Germany* Rulander, Grauerburgunder, Grauklevner, Grauer Riesling, Tokayer. *Italy* Pinot Grigio, Tocai. *Switzerland* Tokayer, Malvoisie. *Romania* Rulanda. *Hungary* Grauer Monch

Sémillon This grape has more name confusions than most. *France* Sémillon Muscat, Malaga, Columbier, Blanc Doux. *South Africa* Wyndruif, Wine Grape, Green Grape. *Romania* St Emilion. *Australia* (except Western Australia) Hunter River Riesling

Sylvaner *France* Gentil Vert, Gamay Blanc, Silvain Vert, Picardon Blanc. *Germany* At least 12 alternative names including Franken, Frankenriesling, Grunedel. *Switzerland* Johannisberger, Gros Rhin. *Italy* Silvaner Bianco. *California* Franken Riesling, Monterey Riesling, Sonoma Riesling

Trebbiano *France* Ugni Blanc (Midi); St Emilion (Charente); Clairette Ronde, Clairette Rose, Roussan (Provence). *Portugal* Thalia. *California* St Emilion. *Australia* White Hermitage, White Shiraz

Welschriesling *Italy* Riesling Italco. *Yugoslavia* Italianski Riesling, Laski Riesling. *Czechoslovakia* Riesling Italianski, Rizling Vlassky. *Hungary* Olasz Riesling. *Bulgaria* Italianski Rizling

MAJOR RED VARIETIES

Cabernet Sauvignon *France* Petit-Cabernet, Vidure (Graves); Bouchet (Gironde); Petit-Bouchet (St Emilion and Pomerol); Sauvignon Rouge (Central France)

Pinot Noir *France* Pineau, Franc Pineau; Savagnin Noir, Savagnin (Jura); Doré or Vert Doré (Champagne). *Germany and Austria* Spätburgunder, Blauburgunder. *Germany and Switzerland* Klevner, Blauer Klevner. *Italy* Blau Burgunder, Pinot Nero. *Hungary* Nagyburgundi

Syrah *France* Sereine, Marsanne. *Australia* Shiraz. *Argentina* Balsamina

OTHER IMPORTANT RED VARIETIES

Cabernet Franc *France* Breton (Loire); Bouchet, Vidure (St Emilion and Pomerol); Veron, Bouchy, Trouchy Noir (elsewhere). *Italy* Bordo

Carignan *France* Catalan, Roussillonen, Monestel. *Italy* Uva di Spagna, Carignano. *Spain* Tinto Mazuelo, Carinena. *Portugal* Pinot Evara. *California* Carignane

Cinsault *France* Malaga (see Sémillon). *Italy* Ottavianello. *Australia* Oeillade, Blue Imperial. *South Africa* Hermitage

Gamay *France* Gamay Noir à Jus Blanc, Bourguignon Noir, Gamay Rond

Grenache *France* Sans Pareil, Alicante, Carignane Rousse, Garancha among others. *Spain* Garnacho, Tinto Aragones, Carignan Rosso, Alicantina among others. *Sicily* Granaccia

Merlot *France* Sémillon Rouge. *Hungary* Médoc Noir

Nebbiolo *Italy* Spanna, Chiavennasca, Picotener, Nebbiolo Canavesano

Sangiovese two major varieties exist:
1 Sangiovese Piccolo and
2 Sangiovese Grosso *Italy* Sangiovese di Romagna, Sangioveto, Sangiovese Gentile, Sangiovese Toscana, Calabrese, Prugnolo (Montepulciano); Brunello (Montalcino)

Tempranillo *Spain* Cencibel (La Mancha and Valdepeñas); Tinto Fino (Ribera del Duero); Ull de Llebre (Penedés); Tempranillo de la Rioja, Tinto de la Rioja, Grenache de Logrono (elsewhere). *Portugal* Aragonez

CONCLUSIONS
Even this brief list of the main synonyms of the most popular grape varieties shows the situation to vary between confusing and farcical!

Ampelography is the science of vine description. If any readers feel that this complex area deserves further study and they see themselves as budding ampelographers I would direct them to Jancis Robinson's technically excellent and highly readable book *Vines, Grapes and Wines*.

GLOSSARY

Words in small capitals are cross-references
to other Glossary entries.

abbocato (*Italy*) medium sweet

abocado (*Spain*) medium sweet

AC/AOC (*France*) Appellation Contrôlée
or Appellation d'Origine Contrôlée. The highest
grade of the French quality control system.
See French wine laws

acetic acetic acid is always present in wine in
tiny amounts. Prolonged exposure of wine to air
allows an excessive amount of acetic acid to
form, rendering the wine vinegary or *piqué*
(pricked)

acidic acids are important in wine to balance
the sweetness and prevent the wine from being
insipid. Volatile acids of which ACETIC is the
commonest are detrimental, while fixed or
stable acids like malic, tartaric and citric are
essential in the right balance

adega (*Portugal*) a cellar or a winery

after-taste flavours and sensations remaining
in the mouth after the wine has gone. Normally
a positive feature (see LENGTH) but in some
wines can be unpleasant

ageing bringing a wine to maturity by storage
in cask or bottle. Some countries have
regulations preventing sale of wine before
certain qualifying periods in cask and/or bottle
have been fulfilled. See also MATURE, LAYING
DOWN

almacenista (*Spain*) literally a stockholder.
In Jerez these merchants deal in small quantities
of the finest sherries which, by careful addition
to a SOLERA, will disproportionately improve the
whole quantity. Also used as a collective noun
for specialist sherries which are of fine
character and which display excellent
characteristics

amabile (*Italy*) semi-sweet; usually sweeter
than ABBOCATO

amaro (*Italy*) very very dry, even bitter

amarone (*Italy*) dry, as in Recioto Amarone
della Valpolicella, the dry Recioto as opposed to
the sweeter version

amontillado (*Spain*) a-montilla-do, in the style
of Montilla. Unfortunately the name is so
abused that now, instead of being a correct
description for an old, matured, fino it has come
to simply mean a medium-sweet sherry

amoroso (*Spain*) a rare sherry produced by
adding MISTELA sweeteners and VINO DE COLOR
to OLOROSO

Amtliche Prufungsnummer, Ap Nr or AP
(*Germany*) all wines of QbA status and above
carry a number which indicates the wine grade,
the vineyard and the year of bottling. In theory
duff bottles can thus be traced back to source in
spite of the generally imprecise German
labelling

Anbaugebiet (*Germany*) sometimes
abbreviated to Gebiet; the wine-growing region,
of which there are eleven

annata (*Italy*) vintage, the year. Increasingly
recognised as important, previously thought of
little consequence except for the very finest
wines

aperitif a beverage taken before a meal to
sharpen the appetite

appellation contrôlée see AC/AOC

aroma see BOUQUET

aromatic describes wines which have a grapey
or flowery character, particularly Rieslings and
Gewürztraminers

arrope (*Spain*) see VINO DE COLOR

astringent acidicly aggressive. Caused by
under-ripe grapes, excess of acids or tannins or
under-matured wines

atmosphere normal air pressure at sea level.
Used as measurement of the pressure in Perle,
CRÉMANT or sparkling wines

Auslese (*Germany*) above SPATLESE, below
BEERENAUSLESE on the German quality/
sweetness scale. Late harvest

azienda (*Italy*) farm or agricultural holding.
Alternatives found on labels are: castello, villa,
tenimento, podere, fattoria, tenuta. See also
CANTINA

back-blending the addition of unfermented
grape juice to a wine before bottling to increase
the sweetness. Naturally the alcohol level is
reduced by this process; used extensively in
Germany and anywhere else that German-style
wines are produced

balance a wine in which all the components

have harmonised

barrique the standard 225-litre Bordeaux barrel now used all over the world

beefy an imprecise term used by tasters to describe red wines of a solidly full character

Beerenauslese (*Germany*) above AUSLESE, below TROCKENBEERENAUSLESE on the German quality/sweetness scale. Hand-selected grapes from late-harvested bunches which, it is hoped, will have some botrytis. Dessert wine sweetness level

Bereich (*Germany*) a medium-sized growing area, usually a town or a group of villages. So general that only QbA wines carry this classification or title

bianco (*Italy*) white

big full or rich flavour; normally applied to red wines, especially those high in alcohol

bin a horizontal space or slot to store a wine bottle. Wine must be in contact with the cork during storage to prevent the cork drying out

bin end(s) normally sale price wines; the remains of a stock or a particular line unrepeatable due to vintage change or rarity

bitter a fault; can be due to many causes but normally excess of acidity allied to cask or cork faults

'black wine' never black! Cahors used to produce very dark red wines by long skin contact during fermentation and by boiling some of the must to concentrate it; no longer produced

blanc de blancs wine produced entirely from the juice of white grapes. Used mainly for champagnes to differentiate from those produced from the normal mixture of red and white grapes

blanc de noirs white wine produced from red grapes. Mainly applied to champagnes to accentuate the fact that only the two permitted red grapes have been used with no white grape content

blanco (*Spain*) white

blended wine virtually every wine is blended. It may be a mixture of grape varieties, of wines from different vintages or of wines from

different growing areas. The objective is to cancel out defects, balance the wine or maintain a certain producer's taste style

Bocksbeutel (*Germany*) the traditional Franken flask; better known as a Mateus Rosé bottle

bodega (*Spain*) literally cellar, but now meaning a wine company

body the weight of a wine on the palate. Light-bodied, full-bodied etc. all relate to an expected optimum for any particular style of wine

botrytis *Botrytis cinerea* or NOBLE ROT. The benign fungus that sometimes attacks grape skins, causing the grapes to become dehydrated. Wines made from botrytis affected grapes are very sweet. Known as Edelfaule in German and *Pourriture noble* in Latin

bottle age many red wines require a balance of cask ageing to bottle ageing to reach full maturity. See also AGEING

bottle sickness a temporary problem in freshly bottled wines, usually associated with the filtration process prior to bottling. Normally passes with time

bouquet technically, the first perfume, the later, more lingering, odour is the aroma. Difficult to detect when the bottle is first opened or the wine is cold

branco (*Portugal*) white

branded wines proprietory wines blended to maintain a consistent house style, eg Hirondelle, Don Cortez. Normally at the cheaper end of the market. See also BLENDED WINE

breathing allowing wine to come into contact with air to release aromas and flavours. Removing the cork and allowing the bottle to stand for a while before serving is almost totally ineffective. See also DECANT

breeding a classic wine or a wine of class. Discretion and delicacy are the traditional descriptions of the attributes of 'breeding' believed to derive from the soil. See also FINESSE

brut term denoting dry wines, usually sparkling ones. In France, officially the driest category of sparkling wine. The terms 'brut zero' and 'zero dosage' are also used, but have no official, or legal, definition

buttery tasting term usually applied to wines, especially whites, which have the vanilla-like flavours associated with oak-ageing, Chardonnay in particular

cantina (*Italy*) a cellar or, more usually, a winery

carafe in France ordinary wines are traditionally drawn straight from the cask into a carafe or carafon – a glass bottle or decanter kept for this purpose

carbonated wine the most basic of sparkling wines. Carbon dioxide is introduced into the wine but only produces a short-lived MOUSSE of coarse bubbles

cava (*Spain*) literally cave. Has come to also mean a cellar but, more importantly, used as a term for Spanish sparkling wines that have been produced using the méthode champenoise: they are 'cava' matured, matured in cellars

cave (*France*) cellar

centrifuging method of cleansing wine of solid matter

chai, maître de (*France*) barrel storage area, may be a warehouse above ground, semi-sunk in the ground for coolness or totally underground. The maître de chai is in charge of all the wine-making operations

chapeau (*France*) the layer of skins, pips and stalks which floats on the top of fermenting red wine. To obtain maximum colour, flavour and tannin this layer must be regularly mixed in by hand or pumped-over

chaptalise/chaptalisation Dr Jean Chaptal, Comte de Canteloup, (1756–1832), Minister of Agriculture to Napoleon I, authorised the addition of beet sugar to wine MUST to raise the sugar level and, thus, the potential alcohol level. This approved practice is still widespread in northern France. See also GALL

character the personality of a wine; normally an attribute of fine wines or wines of especial merit or interest

château bottled bottled at source; 'estate bottled' or 'domaine bottled' mean the same. The ultimate assurance that the wine has not been tampered with

chewey strongly flavoured wines, mainly reds, usually with a high tannin level

chiaretto (*Italy*) a strong rosé colour. Probably better than a ROSATO wine

claret in the early 13th century the English began to ship over the lightish pink wines of Bordeaux which the Bordelaise called Clairet. The wines have changed but the anglicised name has remained

clarete (*Portugal*) light red wine, which was what CLARET was when it was Clairet!

clarification the process of clearing wine after fermentation

classé (*France*) classified; as in *crû classé*, a classified vineyard

classico (*Italy*) the central and best part of a wine-producing region. Roughly corresponds to 'Villages' classification in France

clean normally used for white wines. No faults on the nose or on the palate

clone a living organism produced from one parent and genetically identical to it

coarse or rough, a wine which lacks refinement, usually the result of poor production

cold fermentation essential for the production of well balanced wines in high ambient temperatures. Slowing down the fermentation extracts the maximum flavour from the grapes

collage (*France*) see FINING

collar the neck label

common wine lacking distinction but not necessarily of poor quality

commune (*France*) parish or village. Most usual in Burgundy where the appellations are often linked to individual villages like Pommard, Volnay, Meursault, etc.

con crianza (*Spain*) wood aged. Different regulations apply in different areas regarding the length of time required

corkage the fee charged for opening and serving a customer's own bottle brought to a restaurant. It is supposed to make up for the restaurant's loss of profit on the sale

corked wine spoiled by a bad cork. This can happen to any wine if a faulty cork is used. The wine may be cloudy and will betray a mouldy, musty smell. As this smell is usually immediately discernable no restaurant should offer a customer a corked wine

cosecha (*Spain*) the harvest; Cosecha 1990 indicates the vintage

courtier (*France*) alternative name for NÉGOCIANT in Bordeaux. The wine trades' middlemen

cradle a basket in which the bottle rests having been drawn from the bin in the horizontal position and with the sediment undisturbed.

The theory is that the wine may then be poured off the sediment. A quite useless abomination
crémant sparkling wine with a maximum of four ATMOSPHERES of pressure
crisp normally used for white or rosé wines; refreshingly dry
crû French for growth. Normally used to indicate a wine from a vineyard of sufficient reputation to have been individually recognised by the appellation contrôllée regulations: *crû classé*, 1re Crû etc.
crust the deposit on old ports. So-called because it forms a crust around the bottle. The wine needs to be decanted off this deposit
cultivar the term for a grape variety in South Africa
cuvée (*France*)
  1 the contents of a wine vat – or more than one vat if all the wines were made at the same time and under the same conditions
  2 also applied to a complete parcel, property or vineyard
  3 in Champagne also applied to a finished blended product ready for sale
  In other words, in one form or another, a quantity of similar wine
cuvée close (*France*) method of inducing carbon dioxide into wine by adding sugar and yeast to still wine in a sealed vat. The wine is then bottled from the vat under pressure
decant this essential action for most full red wines fulfills two distinct purposes. If done carefully it leaves the sediment in the bottle and results in the serving of a clear wine and it allows oxygenation of the wine (see BREATHING). Many modern red wines with little or no sediment still benefit enormously from decanting – or even double decanting
decanter a glass vessel used to carry wine which has been decanted to the table. Often, and wrongly, used for long-term storage of ports and sherries
decanting cradle a complicated mechanical device in which a bottle is gradually cranked from the horizonal to about 45% so the wine can be poured smoothly off the sediment
degorgement (*France*) removing the trapped sediment from champagne
delicate gently flavoured; normally indicates a wine unsuitable for ageing
demi-sec approved and controlled sweetness grading for champagne: sweeter than SEC, less sweet than DOUX or rich
depth deep flavour, usually applied to red wines

dessert wine a sweet wine usually served with the dessert course. Fortunately now more frequently available by the glass in good restaurants
Deutscher Tafelwein (*Germany*) table wine – but at least made from German grapes conforming to the conditions of this, the most basic of German wine grades
Deutsches Weinsiegel (*Germany*) an award, normally shown as a seal on the neck label, made by the Deutsche Landwirtschafts-Gesellschaft or German Agricultural Society
digestif a wine taken at the end of a meal, for example, but also applied to proprietary alcoholic products alleged to aid the digestion
DO or, more usually, DOC (*Italy*) Denominazione d'Origine Controllata. The basic quality grade which officially corresponds to VDQS in France as there is a superior level above it but, in reality, corresponds more exactly to AC
doce (*Portugal*) sweet
DOCG (*Italy*) as above but with a 'Guarantia' thrown in. Officially only granted to the greatest of the great
dolce (*Italy*) sweet
domaine (*France*) a wine estate or property
DOS (*Italy*) Denominazione di Origine Semplice. Almost never seen, simply indicates a guarantee of origin
dosage (*France*) the sweetening addition, normally a combination of sugar, wine and sometimes brandy, put into champagne after DEGORGEMENT and prior to despatch to achieve the required level of sweetness
doux (*France*) literally 'soft' but meaning sweet. An official grade of champagne – the sweetest – replaces or used with the older expression RICHE
dry a wine where all the grape sugar has been fermented into alcohol. The acid content will also affect the apparent dryness unless masked by excessive sugar
dulce (*Spain*) sweet
dusty a characteristic especially of southern Rhône red wines; a mildly earthy taste often found in hot countries
earthy a wine possessing some of the character and flavour of the soil. Often applied to wines from Mediterranean-temperature growing areas
Edelfaule (*Germany*) see NOBLE ROT, POURRITURE NOBLE
Edelzwiker (*France*) Alsacian term for wines

produced from a blending of the 'noble' grape varieties allowed in Alsace

EEC wine wine blended from any source country in the EEC

Einzellage (*Germany*) single-vineyard wine area; the smallest unit allowed by German wine law

Eiswein (*Germany*) wine produced from frozen grapes. As the berries have remained on the vine until severe frosts arrive, they are already shrivelled and concentrated. When pressed frozen, the small quantity of water remains with the skins as ice and the sweet juice which has a lower freezing temperature is run off and fermented. Necessarily sweet and horrendously expensive. In the New World they are experimenting with deep-frozen grapes!

en vrac (*France*) method of selling wine in bulk in France. Customers bring their own containers to the producer and fill them from a tank specially designed for the purpose

espumante (*Portugal*) a sparkling wine

espumoso (*Spain*) a sparkling wine

estate bottled see CHÂTEAU BOTTLED

fat a wine often lacking balancing acidity; normally high in glycerine. Well flavoured but lacking firmness

fermentation the conversion of grape sugars into alcohol by the action of yeasts

fiasco (*Italy*) the straw covered 'fiasco' of a bottle containing Chianti and beloved of do-it-yourself table-lamp enthusiasts – or for en-masse wall decoration in trattorias

filtering passing cloudy wine through a filtering medium to cleanse it. See also CENTRIFUGING and FINING

fine wine an imprecise term. Usually applies to classic wines from Bordeaux, Burgundy etc, but, increasingly, to equally praiseworthy wines from newer wine-growing regions

finesse French term for BREEDING or elegance

fining a method of clearing wine. An agent is introduced into cloudy wine to attract the suspended particles and take them to the bottom. Fining agents include organic materials such as blood, casein, isinglass and inorganic materials like fullers earth or bentonite

fino (*Spain*) sherry on which a FLOR has formed to protect the wine from oxidation during the early years of maturation. The dryest and finest style of sherry

flabby a blowsy wine lacking backbone and balancing acidity although having a rich flavour. See also FAT

Flaschengarung (*Germany*) bottle fermentation, ie méthode champenoise

flat obviously applied to sparkling wines which have lost their sparkle, but also to wines, especially whites, which have started to deteriorate. See also OXIDATION

flinty applied especially to wines produced from the Sauvignon Blanc grape. Allegedly due to the smell of gunflint!

flor the skin of yeasts which forms on some sherries, Rueda and Jura wines, so reducing oxidation. In Jerez this leads to the creation of a fino, in Rueda to Dorado or Palido and in the Jura to a vin jaune de garde

flowery normally applied to wines made from grapes of the Riesling family. The scent of spring flowers is said to be present

flute the tall glass which is correct for champagnes and sparkling wines. Retains the bubbles better than the horrid flat saucer-shaped device so often seen

fortified wine wine to which brandy has been added to arrest fermentation, so preserving sweetness and increasing the alcoholic content

fresh any wine which has a light balance of attractive flavour with good acidity

frizzante (*Italy*) fizzing; actually semi-sparkling wines, corresponding to CRÉMANT at around four atmospheres of pressure

fruit wines popular, mainly home-made 'wine' actually using all manner of natural fruits. EEC law officially prevents the use of the word wine for these products

fruity a wine with an aroma suggesting fruits other than grape

Gall (*Germany*) Dr Gall lends his name to Gallation – corresponds to CHAPTALISATION in France

garrafeira (*Portugal*) difficult to translate exactly. It means a matured wine but more than that; often a merchant's best wine – his 'private reserve' – which can sometimes be a blending of different vintages

generic wines wines named after the area of production: Chablis, Sauternes etc. These should display the general characteristics of the area but will seldom be more than a general indication of the typical flavours

generoso (*Italy*) fortified dessert wine

gluhwein (*Germany*) beloved of winter skiing holidaymakers; mulled wine to the rest of us

governo (*Italy*) the traditional system in Chianti involving refermentation by the addition of the juice of semi-dried grapes – the governo.

This softens and heightens the refreshing characteristics and adds a slight prickle to the taste

grand crû (*France*) see CRÛ

gran reserva (*Spain*) the highest quality grade. Normally involves a prescribed period in barrel and/or bottle. See Spanish wine laws

grapey used especially to describe the aroma and taste of wines from the Muscat family of grapes. Also used for other white wines from distinctively flavoured grapes such as Gewürztraminer or Riesling

green really means young. Vinho Verde from Portugal is not literally green in colour, but it's made from barely ripened grapes giving a fresh tartness to the taste

Grosslage (*Germany*) several vineyards grouped under one name

growth allied to CRÛ as in grand crû – great growth. Crû classé – classified growth

gyropallet (*France*) see REMUAGE

hard excessive tannin in a red wine. Characteristic of young quality Bordeaux reds suitable for long ageing

hearty normally applied to red wines with immediate appeal. Warming flavour, often with a high level of alcohol

heavy used for wines of high alcoholic content but more often describes full body without FINESSE

honeyed a rich sweetness to the taste. Even dry wines can taste faintly of honey if sufficiently ripe

house wine normally the cheapest wines on a restaurant's list. May be sold by the bottle, carafe or glass and, if well chosen, can be a bargain

inbottigliatto dal produttore/all origine (*Italy*) bottled by the producer, estate bottled – or both

jammy a derogatory comment applied to red wines which betray high fermentation temperatures by their rather cooked taste or, being fruity, lack balancing acidity

jug wine an American term for simple wines

Kabinett (*Germany*) literally cabinet. Now a quality grade under German law, the first of the QmP grades and the highest grade of wine quality before ascending the sweetness stairway. It is claimed that, in times gone by, vineyard owners would keep their best and most prized wines locked away in their cupboard or cabinet

late harvest wine produced from grapes left on the vine to become over ripe, so encouraging the development of NOBLE ROT

laying down storing wines, normally fine red wines or ports, until they are MATURE

lees the sediment or dregs which settle out of a wine in cask. Leaving some white wines stored on their lees can increase the flavour, e.g. Muscadet sur Lie

length a wine's ability to allow the residual flavour to remain in the mouth; a characteristic of complex, fine, wines. See also AFTERTASTE

light wine(s)
1 EEC parlance for an unfortified, naturally made wine
2 used for wines low in alcohol, normally with less than 5% alcohol
3 used by tasters to describe a wine which is not particularly full bodied

liqueur de tirage (*France*) the solution of sugar, yeast and old wine added to champagne and other méthode champenoise sparkling wines to produce a secondary fermentation

liqueur d'expedition see DOSAGE

liquoroso fortified dessert wine

lively can be used about fresh young white wines but more usually applies to PÉTILLANT or sparkling wines

macération carbonique method of fermentation in which whole grapes ferment in a closed container covered with carbon dioxide to produce light fruity red wines

made wine EEC definition for wines produced from imported grapes, grape juice or MUST, or any grape concentrates. British Wine is made wine, English Wine comes from grapes grown in the British Isles

madeirised describes wines, usually white, which are past their peak due to long or bad storage. They have a brownish tinge and may give a whiff of sherry or madeira on the nose. See also OXIDISED

magnum a double bottle size – 150cl. Popular for champagne in spite of normally costing more than two standard bottles. Red wines in magnums mature more slowly

malolactic fermentation the conversion of naturally present malic acid into the softer lactic acid by the action of bacteria. Now deliberately induced to soften reds but sometimes arrested to keep hot country whites crisp

manzanilla (*Spain*) a FINO matured on the coast at Sanlucar de Barrameda, pale, crisp and

very dry with a hint of a salty sea-tang.
For many, the very best example of FINO
marque (*France*) trade or company name
mature ready to drink. Most wines are in this
state when sold, the exceptions are fine
burgundies, clarets and ports which noramlly
need LAYING DOWN before reaching full maturity,
hence maturation
medium impossible to define. One drinker's
medium-sweet is another's medium-dry.
Officially 4 or 5 on the Wine Development Board
Scale
mellow normally, but not necessarily, used for
a wine at the peak of maturation (see RIPE).
A red wine may reach this condition before it
has reached its peak
millesime (*France*) the year of the vintage
**mis/mise en bouteille a la propriete/au
château** (*France*) can mean almost anything.
The 'property' may not necessarily be the place
the wine was produced – if it's a claret it may
well be a warehouse in Bordeaux! But at least
the wine is unlikely to have strayed too far
before being bottled
mistela (*Spain*) sweetener produced from
a sugary MUST (PX in Jerez) in which
fermentation has been arrested by the addition
of considerable amounts of alcohol and also,
normally, caramel
moelleux (*France*) literally 'marrowy'. A level
of subtle sweetness found especially in the
Coteaux du Layon and Jurançon
mousse the pattern or texture of the bubbles
in a glass of sparkling wine
mulled wine normally red wine heated with
spices, especially nutmeg and cinnamon, with
orange peel or juice and sugar
must grape juice before it is fermented to
produce wine
musty initial mustiness will probably fade quite
quickly having come from a deteriorating cork
or capsule. If the condition persists then
decanting the wine may help, if not, use it
for cooking
mutage (*France*) the artificial cessation
of fermentation. Normally achieved by adding
sulphur dioxide with the intention of retaining
some of the natural sweetness. Used to be
common in Entre-deux-Mers
négociant (*France*) vinous middleman
especially important in Burgundy where many
land holdings are so small that owners are
unlikely to have the necessary space or capital
to process and mature their own wines – hence

négociant-eleveur (*France*) a middleman or
merchant who 'brings up' or develops the wines
by buying-in from a variety of sources, blending,
maturing, selling and shipping
noble rot *Pourriture noble* in French,
Edelfaule in German, *Botrytis cinerea* in Latin.
A benign mould which allows water to escape
from affected grape skins and thus concentrates
the grape sugars to produce sweet wines
non-vintage (NV) a wine assembled or
blended from wines of different vintages
nose (of the wine) is best released and
appreciated by swirling wine around in a
reasonably enclosed glass and taking a deep
breath of the bouquet. Will normally indicate
both the predominant grape and the wine style
nutty most often applied to sherries which can
release a distinct aroma of walnuts or hazelnuts
oakey the taste contributed to wine during
maturation in oak casks. The slightly sweetish
vanilla hints are prized in many red wines and
some fuller whites
Oechsle (*Germany*) System of measuring
sugar content in grapes for the different
categories of Austrian and German wines
oenologue/oenologist a fully trained wine-
maker responsible for all the technical
wine-making decisions
oïdium a disease of the vine. Noticed as
a powdery mildew, the effects are profound and
affect the whole plant
oloroso (*Spain*) no FLOR develops and oxidation
produces a deep brown colour and a soft, full-
bodied fragrance. Naturally dry and often with a
high alcohol level these sherries are normally
sweetened and diluted before bottling
onze degrees (*France*) the name given to
French wines with no pretension to quality. Sold
entirely on their alcoholic strength, the most
usual being 11° of alcohol or onze degrees
Original-abfullung or Orig.-Abfg.
(*Germany*) roughly corresponds to estate or
CHÂTEAU BOTTLED but not all wines on one
estate may be of equal quality as there is a
tendency towards individual fermentation of
grapes from different parcels of land
Ortsteile (*Germany*) a property of such
distinction that the Einzellage or village name is
not used as a prefix eg Steinberger
oxidised a wine so described has started to
deteriorate due to age or poor storage. Mostly
applied to white wines which betray the
condition by taking on an increasingly brownish
hue and tasting flat and 'sherry-like' – a

description very unfair to sherry! See also MADEIRISED

palo cortado (*Spain*) a rarity. A sherry between an AMONTILLADO and an OLOROSO in style. Normally kept separate and unblended

passito (*Italy*) wine produced from grapes that have dried, sometimes on the vine but more normally on drying racks. The resulting wines are naturally sweet or, if used for blending, strengthen the end product

perfume generally similar to BOUQUET, but also used more specifically for wines from Gewürztraminer (see SPICY) and Muscat grapes, both of which are regarded as having a 'perfumed' smell

perlwein (*Germany*) corresponds to petillant, slightly sparkling

petrolly a quality of taste especially associated with mature Riesling wines

phylloxera *Phylloxera vastatrix*, the burrowing plant louse which is indigenous to vines in the United States. Came to Europe in the mid 1800s and decimated virtually every vineyard over a 50-year period. Eventually grafting European vines onto native American rootstocks overcame the problem. Chile is now the only country where this louse has never struck and where they only use ungrafted vines. There was a small outbreak in Somerset in 1987

piquant usually applied to white wines to indicate a pleasant acidity balancing an underlying sweetness or fruitiness

plonk perjorative term but sometimes, in wine bars, bistros and the like, used to indicate good plain, unfussy, wine. Thought to have originated in the First World War as a corruption of 'Blanc'

plummy a pleasant taste somewhat akin to Victoria plums. In general applied to big, well rounded, red wines, often from the New World

pourriture noble (*France*) see NOBLE ROT

prickly the effect of small quantities of carbon dioxide present in the wine. Sometimes deliberate and pleasant. A sign of secondary fermentation which is sometimes a fault

proprietaire (*France*) the owner

punt the depression in the bottom of most wine bottles. Added to strengthen bottles especially for champagnes and sparkling wines

PX (*Spain*) abbreviation for the Pedro Ximenez grape mainly found in Jerez

QbA (*Germany*) Qualitatswein bestimmter Anbaugebiet or Quality Wine from a Designated Region, ie from one of the eleven ANBAUGEBIET. See German wine laws page 108

QmP (*Germany*) Qualitatswein mit Pradikat or Quality wine with Special Attributes. ie unsugared wines from defined areas. The first grade is KABINETT and after that the sweetness increases as well as the quality – to the Germans it's the same thing. . . .

Qualitatswein (*Germany*) any wine graded above TAFELWEIN – can be QbA or QmP

quinta (*Portugal*) estate

racking the movement of wines from barrel to barrel during maturation to get the wine off the lees and to accelerate ageing by exposure to oxygen

récemment dégorgé (*France*) term used for champagnes which have been matured with the yeasts still in the bottle rather than being removed once secondary fermentation is complete. Adds greater depth of flavour – but is expensive

recioto (*Italy*) wine from specially selected and dried well-ripened grapes. Especially used in Valpolicella – see AMARONE

Região Demarcada (*Portugal*) a defined area, similar to AC, DOC, DO etc

remuage (*France*) 'riddling' – the traditional method of persuading the sediment in champagne and M.C. sparkling wines to spiral its way down an upside-down bottle retained in a 'pupitre' (pulpit) – a sandwich-board affair with elongated holes to hold the necks of the champagne bottles. This labour-intensive system is being replaced with unromantic mechanical devices called gyropallets

reserva (*Spain*) the next to top quality grade for Spanish wines. See Spanish wine laws, page 139

reserve sometimes an official qualification, sometimes a meaningless expression. See the information on wine laws, especially the Spanish ones

rich previously used in Champagne to describe the sweetest type released for sale. Otherwise it indicates great depth of flavour in reds or attractive sweetness in dessert wines especially FORTIFIED WINES

riche (*France*) translated as 'rich' and applied to the sweetest grade of champagne. Now only allowed in association with the word DOUX

ripe the point at which a wine has become fully mature; any further storage is likely to result in a decline in quality

riserva (*Italy*) part of the DOC system. Indicates that a minimum ageing requirement has been met

robust normally only applies to reds; a wine capable of long maturation

rosado (*Portugal*) rosé wine

rosato (*Italy*) rosé. There are few Italian rosés and none of note. In this colour-range CHIARETTOS are generally more interesting, especially Chiaretto del Garda

rosso (*Italy*) red

rough very basic wine, for example French ONZE DEGREES wine

round a wine which has no obvious defects. Not necessarily an expensive wine but, by definition, well made

saké *(Japan)* wine made from fermented cleaned and steamed rice, 12% to 16% alcohol, colourless and slightly sweet

Schaumwein (*Germany*) a general and lowly term for any sparkling wine. Qualitatschaumwein is allegedly better quality

sec literally 'dry'. Normally used for sparkling wines. In the case of champagne is sweeter than BRUT and drier than DEMI-SEC

secco (*Italy*) dry

seco (*Spain/Portugal*) dry

secondary fermentation a fault in still wines except a few whites. It occurs when residual sugar and yeast remain in the wine after the fermentation was thought to be over and the wine had been bottled. It is deliberately induced to produce sparkling wines

second label or **second wine** wines which are not up to the standard of an estate's top-quality wines. Often the wines from young vines, and often a bargain!

sediment remains of skins which remain through FINING yet precipitate after storing in bottle. Applies especially to red wines and ports, removed by careful DECANTING

Sekt (*Germany*) sparkling wine. Quality varies, at the lowest level only 60% of the grapes need be German whereas the better sekts clearly define the region of origin

selection de grains nobles (*France*) Alsacian term corresponding to BEERENAUSLESE in Germany. Only hand-selected BOTRYTIS-affected berries are used

semi-seco (*Spain*) medium dry

severe sharp wine, with aggressive attack which probably needs time to mature and soften. Sometimes used where a wine, normally red, lacks fruit. Astringent

sharp a characteristic generally due to excess acidity in the grapes. May be deliberate but more normally due to poor crop condition

short a wine whose taste fades in the mouth. Used especially for red wines where the flavour should linger

sin crianza (*Spain*) without wood ageing; a wine for drinking young

smokey normally present as a result of the deliberate charring of the inside of maturation barrels

smooth similar to VELVETY; high in glycerine and low in 'bite'

soft normally due to an absence of, or muted, acids or tannins. A characteristic of red wines produced by MACERATION CARBONIQUE

solera (*Spain/Portugal*) the maturing system used for sherries and Spanish brandy. Wines for bottling are taken from the oldest barrels – about one third of the capacity of each barrel – which are then topped up from the next oldest and so on until the newest wines go into the youngest barrels

sommelier French title for a wine waiter. Sadly conjures up images of wine snobbery and condescension when it should mean assistance, ideas and professionalism

sour can be applied to TART wines

Spatlese (*Germany*) above KABINETT and below AUSLESE on the QmP quality scale. Sort of semi-LATE HARVEST

spicy normally applied to the Gewürz(spicy)traminer but other grapes also have this characteristic. Difficult to describe precisely but spicy isn't it! PERFUMED is better, the flavour of lychees is a common tasting comment

Spritz/Spritzig (*Germany*) slightly or lightly sparkling; lighter than PERLWEIN

spumante (*Italy*) fully sparkling

stalky strictly speaking refers to the sloppy practice of some wine-makers leaving too much stalk on the bunches and in consequence producing a wine with a rather hard, woody taste

steely an imprecise term. Sometimes used about very dry champagnes and sometimes about very good rieslings

still wine a wine with no sparkle induced. Natural or induced petillance or mild sparkle does not disqualify

stoney perjorative term used about a wine which is empty and dull, especially dry wines

sulphury sulphur in the form of sulphur dioxide is the antiseptic of the wine industry. Some New world countries demand the expression 'contains sulphites' on the label if SO_2 has been

used – which means almost every wine!
Excess of enthusiasm for SO_2 can result in smell when the wine is first poured, but normally this clears

superiore (*Italy*) highest grade of wine of that district

supple difficult to describe. Normally applied to red wines to indicate a balanced roundness on the palate

sur lie (*France*) 'on the lees'. A technique used especially in Muscadet where the wine is stored on its LEES without FINING or FILTERING so as to impart more flavour before bottling

süssreserve (*Germany*) the sweet unfermented grape juice used for BACK-BLENDING

SVdaT Super Vino da Tavola. Term with no legal validity. It indicates a superior quality wine which does not comply with DOC regulations

sweet generally a wine with an OECHSLE reading of at least 100° before fermentation. Drinkers' individual perception of sweetness varies but 7 upwards on the Wine Development Board scale is generally agreed to be sweet

sweet sour nothing to do with Chinese wines! A characteristic most often found in Italian reds with good fruit and good acidity in which the separate flavours have not combined

Tafelwein or TW (*Germany*) table wine. The basic German designation, it has two levels: TW which can be made from grapes grown anywhere and Deutsche Tafelwein when the grapes must be of German origin

tannic tannin is an astringent substance drawn into the juice from the skin, pips and stalks of grapes during prolonged contact, hence normally absent from white wines. Tannins, which promote longevity by their antiseptic quality, should be balanced by fully ripe pulp or allowed to diminish by AGEING. See also LAYING DOWN

tart a very sharp wine suggesting the wine needs to MATURE (if it's red) or that the grapes were insufficiently ripe. See also ACIDIC and TANNIC

thin a weak and watery wine lacking BODY. Too insipid to be enjoyable

tinto (*Spain/Portugal*) red

tough normally used about reds, suggests austerity and excess tannin

transfer system used for sparkling wine. SECONDARY FERMENTATION is induced in the bottle but the residues are removed by discharging the bottles into a pressurised tank where they sink before re-bottling the clean wine

Trocken (*Germany*) dry. Confusingly it is correctly applied to wines which have been fermented through to dryness and without the addition of SÜSSRESERVE. Yet it is also the start of TROCKENBEERENAUSLESE, the sweetest grade

Trockenbeerenauslese or TBA (*Germany*) the highest grade of German wine and therefore the sweetest of the sweet. Means dried, hand-selected late harvested. In the old days suitable grapes were dried on mats in the sun to concentrate the grape sugars, now they are dried more efficiently under lamps

varietal a wine produced predominantly from one variety of grape

varietal labelling a bottle with a label giving information about *what* varieties were used to produce the wine inside, rather than a label telling only *where* it was produced. Much used by New World wine-makers

VDN (*France*) Vin Doux Naturelle. Applied to southern French wines, both white and red, where 10% eaux de vie is added to naturally sweet wines – they must be capable of reaching 15% alcohol without assistance. The addition preserves some natural sweetness and raises the alcohol level to around 18%

VDQS (*France*) Vin Délimité de Qualité Superieur, see French wine laws

vecchio (*Italy*) term allowed under DOC regulations for a matured wine, less than a RISERVA. Stavecchio (very old) is allowed on the labels of a very few wines

velho (*Portugal*) old

velvety normally indicates a high glycerine content leading to a soft feel on the tongue and a soft texture to the wine

vendage tardive (*France*) literally 'late harvest'. Indicates well-ripened grapes, hopefully with some BOTRYTIS present. AUSLESE level of sweetness in Germany

vendemmia (*Italy*) vintage

vendimia (*Spain*) the grape harvest, the vintage

vigneto (*Italy*) indicates the wine is from an individual vineyard

Vin de Pays (*France*) new quality grade introduced into the French Appellation Contrôlée system in 1973 to encourage local pride and character in regional wines. See French wine laws

Vin de Table (*France*) the lowest of Appellation Contrôlée grades. In fact not a grade at all, the product simply qualifies to be called wine, but that is all. See ONZE DEGREES

vinho maduro (*Portugal*) matured wine

vinification the transformation of grapes into wine by pressing and fermenting

Vino Corriente (*Spain*) ordinary or poor wine

Vino da Messa (*Italy*) sacramental wine

Vino da Tavola (*Italy*) table wine. Unlike other countries, this category not only includes the most basic of wines available, but also some (if not all!) of the very best. These are often called Super Vinos da Tavola (SVDAT).

Vino de Color (*Spain*) wine which has been reduced by boiling – often to as little as a fifth of the volume. This treacly product, sometimes called Arrope or Sancocho is used in Jerez for sweetening and colouring; see also MISTELA

Vino de Mesa (*Spain*) table wine

vinosity a vague term. Generally applied to well-made, well-balanced wines

vintage the action of harvesting the grapes. Normally starts in early September in Europe and can continue through to late November in Germany – and early in the New Year for EISWEIN. Naturally in the southern hemisphere it is a half a year earlier!

vintage chart a printed grid showing by symbols or numbers the relative worth of each vintage for any given area. These are obviously very generalised, but can be a reasonable guide for consumers

vintage wine every wine is a VINTAGE wine.

Often used as a term of approbation, probably due to the association with ports and champagnes where the best years are 'declared' as vintage years while wines from other years are sold as NON-VINTAGE

viticulteur (*France*) a wine-grower

Vitis labrusca native American vine. Some wines are produced from this species but the flavours are basically unattractive. However, this is the vine which provides PHYLLOXERA-resistant rootstock for the world's vineyards, so is of immense importance to the wine industry

Vitis vinifera the vine which provides the world's fine wines. Most of the vineyards of the world use this vine grafted onto VITIS LABRUSCA rootstock. See also PHYLLOXERA

weighty a wine of depth and character, usually applied to reds but some whites would qualify

Weingut (*Germany*) a German wine company, a vineyard, a wine estate

wood ageing the accepted way to mature fine wines. The wine is matured in wooden, normally oak, casks gaining complexity and, if the wood is young, flavours of oak. Sometimes overdone to the detriment of the wine

woody sometimes used to describe a positive characteristic in red wines but more normally applied to over-long cask-ageing or a possible fault in the cask

yeasty a smell suggesting that secondary fermentation has, or is about to, take place. Sometimes spoken of as a quality in champagne

WINE TASTE GUIDES

If you buy your wines in a supermarket or one of the major chains of off licences you are likely to see the symbols below. They may be part of the back label on a bottle, but they'll certainly be on the shelf beside the name and price of the wine concerned. These symbols were introduced by the Wine Development Board, an independent organisation, to take some of the mystique out of buying wine. They are a guide to the taste of a wine.

The white wine guide covers the major white wines of the world – as well as rosés, sherry and vermouth – by using a scale of sweetness numbered from 1 to 9. For example, Number 1 signifies very dry white wines (eg Chablis and Muscadet). Number 9 indicates maximum sweetness (eg Malmsey, Madiera and Trockenbeerenauslese). The numbers in between span the remaining dryness-to-sweetness spectrum.

Although similar in principle, the red wine guide works in a slightly different way, using five categories, marked from A to E. These categories identify styles of red wines in terms of total taste – in other words the impression they give to the palate.

They start at 'A' with wines comparable to Beaujolais or German red wines: light, and equally enjoyable with or without food. At 'E', the other end of the scale, are the bigger and more concentrated styles with a greater sensation of depth and fullness. These wines, of which the Italian Barolo is an example, are more suitable to drink with food than on their own. Côtes dy Rhône wines from France and Rioja from Spain are positioned with others in the centre of the guide.

The world of wine is very complex, and there can be variations, due to winemaking, from the taste suggestions. For example, some wines, such as Tokay, are available in varying degrees of sweetness, while the more expensive wines – those which go on maturing in the bottle – are outside the scope of the guides.

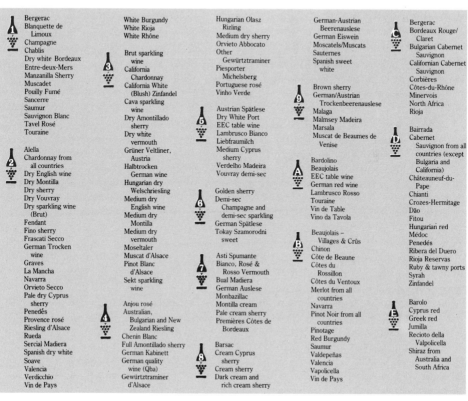

253

INDEX